George Orwell

GEORGE ORWELL

ENGLISH REBEL

ROBERT COLLS

OXFORD
UNIVERSITY PRESS

OXFORD

UNIVERSITY PRESS

Great Clarendon Street, Oxford, OX2 6DP,
United Kingdom

Oxford University Press is a department of the University of Oxford.
It furthers the University's objective of excellence in research, scholarship,
and education by publishing worldwide. Oxford is a registered trade mark of
Oxford University Press in the UK and in certain other countries

© Robert Colls 2013

The moral rights of the author have been asserted

First Edition published in 2013

Impression: 1

Published in the United States of America by Oxford University Press
198 Madison Avenue, New York, NY 10016, United States of America

British Library Cataloguing in Publication Data

Data available

Library of Congress Control Number: 2013940846

ISBN 978-0-19-968080-1

Printed in Italy by
L.E.G.O. S.p.A.—Lavis TN

Links to third party websites are provided by Oxford in good faith and
for information only. Oxford disclaims any responsibility for the materials
contained in any third party website referenced in this work.

I think on the whole you have moved too much away from the ordinary world into a sort of Mickey Mouse universe where things and people don't have to obey the rules of space and time...I have a sort of belly-to-earth attitude and always feel uneasy when I get away from the ordinary world...

(Orwell to Henry Miller, from The Stores,
Wallington, 26 August 1936)

I rather enjoyed your using the phrase 'Mickey Mouse Universe'. The intellectual would have said 'surrealisme'.

(Miller to Orwell, from 18 Villa Seurat,
Paris XIV, September 1936)

Preface and Acknowledgements

Orwell has had a number of fine biographers. He has also enjoyed the services of the best editors a writer could hope for, beginning with Ian Angus and Sonia Orwell in the 1960s and ending magisterially, and definitively, with Peter Davison's *Complete Works*, published by Secker & Warburg in 1986–7 and 1998. There have been other fine studies of Orwell that have followed a particular line, or investigated a particular aspect, or said something special about what sort of man he was or what sort of reputation he enjoyed. And now that Orwell's century is beginning to enter the realm of finished past, we can expect works that parody him, or explore him in non-factual and unreal ways.

My book shares a number of these approaches but is offered here as an intellectual biography that follows his sense of Englishness.

I was encouraged to pursue this theme by two apparently throwaway remarks by Professor K. O. Morgan. The first came *sotto voce* at a conference in Lille in 2004. As I left the podium, Morgan met me by the door. 'Strange thing that, about Orwell,' he remarked. 'You know, putting your belief in the people.' I had never thought of Orwell's commitments in this way—as something quite strange—and Morgan's remark came like a bolt from the blue. It set me thinking. A few years later the Welshman threw another dart, this time in The Lamb and Flag in Oxford, when he charged me there and then to go and write The Englishness of George Orwell. I was told to go forth. Morgan will not remember any of this, but that set me thinking for the second time. This is the result: *George Orwell: English Rebel.*

It is always nice to write the Preface at the end (a light at the beginning of the tunnel) and I want to thank some special people for their part in helping me write this book. I thank Matthew Cotton, commissioning editor at Oxford University Press, who never stopped asking about it. He never stopped asking, it is true, but he was patient as well, and offered significant guidance along the way. I thank as well OUP's anonymous readers for giving me confidence, and the sort of advice I would never have given myself. I thank Jeff New, my copy-editor at OUP, for seeing what I wanted to say—sometimes better than me. I thank Andrew Hawkey, proofreader for OUP, who helped me make the final cut. I thank Emma Barber, Senior Production Editor at OUP, who for a time seemed to be everywhere all at once. I thank the Orwell Archive at University College London, which manages to be friendly, well run, and cramped all at the same time. I thank my third-year students on the Special Subject at the University of Leicester who over the years helped me more perhaps than they (or I) knew at the time. I thank my brother Graham Colls and my friend Albyn Snowdon for always being on hand to talk about everything and anything in bracing and stimulating ways. I thank Professor Wolfram Richter and the Gambrinus Fellowship for giving me the chance to first air my ideas about Orwell and Europe in a public lecture at the University of Dortmund. I thank William Whyte for giving me the opportunity to write an essay in honour of Ross McKibbin that served as a direct try-out for the Englishness theme pursued here. I thank De Montfort University for giving me the time to finish the book, and make good. I thank my colleagues at Leicester and at De Montfort's International Centre for Sports History and Culture who were generous critics: in particular Mike Cronin, Jeremy Crump, Ron Greenall, and Simon Gunn; and Andrew King, an astrophysicist whose taste for the truth has led me round more circuits than I care to remember; and Dick Holt, who felt the full force of the subject. All that said, the book's faults are mine. Where would I be without my prejudices?

A word on the notes. Although the book is intended for the general reader as well as those with an academic interest in Orwell, for the benefit of the latter group there are quite a few of these. My advice to both parties is to suit yourself. If you want to follow the scholarly trail, look to the notes at the back. If you would rather just get on with it, don't bother. The story should carry you through. One of my main reasons for writing the book was a belief that scholars of literature and politics had had a good go at Orwell and now it was another historian's turn. The notes rather support that belief—as does the bibliographical essay, which sets Orwell's reputation in context.

Finally I dedicate this book with all my heart to my father, Bob, who showed me what decency in an English working man looked like long before I read George Orwell; to the women in my life, Amy, Becky, and Rosie, *best friends*; and to my mother, Margaret, who was giving me my life just as Orwell was losing his.

R.C.

Clarendon Park
Leicester
1 May 2013

Contents

List of Plates   xi

Introduction   1

1. Angry Old Etonian   8

2. North Road   46

3. Eye Witness in Barcelona 1937   72

4. Mr Bowling Sees It Through   109

5. England the Whale   130

6. Not Quite Tory   172

7. Last of England   197

8. Death in the Family   217

Life after Death: A Bibliographical Essay   220

Notes   237

Text Acknowledgements   305

Picture Acknowledgements   307

Index   309

List of Plates

1. Orwell in imperial mode, Easton Cliff, Reydon, Suffolk, 1934. (Orwell Archive, UCL Special Collection.)

2. Eric Blair, with school-friends, after a swim at Ward's Mead, Eton, 1919. (Orwell Archive 2B15.)

3. Eric having fun on South Green, Southwold, in the summer of 1922. (Orwell Archive 2C1.)

4. Blair in training at the Police Academy, Mandalay, Burma, 1923. (Orwell Archive 2B25.)

5. Doll's head, nineteenth-century. Nikobar Islanders, Indonesia. (Raustenstrauch-Joest Museum, Cologne.)

6. Book Lover's Corner, 1, South End Road, Hampstead. (Orwell Archive.)

7. Eileen Blair (née O'Shaughnessy), French Morocco, 1938. (Orwell Archive.)

8. Miner at work, 1930. (Woodhorn Museum, Northumberland.)

9. The miner's view of the miner at work: Oliver Kilbourn, *Coal Face Drawers* (1950). (Woodhorn Museum, Northumberland.)

10. The Wigan Orwell did not show: young cotton worker, Eckersley's Mill. (*Picture Post*, 11 November 1939.)

11. Second anniversary of the Catalonian Revolution, Barcelona, 6 October 1936. (Getty Images.)

12. POUM militiamen on the Aragon front. (Orwell Archive 2D7.)

13. The world of George Bowling: Ilford, Essex, April 1936. (Getty Images.)

14. Eileen holding her nephew Laurence, London 1939. (Orwell Archive 3B9.)

15. Orwell with comrades of the St John's Wood Company of the Home Guard. (Orwell Archive 2D33.)

16. London at war—*Dig For Victory, or Allotments in the Park* (1941), Mary Kent Harrison. (By permission of Stephen Howard Harrison.)

17. London in peace—*Victory Day, Richmond Park* (1945), Mary Kent Harrison. (By permission of Stephen Howard Harrison.)

18. Sonia Orwell, 1950. (Orwell Archive.)

Introduction

George Orwell was what they used to call a 'Socialist'. He shared also some of the attitudes to life that used to be called 'Tory'. Right from first principles, therefore, he was not as simple and straightforward as he made out or, indeed, as others made out for him. A deep-seated contrariness marked his writing and contributed to the wide and conflicting range of his appeal. Any attempt to understand his thinking must attend to life as he lived it, a step at a time, in and out of argument, right up to the end.

A step at a time

Born in India in 1903, Eric Blair (George Orwell) was brought up and educated in the south of England. His family was comfortable in a 'lower upper middle-class' sort of way—a way he defined as upper middle class without the money. He attended the country's top public school on a scholarship.

After Eton he joined the Imperial Police and went to Burma. Like many things in his life he did it because he chose to do it. It was not a happy time, however, and he returned to England five years later eager to cross the line. What line? Many lines, as we shall see. His first published works are on the side of the poor and dispossessed and we find him writing, or trying to write, from their point of view. Although England and the British Empire is usually his subject, so is poverty, opposition, and rebellion. He shows no apparent sign of any affiliation to his country or its traditions.[1]

Then, in 1936, he went north and for the first time in his life found an England he could believe in. He saw how the miners kept the country going. He pondered why their labour was the most valuable, but not the most valued. He noted how the working class did not ask for much, and not much was gladly given. But from this point on he knew he belonged. Theirs was another England to believe in and, as time went on, he even came to believe in his own.

Not that Orwell came to England just by thinking about it. Your prose finds you out, he warned. So how he lived mattered to how he wrote, and because he wanted to live and write in certain ways, he took pains to do so. He kept his journal in a neat, purposeful hand. He tried to see situations exactly as they were. He took things in. He took things on. He changed his mind. He wanted to be exact and exacting at the same time. He carefully weighed his experience and tried to turn it into litera- ture. Above all, he fell in line with his country at a critical time in its history. When he died in 1950 his reputation was growing and it has never stopped growing. The literary scholar John Rodden has made Orwell dead almost as interesting as Orwell alive.[2]

Who influenced him? Whom did he influence? How do we read him now? Scan just a single page of the Modern Literary Association's *Inter- national Bibliography* and you will come across studies of Orwell and Som- erset Maugham, Orwell and Samuel Beckett, Orwell and Søren Kierkegaard, Orwell and Salvador Dali, Orwell and Salman Rushdie, Orwell and Evelyn Waugh, Orwell and William Morris, Orwell and Walker Evans (and James Agee), Orwell and Thomas Carlyle, Orwell and Albert Camus, Orwell and Michel Foucault, Orwell and Thomas Pynchon, Orwell and Benedict Anderson, Orwell and Alexander Solzhenitsyn, and Orwell and Virginia Woolf.[3] No one, in the Anglo- American literary world at least, seems to doubt his importance. Rod- den cites him as 'more quoted and referenced than any other modern writer'.[4]

And yet, when it comes to the more general question of what he believed, or how we should see him, this most quoted and referenced of writers is almost impossible to pin down. Scholarly papers on what he is said to have been *against* (from Nazis to Jews) are no guide to what he is said to have been *for* (from Protestants to puddings). He did not appear to believe, for instance, in the existence of God, but he did believe in the importance of continuing to believe in the existence of God. He did not like capitalism, but he believed in the importance of the culture that capitalism produced. That he was both an iconoclast and a tradition- alist is beyond doubt—just about everybody agrees on that—but it is as difficult to decide whether he was a conservative iconoclast or a socialist traditionalist as it is to decide whether he was a Protestant atheist or an atheistical atheist. Orwell spent the best part of his adult life saying he was a socialist and a non-believer, but those who knew him well swore that deep down he was really a conservative, and there are a number of (good) books claiming he was a Christian.

Too young for the last of romanticism, too late for modernism, and dead by the time of the post-modernists, Orwell is not particularly susceptible to aesthetic labels either. Alexandra Harris, in her excellent book on *Romantic Moderns*, finds a slot for almost everyone but him.[5] Nor does he fit easily into any intellectual movement. He might have been a literary Marxist, but he might equally have been a cultural Tory. Indeed, almost all general statements about who or what he was can be matched by equal and opposite statements. For all his gifts of clarity and precision, and for all his ability to persuade you that he was showing you the world as it was, and for all his seriousness, George Orwell is difficult to pin down—a writer who held many points of view, some twice over. He was, after all, the inventor of 'Doublethink': the man who told you that highly civilized human beings were trying to kill him, the man who told you that all animals were equal only some more so. This is not to say that he was fickle, or that he did not believe in anything or that he did not know what he believed. It is only to say he has to be taken a step at a time.

His Englishness

Orwell belonged to a generation who took their Englishness for granted. It is just possible that a boy like him could have grown up free of it, or even against it, but only by chance and only by finding something else to put in its place. Most boys of his class (and not only them) came of age against the gigantic moral backdrop of British global interests and responsibilities. Brought up in a distinctly old-colonial family, he believed in Englishness like he believed in the world. It existed. It existed like ships in the Channel, the king in his castle, money in the bank. It existed as a sort of public poetry to be intoned insistently, regularly, nationally, all one's life through, like the shipping forecast or the football results, to remind you of who you were and where you lived. His was a country, moreover, where a very small group of politicians and other significant figures of state and civil society were trusted, more or less, to stand for the nation and speak on its behalf. In other words, being English was not open to question. It could not be avoided, and, whether one was for it or against it, one was never less than conscious of it. When Orwell thought of other people, he thought of national types. He could see at bottom that such attitudes were probably irrational, yet he never travelled far without them. *Down and Out in Paris and London*, his first book, is rife with foreigners (English types just across the water).[6]

Orwell's first attempt to write self-consciously about such things was probably 'The Tale of John Flory (1890–1927)', written on Burma-police notepaper sometime during the late 1920s. He sketches the story of 'the degeneration and ruin, through his native faults, of a gifted man'.

A second attempt at Englishness followed sometime in 1939, just after his very south-of-England novel, *Coming Up for Air*. 'The Quick and the Dead' is a collection of notes (the book itself was never written) towards another tale of degeneration, this time in a middle-class family. Living without 'colour, pleasure, interest or sense of purpose', their 'guiding principle was to save trouble'. If they do not know how to die, this is a family that has forgotten how to live. 'Steady the Buffs' if you eat too much. 'I hope nobody wants a second helping' if you eat too little. 'Don't dirty a clean plate' before you start.[7]

It was an American who first drew Orwell's attention to the stifling effects of his English upbringing. Writing from Paris in 1936, Henry Miller warned him of his guilt, his 'false respectability', his 'inadequacy', and his 'bloody English education'. In a couple of smarting but affectionate rebukes, the American tried to liberate the Englishman from his sense of responsibility for everything that happened in the world. 'Stop thinking...!' 'Do nothing...!' 'Fuck your capitalistic society!' Thirteen years later, in 1949, alongside some very English advertisements for Rose's Lime Juice and Rudge Bicycles, Lionel Trilling in the *New Yorker* recognized that same 'peculiarly English' idiom in Orwell. But this time the American found strength in his Englishness, not impotence.[8] A lot had happened to Orwell since 1936. Not least, he had found his country.

When he died in 1950, *World Review*'s distinguished contributors made nothing of Orwell's Englishness. Tom Hopkinson too missed it in 1953, but John Atkins was quick to spot it ('stronger than class') in 1954, and got somewhere with it in his idea of a national 'persona'.[9] Raymond Williams in 1958, George Woodcock in 1967, and Jenni Calder in 1968 all spotted Orwell's Englishness again, only to subdivide it into aspects of other things, such as community, or tradition, or patriotism.[10] Williams returned to the theme in 1971, in his short sketch in the Fontana 'Modern Masters' series, where he devoted the first two chapters to this 'most native and English of writers' and Orwell's 'uncertain and ambiguous relationship with England'—only to fade away in the rest of the book.[11] Bernard Bergonzi had picked up on an 'ideology of being English' in Orwell the year before, but failed to take it on and, with two partial exceptions and one full one, the same can be said of a gallery of Englishness-spotters beginning with Lionel Trilling and Atkins in 1949 and 1954, and including Martin Green ('essential', 1961), Richard Rees ('hard-headed', 1970), J. R. Hammond ('acute', 1982), John Rodden ('quintessential', 1989), Malcolm Bradbury ('engrained', 1993), David Gervais ('reminiscent of Priestley', 1993), D. J. Taylor ('shrewd', 2003), John Brannigan ('deep', 2003), Christopher Hitchens ('ambivalent', 2003), and Ben Clarke, who restricted himself to 'interpretive' possibilities in 2006, and national myths in 2007. The one full exception is Michael Walzer, whose 1998 essay 'George Orwell's England' stands out as a fine and original contribution. The two partial exceptions are Bernard Crick and Julian Barnes, who in 1980 and 2009 respectively addressed Orwell's Englishness in ways that suggested there was more to come. In Crick's case, his reference to Orwell as a member of the awkward squad of dissident Englishmen was exactly right, if all too passing. There was to be no adequate follow-up, though he went on to write about national identity in other contexts. For Barnes there is still time. We stand ready.[12]

Nearly all these writers sniffed Orwell's Englishness in the air but were too busy seeing it as other things and did not track it down. When it passed under their noses, as in Orwell's *The Lion and the Unicorn*, or *Coming Up for Air*, or *The English People*, they tended to regard it as an English variant of socialism, or nostalgia, or whimsy, or individualism, or populism, or some aspect of something 'characteristically' and 'indelibly' English, without explaining further.[13] In a lengthy index entry appertaining to Orwell's 'Attitudes, Habits, Characteristics', D. J. Taylor gave 'Englishness' only one mention. In an equally fine work, Gordon Bowker tried to explain the contradictions in Orwell's 'profound sense of Englishness'. That he 'was against private schools' but sent his son to one, that he 'disliked Scots' but chose to live in Scotland, that he 'was a staunch atheist' but 'asked to be buried according to the rites of the

Church of England', and so on tells us something, but by no means enough.[14] Other biographers hardly noticed it, though of course it was there all the time.[15] Not that this should surprise us. Given the kind of men who were its guardians, Englishness was either too familiar to be noticed or, if it was noticed, it was supposed to be held in check. Like their persons or, if you like, like their 'masculinity', being English for this class of men was *supposed* to be held in check, *supposed* to be implicit, assumed, not easily put into words, indefinable.[16] They were so stuck for words for things so personal they used French words instead. Englishness enjoyed a certain 'je ne sais quois'. In the sense that it assumed the dignified part of the constitution, the Englishman's Englishness was there for all to see. But in the sense that it told you something about the man himself, it was a life best kept private.[17] It used to be thought, and to some degree it still is thought, that Englishness made explicit is Englishness exposed, and Englishness exposed is Englishness undone.

In the first place, therefore, I am trying to prove an absence: Orwell saw his identity as his own affair, Englishness as a backdrop, the British Empire in the wings, the state nowhere to be seen. He certainly was not going to talk about it in a personal way. But as he tried to come to terms with himself in times of great threat to his country, England moved centre-stage and front. This is not to say he built his identity out of it. Identities are never 'built' or 'constructed' so much as lived and breathed, day to day, until they run out of meaning and have to change. Driven by his 'need for constant self definition', 'his mind still grinding over the same old political questions' with 'no sense of peace or relinquishment in him', he kept at it right to the end.[18]

Keeping up

This book tries to keep up. Orwell produced no body of work—that came after. Peter Davison's twenty blue volumes might look like a body of work, but Orwell never saw such a thing. He responded to the vagaries of an eventful life. Understanding how this worked is not just a question of doing the research and coming up with new knowledge. Knowledge in the humanities is rarely new in that way, and even if it was, it is not a question of knowledge transfer. It is a question of being convincing. For there is no objective 'England' against which I can measure Orwell's 'Englishness', any more than there is a full and final

'Orwell' who is the standard by which all the other Orwells can be judged. Suffice to say that his Englishness had nothing to do with royalty or regiments, cricket or cucumber sandwiches. It was not about being 'old-fashioned', 'Victorian', or a bit of an 'old fogey'—though he might have been all these things. It was about how at a certain stage in his life he wanted to identify with his country, understand it, explain it, be convinced by it, and reconnect with it in its current and previous manifestations. He thought of a future that could be made more bearable by marching towards it carrying the best of what had inspired previous generations—like the Sikhs carried their holy books aloft into battle. In other words, Orwell's Englishness sat somewhere between what had been lived and breathed in the past and what might be lived and breathed in the future. I am not saying in this book that Englishness is the key to Orwell. I am saying that it was something that he thought *with* as well as about, and that it stayed with him from first to last. If it does not explain all the strands in his thinking, it is at least the strand which runs through all the others. There is no 'key' to Orwell any more than he is a 'box' to open. His Englishness, though, is worth following through.

1

Angry Old Etonian

'Scrub'

In the English left-wing periodical *New Leader* for 30 April 1937 there is
a report from the Spanish Civil War telling of a night attack on the
Aragon front. It describes how a contingent of British Republican volunteers crawled their way across a field up to the edge of the enemy
line, where they crouched listening to the guards before standing up to
throw their bombs. *New Leader* identified the comrades:

> A Spanish comrade arose and rushed forward. 'Por ellos, Arriba!' (For
> the others, charge!) 'Charge!' shouted Blair. 'Over to the right and in!'
> called Paddy Donovan. 'Are we downhearted?' cried the French Captain
> Benjamin. In front of the parapet was Eric Blair's tall figure coolly stroll-
> ing forward through the storm of fire. He leaps at a parapet, then stum-
> bles. Hell, have they got him? No, he was over, closely followed by Cross
> of Hammersmith, Frankford of Hackney, and Bob Smillie, with others
> right after them.[1]

The report goes on to describe how they seized the trench, killing two.
Blair, apparently, was first in and last out. Bayonet fixed, he chased an
enemy soldier who scampered away down the line wrapped in a blanket.
Having taken the trench, there was nothing more for the attackers to do
than relinquish it. They made their way back to their own lines under
cover of darkness.

Rival leftist groups in Britain suggested that this foray was made for
no other reason than to draw attention to the Independent Labour
Party, one of the many *marxisant* parties supporting the Republican side.
The Communist Party in particular claimed that the attack had had no
strategic value, that it was only done for publicity, that it was a 'stunt'.

Well, whatever Eric Blair was doing or thought he was doing that
night in the dark, he was not trying to make friends or influence people

back in England. He was not following, for instance, the rules for getting on as a public figure.[2] He was not enjoying the warmth of a good club. He was not trying to make the right literary contacts which would help him further his career in London. Nor was he comfortably in chambers, or living off a private income, or worming his way onto an expense account, or petitioning for a fellowship—all of which would have given him the freedom to write. Least of all was he carrying a rifle in Spain in order to solve what Stefan Collini calls 'the riddle of Englishness' in England. Englishness was every public moralist's favourite subject in the 1930s.[3] To have been able to say what it was would have rendered a great service to his country and an even greater service to his career.

In the event, under the name of George Orwell, Eric Blair did become a famous public moralist, England's finest, in fact; and he did make a profession out of writing, consummately so, in the end; and he did solve the riddle of Englishness, for a time at least. But he never set out to do these things. He did not intend to be a moralist or a national figure. He had no plan. He had no patron. He was not a 'joiner'. He did not follow an obvious path. George Orwell, the most significant British political writer of the twentieth century, was not even an 'Orwellian'. In his old school slang, he was a 'scrub': someone who liked to do what is not done.

All this makes him a difficult subject. There is little in the way of a trajectory in Orwell's life. It is more a series of intense reactions to peoples and places as he came upon them. Nor is there any trace of a career or much sign of a 'set'. He threw himself into situations, not always to his own advantage. He liked to go against the grain because he believed that was where the truth usually lay. But it led him into all sorts of awkward and angry corners which fed the contrariness in his nature. He loathed nationalism, but defined Englishness for a generation. He was an enemy of the right, but had little to say in favour of the left. He was no friend of the left, but tried to work within it. He was violently opposed to totalitarianism, but had little interest in political parties. He didn't write well about women but tried, in one novel at least, to write about being a woman, and in his last novel he invested his best hope, such as it was, in one woman and (almost) all women. He did not trust intellectuals, but mixed with them, was one himself, and never tried to pretend otherwise, though sometimes he conveniently forgot the fact.

The world as it was

Most of all, Orwell wanted to encounter the world as he found it and tell the truth by turning it into art. As we know from his two most famous books, *Animal Farm* (1945) and *Nineteen Eighty Four* (1949), he least wanted to give way to the blandishments of Fascism and Communism. I say 'blandishments' because he was writing at a time when, for many people in Europe, Fascists and Communists seemed not only necessary and modern, but truthful and attractive too. Only in the summer of 1939 did Nazism become the official enemy of the British people and, once Russia was invaded by Hitler in June 1941, the Soviet Union became Britain's official friend and ally and remained so all through the war. On the whole, he was against both systems almost from the minute he first discovered them. He did not always get things right, but unlike some who lived through the 1930s and 1940s, he did not have to recant, or excuse, his former associations.

He was against capitalism and imperialism too, and reserved some of his harshest criticism for their British variants. All round, he believed that all four systems—capitalist, imperialist, Fascist, and Communist—encouraged the strong to plunder the weak and the few to deceive the many. He made modifications and distinctions within and between them of course, as any serious observer must, and in the end he was forced into siding with one over the other, but in 1946 Orwell claimed that every line he had written since 1936 had been against imperialism and totalitarianism and in favour of 'democratic Socialism' as he hoped it would develop in Britain and Europe.[4]

Orwell was against all the major world systems of his day, including nationalism and Catholicism. Apart from an early gut attraction to a sort of folk Marxism where 'the oppressed are always right and the oppressors are always wrong', he did not believe in political ideologies either.[5] In other words, he painted himself into a very small corner of the things he knew and supported, largely by default, and set his face against the vast ideological spaces of all the things he opposed.

He understood 'ideology' as a form of abstract knowledge which, in order to support a particular tendency or regime, has to distort the world and usually does so by drawing off, or separating out, ideas from experience. Ideology therefore (in Orwell's eyes) could never afford to get too close to the lives of the people. The more abstract the idea and the language that expressed it, the more ideological the work, and vice versa. A key feature of his writing, therefore, was a desire to put himself as far away from abstraction and as close to experience as he could, followed by a meticulous attention to the detail of what he saw, heard, touched, tasted, smelled, and reasonably assumed to be the case. For Orwell, this was the first test of truth. He challenged the world by burrowing into it, and expected to be challenged in turn. He knew that if he was saying something so abstract that it could not be understood, or falsified, then he was not saying anything that mattered. Which is to say, he staked his reputation on being true to the world as it was, and his great fear of intellectuals stemmed from what he saw as their propensity for abstraction and deracination—abstraction in their thinking, and deracination in their lives. Orwell's politics, therefore, were no more and no less than intense encounters turned into writings he hoped would be truthful and important. Like Gramsci, he believed that telling the truth was a revolutionary act. But without the encounters he had no politics, and without the politics he felt he had nothing to say.

If Orwell feared the deracination of intellectuals, it was because he himself was prone to it. So much of his later life was spent ill in bed. So much of his early life was cordoned off. Soon after his birth to English parents in British India—a cocooned life if ever there was one—Eric and his mother Ida and older sister Marjorie returned to England to settle in Henley-on-Thames. There they lived agreeably on Mr Blair's 600 rupees a month, about £440 per year, or over £8 per week—well above the lower range middle-class income of £250 p.a., if not quite reaching the middle range of £500 and over. And in the 1930s, when the Blairs had long since retired to the seaside, what was bad for Indian peasants, it seems, was good for them. The British had grossly overvalued the Indian rupee against the pound at a fixed rate of 1*s.* 6*d.*, and Mr Blair's pension did well out of this.[6] Orwell always said that the British lived off the backs of Indian peasants. Well, at 36 High Street Southwold that certainly seems to have been the case—not forgetting that Blair's pensionable salary had been culled from the opium trade, hardly one of the choicer ends of the imperial project.[7] Orwell went to Burma and came back hating the British Empire. Given his family circumstances, it is not impossible to imagine him walking no further than to the end of Southwold pier and coming to the same conclusion.

At the same time, he regretted how, as a child, his Henley upbringing had forced him to stand apart from the everyday life of the town. He was forbidden to play with neighbouring children because their father was believed to be a plumber. He came to fear manual workers, and never forgot his revulsion on venturing too close. Being invited to swig their beer, or smoke their dog-ends, or smell their sweating bodies ('bacon-like reek') was enough to make a boy retch.[8] Later in life he would force himself to do it. Meanwhile, down in Henley-on-Thames, his mother enjoyed a life of coffee and cards while young Eric was encouraged to make friends with his own sort.[9]

In 1911, when he was 8, he won a scholarship to a boys' private boarding school in Sussex. St Cyprian's seems to have been no different from most English private schools, in that it was set as far away as possible from other people without looking like an asylum—well outside the town, with landscaped grounds, at the end of a drive glimpsed only through a gate. Gilt letters on the board might say 'preparatory school', but only in the sense that it was a preparation for the next school, not for life over the wall.

Looking out on the South Downs, beyond the games-field and miniature parade ground, there was little chance that Eric Blair and the eighty little fellows of St Cyprian's were going to chance upon life as it was actually lived, in Eastbourne, in 1911. He was unhappy here for all sorts of reasons, from the sour porridge to the tepid baths and an early spot of bed-wetting (as reported by him), but most of all he was unhappy because (as he came to regard it later) St Cyprian's was a totalitarian institution which, having lied to him about who he was, proceeded to bully him for being what he thought he had become—snotty, smelly, and unloved.[10] The school was only half a mile from Eastbourne Union Workhouse. Two types of confinement so near and so far would have pleased Orwell's taste for paradox, but as a boy he never knew paupers existed. It may have been that St Cyprian's was his first introduction to ideology. It may have been that St Cyprians was his first small world. It was almost certainly his first strong reaction to a people and a place. He came to hate it for wrenching his character out of shape at such a tender age and for cramming him with large doses of information that was either useless or wrong. In the event it was the useless part (the Latin and Greek) that won him a scholarship to the most prestigious school in the world.

He went up to Eton College in May 1917. He was nearly 14 years old and one of seventy King's Scholars. The six hundred others, the 'Oppidans', were there because their parents could afford to send them. Blair was there because he was clever. Eton scholarships were formidably difficult. Whatever else we learn of Eric Arthur Blair, we should remember his natural gifts.[11]

Although far more open and relaxed than the little prep school, Eton did not teach him much about the outside world either. In 1900 Arthur Clutton-Brock characterized it as a place happy in its customs.[12] In 1905 it had thirty-two classics masters and four science masters. In 1936 it had nine scientists and thirty-nine classicists. Sixth-formers spent half the week construing Latin and Greek verbs and the other half wondering what lay beyond the school bounds. Eton High Street and the principal thoroughfares of Windsor leading up to the Castle and the Park were in bounds; every other street and thoroughfare except Brocas Lane (at such times as boating was allowed) was not.[13] Around the time of Orwell's arrival Eton still believed it had lost a truly great headmaster in Dr Edmond Warre (1884–1905)—though it did not take long for them to forget why they believed it.[14] The headmaster during Orwell's time was the Revd Dr Cyril Argentine Alington (1917–33), formerly of All Souls College, Oxford. Alington had replaced his brother in law, the Revd Edward Lyttelton, formerly of Middlesex County Cricket Club.[15]

Orwell showed no interest in any of it, no more than it showed interest in any of him. He appears to have sidestepped the most powerful boy ideology of the day, sport and the English gentleman.[16] He resisted the Eton cult of oarsman and tutor. Neither headmasters nor housemasters figure in his writing. There are no memoirs of lazy days on the river or cosy evenings in house. One cannot imagine him singing the Eton Boating Song ('we'll still swing together') with the *Anarquistas* in Spain (though you never know).[17] He only ever wrote about sport once.[18] As a King's Scholar he fooled around with other boys (in the grounds), played a bit of football (Eton rules), swam (in a reserved place), learned dead languages (he opted to do a term's science), grew twelve inches, and naturally enough learned nothing more about real life than he had at St Cyprian's. He did, however, stay long enough to earn the right to wear flannels, 'fag fags',[19] and otherwise fit into an institution whose capacious grounds and toleration of what it called 'boys' side' traditions afforded him some measure of independence which over the years grew into a mild delinquency.

For all its cultishness, Eton could show boys how to be awkward and independent too.[20] It also afforded (some of) them the opportunity to think and imagine. When he was about 15, maybe slightly younger, Blair wrote a three-act play, 'The Man and the Maid', about a bunch of useless intellectuals who live on roots and herbs and think that right-eousness lies in the acquisition of a black skin. Their leader, the youth-ful Lucius, son of Mireldo, feels 'the desire for adventure and romance'. He also wishes 'to be quit of this island'. At around the same time, maybe slightly later, Blair also wrote three stories for the college news-paper. 'The Adventure of the Lost Meat-card' is a pastiche of Conan Doyle. The great detective knew the man was not who he said he was because: ' "What American", said Holmes, "would spit on the floor boards when he could spit on the carpet?" ' (a remark which had enjoyed previous literary outings). 'The Slack-bob' has a touch of Richmal Crompton in it, about a boy who only pretends to be a rower and is found out by his cousins—'noisy girls with red hair' and very pronounced opinions. 'A Peep into the Future' concerns a college pro-fessor who announces 'the reign of science' and with it the inferiority of all women. This is pure vaudeville. People eat pills and carry babies in string bags. In the end the mad professor is slapped down by 'a mighty woman' who strides down the chapel aisle to knock him off his perch. ' "A good smackin' is what you want", she said'. And a good smackin' is what he got.[21]

At least young Eric paid enough attention to his lessons to scrape through his exams, and he does not seem to have been particularly irri-tated by the place except, of course, much later in the drawling Old Etonian way about poor form, bad show, and so forth. Even his snobbery was effortless.[22] When he left, he did not try to keep in touch or fondly remember, though Old Etonians kept popping up and became impor-tant to him. But it was no different with the other places that mattered in his life. He was not sentimental. Commentators have struggled to make sense of his time there. Eton claimed to be able to instil in each boy the will to 'to save himself by his sole exertions' while the schoolboy Blair proved the point by coolly observing that there were at least six clerical masters on the staff who made a good living out of the Crucifixion.[23] School friends remembered him as a rebel and a bit of a dark horse:

'certainly able to look after himself from the beginning...obviously a character.' In later life Orwell declared the place a nuisance and an anachronism, but concluded, somewhat surprisingly perhaps, and against Patrick Joyce's expert judgement, that the 'atmosphere...gave each boy a fair chance of developing his individuality'.[24] Public school seems to have left him personally undamaged and might even have given back some of the boyish confidence the prep school had taken away. He put his own son's name down for Westminster.

After Eton, a boy like him should have gone straight to university or into one of the professions, and it is perhaps a sign of the scrub that he didn't. He joined the Imperial Police, and at least one of his tutors at Eton would have taken the view that it was a sign of the scrub that he did.[25] Maybe not going into a well-heeled world represented some sort of snobbery on his part. Maybe he had had enough of being a boy. There were no scholarships this time round, so perhaps it was a simple lack of funds. A friend of his at the time says that Blair wanted to go to university but was forbidden by his father.[26] King's Scholars at Eton traditionally went to King's College, Cambridge (the colleges were joint foundations), but had he gone there he would have learned nothing about England either.[27] True, he might have chatted with porters at the college gates or bedders in his rooms, but by and large life as he might have lived it at Cambridge would have had nothing to do with life as it was generally lived in England in 1922. Most English people could not have named a single Cambridge college, or shown the slightest knowledge of what college life involved. That a young man in a scarf should be chased around the streets by an old one in a hat for staying out late would have struck them as bizarre. On the other hand, if he had gone to King's he might have been taught by John Maynard Keynes, or met E. M. Forster on the stairs.[28] But Eric Blair did not go to Cambridge, or Oxford, or any university. At 19, he went to Burma.

The Empire as it was

At school Orwell played the role of interesting rebel.[29] He recalled it as part of the spirit of the time. But he did not mean it. When he wanted to mean it he played the white man and put on a uniform. One could suppose that he was part of some great imperial plan: that little boys like him were sent away in order to forget their Mummies and remember their Fathers and grow into big boys who would want to run the Empire, or join the army, or teach in a prep school, or *something*. Coarse as it may sound, in Blair's case there was some truth in this supposition. Scrub or not, he was inclined to want to do the right thing.

He chose Burma out of nine Indian provinces, and spent five years there learning something of himself and a lot about the world.[30] At the same time, he had to unlearn nearly everything else. For a young public-school man who had been born in Bengal, whose mother had been brought up in Burma, and whose father had worked his entire life in the Indian Civil Service, this must have come as something of a shock— skeletons in the family cupboard. He went out to Burma in 1922 as part of a great British world system held together by the extraordinary wealth and power of his native country and the extraordinary size and key strategic position of India, his adopted one.[31] When he came back in 1927 that world system had not lost one cubit of its stature, but the point was he no longer believed in it.

First discoveries came in the heat and chaos of everyday life. India comprised 675 states and 824,000 square miles, and administered other places besides. The British were heavily outnumbered in all of them, and not surprisingly saw all of the subcontinent's history as a search for control. So did Gandhi, their main antagonist, who appealed to the British to give self-control to Indians (*Hindswaraj*) by giving self-control (*swaraj*) to themselves. If they looked into their hearts, he claimed, that is what the British would do: there was no need for violence, only an overwhelming spiritual will born of the truth. In M. K. Gandhi the rulers of the world's most formidable imperial power met their most formidable imperial foe—a man who told them they had to withdraw because it was a question of their own identity and freedom that they do so.[32] Burma had its own nationalist movement, but there would not have been a British officer in the territory who did not know about the man in the loincloth who was capable of making all their lives miserable.

Gandhi's message was not just spiritual. It made political sense too. In calling for liberty for India, he was not asking for anything the British did not ask for themselves. And in among the sayings and the 'truths' of his own homespun philosophy, he was simply turning a mirror on his rulers. Do you look like this? Do you look like the man you say you are? If you are freeborn, then why have you not made us free? If you never shall be slaves, why are we your slaves? This was a spiritual version of the Indian National Congress's call upon the *Raj* to honour its own national myths and, in this sense at least Gandhi may have been Blair's first serious encounter with his own Englishness. Orwell remembered as a young policeman reading Gandhi's *The Story of my Experience with Truth* in an Indian newspaper, and how the arguments made a good impression—'which Gandhi himself did not'.[33] Nevertheless, he recalled also a strange degree of respect for the man, even among those who would be only too pleased to throw him into jail.

The British *Raj* (the *rule*) ran on a 'warrant of precedence' that laid down seventy-seven distinctive ranks for officials, not counting caste and racial ranking. By the book, India's provinces appeared to be very carefully modulated systems of administration: from King Emperor at the top to dockside coolie at the bottom, a place for everyone and everyone in their place. Next to the King Emperor was the British high command in London and New Delhi—the India Office, the Viceroy, his staff, their advisors and generals. Then came the princely states, naturally pro-British, covering two-fifths of the territory and containing one-fifth of the population. Then the industrial upper classes, pro-British but increasingly anxious to do better for themselves, possibly in an India that was able to govern itself; then the white-collar classes, a vast collections of desk-*wallahs* from counting-house clerks to city lawyers; then the industrial proletariat, ever growing; then the peasantry—immense. The Indian army and police were paid regular wages, at least.

G. W. Stevens described the District Officer's little court—the fold-up desk, the two chairs, three clerks, and man at the tent door letting in and seeing out the little queue of plaintiffs. Behind the desk, just 30 years old, 'sat the Presence'. 'British Rule incarnate is a young man.' But as a front-line paramilitary police officer in a British Indian province, dealing with people who did not always want to be dealt with, Blair did not see it like that. He remembered instead that hierarchies did not mean much on the ground. When you had to hold a man, or kick him, or punch him, or hang him, or when you were spat at or tripped or bumped off the path, fold-up desks and warrants of precedence did not save you.[34] In a fine, manly flourish John Ruskin once said there was 'no nobler career' than that of imperial service. But Eric Blair returned home from postings where he was hated by large numbers of people knowing that the Empire was not missionary work, and the virtue of young men like him did not lie in its service.[35]

For the British, every hill station was somewhere to escape from. Orwell remembered rather enjoying the company of locals (not counting Buddhist monks), when he could get it, and he made serious efforts to learn the languages, but the ordinary business of being an English *sahib* disgusted him. His great-great grandfather had been a slave-owner in Jamaica. His father-in-law had been a teak dealer in Burma. His father had been an official in the opium trade. These family heirlooms gave him a personal stake in what he witnessed. Presiding over thousands of little ceremonies of control and consent, even the control and consent of a man about to be hanged, Orwell did his duty. But when he came to reflect upon that duty, he laid down his swagger-stick and took on the role of colonial anthropologist instead. Increasingly detached from Burmese and British alike, but exposed to the colonial relationship all day, every day, he came to the conclusion that it was a racket. Or, as he put it, the policeman held the native down while the businessman went through his pockets, and the British Empire pronounced it a good thing for all concerned.[36]

The British had been trading in Burma since the seventeenth century. In the nineteenth century they turned it into a colony, partly for strategic reasons to do with Indian security, and partly for economic reasons to do with raw materials and the Irrawaddy's enormous capacity for growing rice. The country was taken in three bites from the south: the first, taking Rangoon and the Delta, in 1824–6; the second, taking Lower Burma, in 1852–3; and the third, under pressure from the Manchester Chamber of Commerce demanding a trade-route to China, taking Upper Burma, including Mandalay, in 1885.

Cash-cropping started in the late 1860s. The railways came in 1877. Burma Oil commenced operations in 1886. A lieutenant-governor and a non-elected Legislative Council were appointed in 1897, a Department of Jails and Hospitals in 1899, ministries of Public Instruction in 1900, Land Revenue in 1900, Forestry in 1905, Agriculture in 1906, Excise in 1906, and a Judiciary between 1900 and 1905. By 1913 British firms owned 90 per cent of capital assets in grain, timber, rubber, oil, and minerals.[37] A poor neighbour of India and almost as far away from Delhi as from London—or so it must have seemed on station—Burma was ruled by the Indian Civil Service and other institutions of the *Raj*, including the various military and police forces. Joppen's map of 1926 shows it as a thick pink wedge, some 800 miles by 400, with one city at its base and one long river down its middle.[38] Buddhism, the majority religion, was not officially recognized.

The suppression of the Indian 'Mutiny' in 1858 redrew the British presence in the subcontinent. An aggressive trading empire, the East India Company, was replaced by a Viceroy in Calcutta and direct rule from the India Office in London. Attitudes changed. There was less talk now of winning new territories, more talk of steady government and staying on. In particular, there was no longer any question (as once there had been) of turning Indian civil servants into little Englishmen.[39] Macaulay had once hoped 'to form a class who may be interpreters between us and the millions whom we govern; a class of persons, Indian in blood and colour, but English in taste, in opinions, in morals and in intellect'. That was in 1835. By 1876, on the British side at least, that was all over. Lord Salisbury let it be known that Bengali clerks could only be in opposition.[40] In the wake of this complete change of face, the hill station, the compound, the bungalow, the club, and the regimental mess became private places, islands 'secure from noxious India'. When the Prince of Wales visited Burma in December 1921 they held a Military Police Ball at Mandalay in his honour. It was 'a white tie affair'. Such things mattered. They kept you onside.[41]

But having put themselves on the inside, the colonists looked out only to gaze back upon themselves.[42] Were they worthy? Were they strong? Were they keeping face? More to the point perhaps, could they keep control with little more than a gendarmerie as back-up?[43] At any rate, this was how the administrators of the high Indian Civil Service saw it: an India so different that it was only governable in the Oriental manner— which is to say, splendidly, remotely, and strictly hierarchically, with touches of English progress thrown in here and there as was seen fit. Other than that, they faced India down and, depending on how you looked at it, held her down, by force or the illusion of force, by what the Eden Commission in 1879 called 'the grand counterpoise' of a European army backed by the second counterpoise of a country comprised of 'Natives against Natives'. In 1942 Lord Linlithgow's harsh words shocked Clement Attlee, who hoped for finer feelings from a Viceroy:

> India and Burma have no natural association with the Empire, from which they are alien by race, history and religion, and for which as such neither of them have any natural affection, and both are in the Empire because they are conquered countries which have been brought there by

force, kept there by our controls and which hitherto it has suited to remain under our protection.[44]

Except, it has to be said, this was not entirely the case. What Linlithgow said was what Linlithgow wanted to hear, but it was not the case that India was a conquered country, pure and simple. The Indian National Congress, founded in 1885 by high-minded liberals, some of them Indian, some British, but turned into a mass movement by Gandhi from around 1917, held on to the idea that self-rule, or home-rule within a commonwealth of nations, could be achieved along British lines, or at least along the lines that the British had so recently conceded to the Irish and before that, in happier circumstances perhaps, to Canada, Australia, and New Zealand. For all his ragging of British rule, and for all his unlikely (and unpredictable) mixture of old-fashioned political brinkmanship and immovable non-violent resistance (*satyagraha*), Gandhi never asked for more than dominion status for India until 1942, and even then it was negotiable. It had been the *Raj*, not the Congress Party, who had given up on 'natural associations with the Empire', at first refusing, then haggling over dominion status, before opting instead for Oriental hierarchies. Those Indians who wanted Englishness most wanted that which England was least willing to give.

These were Salisbury's and Curzon's *babus*, so-called—Hindi for 'clerk', but a word with a range of meanings, not all of them nice, referring to those politicized, English-speaking Indians who looked to British imperial progress as a higher stage of human development and wanted an Indian share of it.[45] All through Orwell's childhood and youth, men like these had argued for Indian independence on what they took to be British (or English) grounds of liberty. It had been the British, after all, who had made them *babus*, who had given them authority of a kind, and no one could be surprised that, having the pens and the pencils and wanting to join the club, they wanted to sign the book.[46] Against them stood the 'Civilians', the most senior civil servants of the *Raj*, and most British people. Most British people, of course, knew nothing about India, and those who did, in the armed forces or engineering, were glad to leave.[47] As for the Civilians, said to be the most powerful interest-group in Edwardian Britain, they argued that India was India, and unless the British stayed British it would collapse into a heap of castes and fragments. Indeed, they argued that there could be no such thing as an independent 'British India', because the very liberty which such a state sought would be unequal to the task of ruling such a vast and diverse country.

Here they had a point. In 1939 353 million Indians were ruled by around one thousand Civilians, supported by a large under-class of Indian civil servants and a ludicrously lightweight army of 200,000 mixed Indian troops, but mainly Sikh, Gurkha, Pathan, and Punjabi, with 60,000 British to stiffen the mix. With the Royal Navy ready to dispatch them near and far, this force was prepared to keep the peace laterally from Suez to Hong Kong, with long reaches south—which it made in 1875 (Perak War), 1878–80 (2nd Afghan War), 1882 (Egypt), 1885 (2nd Burman War), 1885 and 1900 (Sudan), 1899–1902 (South Africa), and 1900–1 (China). Its main purpose was internal security, but in Bihar province alone, for instance, one of the most populated in India, there were only twelve policemen. For all their talent, the Civilians did not understand what they ruled. They believed in control. They believed in warrants of precedence. In their own way, they believed in caste, and in the virtues of being *pukkah*. But they did not know what Blair knew.

Burma was not only the largest province of India, it was the most crime-ridden and, from an administrator's point of view, the furthest-stretched. Blair was part of a civil force of 13,000 police officers supported by 10,000 soldiers responsible for thirty-six districts and 13 million people. He recalled having to shoot an elephant—which he did with all the *swaraj* he could muster because he was on his own. After initial training, he served in six postings over three years: three of them in the Delta, close to Rangoon, flat, alluvial, swampy, pumping oil day and night; two of them in the jungle—one in Lower and the other in Upper Burma; and one in Moulmein, the third-largest city. He was especially responsible for the discipline and inspection of a police force that was, according to an official report, underpaid, under-employed, poorly trained, badly housed, and low in morale. Constables even disliked their uniforms.[48] But because this was an Empire that outfaced rather than outgunned its subjects, British officials were encouraged to work the channels and never lose face.[49] When Orwell finally did shoot the elephant he felt the strain of being alone in a strange land with an entire global project bearing down on his shoulders. He fired not because he wanted to, but because two thousand jeering Burmese wanted him to—drawing his own conclusions:

> I perceived in this moment that when the white man turns tyrant it is his own freedom that he destroys. He becomes a sort of hollow, posing dummy, the conventionalized figure of a sahib. For it is the condition of his rule that he shall spend his life in trying to impress the 'natives' and so in every crisis he has got to do what the 'natives' expect of him...my whole life, every white man's life in the East, was one long struggle not to be laughed at.[50]

Although it seems Assistant District Superintendant Blair was instinctively drawn to what scholars now call 'the contact zone' of Anglo-Burmese relations, the job in hand made it almost impossible for him to meet the Burmese as friends or neighbours (though they were easier to procure as lovers).[51] He had come upon a troubled country. Infant mortality stood at 20 per cent. Peasant proprietorship was breaking down, with high levels of peonage and debt.[52] There were struggles also between various ethnic groups—between the nationalist Burmese and the colonial British, and between the Burmese and those immigrant Indians who had come to buy land and help themselves. Indian and Chinese businesses dominated Rangoon, a city rich in moneylending and prostitution.[53] Politically, the relationship with India was the key issue. From the Government of India Act in 1919 up to Burma's final separation from India in 1937, Burmese leaders blamed Indian leaders for taking more from the British than they could manage, while peasant Burmese blamed foreign moneylenders for the growing alienation of land, as everybody blamed Rangoon for degenerate Western influences. The police were unpopular with all groups. Gandhi's non-cooperation example, from 1919 up to its abandonment in 1922, had looked increasingly likely to put them to the test. Orwell said he was hated, but when there was deference (as there must have been to the tall young Old Etonian in an officer's uniform), it must have been hard for him to read. Thirty years later Claude Lévi-Strauss would speak of walking through the crowds of Calcutta as 'a permanent repudiation of the notion of human relationship. You are offered everything and promised everything...'[54]

That said, the British in Burma had not made life easy for themselves. Even the best they achieved, such as irrigation and railways, had not always been for the best, and trying to invent a working political system was even harder.[55] In India they had opted to rule by a system based on village stability.[56] But in Burma they had rendered the rural areas unstable by disbanding the village-headman system, while in the towns they faced an increasingly active nationalist movement led by the Buddhist monk U Ottama, an admirer of Gandhi, who campaigned widely from 1921 up to his imprisonment in 1924. Worse was to follow with the Hsaya San armed rebellion in Lower Burma in 1930. Commissions of inquiry came and went, but it was Orwell and his constables who held the front line in a gradually deteriorating situation which included over 700 judicial hangings over the period of his stay.[57]

Under these difficult and sometimes solitary circumstances, the expatriate club was an extremely important place—a 'spiritual citadel', according to Orwell. During the day the British sat in the full glare of their office. At the end of it they could fall back into themselves, cool off, have a few drinks, say what they wanted to say not in front of the servants. This was a tight social round. No matter how small the circle, it had to be joined. Only rarely were locals allowed in. When Clive Dewey wanted to write about the British contribution to *The Mind of the Indian Civil Service*, he devoted a whole chapter to 'Experiments with Friendship'.[58]

In *Burmese Days* (1934) Orwell would come to address all these issues. John Flory is a timber manager in Kyauktada—one of a long chain of managers and officials who hold the Empire together.[59] The British in Burma are only as strong as their weakest link, and Flory is that link. There is friction among them, largely played out at the club.[60] Verrall, for instance, is a cavalry man with the knack of looking down on Flory, usually from a saddle. At the same time it is tartly observed that Verrall only went to a third-class public school. More devoted to his ponies than to his compatriots, when the trouble starts he is not around to deal with it.

Like Verrall, Elizabeth Lackersteen does not want to be in this stupid town and its tin-pot club either. A young woman who has come out to stay with her aunt and uncle, she is willing to make the small sacrifice of a long journey in order to achieve the higher sacrifice of finding a husband.[61] Girls like her were called 'girls of the fishing-fleet' or, if things did not go well, 'returned empties'.[62] At one point it looks as though Elizabeth might make a match with Flory. Having denaturalized himself to the point where almost any vision of Englishness in a cool frock looked beautiful and sounded interesting, the timber man nurses hopes of love and marriage. But they are both caught up in extremely tight racial, class, and gender calculations that centre, for the most part, on the 'dumpy one-storey wooden building' sitting by the Irrawaddy ('huge and ochreous'). Insofar as club life permitted conversation and company, it was somewhere to go in the evening. Insofar as it was a 'bloody hole' pressured beyond belief, Flory couldn't stand it.[63]

Yet this is the club Dr Veraswami wants to join. He has all the right credentials. He is a good sport. He is a good doctor. He pays his tab. He is honourable. His acceptance would make club membership up to eight, but more to the point Veraswami believes in the club just as he believes in the Empire. Possibly he is the only one who does.[64] Yet he cannot be allowed to join the club because he is a *babu*.

He and Flory discuss the problem man to man. No Englishman ever defended the Empire like Veraswami. No Englishman, on the other hand, ever attacked it like Flory:

> The doctor grew agitated, as he always did when Flory criticised the Club members. He was standing with his plump white-clad behind balanced against the veranda rail, and sometimes gesticulating. When searching for a word he would nip his black thumb and forefinger together, as though to capture an idea floating in the air.
>
> 'But truly, truly, Mr Flory, you must not speak so! Why iss it that you are abusing the pukka sahibs, ass you call them? They are the salt of the earth. Consider the great things they have done—consider the great administrators who have made British India what it iss. Consider Clive, Warren Hastings, Dalhousie, Curzon. They were such men—I quote your immortal Shakespeare—ass, take them for all in all, we shall not look upon their like again!'
>
> 'Well, do you want to look upon their like again? I don't...'
>
> 'But, my dear friend, what lie are you living?'
>
> 'Why of course the lie that we're here to uplift our poor black brothers instead of to rob them. I suppose it's a natural enough lie. But it corrupts us, it corrupts us in ways you can't imagine. There's an everlasting sense of being a sneak and a liar that torments us and drives us to justify ourselves night and day. It's at the bottom of half our beastliness to the natives. We Anglo-Indians could be almost bearable if we'd only admit that we're thieves and go on thieving without any humbug.'
>
> The doctor, very pleased, nipped his thumb and forefinger together. 'The weakness of your argument, my dear friend', he said, beaming at his own irony, 'the weakness appears to be, that you are *not* thieves'.[65]

The Professor of History in the University of Rangoon saw the British Empire like Dr Veraswami saw it, as a free imperial association, the only one of its kind in the history of the world.[66] Orwell knew this was a lie, and set his face against it. In his estimate of the Empire as simply a moneymaking racket, however, he overstated his case.[67] It is unlikely that the British economy ever depended on the Empire. Nineteenth-century imperial possessions accounted for only about 25 per cent of imports, 25 per cent of capital investments, and between 25 per cent to 40 per cent of exports. Almost nothing the British did with their Empire (including trade and emigration) could not have been done—and indeed *was* done—elsewhere, at no extra cost or loss of advantage. In addition, world responsibilities burdened the British with higher military expenditures than anybody else—'by a considerable margin'.[68] In Orwell's time imperial markets accounted for just under half of British overseas trade, but in the twentieth century as in the nineteenth, the British propensity to make money and sell things went far beyond their Empire.[69] Orwell spent his life claiming that 'we all live by robbing Asiatic coolies' and that loss of the Empire would mean steep falls in British living standards. But he was wrong on both counts. Imperial trade was neither as large nor as necessary as its promoters suggested, and independence did not spell a collapse in the domestic standard of living.[70]

Orwell said the British did well out of the colonies, but he did not claim that they did it by genocide and murder. As a former colonial policeman he knew the worst (or thought he did), but he could not know, and he certainly could not afford to ignore, how Burma compared, say, to Kenya, or Kenya to anywhere else in a vast imperial mosaic of systems and administrations.[71] Although the British ran their Empire ultimately by force rather than consent, they were not compelled perforce to be systematically repressive. True, India had been hauled back into their system in 1858 by a British army smashing its way up the Ganges, exacting 'savage revenge' as it went. And true, when one speaks of 'system' it is as well to seek Zulu, Ashanti, Maori, and Afrikaaner opinion on what that meant. But on the whole the system was at once too big and too delicate to hold by force alone.[72] The British had known for sure since the first full census of 1881 just how complicated India was. The census's 1,200 folio pages were woven into the very fabric of administration and control. Such a vast country made up of so many religions, languages, castes, occupations, provinces, traditions, and filial loyalties was never going to be ruled by force—let alone outside force, let alone the outside force of a country that did not posssess, and did not desire, large outside forces.[73] Instead, for the British at least, the quotidian duties of contact, cooperation, concession, and equilibrium were far more important, and were cultivated (and not cultivated) in ways that Orwell described in *Burmese Days*. Of course, Burma was not all Britain's imperial possessions any more than Superintendant Blair was all the imperial police. Vast portions of the Empire—settled by ethnically British and Irish populations—were by and large willing and loyal members, and being a policeman in Melbourne was not the same as being a policeman in Moulmein. But there were many Burmese who were unwilling, and what Orwell witnessed in one small part of the Empire he made do for the whole.[74]

The economist J. A. Hobson had famously made the economic case against empire the year before Orwell was born. But he did it mainly on behalf of the British, and his core argument did not concern the rationality of investors but what he called the irrationality—or the 'disease', or the 'pathology'—of imperial identity.[75] In John Flory, Orwell put his finger on the essential (Gandhian) paradox of trying to be true to one's national ideals while trying to serve imperial ones as well. If Flory had stayed on another couple of years he would have seen a socialist Secretary of State finding it just as hard.[76] In *Burmese Days* Orwell identified membership of the club as a metaphor for this central problem of running an empire that was obliged to be British on the one hand and native on the other. The Civilians back in London or in the cool rooms of the new imperial capital at Delhi knew the reasons for being exclusive, but no more than did the timber managers and assistant commissioners sweating it out in the jungle. Without exclusivity, there would be no point. With it, however, there was no future. In this sense, Dr Veraswami's modest and seemingly humble application for club membership is a clever caricature of the Indian National Congress's equally modest application for dominion status within a British configuration. Everybody had a place in the sun (if they wanted it). But nationalists wanted a place in the club—an *Indian Raj* living on equal terms with Britain as an independent nation. Gandhi wanted much the same, though he was prepared to break the rules with his three great campaigns of non-cooperation in 1919–22, 1930–1, and 1942–7. In truth, here was a man building his own club wall round the British club wall, and one day he intended to ask the British to leave by an Indian exit. For the time being few in Blair's day, including Gandhi, could think of India without the British.[77]

Away from the political metaphors, in that complex web of personal attraction, repulsion, and guilt that afflicted John Flory, Orwell was equally good on a number of other home and colonial issues: on petty class rivalries within the British camp; on the impossible otherness of the Burmese; on the Burmese themselves and their intertwining of sexual and economic relationships; and, in the face of a mob attack on the club, on the British calculation whether or not to deploy force.[78] Empire always depended on collaboration in local situations, and *Burmese Days* measures its characters by the nature and extent of their collaboration: the honoured magistrate and devious plotter U Po Kyin; Flory's concubine Ma Hla May, running her own sexual politics; Ko S' La, Flory's manservant, jealous of Ma, but a man who has done well for himself anyway; the esteemed Dr Veraswami, of course; and Mr MacGregor, Deputy Commissioner, awfully decent, terribly diplomatic, the man who gets the girl in the end. Ellis, who collaborates least, gets least, and Flory, who collaborates most, dies by his own hand.

Only in Mannoni's extraordinarily precocious *Psychology of Colonization*, first published in 1950, do we get as near as Orwell in explaining a system that demanded collaboration but loathed it in equal measure.[79] There were many critiques of colonialism written in Orwell's lifetime, but few were written as if the Empire involved real personal exchanges, and nearly all based their audits of empire on standards of metropolitan progressivism which made life in the colonies look backward or bone-headed.[80] In other words, against the orthodox view that the Empire involved duties and responsibilities and even a fine sense of affection and belonging that had to work alongside a much heavier insistence on detachment and control, a lot of metropolitan anti-colonialism took the view that the colonies were simply esurient, unnecessary, irrelevant, and alien.[81] Orwell's anti-colonialism, by contrast, confronted the Empire as a relationship which, for all its frustrations, really mattered to who he was and what he would do next. In this regard he and Kipling were the same, even if they differed on almost everything else.

Blair went to Burma in the wake of the two subcontinental massacres, the greater one at Amritsar, in April 1919, perpetrated by the army, and the smaller but still significant one at Chauri Chaura, Uttar Pradesh, in January 1922, the work of an Indian mob. After firing on a crowd, killing three, twenty-two Indian police officers barricaded themselves in their station, only to be burned alive—an event that prompted Gandhi to call off his first campaign. As Orwell got measured for his uniform in England, the incident at Chauri Chaura must have been on every imperial policeman's mind and, in outline at least, it may have found its way into *Burmese Days*.

Orwell was born in the high noon of British imperial power. First there was Victoria's Diamond Jubilee, 1897, which raised it to the skies. Then there was the Anglo-Boer War, 1899–1902, which dragged it through the gutter. Both events generated unprecedented public debate. As a baby he was brought to England in the year that 'Empire Day' was inaugurated—24 May 1904. He spent his schooldays in the time of the greatest imperial war the world had seen, he came of age in the time of T. E. Lawrence, a new imperial hero, and he returned home in 1927, the year of the Simon Commission, charged with India's future. He lived to see the British Empire's greatest military defeat, at Singapore in 1942, and he lived to see Indian independence, in 1947, the British Empire's first great secession, followed by its first great post-colonial crisis, between India and Pakistan. Overall, he spent his life criticizing a pro-imperialist position that valued Empire too much, and an anti-imperialist position that valued it too little. In 1948 he took Grahame Greene to task for writing a novel set in Africa where Africans counted for nothing: 'the whole thing might as well be happening in a London suburb.'[82] Ten years before he had stood in Morocco and watched a French regiment on the march. His account is not Orwell's greatest piece of prose, but it carries a curious power because it leaves us in no doubt what this great river of armed men meant to him and to the other old colonials who watched it pass. Here at least, Africans counted for everything:

> It was curious really. Every white man there had his thoughts stowed somewhere or other in his mind. I had it, so had the other onlookers, so had the officers on their sweating chargers and the white NCOs marching in the ranks. It was a kind of secret which we all knew and were too clever to tell; only the negroes didn't know it. And really it was almost like watching a flock of cattle to see the long column, a mile or two of armed men, flowing peacefully up the road, while the great white birds drifted over them in the opposite direction, glittering like scraps of paper.[83]

Writer

When Blair left the Imperial Police in August 1927 he felt he had been deceived by a country he did not know (his own) about a country he could not know (Burma), and returned home burdened with anger at one and guilt about the other.[84] In what appears to have been a personal as well as a political crisis, he resolved to start again:

> I felt that I had got to escape not merely from imperialism but from every form of man's dominion over man. I wanted to submerge myself, to get right down among the oppressed to be one of them and on their side…At that time failure seemed to me to be the only virtue. Every suspicion of self-advancement, even to 'succeed' in life to the extent of making a few hundreds a year, seemed to me to be spiritually ugly, a species of bullying.[85]

He came back to stay with his parents in Southwold. The Blairs lived nicely enough on an ICS pension between the golf club and the church. They enjoyed reserved seats at the local cinema. Once upon a time Southwold had been a port town (charter 1489), but the Victorians had turned it into a pleasant place in which to do, well, not a lot. There was the usual double row of shops up and down the High Street, a fraternity of tradesmen, Adnam's brewery, a knitwear factory, a coal wharf, a river and harbour with fishermen and a few boat-builders. The grand white façade of the Swan Hotel dominated the seaward end of the town, while at the other end was the railway station. Locals worked, pensioners did what pensioners do, holidaymakers strolled round taking the air. There was a cramming school, which Orwell attended prior to his police exams. Out of season, things could be dull. All the same, the recently resigned young officer appears to have lived there, off and on, just as agreeably as, if a tad less modestly than, his parents. His sister ran a tea shop. His friends included a set of young men and women with broadly intellectual outlooks. Photographs show him on the beach looking tanned and happy and sometimes even plump. His suit is well tailored, and we know it was made at Denny's the tailors. It says something of his life that Eric Blair had had to reach the age of 25 before making his first friendships with women of his own age and class, but make them he did, and some of them appear to have been brusquely sexual.

For a young man watching the English in Southwold like he had watched the British in Burma, the town's property-owning gerontocracy was a case-study in class relations. Blair had been brought up in a country extraordinarily aware of social class and the attendant problem (as it was seen) of endemic poverty. In 1911 the Census Commissioners had come up with an eight-class model—upper, middle, and working, with inter-mediary classes to bridge marginal differences. In 1921 they revised it into a straight five-class model according to how low the occupation and how high the rate of infant mortality. Between 1901 and 1936 there were at least seven major investigations of poverty in England in the wake of Booth's, the most famous, which began in 1889.[86] In the summer of 1931 this very British awareness of class and poverty turned politically toxic when a run on an overvalued pound forced the government to borrow in foreign markets, which in turn forced them, as they saw it, to seek cuts in public expenditure. A financial crisis made by the very rich led to cuts in benefits to the very poor, and Labour not only fell from office but broke in two when it fell, leading to the election of a Conservative-dominated National Government in October. Nineteen thirty-one was a pivotal year. Labour's political timidity was exposed, and the Tories stepped into government, where they were to remain for the next nine years.[87] Very rarely in the history of British politics had the politics of class, poverty, and nationhood come together so ominously. The Royal Navy mutinied at Invergordon in September 1931 over cuts to its pay, not its loyalty.

Blair had come back to England the year after the 1926 General Strike, but he does not appear to have taken any interest in high politics. He had decided to be a writer and was sticking to the things he knew, which he ground small. Later, in a retrospective essay, he would claim that he had always wanted to be a writer, that it was his 'true nature'.[88] And we know that he had been something of 'a writer' at school, and in Burma had written drafts of novels on the back of police notepaper and so on. But none of this explains or in any way modifies the apparent madness of his decision to resign his commission, leave gainful employ-ment, and return to live with his parents in a modest house in order to pursue a career that was, to say the least, highly unlikely. He might as well have unbuttoned his tunic and declared his intention to go on the stage in a tutu. All one can say is he most certainly meant it, most certainly stuck with it, and prevailed. Within a year he was a published author (albeit of a very short piece in a very small French journal), and within four years he had written his first masterpiece (though a minor one for a periodical).

For the time being, however, he did not like what he saw as the snob-beries of small-town life. In the first instance he may have been pained by his parents' snobbishness. In the second he may have been pained on their behalf. The English class system, home or away, was an exercise in fine weights and measures which only a haunted class like the middle class could understand. But *his* section of the middle class, the Blair sec-tion, the lower but upper section, the upper but hard-up section, the proud but genteel section, was the most haunted. Southwold was a Con-servative town, and for Eric Blair, anti-imperialist, friend of the poor, coming writer, that was reason enough not to like it. But in its scale, which made it knowable; and in its gauntlet of rich and poor, which made it interesting; and in its civility, which scrubbed up well on a sum-mer's day, it stayed in his imagination. When we think of the English-ness of George Orwell, some part of it is forever Southwold.

As for the people, every so often (we are not sure how often, but sometime late in 1927 and again when he came back from Paris late in 1929) Orwell would take his tramping clothes and go off in search of the very poorest, well out of family range, over into deepest Kent, or through the Home Counties, or up to London. He would seek out vagrants, before returning back to base to write about them. His Lon-don base seems to have been 10 Portobello Road, Notting Hill, where he rented a room for a time. The life of tramps was indeed solitary, poor, nasty, and short. They, unlike him, by definition, had no base. He went to Paris in the Spring of 1928, told his agent that he finished a book called *Down and Out in Paris and London* sometime in 1930, and says in the book that the narrator lived in Paris for about eighteen months. It seems he went round wearing a wide-brimmed Breton hat—rather like a black mushroom on a tall stalk. He did other things as well, including book reviews, essays, a couple of failed novels, and a spot of child-minding back in Southwold, but whatever the outcome, and wherever he laid his head at night, it seems that the six-foot three-inch former colonial policeman spent a lot of his time drumming away at his raw ambition to be a writer.[89] From the small upstairs bedroom of 3 Queen Street—which the Blairs rented before moving round the cor-ner to the High Street in 1932—he could savour the contrast between a brightly painted little seaside England on the one hand, and that dark tubercular world where tramping and coughing were synonymous on the other.[90]

Blair's first tour of literary duty, then, was in the 'Darkest England' tradition of seeking out the poor and writing about them. The upper classes never much feature in his writing. When they do, it is usually in an offhand way, as if they lived well apart from the life of the nation, for display purposes only.[91] Government commissioners and other social investigators, on the other hand, had been investigating the lives of the indigent and working poor since the 1830s. If anything, the rate of investigation increased in Orwell's lifetime. But it was the late Victorians who had turned that condition into something generally defined, located, and knowable, and that in turn into a form of alienated life known as Poverty. And 'living in poverty', like living in sin, they turned into a spiritual crisis. Andrew Mearns's pamphlet *The Bitter Cry of Outcast London*, published by the London Congregational Union in 1883, and William Booth's *Darkest England and the Way Out*, published by the Salvation Army in 1890, set the tone.[92] In addition to the urban poor, who for all their faults and alienations were part of 'society', there was also the rural poor, who hardly counted, and the most wretched poor, who took to the road.[93]

In 1903 Jack London published *The People of the Abyss*, a study of poverty in all its manifestations ('I was open to be convinced by the evidence of my own eyes'), with a few of the author's own ideas thrown in as well, including the new race science of eugenics. W. H. Davies published his best-selling *The Autobiography of a Super Tramp* in 1908.[94] Charlie Chaplin's *The Tramp* first came to the cinemas in 1914.[95] Blair saw his integrity as a writer and the integrity of his subject as one and the same. He rejected, therefore, most of the sentiment and sensationalism that surrounded the popular treatment of poverty, preferring instead to turn it from something you petted into something you experienced.[96]

In writing about the lives of the poor Blair had joined a literary tradition of telling it like it was. His findings echoed Mayhew's findings (1848), and Jack London's findings (1903), even down to the detail. He too was sympathetic to the tramp's market preference for common lodging-houses over workhouses (whose wards were far from 'casual').[97] He too felt that the poor were not as bad as they were painted, and was determined to tell the truth. His first published piece was for the small Parisian left-wing newspaper *Monde* (not *Le Monde*)—a no-frills report on 'The present state of affairs regarding censorship in England [which] is as follows'. His earliest published piece in England changed tack slightly to expose the shameless obfuscation of the right-wing French farthing newspaper *L' Ami du Peuple*.[98] However, the writer in him never mistook writing for the literal truth. *Down and Out in Paris and London*, his first published book, published in 1933 under the name George Orwell, is a simplistic and at times crude document which is also capable of bizarre and experimental literariness.[99] Orwell's factual documentation of what it is like to be poor (you think only of money), and hungry (you think only of food), mix with extravagant remembrances of times past, of sex and violence and jobbing in the rue du Coq d'Or, a sort of French Impressionist slum. The book claims to be true to experience—what he would later call 'belly to earth' writing—but this is not entirely the case. He starts by taking you into a modernist painting, 'a very narrow street, a ravine of tall, leprous houses, lurching towards one another in queer attitudes, as though they had all been frozen in the act of collapse', where the people, the Rougiers, Charlie, Boris, the *plongeurs* of the kitchens of Hotel X, are all 'fantastically poor', 'curious beyond words', caught in the 'half mad grooves of life'. Orwell appears to have learnt nothing from the crazy Parisian tenements except how to cope with desperation. With the English tramps, however, it is a different story. Modernism is abandoned for marching. The road is straight. The men move on, the walking wounded of England. He ends the book with a couple of plain tips: '...never again think that all tramps are drunken scoundrels, nor expect a beggar to be grateful when [you] give him a penny.'[100]

Orwell did not just want to write, he wanted to get under the skin of those he wrote about, as close to the grey-skinned experience as he thought he could stand—in the workhouse ('The Spike', *The Adelphi*, April 1931); in the colonial prison ('A Hanging', *The Adelphi*, August 1931); in the fields, just recently quit ('Hop Picking', *New Statesman and Nation*, October 1931); in common lodging-houses ('Common Lodging Houses', *New Statesman and Nation*, September 1932); in jail ('Clink', unpublished manuscript, 1932); amongst the Parisian immigrant poor and the tramps in Kent, and the dead and the dying of 'Hospital X', or Hospital Cochin, 27 rue de Faubourg Saint-Jacques, where he was admitted for two weeks in March 1929. He says he had to go there because he had pneumonia, but he may have gone to write about it.[101] Whatever the reason, he shuffles down the line, signs the form, gets stripped, gets washed, robed, bedded, cupped, strapped in a mustard

poultice, and left to lie in a ward of coughing old men known to the
nurses as *les numeros*.[102]

Down and Out is written in the jabbing style of a man who is keen
to let you know what's what ('Poverty is what I am writing about'),
but Orwell shows he is capable of good work too in scenes such as
those from 'Hotel X', a metaphor for the waste and faded grandeur
of nineteenth-century French capitalism about to fall, or so it seemed
in the crisis year 1932–3. In the shorter, more practical London section of the book he is at his best suggesting alternatives to the workhouse. He is astute enough to catch the great object of the fear and
loathing of the English working class just before its demise.[103] His
description of sleeping arrangements for tramps recognizes that
humiliation does not begin at the workhouse gate. He unveils a hierarchy of London 'kips', an intricate miniature of the lowest levels of
urban life. Sleeping rough on the Embankment is overcrowded, the
police prod you, and you cannot sleep a wink. But it costs nothing.
'The Hangover' costs you twopence to lean on a rope. In 'The Cof-
fin' you lie in a box for fourpence. Next up are Common Lodging
Houses, at sevenpence a night. At eightpence, the Salvation Army
provides a clean bed but a prison atmosphere ('would only appeal to
people who put cleanliness before anything else'), while the best kip
in town costs a shilling but, in Orwell's opinion, ordinary lodgings
are too dear for most men.[104] Is the solution not obvious? Instead of
hating tramps and having rules intended to move them on, the London County Council should introduce one or two simple regulations
for the provision of comfortable beds and clean linen. It's not science, let alone scientific socialism, but it makes sense. 'A tramp is
only an Englishman out of work.'

In 1932, after years of dossing and writing, Orwell moved to west
London to teach in a boys' private day-school. He wasn't the first person, nor would he be the last, to characterize the outer western suburbs
as soulless. Amid the creamy architecture and the wide-open carriage-
ways, he learned to dislike modernist conurbations while at the same
time embracing Modernism's literary forms—the documentary, the
experimental, and the small literary magazines where his first three
great essays appeared.[105]

The schools he taught in, Evelyn's in Hayes and Fray's in Uxbridge,
aspired to the public-school ideal. But Orwell came to the conclusion

that they were not much more than private businesses trading on the lower-middle-class shame of not being sufficiently middle-middle, or upper-middle, or even lower-upper middle.[106] In short, even though they gave him time to write, they were just about the worst places on earth Orwell could have chosen to work in. From their point of view, however, he was something of a catch. Though not qualified to teach, and without a university degree, the schools invested in his famous former school and posh accent. A future generation of sociologists would call it 'cultural capital', and such schools put it in their prospectuses. Parents could hardly ask for more from a gentleman, and in his case they didn't know the half of what they were getting.

By this time Orwell had growing reason to believe in himself as a writer. He had acquired an agent.[107] He seemed to have acquired not just a publisher but an up-and-coming publisher at that. He was getting work with *The Adelphi* magazine. *Down and Out in Paris and London* had enjoyed good national notices.

Then, in December 1933, he caught pneumonia. Never one to bother much about his health, he drove his motorbike in the freezing rain and found himself spending Christmas in Uxbridge Cottage Hospital. In January 1934 he moved back to Southwold, where he spent the spring and summer convalescing—the first of many such interludes that would come to characterize his life. There he lived quietly and wrote his next book, *A Clergyman's Daughter*, before moving back to London in October 1934, this time to a slightly better address and a slightly worse position. He was now an assitant in a West Hampstead bookshop. For all that he was on the side of the poor, Orwell seems to have enjoyed private school-mastering. At the same time, he noticed the exploitation, including the exploitation of impecunious private schoolmasters like him.

So, after a year of hypocrisy in Hayes, and a spot of sunbathing in Suffolk, Orwell went in search of happiness in Hampstead. He wasn't much happier working at Booklover's Corner—more bowing and scraping, never enough respect, never enough money. Who were these English anyway? When they weren't thrashing their children or sending them away to school, as he had been, aged 8, they were holding down foreign natives and lecturing them about liberty. What a country! Still, he was astonishingly well read, must have liked talking about books as well as selling them, and was beginning to mix with a similar crowd.[108] They called themselves the Kentish Town Junior Republic.

Cigarette smouldering, he continued to hammer at the typewriter. Three more books followed in quick succession. Like *Down and Out*, they were all based on Orwell's own experiences and they were all angry— angry about all those things which, as a budding writer with a social conscience and no money or prospect of money, Orwell so easily opposed. *Burmese Days*, published in 1934 in the United States and in 1935 in Britain (there had been publisher's fears about libel), is the best. An unsigned review for the *Times Literary Supplement* drew attention to Orwell's unrelenting pessimism, *The Times* called it a bitter book, and his friends Richard Rees at *The Adelphi* and Cyril Connolly at the *New Statesman* saw him as a 'good hater' and 'extremely biased'. But they were good reviews anyway, and more were to come in the *New York Times* and the *Boston Evening Transcript*.[109] *Burmese Days* has its faults, but following *A Passage to India* it is Britain's second post-colonial novel.

A Clergyman's Daughter, published in 1935, is the story of Dorothy Hare, a 28-year-old spinster who spends her days working in a way that a later generation of middle-class women would come to see as demeaning. Dorothy has no savings, no income, no property, no job, and no resources of her own. She looks after her father, in other words, and minds his parish. The country town she lives in is pleasant enough if you can pay your bills, but hard-faced if you cannot. Dorothy runs the gauntlet of High Street creditors every morning, and every minute she is mindful of her duties, her reputation, and her gathering disbelief in a male trinity of father, God, and holy church.

After *Down and Out*, Orwell's writing turned misanthropic. Flory has a large birthmark across his face. The characters in *Down and Out* are not exactly attractive, but in *A Clergyman's Daughter* Dorothy is a 'Hare', Mrs Creevy looks like a toad, Mrs Pither a rabbit, and the postmistress is a dachshund. The men are not pretty either. The Revd Charles Hare is cold and controlling. Mr Warburton wants to have sex and refuses to give up. He tells Dorothy it will be good for her. When it all becomes too much, she loses her memory and goes absent. Orwell injects some experimental writing at this point, possibly in the manner of James Joyce's *Ulysses*, a book he said he loved but also said that it made his own writing look like the work of 'a eunuch'.[110] He wasn't wrong. After many adventures with tramps and hop-pickers and others, Dorothy gets her memory back and returns to the rectory. In a strong show of emotion, her father pats her on the shoulder. Orwell loathed the book while he was writing it and loathed it when he had finished it. He claimed he only did it for the money, but that does not explain why he tried something so difficult. Nor does it account for the strong descriptions, venturing here into the rhythms of twopence a bushel hop-picking and big-dipper singing:

> It gave you a physical joy, a warm satisfied feeling inside you, to stand there hour after hour, tearing off the heavy clusters and watching the pale green pile grow higher and higher in your bin, every bushel another two pence in your pocket. The sun burned down upon you, baking you brown, and the bitter, never-palling scent, like a wind from oceans of cool beer, flowed into your nostrils and refreshed you. When the sun was shining everybody sang as they worked; the plantations rang with singing. For some reason all the songs were sad that autumn...like gutter versions of *Carmen* and *Manon Lescaut*. There was:

> 'There *they* go—in *their joy*—
> 'Appy *girl*—lucky *boy*—
> But 'ere am I-I-I—
> Broken 'a-a-arted!'[111]

Flory's war on British imperialism (of which he was a part), and Dorothy's war with small-town narrowness (of which she was a part), was succeeded by Orwell's *Keep The Aspidistra Flying*, published in 1936, the story of Gordon Comstock and (as he sees it) capitalism's war on him. In his less bashful moments Gordon refers to the enemy as 'The Money God', by which he means a range of businesses, from the advertising industry to the City of London, but including all the appurtenances of English middle-class life that he cannot afford—including an aspidistra in the front window. This is not a comedy. The message is serious, although as in all Orwell's early novels the tone is jocular. What are we to make, for instance, of the 'peculiarly mangy' aspidistra belonging to his landlady? It only has *seven leaves*, but what that signifies, if anything, is hard to say. Sometimes in literary criticism it does not pay to go too far: 'Many a time he had furtively attempted to kill it—starving it of water, grinding hot cigarette ends against its stem, even mixing salt in its earth. But the beastly things are practically immortal. In almost any circumstances they can preserve a wilting, diseased existence.'[112]

Comstock thinks he is a political animal but in truth, he has turned his personal inadequacies into something he only mistakes for politics. He wants to be known by people who do not want to know him. He wants to have sex with women who do not want to let him. He wants to have a badly paid job while resenting those who have well-paid jobs. He wants to have an aspidistra and he wants to kill the aspidistra. He envies his enemies and he exploits his friends—including Julia, his hard-working sister, who lends him money, and Rosemary, his hard-working girlfriend, who lets him. Gordon whinges a lot in the belief that this makes him left-wing.

It is hard not to see Orwell mixing some of his own self-doubt into the 29-year-old, 'moth-eaten' Comstock.[113] They are both bookshop assistants. They both know their way home up to cold bedsits. They are both poets, mainly unpublished. They go to play-readings and, very occasionally, to Italian restaurants. Politically minded but not politically informed, they are on the side of the underdog and they have trained themselves to see underdogs everywhere. 'And I see people thronging the street | The death-marked people... | Goalless, rootless, like leaves drifting.'[114] But it would be a mistake to confuse Orwell for Comstock. Orwell in 1935–6 had friends, contacts, some hard-earned money, and, in literary terms at least, a lot of drive and some not insignificant success. He was onto his fourth book and had been reviewed by the big nationals and quality journals for all of them—including in the United States.[115] In other words, he was by now an 'ambitious, non-stop, hard-working professional writer' who knew his business.[116] Comstock, by way of contrast, had one slender publication, *Mice*, and certainly did not know his business. You might say that Gordon Comstock was George Orwell in hindsight; the Orwell/Blair of the late twenties and early thirties as seen from an altogether better vantage. As for all the hating and whingeing, Orwell was certainly capable of that, but Comstock is toxic. His own righteousness distorts the world as it is and, in Orwell's literary rule-book at least, this is the worst crime. Talk of 'The Money God' is just a decoy. Orwell's real taboo is the man who has lost his better nature fighting it. Worse than the poor and the unemployed, the men on the rope and the men in the coffin, and John Flory and Dorothy Hare and that whole cast of people struggling with their fate, Comstock has a way out if he wants to help himself, and a way in if he wants to help others, but he chooses neither. Instead, he stands aside and has great thoughts:

> Gordon watched them go. They were just by-products. The throw-outs of the money-god. All over London, by tens of thousands, draggled old

beasts of that description; creeping like unclean beetles to the grave. He gazed at the graceless street. At this moment it seemed to him that in a street like this, in a town like this, every life that is lived must be meaningless and intolerable. The sense of disintegration, of decay, that is endemic in our time, was strong upon him. Somehow it was mixed up with the ad-posters opposite... For can you not see, if you know how to look, that behind that slick self-satisfaction, that tittering fat-bellied triviality, there is nothing but a frightful emptiness, a secret despair? The great death-wish of the modern world.[117]

A lot of Orwell's writing at this time is uncomfortable with itself and its subject. Although purporting to be on the side of the people, the sentiment is more misanthropic than political, and there is no voice. If there *is* a politics, it is recognizable only in capital letters or abstract nouns. All of his four published books up to 1936 have no political point other than that England is wrong. Not what is wrong with it—but *that* it is wrong. Orwell at this stage is not concerned with England and Englishness, but with what is wrong with all that is Wrong. He is good on certain facts (what it feels like to starve, for instance),[118] but there is little light and shade, not much complexity, and, for the most part, over-simple messages. Destitution is wrong. Poverty is wrong. Gentility is wrong. Genteel poverty is wrong. Empire is wrong. Racism is wrong. The Masses are wrong. The Elite is wrong. Capitalism is wrong (but you may have to go with it). Only *The People* unto whom wrongs are done are right, but we do not know them. It is true that occasionally Orwell's closely observed traits can be unforgettable, and in his early reviewing it is possible to see the makings of a great essayist, but in spite of the obvious talent it is impossible to know what he wants.

This is just as true of his characters. The narrator of *Down and Out* (1933) remains obscure. We remember his adventures, but we do not remember him. Similarly with Orwell's attempt to get inside the mind of Dorothy Hare. There are thoughtful passages, but the project as a whole is a cross-dressing disaster. Orwell's attempts at experimental writing fare no better. After her adventures among tramps and what-not, Dorothy ends up exactly where she began, the clergyman's daughter and an old maid before her time. Hardly an experimental ending. We know what is wrong with her life; but we do not know, and nor does she, what sort of life she wants instead. It is the same with

John Flory, who is a study in self-disgust. We are told he wants a life with the young English visitor, but we cannot trust his judgement. He is in a bad place. He is in a negative frame of mind. He can do nothing but get his life wrong and more wrong. Attempting to break free by marrying Elizabeth is a mistake from the start, and would have been even if he had succeeded. If John Flory is the first colonial depressive before Graham Greene, Gordon Comstock is the first angry young man before John Osborne. He works in a small North London leftist bookshop and aspires to be a small North London leftist poet. He could have had another life working for a living, marrying his girlfriend, and living with her and the aspidistra makes three somewhere in North London. And still have written his poems. Instead, he aspires to be an intellectual.

Comstock is Orwell's least sympathetic character to date, and a warning that even at this stage in his politics Orwell's feelings about the intellectual left are not good. Comstock is an idiot. Too self-pitying to see the world as it is, and standing away from it, he is cruel even to his girlfriend, whom he blames for most of his woes, especially his sexual woes. Herein may be a rare joke in Orwell—'Comstockery'.[119] Orwell expressed some of this in a poem he wrote in 1934. It is painstakingly called 'On a Ruined Farm Near His Master's Voice Gramophone Factory (somewhere near the A40)'. It is the sort of poem Gordon might have written, and I do not think it is intended as ironic:

> I feel, and with sharper pang
> My mortal sickness; how I give
> My heart to weak and stuffless ghosts
> And with the living cannot live.

> The acid smoke has soured the fields,
> And browned the few and windworn flowers;
> But there, where steel and concrete soar
> In dizzy geometric towers—

> There where the tapering cranes sweep round,
> And great wheels turn, and trains roar by
> Like strong, low headed brutes of steel—
> This is my World, my Home; yet why

> So alien still...?[120]

Orwell and Blair

Brenda Salkeld once complained about the gloominess of his letters, and in his reply he blamed it on the gloominess of his life. He told her he had once gone to Kensal Rise cemetery in order to produce a 'gloomy frame of mind in order to get on with what [he] was writing'. But in the event it did not work, and 'the inscriptions on the tombstones sent me into such paroxysms of laughter that all gloom was gone for the day'.[121] Clearly, for George Orwell, published author, being gloomy as a writer and being gloomy as a private person was not necessarily the same thing.

He published under the name 'George Orwell' from 1933. He told his agent on 19 November 1932 that he favoured it over P. S. Burton ('the name I always use when tramping'), Kenneth Miles, and H. Lewis Allways. We can be sure he made the right choice.[122] The Orwell is a river in Suffolk. 'Orwell' was also the favourite for the 1932 Epsom Derby (a 'certainty', according to British Pathe News). Two years later he made the switch complete by writing book reviews under that name.[123] But the switch may have meant more than a change of name.[124] It is not at all clear that Orwell and Blair are the same man. 'George Orwell', author, is the decent Englishman who goes into corners, puts himself to the test, and can be relied upon to speak the truth, or try to. He is not bookish, but intelligent. He is not classless, but he is fair, and you can trust him. Blair, on the other hand, seems more like the writer Orwell left behind, the metropolitan intellectual who thinks in a high register and knows what he wants before he finds it; the man who spends his days and nights at the typewriter.[125]

'Who am I?' and 'Can I change?' are questions that run through all Orwell's writings. Sometimes they are asked explicitly, as in his personal relations with people of other classes or cultures. Sometimes they are implicit, as when the questioning shifts from him to his fictional characters. Occasionally the questions are ducked, as when he tries to conceal who he is and get away with it. At other times they are taken full on, as when he has to save face in order to save his reputation. Whichever way these questions are posed—in his dealings with English coalminers for example, or tramp majors, or peasants, all waiting for him to play a certain role—questions of identity are never far away. Orwell was a left intellectual, yet he did not like left intellectuals. There were times when he could hardly bring himself to believe a word they said. *Yet he was one*, and somehow had to conceal it in his writing. Walter Bagehot put concealment at the heart of the English constitution, just as Lord Chesterfield had put it at the heart of English gentlemanliness.[126] Orwell was not unaware of gentlemanly concealment and its other side, performance. He summed it up in 1948 as two persons in one: the author who struggles to be free; and the man who *is* the author, 'the saner self that stands aside, records...refuses to be deceived'.[127]

So here we have 'Orwell' the decent Englishman, the man 'not guided by ideas'—the man Blair thought he would have liked to have been if he had not been what he was already, that remarkably unattractive figure, the left intellectual.[128] Although as time went by the performance grew inwards to bring both Blair and Orwell together as one (he came to use both names interchangeably), it is possible that he never did rid himself of the basic split in who he was and who he wanted to be, and indeed drew on it for insight and empathy.[129]

Orwell is not reluctant to write in the first person—after all, he started out writing like that—but his early work is curiously impersonal.[130] In *Down and Out* the narrator does not have a name, let alone a personality. In 1933 Blair could not be Blair, and 'Orwell' had yet to be born, but the French translator of *Burmese Days* remarked how 'your second book shows an enormous progress on the first'. Translators know a lot. They do not just read the text, they labour over it: 'In *Down and Out*, the events dominated and controlled you, you were only a truthful narrator and a wise observer. Here, in *Burmese Days*, you control your subject, you are the creator, you raise yourself admirably, and your analysis shows a sharp sense of observation right through...'[131] His first published writing is journalistic reportage, signed Eric Blair, mainly for the French press, on British social and economic conditions—'Unemployment', 'A Day in the Life of a Tramp', 'Beggars in London', 'The British Empire in Burma', and so on. There are two minor masterpieces buried in this early work—'A Hanging', and 'The Spike'—both published by *The Adelphi* in April and August 1931 respectively. 'The Spike' tells the story of a night in an English workhouse with forty-eight male tramps and one female, that starts late one afternoon with them grazing on the village green and ends early next morning when they are herded back onto the road. In amongst it all is 'Orwell', the decent man, clearly not a down-and-out insider because he is the reporter, but not an intellectual either. There is no politics in the piece, though we know where his sympathies lie. Nor is there any sentiment. It is very simple and restrained, and yet, everything that has to be said is said. The piece is signed Eric Blair, but this is Orwell for sure, personal and impersonal at the same time, controlling his material, shaping his reader, squinting through the human condition at the politics of it. Old Daddy appears here and will reappear in *Nineteen Eighty-Four.*

> After breakfast we had to undress again for the medical inspection, which is a precaution against smallpox. It was three quarters of an hour before the doctor arrived, and one had time now to look about him and see what manner of men we were. It was an instructive sight. We stood shivering naked to the waist in two long ranks in the passage. The filtered light, bluish and cold, lighted us up with unmerciful clarity...Shock heads, hairy, crumpled faces, hollow chests, flat feet, sagging muscles— every kind of malformation and physical rottenness were there. All were flabby and discoloured, as all tramps are under their deceptive sunburn... Old 'Daddy', aged seventy four, with his truss and his red, watering eyes; a herring-gutted starveling...[132]

There are two great moments in these essays. One when the Tramp Major sees in Orwell a real gentleman, and asks him if it's true:

> He was a gruff, soldierly man of forty, who gave the tramps no more ceremony than sheep at the dipping pond, shoving them this way and that and shouting oaths in their faces. But when he came to myself, he looked hard at me, and said:
>
> 'You are a gentleman?'
>
> 'I suppose so', I said.
>
> He gave me another long look. 'Well, that's bloody bad luck, guv'nor', he said, 'that's bloody bad luck, that is'.[133]

The other moment is in 'A Hanging' when Orwell glimpses the full horror of what he is doing. Essays and short stories must never labour the point. What you are shown is always more important than what you are told. Orwell makes the walk to the gallows a moment for the living, not the dead. The writing trots along with the prisoner, on his shoulder almost, as he bobs his way to the rope:

> He walked clumsily with his bound arms, but quite steadily, with that bobbing gait of the Indian who never straightens his knees. At each step his muscles slid neatly into place, the lock of hair on his scalp danced up

and down, his feet printed themselves in the wet gravel. And once, in spite of the men who gripped him by each shoulder, he stepped slightly aside to avoid a puddle on the path. It is curious but till that moment I had never realized what it means to destroy a healthy, conscious man.[134]

Up to 1937 Orwell the essayist had not been seriously tried, at any rate at book length. But he is there almost from the start, his outline gradually emerging in book reviews from a man who likes to test what he is told against what he knows; then in reports from a man who has decided to make plain speaking his moral duty, as in 'The Spike'; then its clearest outline to date, here and there in *Burmese Days*, its impact dulled because Flory and all the rest are, after all, only fiction.[135] Blair was trying to be a writer. Orwell, on the other hand, was trying to write.

At first Blair and Orwell both wrote against the awfulness of life as they knew it—inequality at home and aggravated inequality abroad. One of Blair's earliest musings, an untitled play, set the tone: 'Scene One: a mean and poverty stricken room.'[136] By 1936, however, in the sheer perversity of Gordon Comstock, there is clear evidence of Orwell's mistrust of those who said they were fighting an abstraction, and by the time of his full maturity it is fair to say that of all the people Orwell did not trust, he did not trust left intellectuals. And yet Eric Blair, who was a left-wing intellectual, reinvented himself in 1927 as a man without a home, and in the end, and not without irony, Orwell's fundamental charge against left intellectuals was that they were people without a home. They had been 'Europeanized', he said. 'The really important fact about so many of the English intelligentsia [is] their severance from the common culture of the country.'[137] Orwell feared severance and displacement in himself and his characters: the phantom narrator in *Down and Out* ('drifting at two miles an hour through the crowds'); the solitary John Flory in *Burmese Days* ('If he had one person, just one, to halve his loneliness'); the lost and forgotten Dorothy Hare in *The Clergyman's Daughter* ('a creditor behind every window'); the wandering Gordon Comstock in *Keep the Aspidistra Flying* ('The thought of his cold lonely bedroom...like a doom before him'). These, and all the others without a home—the down-and-outs, the lonely schoolmasters, the impoverished curates, the penniless intellectuals, the expats, bedsitters, bedwetters, and all those with nothing to lose but their chilblains—all drew Orwell's early attention because he knew them all as well as he knew himself. But they were not representative of the common culture of England.

Orwell's book on the north of England began this way. In the publisher's mind at least, Orwell the angry Old Etonian would go north to describe the awfulness, say something about the common culture, do penance, and offer some simple, heartfelt remedy. And from the way the book is structured, one might suppose that this is how it will read. But it turns out the other way. The publisher had not noticed that Gordon Comstock was not so much anti-capitalist as a failure in life, and, what is more, since writing *Keep the Aspidistra Flying* Orwell had read Henry Miller and been reminded of other ways of engaging with the world than Comstock's highly strung avoidance of it. In his review of Miller just before heading north, Orwell praised *Tropic of Cancer* for its intimate engagement with the world as it really was. Although Miller's down and out Paris is not Unlike Orwell's (whoring, starvation, *ennui* etc.), the American's 'world' consists mainly of a man's thoughts and fantasies. Then, in a letter to him a few months later, and written while he was in the middle of work on *The Road to Wigan Pier*, Orwell criticized Miller's *Black Spring* as a failure in this very regard. Either way, a new idea was in the making—or at least an old idea made good. 'Belly to earth' was about to become not just the mark of what Orwell demanded in himself, but what the world demanded in times such as these:

> Probably, although he chooses to describe ugly things, Mr Miller would not answer to the name of pessimist. He even has passages of rather Whitmanesque enthusiasm for the process of life. What he seems to be saying is that if one stiffens oneself by the contemplation of ugliness, one ends by finding life not less but more worth living. (Orwell on Miller, 14 November 1935)[138]

> I liked *Tropic of Cancer* especially for three things, first of all a peculiar rhythmic quality in your English, secondly the fact that you dealt with facts well known to everybody but never mentioned in print...thirdly the way in which you would wander off into a kind of reverie where the laws of ordinary reality were slipped just a little but not too much...but I think on the whole [in *Black Spring*] you have moved too much from the ordinary world into a sort of Mickey Mouse universe where things and people don't have to obey the rules of space and time. I dare say I am wrong and perhaps have missed your drift altogether, but I have a sort of belly-to-earth attitude and always feel uneasy when I get away from the ordinary world where grass is green, stones are hard etc. (Orwell to Miller, 26–7 August 1936).[139]

2

North Road

Wigan

> The first sound in the mornings was the clumping of the mill-girls'
> clogs down the cobbled street. Earlier than that, I suppose, there
> were factory whistles which I was never awake to hear.[1]

Orwell arrived in Wigan to hear the mill-girls but decided to concentrate on the miners. All contacts led to them. Just as northern England had come to stand for the Industrial Revolution, so the miners had come to stand for the British working class.[2]

The inter-war depression brought a form of structural unemployment not seen in Britain for over a hundred years. The regionally concentrated coal industry was particularly hard hit.[3] The miners had lost battles with coal-owners and the state first in 1919–21, when they lost their case for public ownership of Britain's mines,[4] and again in 1926, when the country suffered its first General Strike, which was mercifully short, followed by a six-month national coal strike, which was merciless. The miners said they would eat grass before going back, but go back they did. Coal had lost crucial export share when sterling went back on the gold standard in 1925, and in the financial crises of 1929 and 1931 there were further wage-cuts and redundancies.

Spirits rose briefly with the election of a Labour government in 1929, but after two years trying to decide between the interests of its own people and the interests of the economy as a whole (as defined by bankers and financiers), Labour found itself still in government but out of office. The Prime Minister and a few acolytes hung on, but coalition with the Conservatives was not a pleasant sight. The miners' unions meanwhile remained Labour's strongest link with the labour movement, but their membership had fallen massively from around 1 million in 1920 to half a million in 1930, and by 1933, in the trough of the depression, nearly 42 per cent of that much-depleted number was unemployed. In 1937 one in four miners remained unemployed: 15 per cent of all the unemployed.[5] Throughout the 1930s Britain was governed with mortgages in mind, not wages, though industry did eventually recover on the back of a housing boom. By the time Orwell arrived in the north in February 1936 unemployment in Wigan had begun to fall from a peak of 32 per cent at the beginning of the decade. All trends were looking better. But he had not gone north to study economics.[6]

Nor had he gone to make statistical investigations into calorific intake, in the manner of other poverty surveys.[7] The miners carried a heavy symbolic load. Nothing in the annals of British economic and social history compared. Coalminers and cotton-workers had always been at the centre of the Industrial Revolution—and Wigan had plenty of both.[8] But it was a revolution that continued to show its dark side. In September 1934 Gresford Colliery near Wrexham blew up, killing 256 men and boys. In a matter of minutes 200 widows and 800 orphans were left wondering what would become of them. The commission of inquiry was still deliberating as Orwell set out. Not only did coal remain vivid in the popular imagination, and vital to the national economy, but the Miners' Federation of Great Britain remained Britain's most powerful trade union—still influential, still combative. Mining communities, too, were rich in history and identity. It is said Orwell chose Wigan on the strength of an old music-hall joke about its 'pier' (it didn't have one), but he was there because *The Adelphi*, which announced in 1932 that it would represent the views of the Independent Labour Party, had contacts in the Lancashire coal-and-cotton belt. There had been a time, in Burma, when Orwell had used a copy of *The Adelphi* for target practice. Now he was using it to make friends and influence people.[9]

He was 33 years old and had been to the north of England only once, when he stayed with his sister and her family in Bramley. But he had never stuck his nose into what people like him called 'the industrial districts'; had never stood under a factory chimney and breathed in; had never met working-class people on their own terms in their own streets, or watched them work, or written about them. Though his girlfriend Eileen O'Shaughnessy came from South Shields, a town built on collieries, railways, and shipyards, and his friend at *The Adelphi* Jack Common was another Tynesider, Orwell showed no interest in going there and there is no evidence that he ever did go there except to bury his wife and visit her grave. His publisher Victor Gollancz was thinking of starting a 'Left Book Club'. Part cheap lending-library and part debating society, Left Book Clubs were going to sell books and advance the cause. What cause? Gollancz, a Communist-party sympathizer, possibly member, certainly insider, was looking for a broadly based Popular Front initiative, and may have seen Orwell as his man, signing him up for the Club list once they had received the manuscript on 21 December 1936.[10] Had this young author not written against the Empire? Had he not inveighed against the Money God? Had not he fretted over the unemployed of Middlesbrough? Well then. Send him up there. Wherever it is.[11]

So, here was Orwell ready to go down the mine for literature, for Victor Gollancz, for a £100 advance on a book, and for the problem, which was Unemployment, and for the solution, which was Socialism. Orwell had definitely got his man. Gollancz only thought he had.[12]

He began his journey on 31 January 1936, travelling by bus and on foot from Coventry to Birmingham ('frightful'), Stafford to Hanley ('bleak'), and on to Manchester ('beastly'),[13] where he made contact with the men from *The Adelphi* before finding lodgings in Wigan on 11 February. He stayed four days at 72 Warrington Lane with the Hornbys, an ex-miner and his wife and their three lodgers, followed by two weeks at 22 Darlington Street with the Forrests, another former miner, his wife, and their six lodgers.

Orwell's road north was par for the course. It was a road everyone in the south of England had to face at some time in their lives. The BBC spoke from south to the north. *London Calling!* So did Buckingham Palace and the Bank of England. So did Fleet Street, Wardour Street, and the City of London. So did WC1 and every branch of government and the civil service. So did the nation's most prestigious cultural, religious, and moral institutions, not least Lambeth Palace, and its most fashionable universities, schools, art galleries, regiments, and clubs, not least the Marylebone Cricket Club. So did the middle class, most of whom lived in the interestingly named Home Counties. So did money and commodities in all their forms.[14] One could always see oneself leaving the south for the north, if only to take a look.

For the Victorians, the industrial north had its problems, but not as many as London. For much of the nineteenth century and some of the twentieth modernity, democracy, urbanity, progress, inventiveness, engineering, and the like were identified as northern attributes.[15] Northern technology had changed the world. Northern towns had set the standard for civic pride. Northern work-and-leisure patterns had become the modern norm. By 1936 however, once so healthy, it seemed the economic depression was the north's personal terminal illness. The midlands and the southern regions were hardly affected, while the salaried classes, wherever they lived, were enjoying steady growth and rising real incomes. No wonder they went north to see what was happening. If it was suburban, or southern, or rural, it was bound to be English. If it was terraced, or northern, or industrial, it needed a second look.[16]

Apart from the social investigators, those who went kept to the England they knew already. S. P. B. Mais went in search of *This Unknown Island* for the BBC and steered well clear of the industrial districts. The *National Geographic Magazine* went in search of England for American tourists and did the same, preferring the servility of rural England. ' "It is too bad that you should see the Lake District under such unfavourable circumstances", said the solicitous hostess at the commodious lodge in Grasmere.' H. V. Morton, in his best-selling book *In Search of England*, did everything in his power to head north but avoid workers. He drove past factories in Bristol and Birmingham and entered Lancashire sideways so as not so see too much of that which 'blinds us to the real north' (which was rural). Though Morton did manage to smell fish-and-chips in Warrington, it was from afar. And though he did find time for a walk round Wigan town centre, it was in the company of the Town Clerk, who pointed out the pre-industrial bits. Next stop Lake District. No factory chimneys there. A 'Right Book Club' followed Gollancz's Left Book Club initiative, only to take its journey round Wigan, not through it. Of the popular works, only J. B. Priestley's 1934 *English Journey* (also commissioned by Gollancz) got stuck into industrial England.

Unlike Orwell, however, who just alights on Wigan out of the blue, Priestley journeyed north as a homecoming. This is his England, and his North, and he takes you round. But the north was in bad shape in 1934, so bad that Priestley is clearly ashamed. When Thomas Sharp took himself to the Durham coalfield in 1935, he concluded that 'theoretically the simplest plan is to evacuate the whole territory'. A dozen years later a particularly unprepared observer would say that the Durham coalfield was nearer to hell than anything he had seen since Belsen.[17] It was not just the unemployment. Many sympathetic observers, including Priestley and Sharp, objected to the mess just as much. Their response was more aesthetic than economic. They looked forward to a complete tidy-up, also known as 'planning', sometimes known as 'socialism'.[18] 'Planning' in England was essentially about land-use, and 'regionalism' was about geographic and demographic land-use. Neither was interested in trying to understand what made successful economies, let alone successful businesses.[19]

Orwell shared all these faults. His Diary (which was in effect a draft work), and his book, *The Road to Wigan Pier*, are not short of the standard inter-war criticisms of industrial blight, rural waste, regional mess, and so on. Nor did Orwell show any real interest in what might be done about it—through planning measures or state intervention, say—and only a passing interest in the politics and economics. He lets the Lancashire Steel Corporation, the Wigan Coal Corporation, and the Wigan Coal and Iron Company go by. Earl Peel (also of London Midland, Scottish Railway) and Sir W. P. Rylands, Bt. (also of Pearson & Knowles Coal and Iron Co.) get a completely free pass. Orwell's subject is not capitalism or the Depression but the condition of the English working class. He takes the same line as Arnold Toynbee did fifty years before. He sees the Industrial Revolution as 'a period as disastrous and as terrible as any through which a nation ever passed', and asks similar questions to those asked by Thomas Carlyle fifty years before that:

> Meantime, the questions, Why are the Working Classes discontented; what is their condition, economical, moral, in their homes and their hearts, as it is in reality and as they figure it to themselves to be; what do they complain of; what ought they, and ought they not to complain of?— these are measurable questions...[20]

Orwell is sympathetic and eager to get close, but he is not prepared to get as close to, or inside, the people of Wigan as Henry Miller might have done. The miners and their families are over *there*, not over here; they are people to be approached, and won over, and empathized with in one or two remarkable passages, but they are not on the same side of the railings as him, and they are not the same sort of people as him. In other words, Orwell is not interested, as later sociologists would be interested, in 'the objective importance of the actors' subjective interpretations'.[21] Early in the book he says terrible things about people, as harsh as you could get in talking about the degenerative poor. In the very next paragraph, however, as if recoiling from his own brutality, Orwell identifies with them and even says that they identified with him. First he is talking about people who crawl around like beetles. Then he is talking about a young woman's tenderest feelings as she tries to clear a blocked waste pipe with a stick:

> The place was beginning to depress me. It was not only the dirt, the smells, and the vile food, but the feeling of stagnant and meaningless decay, of having got down into some subterranean place where people go round and round, just like black beetles. But it is no use saying that people like the Brookers are just disgusting…for they exist in tens and hundreds of thousands; they are one of the characteristic by-products of the modern world…labyrinthine slums and dark back kitchens with sickly, ageing people creeping round and round them like black beetles.
>
> …I had time to see everything about her—her sacking apron, her clumsy clogs, her arms reddened by the cold. She looked up as the train passed, and I was almost near enough to catch her eye…the most desolate, hopeless expression I have ever seen. It struck me then that we are mistaken when we say that 'It isn't the same for them as it would be for us', and that people bred in the slums can imagine nothing but the slums. For what I saw in her face was not the ignorant suffering of an animal.[22]

Or a cockroach perhaps? What kind of person Orwell was at this stage in his life is not clear—except that he is beginning to be someone you can follow if you have a mind to. If H. V. Morton takes you round England like a bad landlord, only showing the charming parts, and J. B. Priestley takes you round like a good landlord, full of care, Orwell marches on ahead, a fugitive figure, making no suggestions about what can be done or not done until, in the second half of the book, he comes clean about who he is and what he is doing there.

Overground

The Road to Wigan Pier starts in low spirits, strangely incurious about the people along the way. In his Coventry bed-and-breakfast the owner has his Friendly Society certificate proudly framed on the wall, but Orwell doesn't enquire further. In Stafford he says he slept miserably in grey twill sheets (not a hardship, surely, for a man who had lived as a tramp?). In Burslem he hears broken ice lapping against the reservoir bank (the most melancholy sound he has ever heard, apparently). In Manchester he stays with the Meades. Frank Meade is an official of the Amalgamated

Society of Woodworkers and an active socialist, but Orwell shows no interest. 'Meade is some kind of Trade Union Official.' On reaching Wigan, the town has just been through the threat of a miners' strike, called off at the last minute—but he doesn't notice.[23] He wakes to the rattle of clogs on cobbles. He takes a long walk along the canal bank ('one-time site of Wigan Pier') to observe that in this town, a town where he can count thirty-three factory chimneys from a single spot, even the rats lacked energy.[24] He will learn, eventually, that this is a town with serious overcrowding, where every miner has had an accident or knows someone who has, and where the slag-heaps are constantly moving and sinking, 'like a choppy sea suddenly frozen'.[25] When he finally leaves and sees the girl poking the pipe with a stick in a Henry Miller moment of dumb endurance, this serves as Wigan's final image before Sheffield is upon him and the train is rumbling past 'villa civilization', 'the outer slums', and 'the slag-heaps, belching chimneys, blast-furnaces, canals, and gasometers of another industrial town'.[26]

Sheffield is an ugly town, 'the ugliest town in the Old World', according to our correspondent, but at night it has a 'sinister magnificence'. Just as he did in Paris, Orwell contrives to turn a slum into a modernist painting. He picks his palate from Sheffield's bright sulphurous hills, its yellow rivers, red rivulets, blue flames, and gaunt little streets. He notes that white-hot iron is not white, but lemon. He notes the social significance of the shawl, and the colliery pay-clerks' 'Death Stoppage' rubber stamp: which is inky purple-blue. As in Burma, he sees life anew—a life of boiled sweets, bad teeth, and pink tinned salmon.

Wigan is an obedient town, not given to excitements. The bulk of Orwell's research concerns the day-to-day lives of the unemployed. He mooches round and collects door-to-door with the National Unemployed Workers' Movement (NUWM), a Communist front which he admires for doing the work the Labour party and trade unions would not do. One afternoon he watches unemployed men scree down pit-heaps to win small coals from the dirt train passing beneath. In the evenings he keeps his diary, checks proofs of the Comstock novel, writes letters to friends and accounts for his expenditures. There is no record of going to the pub or the cinema or up to Central Park. He seems as poor as his subjects. Although there was talk all through the 1930s of malnutrition in the industrial districts, by his standards he is struck by the size and frequency of the meals. He tells Cyril Connolly, an old

Etonian pal, 'the miners are very nice people, very warm hearted'.[27] As someone who had been trained to see the working class as 'almost sub-human', this must have come as a relief.[28]

Orwell wanted to know how people got by on so little money in such small spaces. We find him stooping into what for him were very small houses, prodding around, making notes:[29] one room up, one room down, 12 by 10, with alcove, larder, scullery, coal-hole, window, lavatory, rent, and rates. He presses his housing chapters into ways of talking about the lives of women, where he finds corners of poverty he never would have guessed at. These were women with rooms of their own alright. Standing in a tiny scullery, he notes the constant demands, clutter, and 'infinity of jobs' that dominate a mother's life. Going upstairs, he learns that bedding can be pawned, so overcoats will do instead. Sitting downstairs with a nice cup of tea on his knee, he is made to understand why women 'cling to their living rooms' and best china. Out the back he notes there is no hot water, that the door jams, and, because there is no back lane, the toilet is a walk round the block. Unlike nearly every London journalist there is (and has been), Orwell not only understands the difference between a terraced house and a back to back, he understands the variants of a back to back:

> Back to back houses are two houses built in one, each side of the house being somebody's front door, so that if you walk down a row of what is apparently twelve houses you are in reality seeing not twelve houses but twenty four. The front houses give on the street and the back ones on the yard, and there is only one way out of each house. The effect of this is obvious. The lavatories are in the yard at the back so that if you live on the side facing the street, to get to the lavatory or the dust-bin you have to go out of the front door and walk round the end of the block—a distance that may be as much as two hundred yards; if you live at the back, on the other hand, your outlook is onto a row of lavatories. There are also houses of what is called the 'blind back' type, which are single houses, but in which the builder has omitted to put in a back door...'[30]

He is particularly interested in take-home pay.[31] Disregarding company figures and piece rates, he inspects miners' pay-stubs instead and works out an average of £2. 15s. 2d. per man per week, or just over 9s. per shift. He estimates too the cost of weekly 'stoppages', the money taken off pay in order to cover various extra labour costs carried by the miner, including hospital and friendly-society subscriptions, trade-union dues, company charges for tool-sharpening, lamp hire, and the like, plus 9*d.* to the 'checkweighman'—the man who weighs the miners' coals on the union's behalf, because there had been a time in living memory when the company's scales were not to be trusted.

Against the 50*s.* per week of a working miner, Orwell calculated that an unemployed man and his wife and three young children would take home about 35*s.* per week on full benefit, 33*s.* when they moved to transitional benefit, and 32*s.* on the 'PAC', otherwise known as the Public Assistance Committee or 'dole'—the lowest step on the ladder. Orwell wanted to know how these people made ends meet. More than that, he wanted to know how they could eat so little, work so hard, and stay so spirited. At this point we see him questing beyond things into the emotional meaning of things, turning from someone who has not read Henry Miller into someone who has (albeit modestly). Here he can turn a bread-and-marge question into a sense-and-sensibility question:

> The basis of their diet, therefore, is white bread and margarine, corned beef, sugared tea, and potatoes—an appalling diet. Would it not be better if they spent more money on wholesome things like oranges and wholemeal bread or if they even, like the writer of the letter to the *New Statesman*, saved on fuel and ate their carrots raw? Yes it would, but the point is that no ordinary human being is ever going to do such a thing...A millionaire may enjoy breakfasting off orange juice and Ryvita biscuits; an unemployed man doesn't...When you are unemployed, which is to say when you are underfed, harassed, bored, and miserable, you don't *want* to eat dull wholesome food. You want something a little bit 'tasty'...Let's have three pennorth of chips! Run out and buy us a two penny ice cream! Put the kettle on and we'll have a nice cup of tea![32]

On 19 February Orwell went to a dance at the Cooperative Hall organized by the National Unemployed Workers' Movement in support of the Ernst Thälmann Defence Fund.[33] He is sympathetic to the anti-Fascist cause—of course he is—but he is also surprisingly unsympathetic to what is happening in front of his nose. More used to the tight male hierarchies of left politics than the looser, more diffuse, more inclusive politics of the women's 'social', Orwell does not think the event is serious enough. He wants class struggle, not social dancing. So he sees only young girls on the floor and old ones round it, knitting and singing. He thinks that a gathering of 'shapeless middle-aged women' and 'gaping girls' is 'rather pathetic'. He concludes that the British people have lost their turbulence.[34] He looked but did not see: did not see that it was not just male intellectuals who could be 'political'; did not see that the NUWM had brought people together, cheaply and convivially, with supper and speeches, in order to raise money for a man they had likely never heard of.

Orwell was genuinely interested in working-class life, for sure, but from the vantage-point of a lodger and a visitor he seemed to think it was all endurance. He saw the women at work, but missed the more joyful aspects of their lives—perhaps even of their working lives? Perhaps the young woman in the back lane liked to dance? Perhaps she had danced at the Thälmann benefit? Orwell's sister Marjorie and brother-in-law Humphrey Dakin used to josh him that if he really wanted to mix with the workers he ought to get out more, and made sure he did.[35] It is worth noting, however, that Orwell was operating according to chance encounters, not a research programme. He was thinking like a journalist, not a sociologist. But John Beavan was probably right when he said it would have been far better all round if Orwell had got a job as a clerk (not easy, one has to admit), joined a trade union, and spent his Saturdays watching the rugby.[36]

For all his sympathy, Orwell's lack of curiosity about the thoughts of ordinary people led him quite unwittingly into a Leninist position on their inability to think for themselves.[37] That they shared a certain organizational talent he accepts, but there is no sense of leadership or thought or even point of view in his account. For a man on the brink of breaking his ties with 'bourgeois intellectuals', it is strange that Orwell does not know any labour history, seems to regard socialism as some sort of fad, and shows no knowledge of the Socialist Sunday Schools and Leagues of Youth, for instance, which existed albeit as minority forms, and no interest whatsoever in the more gregarious aspects of life in the industrial town—the chapel oratorios and concert parties, or the rambling and cycling clubs, or the boxing booths, banjo bands, and brass bands, the weekly hops, the free-and-easies, the charabanc outings, and Lancashire's famous Wakes. He is taken to an afternoon meeting in a Methodist church ('some kind of men's association, they call it a Brotherhood'), but shows no interest in this most proletarian of religious movements, and would have been horrified to know that the Brotherhood had once been called the Pleasant Sunday Afternoon movement. Lancashire was the home of football, but there is no football in Orwell. Yorkshire was a stronghold of the Workingmen's Club and Institute Union, but when he attends their delegate meeting in Barnsley he does not approve of the free beer and sandwiches, and thinks the organization might go Fascist. The friendly societies took the subscriptions of half of all British working-class men in 1914, but Orwell says not a word on how they had managed to organize such a vast undertaking, nor indeed on how, along with all the other mutual societies, sick clubs, and boxes, they had secured their place in law to allow them to do so. There is no fun, no ambition, no zest, no obscenity, and precious little sociability in Orwell's north. A night out in Blackpool would have done him (and English Literature) the world of good. Where are the comedians? Where is George Formby, Wigan's favourite son? Where are the factory lasses? Where's our Gracie? He says that all trades-union and Labour party officials are middle class, automatically so, and shows almost no time for those bulwarks of working-class defence—the Miners' Federation, the cooperative societies and guilds, the trades councils, the Labour party, and the many-layered and infinitely resourceful female communities of the street.[38] He notes the poverty, but where is the thrift?[39] He notes the grind, but where's the Ritz Super, soon to be Lancashire's most luxurious cinema?[40]

Orwell was not much interested in institutions of any kind, but when his neglect of institutions is aligned with his lack of faith in those who ran them, then it all begins to look a bit self-centred. In his essay 'Looking Back on the Spanish Civil War', probably written in 1942, just before or at the same time as his *The English People*, Orwell reiterates his belief in the regenerative powers of the poor. They will always be sworn enemies of Fascism, he says—though without much evidence for saying so. He likens their struggles to the growth of a plant. 'The plant is blind and stupid, but it knows enough to keep pushing upwards…'[41] Blind and stupid?

It is worth remembering that Orwell was not the only writer with a left-wing conscience going north at this time.[42] John Newsom's *Out of the Pit: A Challenge to the Comfortable*, published by Oxford University Press in 1936, got the idea. As well as this, and Gollancz's ventures in the Left Book Club, there was the Surrey Appeal for Jarrow, the Hertfordshire Campaign for County Durham, and Julian Trevelyan, that leftist scion of a Northumbrian landed family, who set out to save the workers from their blindness only to find that they saved him from himself.[43] There were also the boys from Mass Observation. While Orwell was in Wigan,

Messrs Harrisson (educated at Harrow), Jennings (The Perse), Spender (Gresham's), Madge (Winchester), and Trevelyan, the man saved by miners' paintings (Bedales), were all getting busy in and around Bolton, trying to be anthropological.[44] In the summer that Orwell wrote *The Road to Wigan Pier* Mass Observation had over sixty young men taking notes over the Oxbridge vac, while another young man, Geoffrey Gorer (Charterhouse), was writing to Orwell trying to turn him into an anthropologist too.[45]

Underground

After twelve days in Wigan, on 23 February 1936, Orwell went down the mine. He was three hours down, 300 yards below, two miles out, and the event was a landmark in his life. He made his way to the face to see the cutters in action, and in the dark and the heat took his first glimpse of an England he never knew. Here were men who confirmed all his doubts about people like him, and all his growing faith in people like them:

> ... what I want to emphasize is this. Here is this frightful business of crawling to and fro, which to any normal person is a hard day's work in itself; and it is not part of the miner's work at all, it is merely an extra, like the City man's daily ride in the Tube. The miner does that journey to and fro, and sandwiched in between there are seven and a half hours of savage work. I have never travelled much more than a mile to the coal face; but often it is three miles, in which case I and most people other than coal miners would never get there at all. This is the kind of point that one is always liable to miss. When you think of a coal-mine you think of depth, heat, darkness, blackened figures hacking at walls of coal; you don't think, necessarily, of those miles creeping to and fro. There is the question of time, also. A miner's working shift of seven and a half hours does not sound very long, but one has got to add on to it at least an hour a day for 'travelling', more often two hours and sometimes three. Of course the 'travelling' is not technically work and the miner is not paid for it; but it is as like work as makes no difference. It is easy to say that miners don't mind all this. Certainly, it is not the same for them as it would be for you and me. They have done it since childhood, they have the right muscles hardened, and they can move to and fro underground with a startling and rather horrible agility... at the workings you see them on all fours, skipping round the pit props almost like dogs. But it is quite a mistake to think that they enjoy it.[46]

Orwell puts himself forward as the man who wants to save you with the truth, just as he was saved. But who is this 'you'? Not the miners, that's for sure. They may need saving, they may even need socialism, but they don't need George Orwell. Orwell is writing on behalf of miners, but he is not writing for them. Rather, he is writing for himself, because he has seen great things; and then he is writing for those on the left, who need to see great things. Only then would socialists be able to put socialism right and make it popular. Orwell never proposed socialism as something that might be done unto him. Rather it is to be done unto *them*, with Orwell taking care of his own business. He even doubts that he would be able to live under socialism at all, because it is, or should be, the politics of the working class, and Orwell (he has decided) is irrevocably middle class. It is the duty of all socialists to bring on the change—but it may not be in their personal interest.

What Orwell said about the miners in *The Road to Wigan Pier* is not necessarily what he felt about them at the time. His Diary gives no hint. Indeed, he takes two more underground trips, one to Barnsley's 'day hole', or drift mine, on 19 March, and another to modern Grimethorpe two days later in order to get his copy. But when he had garnered his experience, and shaped his response, and fashioned it into art, what he suggests is not something that could be given by the south to the north, as was usually the case, but by the north to the south—a reorientation which in Thirties writing virtually stands alone.

So he goes underground, and having journeyed through the darkness past the stations of the cross he comes upon those who bear the stigmata of their labour, and in a chiaroscuro of lamplight, everyone on their knees (Orwell pondering his middle-class soul, no doubt), he looks up and sees the truth. He makes the coal-face look like Calvary, but his notes describe it as hell. In the gloom, crawling on his belly, he drops his lamp and knocks out another. He is engulfed in total blackness. Then there is light, and note that it is not Orwell's *opinions* which are redeemed here, it is his *faith*—his faith in what is true. And what is true for 'You and I' (we are clearly not the same species as coalminers) 'and the editor of the *Times Lit Supp*, and the Nancy poets and Comrade X', is true for all men *like us*. Gollancz had expected another Comstock rant against the capitalist class. What he got was a man on his hands and knees crawling about in the dark thinking about people like Gollancz and not a word about coal-owners:

When you have finally got there...you crawl through the last line of pit
props and see opposite you a shiny black wall three or four feet high. This
is the coal face. Overhead is the smooth ceiling made by the rock from
which the coal has been cut; underneath is the rock again, so that the gallery you are in is only as high as the ledge of coal itself, probably not much
more than a yard. The first impression of all, overmastering everything
else for a while, is the frightful deafening din from the conveyor belt which
carries the coal away. You cannot see very far, because the fog of coal dust
throws back the beam of your lamp, but you can see on either side of you
the line of half-naked kneeling men, one to every four or five yards, driving
their shovels under the fallen coal and flinging it swiftly over their left shoulders. They are feeding it on to the conveyor belt...Down this belt a glitter-
ing river of coal races constantly...the fillers look and work as though they
were made of iron...You can never forget that spectacle once you have
seen it—the line of bowed, kneeling figures, sooty black all over, driving
their huge shovels under the coal with stupendous force and speed.

In a way it is even humiliating to watch coal-miners working. It raises
in you a momentary doubt about your own status as an 'intellectual' and
a superior person generally. For it is brought home to you, at least while
you are watching, that it is only because miners sweat their guts out that
superior persons can remain superior...all of us *really* owe the compara-
tive decency of our lives to poor drudges underground, blackened to the
eyes, with their throats full of coal dust, driving their shovels forward with
arms and belly muscles of steel.[47]

He says it took him a week to get over his trip down the mine (though he
was on his way to Liverpool two days later), and he piles on the usual
adjectives—'frightful', 'bloody', 'beastly', and so forth. But hundreds of
feet beneath its surface, in the gloom, with his spindly legs buckling
every few hundred yards, Orwell found an England he could believe in.
He had written to his Old Etonian friend Richard Rees to say he was
getting into '*partibus infidelium*'. Now he was a barbarian himself.[48]

England began to look better. He left Eton without sorrow or regret.
He rode out of Burmese villages without so much as a cheerio. He shuffled in and out of tramps' lives hardly noticed. He did an about turn in
Suffolk to turn up in London, all without too much difficulty. But Wigan
was a closed shop. Wigan was poor, but it certainly did not want his
sympathy and charity he had none. In this town, if you could not handle
a shovel you could not support a family, and if you could not support a
family what were you doing there? He looked like an outsider, talked like

a toff, and needed taking round. One woman thought he had come from the council. Unlike Burmese villagers, or Parisian dishwashers, or Kentish tramps, or Suffolk spinsters and all the other people he had tried to know and write about, here was a class who would not let him in. And for once he was genuinely impressed. How could he feel sorry for miners when it was they who felt sorry for him? How could he patronize men who were stronger than him? He could not even join their world, let alone opine that it was 'wrong'. Not that it was wrong. As Orwell made clear, it was 'the absolutely necessary counterpart of our world above', and the sooner 'we' knew about it, the better.[49] The labour of hotel dishwashers was absolutely pointless.[50] The labour of miners, on the other hand, was the source of all value.

Even if he wondered about his exclusion from this world of blue-tattooed men, he was also excited by it.[51] Richard Rees recalled 'there'd been a kind of fire smouldering in him all his life which suddenly sort of broke into flame'.[52] While it is true that Orwell stood with the Poor, and had done so ever since resigning his police commission, he had no real faith in their powers. In Paris, he had worked as a hotel dishwasher and was on their side. Still he noted the filth. In Wigan, he stayed at the Brookers and in the end the impotency of their lives got him down. He called them beetles and was more than familiar with the regular way of identifying depressed people with depressed places: 'simple lines, merged masses, dim colours.'[53] Orwell's reporting is conventional in one sense— the people are taking flak and the industrial front is in danger of breaking up. But it is unconventional in the way it takes the miners off the streets and corner-ends, out of their ill-fitting clothes and dole queues, and puts them in the lower deck where the battle is hot and they are heroes stripped as heroes.[54] These were the men who turned the modern world. Just as he needed Wigan more than Wigan needed him, so he reckoned the south needed the north.[55]

And yet, for all its strength, the north remained a heavily exploited region and the miners a heavily exploited class. Orwell lived in a country where the difference in the lives of the propertied rich and the propertyless poor was shameless. Even when the poor were old or sick and in need of a hospital bed, it had to be begged for.[56] How could that be? How could those who produced everything end their lives with almost nothing and those who produced nothing begin their lives with almost everything? Orwell thought asking this turned him into some kind of socialist. But what kind of socialist? *The Road to Wigan Pier* is Orwell's most difficult book, made more difficult still by his attempt in Part Two to translate all this seeing and believing into politics. Part One is about the miners and their families. Part Two is about socialism. We know who *they* are, but what is *that*?

Socialists: working class or middle class?

What 'socialism' meant was no more clear to Orwell in 1936 than it had been to any member of the Labour party since its foundation in 1900. To Sidney and Beatrice Webb, it was about 'common ownership' of the entire economy 'by the best obtainable system'. This was enshrined in the new Labour constitution of 1918, which Sidney had drafted, but to the socialists who had gone before it had been less about ownership and more about 'Fraternity' and 'New Life' and 'Fellowship', while to the Plebs' League and the Syndicalists and other neo-Marxist groups up to the formation of the Communist party in 1920, it had been about workers' control in some form. In the 1920s R. H. Tawney said socialism was about equality, with a Christian edge. In the 1930s that cadre of young Labour party intellectuals Orwell so studiously avoided—Evan Durbin, Hugh Gaitskell, and Douglas Jay—said it was about planning and modernization. Ramsay Macdonald once said that socialism was about going 'on and on and on' and 'up and up and up', as well he might, because all these meanings and not a few more can be found in Labour party thinking in any year of Orwell's life.[57] Then there was 'Nationalization', supposedly present in the 1918 constitution under clause IIId (later IV), and ready to form the basis of Labour's programme into the 1940s, albeit with scant practical examples on board except the London Passenger Transport Authority: not a body likely to interest Orwell beyond the cost of his ticket.

At first *The Road to Wigan Pier* wants to show us the problem, which is unemployment and exploitation, and then to show us the remedy, which is socialism.[58] Orwell sets it up like this because that is how he wants us to read it. But in fact this is not how the book does read. Instead, socialism emerges not as the solution but the problem, and the unemployed and exploited emerge not as the problem but the solution. At the same time, his subject switches from the condition of the English working class to his own response to the condition of the English working class. This puts him (and us) in something of a quandary.

Drawing on his family background, he starts by describing a rich tradition of English middle-class snobbery. The middle classes are not all rich, he says. But they do have standards, and their most basic standard is that they are not working class. Deep down, they loathe that class for all sorts of reasons, not least because they smell. Orwell attempts to qualify this by saying that the middle classes are brought up to believe the working classes smell. 'You cannot have affection for a man whose breath stinks,' he says; 'habitually stinks, I mean'.[59] And there we have it. In this, his first sustained piece of political writing, Orwell puts instinct, personal experience, and convention at its core. He says that nothing is more basic, unforgettable, and contrary to our pleasure than the habitual stink of another human being. He remembers from childhood the 'faintly unappetizing' odour of servants and the imagined reek of navvies. Which is to say: he starts by putting class consciousness where it firmly belongs; not with the capitalist stage of production or the ownership of the means of production or anything theoretical like that, but in personal encounters with people of another class.

He was not thanked for his efforts. Harry Pollitt, General Secretary of the Communist Party of Great Britain, took him to task in the *Daily Worker* (17 March 1937) for saying workers were smelly, and the *Worker* repeated the charge over the summer. Orwell was at pains to refute it. He told Gollancz to tell Pollitt that it was untrue, that he never had and never would say such a thing, and unless he stopped saying he had he would tell tales about the General Secretary and his friends as well.[60] But he *did* seem to believe it. Had he not written in his *Wigan Pier* Diary that the Meades' house in Manchester was 'the only house I have been in since leaving London that did not smell'?[61] And though one can qualify this by saying that a smelly house and a smelly person are two different things, or that his experience of Wigan had been mainly in boarding-houses, not family homes, or that the Meades lived in a new house and Wigan was full of old ones, or that he had only sought out the old ones and had not been in Wigan very long anyway, and so on and so on, these qualifications miss the point.

What was the point? Working-class people did not smell to themselves and not necessarily to others, and although there were good reasons why overcrowded houses should be smelly, there were many millions of hard-scrubbing wives and mothers who would have been mortified by the charge, not least the millions of cleaners, nannies, and domestic helps whose entire lives were devoted to making sure the middle classes did not smell either. But Orwell's point is not a lesson in personal hygiene. It is a lesson in class relations, which apply whether or not the people involved are smelly or not, socialists or not. The battle of the classes, he says, will not be won in the abstract, or in some future state, but in the present, in how people actually are, and what they actually think of each other. Fought more on behalf of others than himself, and only about the world as it actually was, not about making it over again, in this regard at least Orwell's socialism was consistent.

Class feelings are clearly ineradicable in people who have been brought up to believe they are a class. The problem for Orwell is that although socialism is undoubtedly a good idea, because all thinking socialists are middle class, and all middle-class people are snobs, all socialists are snobs. Workers cannot be thinking socialists because, for whatever reason (and he offers a few), they lack the necessary intelligence. Miners cannot be socialists either, because, in Orwell's account at any rate, they are statues, and statues never speak. Union leaders *are* socialists, call each other 'comrade', and so on, but he reckons they stopped being working class years ago. Other types of working-class socialists, such as writers and activists, cannot be typical of their class either because they over-intellectualize and harbour deep resentments about middle-class intellectuals, who patronize them.[62] As for the ranks of the genuinely self-taught, they are remarkable people, but most workers are not like them, and the trouble with people like the Brookers— and there are millions and millions of people like the Brookers—is that they say the same thing over and over again.[63]

Middle-class socialists, then, according to Orwell, define the brand. They may speak for the workers. They may go in search of the workers. They may praise the workers. But secretly they detest the workers for being working class, just as they loathe themselves for being middle class (but are unable or unwilling to give up the prejudices and privileges that brings).

When talking about socialism, therefore, Orwell brings the classes together in theory before prising them apart in real life. He speaks shrewdly about working-class community, noting sharp differences of opinion in what constitutes a 'slum' and accepting that 'in destroying the slum you destroy other things as well'—such as a sense of belonging, and strong social networks. By contrast, he depicts socialist intellectuals as displaced persons. And because you are never sure where they come from, you can never be sure who they are.[64] In Barnsley, he hears Sir Oswald Mosley, leader of the British Union of Fascists, speak from a socialist angle and 'bamboozle' his audience into believing he stands with them.[65]

Then there are the ranks of the cranks, targets of a volley of vituperative fire covering 'every fruit-juice drinker, nudist, sandal-wearer, sex maniac, Quaker, Nature Cure quack, pacifist and feminist in England'— people, he said, 'who come flocking towards the smell of "progress" like bluebottles to a dead cat'. The year before there had been some sharp exchanges in the pages of the *Daily Worker* over dress codes for Communist women. Some comrades reckoned that a beauty-tips column was unbefitting. They preferred a natural complexion and simple clothing over sex and make-up. Other comrades were keen 'to show the young women whom we wish to get inside the party that communists are not wearers of red shirts or vegetarians or other "cranks", but normal working-class people'.[66] Orwell was an unlikely contributor to this unlikely debate, but when he saw two pistachio Reds get on the bus in Letchworth in 1936 he could not help but make his own small contribution. He mocked them as members of an Independent Labour Party summer school, but omitted to mention that during that very same summer he too had attended a socialist summer school at Langham with the same sort of people. The following year he would attend the ILP School at Letchworth.[67] 'No genuine working man grasps the deeper implications of Socialism', Orwell declared, and no wonder.[68] Having mixed with the miners, who hardly wore clothes at all, let alone the latest fashions, and now having witnessed these two strange specimens of socialist fashion sense get on a bus, he could say no other:

> One of them was obscenely bald, the other had long grey hair...They were dressed in pistachio-coloured shirts and khaki shorts into which their huge bottoms were crammed so tightly that you could study every dimple. Their appearance created a mild stir of horror on top of the bus. The man next to me, a commercial traveller I should say, glanced at me, at them, and back again at me, and murmured 'Socialists', as who should say, 'Red Indians'. He was probably right...but the point is that to him, as an ordinary man, a crank meant a Socialist and a Socialist meant a crank.[69]

Jack Common

Orwell did not have happy memories of progressive summer schools, though they did not stop him attending them, and what exactly was an 'ordinary' working man anyway—and did he know any?[70] It is here that his friendship with Jack Common is interesting. Orwell first met him in 1930 in *The Adelphi* offices in London, and got to know him better as Common rose to the deputy-editorship under Richard Rees. Son of an engine driver brought up in Heaton, Newcastle upon Tyne, Common spent his life doing odd jobs by day in order to pay for his writing by night. Into his sixties, he was worried about the gas and electric and not being able to afford cigarettes. But he was also extremely talented and the perfect foil for Orwell. Here he is describing our man turning up on a bicycle. The two of them had agreed to meet for a drink in a country pub. Leaning on a three-armed signpost, Common observed the cranky scene:

> From that last direction, and very much downhill, there presently appeared a solitary cyclist, a tall man on a tall bike. He could have got off and walked at the worst gradient. Not he. This Don Quixote weaved and wandered this side, that side, defeating windmills of gravity till he grew tall on the hill brow and tall too was that *Rosinante* of a bicycle, an ancient Triumph that could have belonged to his father. Fellow-countrymen of Herts, we made greetings.[71]

Common had the wit to make an impression. Soon after Wigan we find the two men discussing what Orwell called 'this business of class-breaking'—by which he meant the problem (his problem) of being middle class and socialist at the same time. For the Old Etonian, riddled with class and colonial guilt, this was a serious issue. For the Old Heatonian, who liked a laugh, it was a hilarious and paradoxical episode in the history of a class given to moral constipation. In 1934 Common had offered his readers a choice of purges for their affliction. They could either have 'lavender water of Buchmanites', or 'laudanum of Rome', or 'castor oil of the Fascists'—a drastic remedy which promised quick relief, 'though one notices that bourgeois sufferers are much more constipated after treatment than they were before'. The best cure for a bad bourgeois conscience? 'A good, stiff, toddy of Marxism, many times repeated', though not the sort of cure that goes down easily:

> If you have any reason to suspect yourself of being bourgeois in some way, if your bowels are sluggish, if you have a tendency to sell things, or

save money, if you find yourself attached to your possessions or interested
in credit schemes, if you think you would like to lead the workers, then
you cannot do better than to take a good stiff dose of anti-bourgeois
cathartic. This is the invention of Karl Marx, a man himself considera-
bly afflicted.[72]

Between them, the two men played out the paradox: one too posh to be
a worker, the other not posh enough to be an intellectual. According to
Common, 'we got on fairly merrily by this method of regularly turning
over one another's statements to look for the bug underneath, integrity
undamaged by intellectual contact'. Common could have been a model
for Orwell's genuine working man—an entirely theoretical construct, by
the way, but clearly someone not afflicted by bourgeois tendencies who
nevertheless was clever and socialistic at the same time. It may even be
that Orwell got his best notes on cranky socialists from Common's literary creation, Uncle Robin.[73]

Socialism: problem or solution?

So much for the socialists; what about socialism? In Orwell's eyes, 'as
everyone who has brains knows', socialism was undoubtedly the solution
to society's problems, but he hardly helped the cause by making it no
more appealing than the socialists who promoted it. Part of a 'nexus of
thought' that included the immense organization of every aspect of a
person's life—including the huge new future leisure areas of one's life to
be reclaimed from work by machinery—Orwell argued that modern
socialism was contrary to our deepest instincts. He was not talking here
of any of the plausible understandings of socialism that had entertained
the Labour party since its foundation. He was talking instead of the way
a few very senior English nineteenth-century moralists (Arnold, Newman,
Ruskin, and Morris among them) had written against machines or at any
rate against mechanical ways of realizing oneself, *and* of the way a few
self-styled scientifically minded people had talked about future Utopian
states. He was talking, in other words, of a sort of English moralism
wrapped up in French positivism wrapped up in Soviet progressivism
which, according to Orwell, threatened to deliver the organization of
everything, for everybody, everywhere, all of the time, until there would
be nothing left to live for. He concluded that this must be wrong, that
surely people would still want the challenge and uncertainty of life.[74]

How could you be happy when you had everything? This was not socialism so much as a fantastical authoritarian dream conjured up by people who wanted to control the world. Or was this maybe socialism after all? There's that smell of cranks again: 'Socialism, at least in this island, does not smell any longer of revolution and the overthrow of tyrants; it smells of crankishness, machine-worship, and the stupid cult of Russia. Unless you can remove that smell, and very rapidly, Fascism may win.'[75]

What did he think? What was socialism really? Again, Orwell preferred to draw on his own recent experience and to bind his politics to a sense of what was 'genuine' (favourite word, but meaning unclear) and 'decent' (favourite word, but meaning unclear). Needless to say, all this comes very close to his view of what the ordinary working man wanted from life, which is 'present society with the worst abuses left out'. If this is socialism—and Orwell never wavered in his view that it was—it will make bad things better but continue in the meantime to take its cue from the everyday. What might this mean for the miners exactly? Fewer accidents? More money? Hot baths? What miner did not want these things, socialist or not? And what about the women? What did they want? A modern kitchen? A night off? A back door? What working-class mother would not want a scullery-maid (unless she had a daughter to do it)? And because the English working class rarely saw their lives as anything other than common, and commercial too, then local life, real people, and actually existing pleasures (some of them actually existing Tory pleasures) would have to be allowed under socialism.[76] Orwell's reasoning here is fundamental to his belly-to-earth Englishness. But Englishness is for later. For now, there's the problem of changing capitalism into some acceptable form of socialism that reflected not only what the people actually wanted, but how they actually were. How were socialists to make the transition?

If the common and commercial culture that is part of the transition is not different from the common and commercial culture that simultaneously prevents it ('fish and chips, art-silk stockings, tinned salmon, cut-price chocolate, the movies, the radio, strong tea, and the Football Pools have between them averted revolution'),[77] who will be able to think beyond it in order to bring in the new? Here, somewhat unconvincingly, Orwell was forced back to his much-criticized middle-class socialists, calling on them to drop their crankiness, build an effective political common sense, and unite with the working class (in some as yet unexplained way). It is true, he says, that socialism may never have written a good popular song, or organized a day at the races, but it is still an institution we cannot do without.[78] At the end of *Wigan Pier* it is clear that Orwell has addressed his book not only to middle-class socialists but to the middle class as a whole, to the teachers and civil servants, to the ship's officers and commercial travellers, to the small businessmen and engineers who actually steer the world that the miners and other workers turn, and who have suddenly appeared on Orwell's political horizon to give reinforcement to his beleaguered and incompetent league of left cranks and casuists. 'Orwell' includes himself in their number. 'We have nothing to lose but *our* aitches', he says, and these are his last words on the subject.

It was part of the Orwell performance to write as the loner, the outsider, the decent middle-class man who sees it all. But you would not know from reading *The Road to Wigan Pier* that the issue Orwell appeared to have made his own (the left's relations with the working class), along with the idea he was to make his own (working-class culture as the basis of ethical socialism), were each at the heart of the *Adelphi* movement and familiar across the intellectual left as a whole.[79] Nor would you know from his dystopian ruminations on socialism that Labour and the TUC were at that very moment formulating an 'Immediate Programme' which offered as good and as practical a plan for socialism as you could find. For all Orwell's soul-searching, and for all his castigations of what he deemed to be of the 'left', he was a man writing from very narrow political experience, who knew nothing of labour traditions and who found it difficult to mix with workers. As he wrote to a friend in 1931, 'I haven't anything of great interest to report yet about the Lower Classes'.[80]

To be or not to be? Was he to be a socialist or not a socialist? Was he to be part of the problem or part of the solution? The French Communist and Surrealist André Breton offered his opinion on such matters in 1927. Breton saw bourgeois art as the means of bourgeois self-destruction, and bourgeois self-destruction as the road to socialist reconstruction. According to him, therefore, bourgeois intellectuals could only contemplate overthrowing the bourgeois system once they had overthrown themselves. Whatever that meant. Orwell in 1936 most certainly saw his own writing as 'bourgeois art';[81] and he wanted to overthrow the system; and there can be no doubt he was in difficulty over what class he belonged to. He knew from his policing and tramping days that in real life self-destruction is not easy:

> Our aim must be the absolute destruction of all the pretensions of the caste to which we involuntarily belong, pretensions which we can only help to abolish ourselves when we have managed to abolish them within us. (Breton in 1927)[82]

> With loving though slightly patronizing smiles we set out to greet our proletarian brothers, and behold! our proletarian brothers—in so far as we understand them—are not asking for our greetings, they are asking us to commit suicide...this class-breaking business isn't so simple...If you are a bourgeois 'intellectual' you too readily imagine that you have some-how become un-bourgeois because you find it easy to laugh at patriotism and the C. of E. and the Old School Tie and Colonel Blimp and the rest of it. But from the point of view of the proletarian 'intellectual'...very likely he looks upon you and Colonel Blimp as practically equivalent persons.' (Orwell in 1937)[83]

Orwell's time in the north of England combined with exchanges with Jack Common and Henry Miller to heighten his self-awareness. True: he was different from the proles and could not be one of them. Not true: this prevented him from joining the struggle. The time was coming anyway when the 'we of the sinking middle class', 'the private school-master, the half-starved free-lance journalist, the colonel's spinster daugh-ter', would soon be relieved of their self-destroying duties to find themselves going down, down, 'without further struggles into the work-ing class where we belong'.[84] *The Road to Wigan Pier* gets there in the end. The conclusion is obvious, if unexpected. Except for a few base reaction-aries and plutocrats, socialism needed all the people. All workers now.

Not alone

Orwell had been in Wigan for just under three weeks when one morn-ing a full chamber-pot was left under the breakfast table and he packed his bags and left. He made for Sheffield, where he stayed for three days, 2–5 March, with the Searles ('I have seldom met people with more natu-ral decency'), walking round in the company of a man called James Brown, before taking the train to stay for a week with his sister Marjorie and her family in Headingley, Leeds. He enjoyed the comfort and light of 21 Estcourt Avenue. 'The children make peace and quiet difficult, but if you definitely want to be alone you can be so—in a working-class house never, either by day or by night.'[85]

Then he headed back south into the Yorkshire coalfield, lodging for two weeks (13–26 March) with the Greys at 4 Agnes Terrace, Barnsley. Mr Grey, age 50, was a filler, a 'short, powerful man' with 'coarse features' and a 'very fatigued look'. Mrs Grey, age 38, Orwell tells us, was a smart and skilful housewife. They had two daughters, Doreen, 12, and Irene, 10. They also had other lodgers—a widowed joiner and his son, and a professional pub singer—but it appears to have been Orwell who was taken into the family circle. He went to more meetings, including hearing Mosley speak and attending a Workingmen's Club and Institute Union delegate meeting, both previously mentioned. He also went down two more pits, including Grimethorpe on Saturday the 21st, where he saw the fillers in action.

The day after he arrived at Agnes Terrace, Orwell declared in his Diary that 'I am very comfortable in this house'. In the evenings he would sit awhile, the girls watching him type, before he and Mr Grey would chat about the war, or life on 2s. 2d. per ton filled. When it came to describing these scenes there is no doubt that for Orwell writing what you saw included writing what you felt. He drew upon his emotions as much as his memories. We have to beware his *narodnik* tendencies here,[86] particularly his new-found belief in the holy worker. He was searching not only for the truth, but true belief. We find his observations on life at 4 Agnes Terrace testifying on behalf of women what the pit chapter testified on behalf of men.[87] Orwell offers the natural symmetry of the family out of the hard-won peace and comfort of the home. Mr Grey's pit-work complements Mrs Grey's housework: the one hard and muscular, the other of a 'sane and comely shape'. Happy was the man, Orwell must have felt, who had both. Certainly he had had neither:

> I should say that a manual worker, if he is in steady work and drawing good wages—an 'if' that gets bigger and bigger—has a better chance of being happy than an 'educated' man. His home life seems to fall more naturally into a sane and comely shape. I have often been struck by the peculiar easy completeness, the perfect symmetry as it were, of a working-class interior at its best. Especially on winter evenings after tea, when the fire glows in the open range and dances mirrored in the steel fender, when Father, in shirt sleeves, sits in the rocking chair at one side of the fire reading the racing finals, and Mother sits on the other with her sewing, and the

children are happy with a pennorth of mint humbugs, and the dog lolls roasting himself on the rag mat—it is a good place to be in, provided that you can be not only in it but sufficiently *of* it to be taken for granted.[88]

Of course there is sentimentality and contrivance in this. It is as if we are looking at the Greys' family album. We can imagine the fixed positions, the frozen smiles, the shutter, the flash, the still-life, and then the whole tableau breaking up. Father stretches and declares he's off to the pub. The dog is too hot, and stands unsteadily. Mother carries on sewing but not looking up, and not before some sharp words for the man who bangs the front door. The kids argue over the last mint and the lodger sees it for what it is. Humbug. All gone now. Even so, Orwell catches the family at rest just as he caught the fillers at work. An alternative English are in the making. And they are a family.[89]

After Barnsley he went back to Marjorie's for three days' respite and then, on 30 March 1936, caught the train back to London and never, as far as we know, returned to Wigan, Sheffield, or Barnsley again.[90] He had spent fifty-six days away; forty-six of them with working-class people, but only thirteen with a working miner and his family. When he was leaving Wigan and the train bore him away and the slag-heaps gave way to open moorland, and the sun came out, and the snow shone bright, he reflected on the land he was leaving: 'a crowded, dirty little country [where] one takes defilement almost for granted.'[91] Yet it was here, in such a place, that he had found an England to believe in; a northern England vested in an exploited and exhausted class whose lives were valuable all the same—the most valuable he had seen. In the face of so much endurance, the prevailing myth that the English people were 'not intellectual' and shared 'a horror of abstract thought' suited him.[92] He would go home and write about them as a way of showing intellectuals they did not know everything. And he would write about them as a regenerative force who, because the Depression was pushing Orwell's sinking section of the middle class down into their ranks anyway, relieved him of all existential worries about his being middle class and all that. From now on all hope lay with the proles. Very soon Orwell would be one himself. But equally, his thoughts on class could sound like G. K. Chesterton's—and G. K was no socialist. In the meantime he got married like an ordinary man should, dug his garden over the autumn, and wrote *The Road to Wigan Pier* as the Jarrow Marchers made their way to London.[93] At last he was not alone.

Eye Witness in Barcelona 1937

Anti-Fascist

Spain was to prove the fundamental political experience of Orwell's life. It was here that he witnessed cold-blooded murder and terror. On a couple of occasions, the blood and terror was his own.

He arrived in Barcelona on Boxing Day 1936 in order to offer his services to the second Spanish Republic.[1] After delivering the manuscript of *The Road to Wigan Pier* to his agent in London, he looked up Henry Miller in Paris. He did not get much encouragement from the American about going for a soldier, except a warm corduroy jacket which was maybe encouragement enough, but at least he kept his tryst with a writer who had helped him feel his way in the world. Then he took the train south to a country in turmoil.

With a letter of introduction from the British Independent Labour Party (ILP), Orwell made his way to the militia barracks of the *Partido Obrero de Unificacion Marxista*, otherwise known as the POUM, a party of the far left.[2] There, and without fuss, he signed on as 'Eric Blair, grocer'. *Grocer*. How unheroic can you get? He was not really a grocer. He could have signed on as 'Author' with far more justification, or bookshop assistant, or even schoolmaster. He was renting a Hertfordshire cottage that used to be a grocer's and he and his wife had kept the shop going as a sideline, making a little money selling mostly sweets to kids in halfpenny packets. But when it came to signing on to fight in a socialist revolution, being one of the 'we of the sinking middle class' suited him best. He was a grocer now and, naturally enough, first cue was yet another encounter with heroes he could believe in:

> In the Lenin Barracks in Barcelona, the day before I joined the militia, I saw an Italian militiaman standing in front of the officers' table. He was a tough-looking youth of twenty five or six, with reddish yellow hair and powerful

shoulders. His peaked leather cap was pulled fiercely over one eye. He was standing in profile to me, his chin on his breast, gazing with a puzzled frown at a map which one of the officers had open on the table. Something in his face deeply moved me. It was the face of a man who would commit murder and throw away his life for a friend—the kind of face you would expect in an Anarchist, though as likely as not he was a Communist. There was both candour and ferocity in it . . .

'*Italiano?*'

I answered in my bad Spanish: '*No, Ingles. Y tu?*'

'*Italiano.*'

As we went out he stepped across the room and gripped my hand very hard. Queer, the affection you can feel for a stranger! It was as though his spirit and mine had momentarily succeeded in bridging the gulf of language and tradition and meeting in utter intimacy. I hoped he liked me as well as I liked him. But I knew that to retain my first impression of him I must not see him again. One was always making contacts of that kind in Spain.[3]

Orwell would write a poem in this man's memory. After the bad days of Comstockery, the quality of his poetry was improving with the quality of his encounters:

> The Italian soldier shook my hand
>   Beside the guard room table;
> The strong hand and the subtle hand
>   Whose palms are only able
>
> To meet within the sound of guns,
> But oh! what peace I knew then
> In gazing on his battered face
> Purer than any woman's![4]

Eric Blair, grocer, spent six months in Spain, mainly on the Aragon front with the eighty men and assorted dogs and uniforms of an under-strength *centura* of the Lenin Division of the POUM militia. He was prepared to die with these men, and for them if necessary. Not everything was to his liking. Military training was useless, modern weapons were rare, the barracks was filthy, standards were low. Even the buglers couldn't play properly.[5] The usual adjectives came out and did duty: 'frightful', 'disgraceful', 'wasteful', and so on. So did the smells: this time, the horse-piss and rotten oats of a former cavalry barracks. He noted in passing how some magnificent chargers had been captured and handed over to the militia, who were busy riding them to death. This was not a free society nor even an attractive one, nor could it be, but in those first few days Orwell was convinced that it was the most equal society he had known. Just as he saw the English miners as 'genuine working men', so he saw the Spanish militias as 'genuine revolutionaries', 'microcosms of a classless society'. At the front he reckoned complete equality, or something not far from it, had been achieved. 'Snobbishness, money grubbing, fear of the boss etc.' had ceased; class prejudice had gone; comradeship was real and unaffected. Above all, he was struck by the 'essential decency . . . straightforwardness and generosity' of the Catalans.[6]

In other words, he thought he had found what he had been looking for in Part Two of *Wigan Pier*: a socialism that did not need its 'sleek little professors' to tell it what it was. He intuited the same instincts in the Spanish working class which he had found in the English.[7] In Lancashire and Yorkshire he believed he had found the real England in a class of men whose loyalty was not to something abstract, as it tended to be with intellectuals; or to something he could hardly comprehend, as it was with the Burmese; or to something unknowable, as it was with the tramps—but a loyalty to each other, face to face, here and now, without question, whatever the odds. And so it was with the Catalans, except they were not only loyal, they were armed and loyal. The English miners were a class in themselves. The Spanish militias, on the other hand, were a class *for* themselves. Having saved the Republic from 'Black' Spain, the land of colonels, priests, and landowners, they now seemed ready to establish Red Spain, a land fit for workers and peasants. Here began Orwell's first lesson in Revolution:

> when one came straight from England the aspect of Barcelona was something startling and overwhelming. It was the first time that I had ever been in a town where the working class was in the saddle. Practically every building of any size had been seized by the workers and was draped with red flags or with the red and black flag of the Anarchists; every wall was scrawled with the hammer and sickle and with the initials of the revolutionary parties; every church had been gutted and its images burnt. Churches here and there were being systematically demolished by gangs of workmen. Every shop and café had an inscription saying it had been collectivized; even the bootblacks had been collectivized and their boxes painted red and black. Waiters and shop-walkers looked you in the face and treated you as an equal. Servile and even unceremonial forms of

speech had temporarily disappeared. Nobody said 'Senor' or 'Don' or even 'Usted'; everyone called everyone else 'Comrade' and 'Thou', and said 'Salud!' instead of 'Buenos dias'. Tipping was forbidden by law; almost my first experience was receiving a lecture from a hotel manager for trying to tip a lift boy. There were no private motor cars, they had all been commandeered, and all the trams and taxis and much of the other transport were painted red and black. The revolutionary posters were everywhere flaming from the walls in clean reds and blues that made the few remaining advertisements look like daubs of mud. Down the Ramblas, the wide central artery of the town where crowds of people streamed constantly to and fro, the loudspeakers were bellowing revolutionary songs all day and far into the night. And it was the aspect of the crowds that was the queerest thing of all. In outward appearance it was a town in which the wealthy classes had practically ceased to exist.[8]

He saw action twice.[9] First in early April as part of a wider Republican drive—as reported in the *New Leader* at the beginning of this book. Orwell's own account of the action is in chapter 7 of *Homage to Catalonia* and is a masterpiece. If the attack was part of the revolution, he is saying, no politician could possibly comprehend it because we who made the attack could not comprehend it either. Their rifles jam, their bombs stick, they crawl on their bellies sick with fear there, and they crawl on their bellies sick with fear back, and they achieve nothing in between but casualties. None of this was predictable before the attack. None of it made sense after. Orwell gets back to his lines, quite incongruously remembering only 'the bare misery of the Fascist dug outs'. They are told by their superiors that the attack was a great success, but he hardly believes it. They always said such things.

He never made of the war more than a matter of being there. When he looked back, what mattered most was 'first of all the physical memories, the sounds, the smells, and the surfaces of things'.[10] The rest was a question of getting through it with all the experience, instinct, and common sense you could cup in your hands. If you have no heavy weaponry and face an enemy who has machine-guns, there are only three things you can do. You can dig in at 400 yards. You can advance and get mown down. Or you can make pointless small-scale night-attacks of the sort described. The common-sense alternative to all this, and what matters most, apart from a weapon that doesn't jam, was firewood, food, tobacco, candles, warm blankets, good boots, and a daily alternative to the boredom and the vermin.[11] Always drawn to the little platoons and the little platoons to him, his comrades made him their corporal. After 115 days away, Eileen remembered him back from the front. 'He arrived completely ragged, almost bare-foot, a little lousy, dark brown and looking really well. For the previous 12 hours he had been in trains consuming anis, muscatel out of anis bottles, sardines and chocolate.'[12]

No sooner was Orwell back in Barcelona than he was in action again. This time, however, he found himself fighting his own side. After months of left factionalism in government circles, a new Republican army was on the streets of Barcelona while the old Caballero regime was falling apart in Valencia. By the middle of May, after perhaps 500 had died in what Orwell later referred to as a 'dust up' between the army and the militias, Juan Negrin was in, Caballero was out, and the POUM was on its way out.[13]

Internecine struggles had been simmering all winter. They boiled over on 25 April, after Caballero dismissed the Communist-controlled defence committee of Madrid and fighting broke out between Anarchists and Communists in the Catalan border town of Puigcerda, and Roldan Cortada, a well-known Communist, was assassinated in Barcelona. When Orwell arrived back on the 26th mass rallies were taking place in memory of Cortada, while Anarchist suspects were being rounded up. Orwell was due to return to the front in a matter of days, but opted to stay put while the POUM militia—officially subordinate to the mass Catalan Anarchist trade union the CNT, but fiercely independent too—stood its ground and refused to surrender its weapons. Fighting broke out in and around the Telephone Exchange on 3 May, after police tried to dislodge telephone workers who had been carrying out their duties in a conscientious Anarchist fashion.

He looked on amazed at the sudden turn of events. While the POUM was fighting Fascists at the front, the Republic was fighting, or at any rate hassling, the POUM in its own backyard. 'Anti-Fascism' was a Communist concept subject to an array of Soviet interpretations, but this was ridiculous.[14] Loyal to his comrades, and loyal to the anti-Fascist cause as he saw it, Orwell took his rifle, an old Mauser, up onto a cinema roof overlooking the Ramblas and loitered there looking for a kill. In so doing, as a well-educated man at the heart of a revolution, he mused that he should feel part of history. But he never did. 'At such times the physical details always outweighed everything else':

Throughout the fighting I never made the correct 'analysis' of the situation that was so glibly made by journalists hundreds of miles away. What I was chiefly thinking about was not the rights and wrongs of this miserable internecine scrap, but simply the discomfort and the boredom of sitting day and night on that intolerable roof, and the hunger...If this was history it did not feel like it.[15]

Orwell had not come to Spain to fight a left-wing government. After his initial infatuation with a classless society, he knew by now how perplexing Spain could be, and how squalid, but he had warmed to his comrades and was shocked and distressed at the lies that were being told, slandering them as Fascists and fifth-columnists. At the same time, he knew the military limitations of the militias, was never going to be convinced by his own side's incipient Leninism, and remained a supporter of the Republic. He still wanted to join its army once he had stopped resisting it. Just before the street-fighting broke out on 3 May he told a Comintern representative that he hoped his connections with the POUM would not count against his application to join the International Brigade, then fighting in defence of Madrid.[16] Subsequently he applied for a discharge from the POUM and did not report to their Barcelona barracks as instructed. He only wanted to get to Madrid and do some hard fighting, and probably some hard reporting too. Up to this point Orwell had inclined to the Republican and Communist-party 'fight-the-war' line over the POUM's 'fight-the-war-*and*-the-revolution' line.[17] But equally, he never had any illusions about growing Soviet influence on the Republic, and could not help noticing how capable Republican security forces looked compared to his own tattered comrades in the militia. After a few days street-fighting and stand-off, the shooting died down and a deal was struck. Assault guards came in from Valencia to patrol the streets, carrying their new Russian automatics with pride.[18] At the front, the POUM's ancient rifles exploded on their shoulders.

Then it was back to the front on 10 May. Later in May, however, he was in Barcelona again, just out of the military field hospital at Lerida. Contrary to his claim that enemy snipers couldn't hit a bull in a passage, Orwell had caught an early morning *hola* right through the throat: a high-velocity 7 mm-calibre bullet between the trachea and carotid artery. This time the war finally hit home. It was not long since he had described shooting an elephant in Burma. Now he was describing being shot himself in Spain. We should not be surprised that the sensations for Orwell and his elephant were the same. The writing always comes first:

> When I pulled the trigger I did not hear the bang or feel the kick—one never does when a shot goes home...In that instant, in too short a time, one would have thought, even for the bullet to get there, a mysterious, terrible change had come over the elephant. He neither stirred nor fell, but every line of his body had altered. He looked suddenly stricken, shrunken, immensely old, as though the frightful impact of the bullet had paralysed him without knocking him down...he sagged to his knees. ('Shooting an Elephant', *New Writing*, 1936)[19]

> Roughly speaking it was the sensation of being at the centre of an explosion. There seemed to be a loud bang and a blinding flash of light all around me, and I felt a tremendous shock—no pain, only a violent shock, such as you get from an electric terminal; with a sense of utter weakness, a feeling of being stricken and shrivelled up to nothing. The sand bags in front of me receded into immense distance...The next moment my knees crumpled up and I was falling. (*Homage to Catalonia*, 1938)[20]

He was lucky to survive. As he said, Spanish marksmanship saved his life a few times. It took eight days to move him down the line from field stations to hospitals to a sanatorium in Barcelona where, after two weeks' convalescence, he was released. Released, but as a soldier not discharged, and by no means at liberty. For its part in resisting the May demilitarization the POUM was being accused of treason in the press, and on 16 June, the day after a sick and heavily bandaged Orwell set out back to the front to secure his discharge papers, the government finally declared it an illegal organization, raiding its offices and closing its newspaper, *La Batalla*. Security police and others were making arrests. POUM's leader, Andres Nin, was taken on the same day, and held in a Communist private prison, or *checa*, where he was tortured, possibly with some government knowledge (though it was still early for the Negrin government which had only been in power three days).[21] Other comrades, including Georges Kopp, formerly commandant of the Lenin division, and Bob Smillie, from Orwell's old platoon, had also been arrested, Kopp on 20 June.

It took no time for Republican security forces to identify Orwell and his wife as spies. On 18 June, the same day her husband was issued with a medical discharge and safe passage by the 29th Army Division, security men raided Eileen's room at the hotel.[22] She stayed in bed, concealing their ILP papers. When Orwell got back from the front on the 20th the Blairs expected to be arrested at any minute. Because Eileen was clearly the bait, she stayed at the hotel while Orwell slept rough. They pestered the British Consulate for visas and looked for a way out, while at considerable risk to themselves they also went to see Kopp in jail, where they lobbied on his behalf. To no avail. Kopp spent eighteen months in prison. Bob Smillie was already dead—murdered, or allowed to die in custody, whichever way it was.[23]

On 23 June, along with Stafford Cottman, another British volunteer from Orwell's old platoon, and the ILP official John McNair, the Blairs left Barcelona by train, posing as war tourists.[24] If they had been caught they would most certainly have been arrested. Three weeks after crossing over into France a full indictment was published against them for High Treason and Espionage: 'One must consider them ILP agents of the POUM.' 'Eric Blair took part in the events of May.' It seems they had been spied upon by men they took to be their comrades.[25] Here ended Orwell's second lesson in Revolution.

Man to man

Orwell claimed later that he had gone to Spain knowing nothing of Spanish politics and with no idea what kind of war he was joining. He saw it as a war against Fascism and that was that. But this was not quite true. *The Road to Wigan Pier* is not exactly politically innocent, and there are strong similarities in the stance he took against left-wing intellectuals in that book and the stance he took against them in *Homage to Catalonia*. In other words, he was keen to write a book about Spain just as he had written one about England, and just as he drew powerful conclusions from his English experience, so he drew them from his Spanish, with exactly the same reversals of expectation. He goes to Wigan with grave doubts about capitalism, and leaves it with grave doubts about socialism. He goes to Spain an out-and-out anti-Fascist, and leaves it an out-and-out anti-Communist. Orwell's politics was developing now as a matter of truth to action. The miners had shown him a better England and made him a better man. The Spanish people had saved the Republic and shown him a new Spain. Twice he had seen the truth for himself. Now he was going to act on it.

So, in a small footnote to the history of the Spanish Civil War, George Orwell returned to London to defend the actions of the POUM and to sever his links, such as they were, with Communist and Communist-influenced sections of the British intelligentsia. He was not alone in this. The ILP and the Glasgow POUM Defence Committee both launched campaigns to defend their arrested Spanish comrades.[26] More important, during the summer and autumn of 1937, goaded by letters from Kopp about the squalor and brutality of life inside a Republican prison,[27] Orwell forged an aggressive, unrelenting essay style that would come to be his trademark: establish the truth of the encounter; show its wider political significance; challenge the reader's moral integrity. This style had started surprisingly well in 1931, in 'The Spike' and 'A Hanging', but had deteriorated somewhat in *Down and Out in Paris and London*, only to languish in the novels but stay alive in the book reviews, to show new life in *Burmese Days*, and look promising again with *The Road to Wigan Pier*. Unlike that work, however, which simply bolted his politics onto his experience, *Homage to Catalonia*, as Richard Keeble shows, blended them together in ways that mixed into a single, absorbing story.[28]

Homage to Catalonia is told in the first person. It rarely speculates beyond that, but equally there is hardly a sentence which does not carry some wider nuance. Consider how his description of the attempt to save Georges Kopp turns from a matter of first-person fact into the wider significance of why it matters at all. The narrative starts, 'My wife and I visited Kopp that afternoon'. They try to retrieve from the police documents that had been taken from Kopp and might serve to save his life. An army officer helps. He is entirely sympathetic, if entirely proper, in his response to Major Kopp. The police, by contrast, are corrupt. Having retrieved the army documents but having failed, nevertheless, to obtain Kopp's release, Orwell and the army officer accept the situation, bow slightly to each other, 'and then there happened a strange and moving thing, the little officer hesitated a moment, then stepped across, and shook hands with me'. Orwell says he records this encounter because, 'trivial though it may sound... it is somehow typical of Spain'.[29]

Note the 'somehow'. As in Orwell's exchange with the militiaman at the start of the book, the passage may be rooted in chance encounters and quicksilver reporting, but it is also reaching out with a wider meaning, a meaning which in a lesser writer or a lazier journalist would look tendentious.[30] Encounters like this are repeated all through;

they are his homage. Orwell is feeling his way not only towards an anti-politics politics, but also towards an anti-literary literariness that ultimately becomes his house style. I have not got the time to make the story into literature, he seems to be saying. But he only *seems* to be saying it. In Orwell, the writer always beats the journalist to the story.

Rather than identify 'Orwell' as like them, we do better to identify a coming generation of journalists as like him. Always a better essayist than a novelist, in *Homage to Catalonia* he is a book-length essayist trying to capture the intimacy of the first-person novelist. Jenni Calder has called this 'the necessity of action' in his writing.[31] The style was not entirely original. Documentary film-makers had been trying to do first person for ten years or more.[32] Social investigators had been taking readers into London slum life for well over fifty, and a few before that. Modern war reporting had relied on personal witness for even longer.[33] Orwell's notebooks bulged with cuttings and pamphlets and duplicates.[34] He had always been an immediate, there-and-then kind of guy; keen to know, find out, explain, move on. His nieces and nephews remembered him that way. So did the Peters brothers—'A walk was a mixture of energy, adventure and matters of fact. The world, we felt, was just like this.' So did the boys he taught at prep school. He was a good teacher. His flatmates, schoolfriends, and Spanish comrades too, all remembered him as someone who 'always reacted to situations', was 'awfully personal', and who wanted to get involved and understand people. 'He was not, I repeat, *not* a snob.'[35]

You might say, therefore, that even though he hardly ever worked to deadlines from the front, there was something of the journalist in him. But you might also say that a man who went in search of the truth was bound to react strongly when his own side told lies, not only against himself but against his wife and comrades too, *as a matter of course*. Orwell felt trashed by Republican Spain. Fascism could never have hurt him like this, because he had no interest in Fascists. It was as if in Barcelona his taste for life and his taste for art and politics came together, once at the outset to be exalted, once at the end to be disgusted. In defence of the Revolution and against those who had betrayed it, Orwell found his voice. No English journalist, with the possible exception of Hazlitt or Cobbett, had been so personally driven or self-possessed.

So, in his urge to tell it like it was whatever the cost, Orwell had a lot of the journalist in him. But the theory was that the modern press had learned not only to invent 'the masses', but to comfort and deceive them too. The first British instance was generally thought to be the Anglo-Boer War (1899–1902), a literary war with Kipling taking special briefings from the generals while Edgar Wallace (*Daily Mail*), Henry Nevinson (*Daily Chronicle*), Winston Churchill (*Morning Post*), and J. A. Hobson (*Manchester Guardian*) reported back from the action. South Africa was a unique war in British history. For the first time, a tight relationship between pressmen and politicians was apparent.[36] In the United States, Walter Lippman talked in 1922 of 'the manufacture of consent' out of newspaper stereotypes and fictions, while Norman Angell talked in 1914 and again in 1926 of the newspaper industry's daily drive for 'the quickest reaction from the very largest number'. In Great Britain, Harold Lasswell warned in 1927 against too much emotion in the press—though not without admiration for newspapermen's 'terse, vivid' style and rapid storytelling. Orwell's first published pieces, as we have seen, followed these sociological lines by addressing the twin problem of state censorship in Britain and mass commercialization of the press in France. The view from the left was that in the capitalist news kingdoms of the world—pioneered by Northcliffe in England and Hearst in the United States—everything was bland and mass-manipulated.[37] This view was endorsed by the press lords themselves.[38] But there were countervailing developments too, in particular a growing personal and professional commitment among journalists to getting as close to what was happening as possible, and telling it in their own name, whatever the cost. Long before Orwell, therefore, and in a way which suited his dissent from the orthodoxies of both the right (mass news is popular opinion) and left (mass news is manipulation), 'being there' in order to tell the truth had grown to be part of the journalist's trade. By the time he was thinking of going to Spain, 'with some notion of writing newspaper articles',[39] the greatest living practitioner of the trade was Ernest Hemingway.

Like Priestley and Chesterton, Hemingway was one of those writers whom Orwell never gave his full attention but with whom he had a lot in common.[40] Both men had lived in the same area of Paris in the 1920s; both were anti-Fascist and anti-Communist, not party men but pro-Republican and pro the masculine virtues too, not only in their lives but in their prose. When they speak, you listen. When you listen, it is in that man-to-man, democratic way that so impressed Thomas Paine in revolutionary America in 1776 and Orwell in revolutionary Spain in 1937. That said, while Orwell served in a trench on twopence a day, Hemingway was in and out of Spain (five times), staying at the Hotel Florida courtesy of the North American Newspaper Alliance on a dollar rate of $500 a cable. He even had a chauffeur (in Madrid he had four), and his girlfriend Martha Gellhorn had a direct line to the White House.[41] All the same, man (and girlfriend) could really write. Although Orwell affected disdain for Hemingway's tough-guy prose, it is hard to believe he did not learn from it.[42] Years later, when they were both serving as newspaper war correspondents, they met briefly in Paris at the Hotel Scribe, an incident that the American felt obliged to inflate as time went by.[43]

Orwell also had much in common with two other great left-wing American writer-reporters—Upton Sinclair and John Steinbeck. He, like them, never saw himself as anything more than a jobbing writer and shared something of their 'ordinary Joe' prose style. Steinbeck would come to be seen as 'uniquely American', just as Orwell would come to be seen as uniquely English. More than Hemingway perhaps, and along with two other belly-to-earth Americans, Miller and Faulkner, Sinclair, Steinbeck, and Orwell were committed to trying to tell the truth about ordinary lives.[44] Miller's Avenue Clichy, Faulkner's Yoknapatawpha County, Sinclair's Packingtown, Steinbeck's Salinas Valley, and Orwell's Aragon Front all came out of being there and getting it right. Orwell never could and never did write a novel as good as *The Grapes of Wrath*, but Steinbeck's taste for 'the shock of first hand observation' and 'complex, self-contained, imaginative worlds' matched Orwell's politics, and Sinclair's Chicago Union stockyards prefigured twentieth-century totalitarian genocides not a world away from *Nineteen Eighty-Four*.[45] All these writers knew how very small worlds could contain very big ones.[46] Orwell got out of Spain believing that it was just a rehearsal for the next big war to come. Along with civilian bombing, mass mobilization, and the inexorable shift towards total government and a new kind of politics, he was convinced that another key feature of war would be how intellectuals would seek to deceive the masses. Not for the first time, he was taking his arguments, as well as picking his fights, from the left, on the left.[47] Determined to tell the truth about Spain, at the same time he was sympathetic to the Left Book Club line that in the age of the masses the truth was impossible:

In the last quarter of a century the whole picture has changed. Political propaganda has become the chief internal weapon of governments, and it is employed not only to persuade a sufficient number of people that a particular course of action is expedient or right, but to keep whole populations in a complete, and it is apparently hoped, a perpetual emotional subjection.[48]

He increasingly adopted Julien Benda's argument that, as they were drawn into politics, intellectuals would find that if they told the truth they would not be able to go on being political, and if they went on being political they would not be able to tell the truth. Culpable if they did, and culpable if they did not, Orwell argued that in an age of opinion, these trends were clear for all to see across Europe's intelligentsias: evidently so in the capitalist news and advertising industries, and flagrantly so in the one-party states—whether of the right or the left or the Vatican—where ambitious, rootless party intellectuals were in power through lies and deception.[49] Orwell raged against them, starting with Gordon Comstock (an intellectual and victim of intellectuals) in *Keep the Aspidistra Flying*, and going on right to the end with Winston Smith (the same) in *Nineteen Eighty-Four*.

In England he had known that all was not well on the metropolitan left long before Kingsley Martin's *New Statesman and Nation* refused to publish his review of Franz Borkenau's *The Spanish Cockpit* in July 1937.[50] Comstock had shown a worrying propensity for self-deception—first sign of mass deception—and *Wigan Pier* had been intensely critical of left intellectuals for much the same reason. But what Orwell found pathetic in Comstock and repulsive in Kingsley Martin, he found murderous in Barcelona. His 'Eye Witness in Barcelona' (*Controversy*, 1: 11, August 1937) set the tone, and a good example of his desire to set the record straight can be found in his clinical, point-by-point sectional removal of F. A. Frankford's charge of POUM treachery as published in the *Daily Worker* on 21 August 1937.[51] At least Frankford had been to Spain. For those who had not been there and seen for themselves, Orwell took the opportunity to administer careful beatings. Stalinist duchesses were particularly welcome.[52]

Anti-Communist

Orwell's reflections on the revolution in Spain, as told in chapter 5 of the first edition of *Homage to Catalonia*, are straightforward. In the summer of 1936 Spanish workers had taken up arms and aligned with loyal

Republican forces in order to prevent a Fascist takeover by units of the professional army and police. In Catalonia these actions were accompanied by the spontaneous collectivization of farms, businesses, and local government. What had begun as the prevention of an army *coup d'état* therefore, turned into a full-blown revolution, a revolution made conscious by the myriad anarchist, socialist, and trade-union organizations—the PSUC, UGT, CNT, FAI, PCE, POUM, and so on—who steered it. A 'plague of initials', Orwell called them. Then, within a year of these momentous events, the USSR was trying to run the show according to its own ends, which were not (necessarily) those of the Republic or the revolution. Which is to say, according to Orwell at any rate, all that had been won in 1936 was being lost in 1937. His specific charge was that, under the new dispensation, the Republic was actively suppressing revolutionary groups and dismantling revolutionary achievements in order to reconstitute a bourgeois 'popular front' able to defend itself from Franco on the one hand while attending to its own (and Soviet) worries about the prospect of an extreme-left popular government on the other. Because this involved disarming and imprisoning men he had fought alongside, in Orwell's eyes the government, and especially the Communists who were increasingly influencing the government, were little better than the enemy. 'The point to notice is that the people who are in prison now are not Fascists but revolutionaries ... and the people responsible for putting them there are ... the Communists.'[53]

According to Orwell, then, militias such as the POUM and the CNT who had resisted being disarmed on the streets of Barcelona in May 1937 were clear defenders of the revolution, while those who had tried to disarm them were its enemies. To him, these were grand facts— heavy beasts roaming an otherwise vague and indeterminate political landscape. Counter-revolutionary moves by a Communist-backed government had led to his comrades-in-arms being traduced, arrested, and imprisoned, their leader murdered, their offices closed, and their party declared 'Trotsky-Fascist'. In response, in a flurry of essays and reviews, most notably 'Spilling the Spanish Beans' (*New English Weekly*, 29 July and 2 September 1937) and 'Eye Witness in Barcelona' (*Controversy*, August 1937), followed by *Homage to Catalonia* in April 1938, Orwell told against those on the ideological left in Britain who had sold the revolution short by shutting their eyes to what was really happening.

What was really happening? Orwell stuck to what his eyes did see and to the POUM position—though not necessarily in that order. Sometimes he went beyond what he could actually have seen. Often what he actually did see was viewed in the light of the POUM position. He hardly considered Labour party policy on Spain as policy at all, vacillating as it did between supporting 'democracy' on the one hand and the 'Republic' on the other: both positions entirely rhetorical.[54] And in a moment of high revolutionary ardour that would stay with him for the next three years, Orwell pronounced all Popular Front governments like Negrin's freaks (bourgeois head, workers' body), threw the charge that the POUM was Fascist back in Negrin's face ('the present government has more points of resemblance to Fascism than points of difference'), and insisted that even in time of war—*especially* in time of war—the revolution must come first. If you do not free the people, he argued, you will not win the war; and if you do not win the war, you will surely not free the people. All opposing views he dismissed as lies, or contrary to how the people on the ground actually saw things, which was in accord with how he saw things, which was usually in accord with his moment of ideology:

> My reading of the situation, derived from what people were actually doing and saying at the time, is this—
>
> The workers came into the streets in a spontaneous defensive movement, and they only consciously wanted two things: the handing-back of the Telephone Exchange and the disarming of the hated Civil Guards. In addition there was the resentment caused by the growing poverty in Barcelona and the luxurious life lived by the bourgeoisie.[55]

This was the POUM line at least, and although Orwell started out sceptical in the end he came down in favour of it, not so much because he believed the line but because believed in the men who believed the line.[56] What mattered to him in Catalonia and Aragon was the same as what mattered to him in Yorkshire and Lancashire: not so much the politics as the people—the unbeliever who came to believe, the uncommitted who came to commit, the man who was blind who came to see. In this extract, note the withering away of what Orwell reasons to be the case and the slow, incipient growth of what he knows to be the case simply by his commitment to it:

> On the surface the quarrel between the Communists and the POUM was one of tactics. The POUM was for immediate revolution, the Communists

not. So far so good; there was much to be said on both sides...But here the peculiarity of Communist tactics came in. Tentatively at first, then more loudly, they began to assert that the POUM was splitting the Government forces not by bad judgement but by deliberate design. The POUM was declared to be no more than a gang of disguised Fascists, in the pay of Franco and Hitler, who were pressing a pseudo-revolutionary policy as a way of aiding the Fascist cause. The POUM was a 'Trotskyist' organization and 'Franco's Fifth Column'. This implied that scores of thousands of working-class people, including eight or ten thousand soldiers who were freezing in the front-line trenches and hundreds of foreigners who had come to Spain to fight against Fascism, often sacrificing their livelihood and their nationality by doing so, were simply traitors...It is not a nice thing to see a Spanish boy of fifteen carried down the line on a stretcher, with a dazed white face looking out from the blankets, and to think of the sleek persons in London and Paris who are writing pamphlets to prove that this boy is a Fascist in disguise...all the usual war-stuff, the tub-thumping, the heroics, the vilification of the enemy—all these were done, as usual, by people who were not fighting and who in many cases would have run a hundred miles sooner than fight. [In this regard] one of the dreariest effects of this war has been to teach me that the Left-wing press is every bit as spurious and dishonest as that of the Right.[57]

This is highly charged writing, but the truth is that Orwell might have spent a little less time responding to his own experience and a little more time thinking carefully about the art of the politically possible. To begin with, not all Communists at home or abroad shared his sense of urgency. They thought that 'The Revolution' (an almost mystical act of transmutation that would solve the problem of class) could wait on the forces of History (capital 'H' and inevitably moving in the direction of Communism). In the meantime, the Communist International had a regional struggle to pursue and trusted Russia's big battalions to help them pursue it. If that involved Popular Front policies, so be it. If it involved 'all the usual war-stuff', so be it.

Moreover, in Spain the situation was more complicated than Orwell allowed. The Spanish Communist Party had assumed a key role in government, but it would be wrong to suppose that all Spanish Communists were intellectuals, or bureaucrats, or that the PCE was the only party in the history of the Spanish left to declare its rivals traitors. Even if the International Brigades were Communist-controlled, their soldiers were there like Orwell was there, to fight the enemy, not each other. International Brigade Communists had been street-fighting Franco in

Madrid while Orwell had been safely tucked up in his grocery. The
British battalion of the XV Brigade, formed in January 1937 (which
Orwell tried to join), took hammerings at every battle it fought—at Jarama in February 1937, at Brunette in July 1937, at Aragon in August
1937, and at Ebro in July 1938. And long before Spanish Communists
got their way (May–June 1937) the Second Republic had been born in
sectarian conflict not only between left and right, but between left and
left—between regionalists and centralists, syndicalists and socialists,
liberals and Leninists, and all varieties of Leninist, including the two
factions which had clashed at the heart of Orwell's politics—the pro-
Anarquista POUM and the pro-*Moscovita* PCE.[58]

These rivalries had frequently been violent in word and deed. The
POUM and Catalan and Spanish Communists had been at each other's
throats since at least December 1936, and government agencies in
Madrid, Barcelona, and Valencia had been trying to disarm the militias
and normalize due process since before that. At times the Republic
could look like a war of all on all. That it saw far fewer extra-judicial
killings than the Nationalist territories was only because Franco and his
friends were better at it.[59] Not only that, there had been clashes between
left republican governments and those they saw as their natural supporters, the workers, almost from the beginning of the Second Republic—at
Castiblanco in 1931, at Arnedo in 1932, at Llobregat in 1932, and in
the sickening burnings and shootings of the 'Casas Viejas' incident of
8 January 1933, which led to the withdrawal of Anarchist support for
the government and the return to government of the right. When a
right-wing government used a colonial army to trample the Asturias in
1934, they were only improving upon an incipient republican taste for
rising and repression amply played out two years later.[60]

The Second Republic had never been able to keep its house in order.
That it included 'at least twelve different leftist and liberal revolutionary
or reform projects' shows the scale of its problems. The wonder was not
that it handled these projects badly but that it dared handle them at
all.[61] Given that, and given that in May 1937 it was surrendering territory and losing the war, it was not unreasonable for Negrin's new government to want to try again to assert its authority, disarm the militias,
and build a new army. The Communist 5th Regiment's motto,
'Discipline, Hierarchy, Organization', may have been a touch excessive,
but we get the point. From Negrin's point of view doing away with

private revolutionary patrols, crossings, checkpoints, holding centres, safe houses, *paseos*, persons missing, persons dead, paramilitaries, *all that*, was not only worth a try, it was 'crucial to the constitutional credibility of the government' and the winning of the war.[62] Violations of the democratic state, after all, were the actions of the right. The intimidation of civil society, after all, was how Franco's *Africanistas* did it.[63] That Communist politicians pressed for order and discipline in order to scatter rivals in their way was clearly dangerous for Anarchists and Trotskyists, particularly in view of what was going on in the Soviet Union, but it could not have been unexpected. The Soviet Union was the only country actively supporting the Republic in men and arms, and it had been their battle tanks, not militia rifles, which had stopped Franco in his tracks outside Madrid in November 1936. After that, the Republic's few victories—at Jarama in February and at Guadalajara in March 1937—could not have been won without Soviet armour. Franco had plenty of German materiel and a hefty Italian army of occupation on his side, and before he ran into the Russians his colonial army had swept up from the south in less than four weeks. While the British, French, and Americans stood aside, the Republic took what it could and paid for it in gold and in the channelling of Soviet aid through the PCE. Against this, the POUM strategy of continuing to look to the militias and *incontrolats* while fighting an increasingly capable enemy at the front and an increasingly complicated workers' revolution to the rear looked like so much wishful thinking. According to one historian at least, it 'would have brought disaster'.[64]

Orwell was unrealistic about the Spanish revolution, and it took him too long to work out why.[65] And because he was unrealistic on the revolution, he was unrealistic on the politics. That he came back from Spain to join the ILP (and by association its absurd global posturing) is surprising for a man who had written Part Two of *The Road to Wigan Pier*.[66] Yet not for the first time—and nor would it be for the last—he took a far left line only to use it to pick a fight with the left. 'Bourgeois democracy is only another name for capitalism,' he declared. 'And so is Fascism.' And so, out of this dismal equation, came the dismal deduction: 'to fight against Fascism on behalf of democracy is to fight against one form of capitalism on behalf of a second which is liable to turn into the first at any moment.' This put Orwell out of step not only with most of the Labour party, but with Labour's very reason for existence. On the other hand,

although they wrote very different books on the subject, and although
Orwell did not trust him, he shared John Strachey's essential point that
in a fight with Fascism it was a wager whether the British political
class would turn Fascist before the British working class would turn
revolutionary—a point of view shared by Stafford Cripps on Labour's
hard left, and held by Orwell for the next three years.[67]

In its fight against Fascism, Orwell seemed to believe that the Republic was turning Fascist. He joined the ILP in 1938, he said, because
never again would he 'be led up the garden path in the name of capitalist democracy'.[68]

Someone less instinctively drawn to the little platoons might have
made more sense of the situation. The new man in charge of the army,
General Vicente Rojo, was a talented soldier and a genuine republican.
Time and again his army would prove its worth against the odds.[69] Juan
Negrin was another man of talent. While Orwell was accusing his government of behaviour tantamount to Fascism (that is, accusing it of
Fascism), the hapless Prime Minister—'a man of the *grande bourgeoisie*'
according to Hugh Thomas[70]—was deploying his considerable linguistic and diplomatic skills trying, unsuccessfully one has to admit, to raise
French and British assistance to fight Fascists. In almost impossible circumstances Roja got the army moving again and Negrin got the government moving again, succeeding to some extent in his efforts to
re-establish cabinet responsibility, build an effective administration, discipline dissidents, accommodate the church, restore the justice system,
and pay off or otherwise diminish what he owed his Soviet creditors.[71]
Special courts were opened to deal quickly and, it has been estimated,
not unfairly with minor cases. Trained judges replaced popular tribu-
nals. Priests were released. The police was restored to normal duties.
The Red Cross was allowed full access to prisoners, including enemy
prisoners. There were to be no Moscow show trials in Spain. Helen
Graham tell us that when the POUM leaders were (finally) brought to
trial in October 1938, charged with supporting the illegal rebellion of
May 1937, the trial was fair, 'in spite of the PCE's best efforts' and a
horrendous collapse in the Republic's military capacity after defeat at
the battle of the River Ebro.[72] Negrin was unable to prevent the Soviet
secret police's persecution of foreign Trotskyists in the militias and the
International Brigades, which went on all through 1937 and which, as
we have seen, nearly swept up the Blairs. Andres Nin was arrested by

police-chief Burillo on 16 June 1937, and shot and dumped in the road by Soviet agents on the 22nd.[73] On the 23rd Orwell and Eileen fled the country.

Anti-Soviet

Orwell's anti-Communism was not just about Spain. It stretched naturally enough to the Soviet Union. We do not know exactly when he began thinking about Russia, but it was probably in Paris in 1928, when he saw a lot of his aunt, Nellie Limouzin, and her partner Eugene Adam, a former Esperantist-Communist who had gone to Moscow in 1922 and come back disillusioned, not having taught the world to speak. Adam was well connected. He introduced Orwell to his friends on the French internationalist left, including journalists who gave the young English writer a start.[74] Later Orwell would say that he had viewed the Soviet regime 'with plain horror' since 1932, that he could feel it in his bones, that he 'could feel it in their literature'.[75] *Wigan Pier* and *Homage to Catalonia* are scattered with side references to Marxist-Leninism. Even so, Orwell's first full critique of the Soviet system came late, in 1938 reviews of Eugene Lyons's *Assignment in Utopia* and Franz Borkenau's *The Communist International*. What Orwell says here about the Soviet Union is unequivocal: that it is a country run by a tiny minority of the population; that it seeks international hegemony; that there is no freedom of speech or movement; that people go in fear of informers and the police; that the country is in the grip of 'monstrous state trials'; that Stalin is rarely seen but formally worshipped; that it has its apologists in all countries ('fifty thousand gramophones'); and all in all, that 'the system Mr Lyons describes does not seem to be very different from Fascism'.[76]

Orwell was no specialist, but Edward Crankshaw, the great historian of Russia, considered Orwell's 1938 essays the 'best short comment on the Moscow trials' and the 'best short summary of Stalinism in foreign policy offered by anyone for years to come'. 'Astonishingly right for that time.'[77] Ten years later, and after four years of war filled with official adulation in Britain for its Soviet allies, Orwell's criticism had only deepened.[78] The Soviet Union remained, he said, a country ruled by terror and deception, led by 'experts and fanatics' living a life cut off from the vast majority of the population and running a security system where there was 'no restraint, no limit'.[79]

Orwell's prescience is impressive, particularly so for a man who did not know the Soviet terror and had only felt its beating wings from afar. In 1929 Stalin began the process of herding 60 million people, or half the peasantry, into collective farms. Orlando Figes identifies this as 'the great turning point in Soviet history': no accident, but a disastrous policy which resulted in the death of between 4 million to 8 million people, the scattering of families, and the creation of a nomadic population of many millions who would help stock the camps and settlements of Stalin's programme of forced industrialization, of which the Gulag system of slave-labour camps was one form.[80] As central state policies 'uprooted', 'destroyed', and 'abolished' (Figes) actually existing classes, and because politics was 'bourgeois politics', associated with the thinking of those whose consciousness was old and 'false', the country found itself with no means of dealing with the resulting confusion.[81] Classes in the real sense had been abolished, and because there was no longer a politics or a property to represent what remained, what remained became like the estates of the Tsarist regimes—defined solely by their relationship to the state and granted (or denied) their rights and privileges accordingly. The industrial proletariat was the most favoured and most correct class; the bourgeoisie the least favoured and least correct. All this destruction and nihilism Orwell translated into *Nineteen Eighty-Four*. Politics was impossible. The party, which was supposed to have replaced the old politics with the new, was itself not trusted. Denied an old party politics he himself had destroyed and confronting a new political party he did not trust, Stalin tried to rule instead by special campaigns, parallel bureaucracies, armed bodies of men, and so on. When these did not work either, in order to atone for its sins he obliged the party to turn on itself.[82] This too Orwell translated into *Nineteen Eighty-Four*.

Five Soviet terror campaigns were carried out in Orwell's lifetime: 1928–31, 1934–5, 1937–8, 1943–6, and 1948–53. Under Special Operational Order 00447 of 30 July 1937, eight anti-Soviet groupings were defined in such a way as to include anyone the security forces targeted, while all state apparatuses, including the schools and courts, preached the rejection of all loyalty that was not party loyalty and the dissolution of all morality that was not Soviet morality. 'Terror managers' were appointed to draw up production quotas for hundreds of thousands of arrests, convictions, deportations, and executions. As with quotas for grain, or boots, or any other product, higher-ranking ministers wanted the managers to produce more terror; hard-pressed lower-ranking officials wanted them to produce less. Either way, the 'terror was planned much as the Soviet economy was planned'.[83] Under article 58 of the Russian Criminal Code, covering 'anti-Soviet propaganda' and 'counter-revolutionary activity', between 1921 and 1938 nearly 5 million people were arrested for criminal offences, and of these over 3 million were charged with treason under a list that was long as it was wide. Offences included 'subversion', 'diversion', 'weakening', 'failure', and 'negligence'. Over the period of Orwell's adult life it is estimated that in the Soviet Union more than one person in every one-and-a-half families was a victim, and more than one person in every eight, or over 25 million people all told, were either shot, enslaved, or deported. The worst years were 1937–8, when 681,692 'former people' (as they were called) were shot, along with 85,000 Russian Orthodox priests and 634,820 other former persons who were sent to the Gulag, and 18,208 others who were exiled.[84] Murderous under the law on the one hand and murderous outside the law on the other, Stalin's Soviet Union was a two-model state that did what it wanted without knowing what it wanted to do.

Orwell was in Spain during the worst years of the terror. While he was writing *The Road to Wigan Pier* the first Moscow show trials (19–24 August 1936) were convicting Kamenev, Zinoviev, and Bukharin of counter-revolutionary acts, and while he was calling in that book for more honesty on the left, Bukharin was pleading guilty 'to the sum total of crimes committed by this counter-revolutionary organization irrespective of whether or not I knew of, whether or not I took direct part, in any particular act'.[85] Before Orwell arrived in Spain, *Pravda* had announced that the elimination of Spanish and international Trotskyists and Anarcho-Syndicalists had begun there, and would 'be carried out with the same energy as in the Soviet Union'.[86] While Orwell was digging in on the Aragon front, the second Moscow show trials were taking place (23 and 30 January 1937). When he was recovering from his bullet in the throat, the NKVD bureau in Barcelona was giving the order (14 June 1937) for the Spanish terror to begin. On 21 June the Blairs found themselves on the run, their friends and former comrades in prison. It would have been cold comfort to them to know that the man who presided over the Spanish terror, the Russian Consul-General in Barcelona, would himself become a victim of the Soviet terror.[87]

Georges Kopp, another victim, wrote from prison to the chief of police to complain about his eighteen days without charge in a tiny cell crammed with prisoners, some of them common criminals, all of them subjected to assault and starvation. Kopp threatened to go on hunger-strike. He said he would kill 'with bare fists' any guard who approached him. He also pleaded his anti-Fascist credentials, but to no avail. Kopp endured eighteen months in jail, where he underwent severe interrogations.[88] Although the Blairs knew all about this, and had risked their lives to try and save him, it is interesting that they blamed Negrin, not the breakdown of a state whose proper functioning Negrin was trying to restore.

So much for the revolution. As for the war, while the Soviets were claiming to build an effective military force in Spain, at home they were busy cutting their own military elite to ribbons. Between 1937 and 1938, eleven out of eleven Soviet deputy commissars of defence, seventy-five out of eighty members of the Supreme Military Council, eight admirals, and 35,000 army officers were executed. At the moment that the Comintern was struggling to destroy the anti-Stalinist POUM in Spain, they were trying to obliterate their own *pro*-Stalinist Communist parties in Germany, Poland, and the Baltic. At Albacete, headquarters of the International Brigades, the *Servicio Investigacion Militar* watched over party members in the interests of party loyalty, while party commissars operated at every level from company level up. Peter Davison reckons that some 500 men of the International Brigades were executed in these years by their own side—about the same number of British volunteers who were killed in combat.[89] Orwell had originally wanted to join the Brigades. Had he managed it, there can be little doubt that if he had not died a hero in defence of Madrid he would have died a traitor up against the wall in Albacete.

Some of these things he saw with his own eyes. All of them he sensed, sensed what happens when people go mad with ideology.

Anti-Marxist

On the left there was plenty to be ideological about. The Soviet Union comprised one-sixth of the Earth's surface, and was considered by some in Britain—not just Communists—to be the 'Socialist Sixth', the only country in the world run by associations of the people for the people.[90]

Those who believed this naturally included members of the Communist party, but also many prominent intellectuals.[91] Here is George Bernard Shaw on the BBC in October 1931. He is speaking of a country in the middle of a famine:

> Russia flaunts her budget surplus of 750 millions, her people employed to the last man and woman, her scientific agriculture doubling and trebling her harvest, her roaring and multiplying factories, her efficient rulers, her atmosphere of such hope and security for the poorest as has never before been seen in a civilized country on earth.[92]

This was the great sage of English and Irish letters speaking, but 11-year-old William Brown, who lived in Kent and whose standards were hardly demanding, knew better.[93] And Liberals and Conservatives knew better. And some socialists, including Orwell, knew better, because far from what its ideology claimed, the USSR was built on the state's most extreme *dis*association from the lives of the people. For William Brown, as for Orwell, their contempt stretched to all the higher, Universal forms of English disassociation as well, including World Harmony, Higher Thought, Flowing Robes, Perfect Love, Spiritual Novels, Vegetarianism, and schemes for the Reformation of Bolsheviks and the Adoption of Poor Northern Families by Rich Southern Ones. How do you represent the people? As William Brown's friend Henry put it:

> There's four sorts of people tryin' to get to be rulers. They all want to make things better, but they want to make 'em better in different ways. There's Conservatives an' they want to make things better by keepin' 'em jus' like what they are now. An' there's Lib'rals an' they want to make things better by alterin' them jus' a bit, but not so anyone'd notice, an' there's Socialists, an' they want to make things better by takin' everyone's money off 'em, an' there's Communists an' they want to make things better by killin' everyone but themselves.[94]

During the 1930s Stalin was able to move Marxism away from its emphasis on class and social change in the direction of the rebuilding of human nature by the state. In 1932 he referred to Soviet writers and artists as 'Engineers of the Human Soul'—the men and women who would rebuild humanity and make it fit for Communism. What Communist intellectuals in the 1930s called 'Historical Materialism' was the science of that transformation, while the state-sponsored movements of *Proletkult* (1920–32), and Socialist Realism (1932–45) served as its technical manuals, with drawings. The trouble was that in real life *Proletkult* had nothing to do with proletarian culture, any more than Socialist Realism had anything to do with social reality. Communism was supposed to be making a completely new sort of man and woman, a new species more dignified and more realized in their humanity than ever before. In point of fact, *Homo Sovieticus*' most developed skill involved 'a whole range of supplicatory and dependent behaviours' derived from the 'hunting and gathering of scarce goods in an urban environment'.[95] Orwell would seize on these miserable deceptions in *Nineteen Eighty-Four*.

All these ideological abstractions were held together by the master ideological abstraction of Marxism itself. In its so-called Laws of Motion; in its linear understanding of the phases of human development; in its rigid distinction between ideology and its underlying material structure; *and* in what Orwell mockingly referred to as the old pea-and-thimble trick of 'Dialectical Materialism', where what is one thing one minute becomes another thing the next (as, for instance, how a government becomes Fascist by fighting Fascists?)—the body of writings that came to be known as Marxism was a theory capable of interpreting the world regardless of the actual lives and thoughts of the people who lived it. In short, Marxism was as far away from Orwell's belly-to-earth thinking as you could get.[96] Its claim to be scientific was not based on the world as it was, and is, but on an idea that took the phases of Hegel's philosophical dialectic as *analogous* to the phases of historical development as outlined by Marx and others, and proved them by further analogy, this time with the natural sciences, to give them the status of 'laws'. In his *Dialectics of Nature* (1885) Engels proved the scientific laws of the 'struggle of opposites' and 'quantitative into qualitative'—to his own satisfaction at least—by any analogy he could think of.[97] Given such levels of abstraction, anything was possible for those who believed it. Orwell did not believe it.

Marxist theoreticians talked about laws of historical development, but they could make no sensible calculations, let alone predictions, based on those laws.[98] They talked about the rate of extraction of surplus value, but they could not measure one single unit of that value, let alone its rate of extraction. When they tried, their analysis was no different from that of orthodox economists.[99] They talked about the rise of class consciousness, but they could not predict a single instance of where, or when, or to whom. They saw the world in theory first and facts second, and when the facts falsified the theory, they simply changed the theory. That was their job. Engels once wrote to Marx saying he had made an 'ass' of himself in something he had written on India. Marx reassured him that, 'in that case one can always get out of it with a little dialectic. I have of course so worded my proposition as to be right either way.'[100] And when people thought otherwise, or argued back, or presented alternative evidence, it was not necessarily the Marxist case that they were wrong. They might be right in detail (according to Marxists, an inferior form of argument called 'empiricism'),[101] but they were pronounced wrong, or 'false', in their consciousness, in the sense that beards can be false, or teeth can be false—which is, not real, not fitting. It was not up to the individual to find out whether one's consciousness was real or fitting or not. Marxist theoreticians made that judgement for you.[102] In the years after 1945, quite against the odds, English Marxist historians produced a type of history that flew in the face of much of this dogma. Marx, not Marxism, was their inspiration. But so was an indigenous English Tory radical tradition which in many ways Orwell shared.[103]

Marxism put an awful lot of reality into the hands of those who claimed to know the laws of historical development, and an awful lot of philosophy into the hands of those who claimed to know the secret of alienation, but very little reality and no philosophy whatsoever into the hands of the people. Orwell could not have lived and breathed in such a world. The proletariat were propertyless.[104] He knew that, and Marx seems to have helped him understand why, though by how much is open to question. Eileen Blair told a friend in 1938 that they had called their poodle puppy 'Marx' in order to remind them that they 'had never read Marx and now that we have read a little and taken so strong a personal dislike to the man . . . we can't look the dog in the face'.[105] It was certainly not true that Orwell had not read Marx.[106] Eileen liked to tease. But however much he had read, and whether or not he was self-consciously supporting a hard Marxist line in Spain or just the men he had fought alongside, Marxism was not Orwell's way. Contrary to his deepest personal and political instincts, it did not suit the rebel in him, or the anti-intellectual side of his temperament, or his taste for free enquiry and expression. He did not say that journalism was the first draft of history, but for him it was. He was certainly less interested in the pronouncements of those who had not been there, and more forgiving of those who had.

The Road to Wigan Pier was delivered to him in a Spanish trench on 8 March 1937. Though favourable, the reviews from the left bore all the marks of those who did not know and did not bother to find out.[107] Arthur Calder-Marshall in *Time & Tide* reviewed the book as 'a description of life in the North of England'. Goldring in *Fortnightly* found it remarkable that Orwell had 'lived entirely in coal miners' houses'. Walter Greenwood in *Tribune* and James Stern in *New Republic* looked only as far as the plates to conclude that *The Road to Wigan Pier* led also to Durham and South Wales (Greenwood), and 'the sprawling slums of Newcastle...and the unemployed mining districts of South Wales' (Stern). All untrue. In the *New Statesman and Nation* Hamish Miles observed, quite properly, that Orwell had missed the mining village's strength of community, but then showed his complete misreading (or no-reading) of the argument by saying that Orwell had depicted the miners as hungry for left-wing leadership.[108] Even more dismaying, the book was prefaced by what must be the worst introduction ever written by a publisher on behalf of one his own publications. Gollancz introduced the book by asking Left Book Club readers and study groups not to take it seriously. Amazingly, or ironically, Orwell told Gollancz he liked the introduction.[109] Only Harry Pollitt, General Secretary of the Communist Party of Great Britain, gave Orwell what Orwell the writer secretly thought Blair the intellectual deserved. In the *Daily Worker* for 17 March 1937 Pollitt said that Orwell had come to Wigan slumming it—'a disillusioned little middle class boy' grown tired of imperialism.[110]

All this was par for the course, and anyway, dug in outside Huesca, he had other things on his mind. Orwell was an experienced reviewer, and he knew how these things went. Reviewers did not always read what they reviewed, and authors were fair game. He had done as much himself. He was not always fair on the people he attacked, and sometimes he looked both ways.[111] However, he had created 'Orwell' in order to tell the truth and draw the line, and the line he was drawing in 1937 was where Communists and Communist sympathizers were telling lies or avoiding truths on behalf of what they estimated to be higher causes. Frank Jellinek was Special Correspondent of the *Manchester Guardian* in Barcelona at this time. Orwell praised his *Civil War in Spain* (1938), even though Jellinek toed the party line. At least he had been there, and for Orwell, at this stage in his life, that was hugely important. But Orwell seemed to think that the *Guardian* man had been there and knew the score in ways that W. H. Auden did not, and although Auden was an innocent, and had not a word to say this way or that about keeping to Communist or any other party lines, and did not do so anyway, Orwell sensed fraud and degeneracy in the young poet and went in for the kill.[112] Writing a poem, still more writing a review of a poem, might seem small beer in an otherwise tumultuous year. But Orwell's attack on a man, a rival perhaps, who had dared speak of murder *in a poem* tells us much about Orwell's personal and political volatility at this time.

Anti-Auden

W. H. Auden went to Spain just after Orwell, in February 1937, ostensibly to drive an ambulance for the Spanish Medical Aid Committee. From the point of view of his Communist controllers, however, he was taken there in order to write pro-party propaganda.[113] Auden did neither, as it happens. After being taken round—Valencia, Madrid, Aragon—he returned to England in March to write his major poem 'Spain'.[114]

Orwell started his review by saying, 'incidentally', he thought 'Spain' was 'one of the few decent things that have been written about the Spanish war'. Yet, although he could not have known the real purpose of Auden's five-week visit (because neither did Auden), he thought he sensed that purpose in the famous young poet's Communist party connections and in the company he kept.[115] After sniping at him in *The Adelphi* in 1938 ('yearning for bloodshed'), Orwell gave him both barrels in 'Inside the Whale', published in March 1940.[116] In that essay he quotes two stanzas from Auden's twenty-six before drawing the crucial distinction between being there and having seen things and drawing an opinion, and not being there and not having seen things and still drawing an opinion. The first of Auden's stanzas sketches pleasant scenes from English middle-class life. This is how the young will live tomorrow—bursting with poetry and fun—once the struggle is over. The second stanza describes today.

> Tomorrow for the young, the poets exploding like bombs,
> The walks by the lake, the weeks of perfect communion;
>   Tomorrow the bicycle races
> Through the suburbs on summer evenings. But today the struggle.

> Today the deliberate increase in the chances of death,
> The conscious acceptance of guilt in the necessary murder;
>   Today the expending of powers
> On the flat ephemeral pamphlet and the boring meeting.

Orwell was outraged by these lines:

> The second stanza is intended as a sort of thumbnail sketch of a day in the
> life of a 'good party man'. In the morning a couple of political murders, a
> ten minutes' interlude to stifle 'bourgeois' remorse, and then a hurried
> luncheon and a busy afternoon and evening chalking walls and distributing
> leaflets. All very edifying. But notice the phrase 'necessary murder'.[117]

Auden had used the phrase 'necessary murder' humbly, to accept his
vicarious guilt in a war that he, like Orwell, considered just but also
knew to be murderous. Though Orwell did not doubt Auden's honesty
(even if he failed to praise him for it), it is instructive as to his state of
mind at the time that he ended the decade brawling on the far political
margins with the left's greatest poet over two words that captured for
him the difference between what *he* had seen with his own eyes and then
written about, and what the poet had possibly *also* seen, with his own
eyes, and also written about. Orwell was sure he knew the difference
between being killed and being murdered, and the other man, apparently, did not. Nothing Auden could say in his defence could change
that. Orwell knew the difference, Auden did not. His anger at the poet
fed on a moral righteousness he had been deliberately nurturing for
some years. As he told Stephen Spender the year before:

> I was willing to use you as a symbol of the parlour Bolshie because...I
> looked upon you as a sort of fashionable successful person, also a Com-
> munist or Communist sympathizer, & I have been very hostile to the C.P.
> since about 1935, &...because not having met you I could regard you as
> a type & also as an abstraction...It is partly for this reason that I don't
> mix much in literary circles, because I know from experience that once I
> have met & spoken to anyone I shall never again be able to show any
> intellectual brutality towards him...[118]

This admission to one leftist poet did not stop Orwell showing intellectual brutality to another. Given what he had been trying to do to set the
Spanish record straight since his return in 1937, it is one of the paradoxes of Orwell's intellectual biography that Auden found himself
libelled as a coward and a fool for writing honestly:

[Auden's poem] could only be written by a person to whom murder is at most a *word*. Personally I would not speak so lightly of murder. It so happens that I have seen the bodies of numbers of murdered men—I don't mean killed in battle, I mean murdered. Therefore I have some conception of what murder means—the terror, the hatred, the howling relatives, the post-mortems, the blood, the smells...The Hitlers and Stalins find murder necessary, but they don't advertise their callousness, and they don't speak of it as murder; it is 'liquidation', 'elimination', or some other soothing phrase. Mr Auden's brand of amoralism is only possible if you are the kind of person who is always somewhere else when the trigger is pulled. So much left-wing thought is a kind of playing with fire by people who don't even know the fire is hot.[119]

Catching him in this mood, it would have taken a brave man to ask Orwell exactly when and where he had seen the bodies of numbers of murdered men. He said elsewhere that he had seen little evidence of such atrocities.[120] But apart from that, his response tells us a great deal about the way Spain had turned his Spanish war away from a matter of principle to a matter of witness. Auden is dragged to the front only to prove Orwell's superior testimony. But Auden *does* speak of civil war as 'murder' (for what else is it?), and he does *not* try to hide his guilt. If he speaks vicariously, it is deliberate, free from self-deception. In other words, Orwell attacks Auden for doing what poets are charged to do. When he says that for Auden 'murder' is only a 'word', too true it is, because poems do not actually commit murders. And when he says the stanza describes a day in the life of a good party man, maybe it does, but Auden was far from that. As with Hemingway, Priestley, and Chesterton, he was far closer to Orwell than Orwell could accept, in life as in politics. Estranged from his social class, and searching for an authentic English voice, Auden was never political in the party-political sense, and although a defender of the Spanish Republic he was sullen about its failures. Indeed, Orwell's POUM stance in 1937 was far closer to the good party man's position than Auden's poem—for 'Spain' clearly rejected the Marxism of the dialectical inevitability of history, to declare itself in favour of the burden of human choice.[121] 'History' enters Auden's poem with a capital 'H', but it is a History that moves in many directions, not only forward, and it is not what the dialecticians say it is but what people choose. 'I am not the Mover.' 'I am whatever you do.' 'I am your choice, your decision: yes, I am Spain.'

Orwell charged Auden with defending murder. So he did, for that was the fact they were all offered. Only Orwell did not choose to call it that and Auden did, and there was nothing more to it than that.[122]

All this bloody-mindedness Orwell heaped on Auden. Frank Jellinek, the *Guardian*'s correspondent, meanwhile, got off scot-free. He advocated murder in the name of the dialectic without a word of criticism from our eyewitness in Barcelona. What on earth was Orwell thinking?[123] Where was his fairness now? It is difficult to guess why Auden got such a kicking, other than maybe he reminded Orwell of his year-group at Eton, filled as it was with so much brilliance—a certain sort of unmanly 'brilliance' at that, which embarrassed Orwell almost as much as it challenged him.[124] Public-school traditions were certainly on his mind. In 1940 he would mock them one minute only to praise them the next.[125] But there is another point. Auden and Christopher Isherwood dropped off in the United States in January 1939 and stayed there for the duration. Orwell, on the other hand, by that time, was gearing up to fight in another war against Fascists. He says in his essay that Auden is the sort of dodger who is always 'somewhere else when the trigger is pulled'. It might be that Orwell's case against Auden was more about him being alive in the United States than about those who had died in Spain.[126] Other poets had died there, why not him? Indeed, why not both of them? Orwell would return to this.[127]

Wrestling with the left

Orwell was fixated with the London revolutionary left. Great things were happening in Roosevelt's America, but he hardly noticed. Some New Deal ideas were having a critical influence on the Labour party, but he always wrote as if Labour had no ideas to speak of.[128] Indeed, he had shown little interest in the Labour party altogether, even though its lack of interest in the finer mysteries of the dialectic would have impressed him, as would how a left-of-centre party managed to live with a working-class constituency that was more interested in football than politics. Labour's regional concentrations, its heavy-industrial base, its taste for practical solutions, and most of all, through the trade unions, its organic connection to the lives and interests of millions of workers and their families—all these features would have taken Orwell away from the London revolutionary left.[129] He was drawn to Labour's sort of Englishness in the end, but not yet. For the time being he never showed any interest in the party, its history, or organization. Anyway, his timing was all wrong. The general election of 1918 was notoriously lacklustre. Ten million people failed to turn out. Orwell was 15 years old. The 1923 and 1924 elections were lively, seeing the first Labour government, but he was sweating it out in Burma. When Labour came to power for the second time, in 1929, he was pretending to be down and out in Paris, but this administration had the double misfortune to be desperately unlucky and desperately dull. Ramsay MacDonald presided over the worst financial crisis in modern times, but his cabinet was bereft of economic ability (it was the Liberals who had the talent in that department) and in 1931 he was persuaded into siding with the bankers and Conservatives. All through the 1930s Labour was noticeable by its absence—'a party doomed to frustration', according to its official historian.[130] The 1935 general election was 'the quietest on record'.[131] Baldwin's Conservatives claimed not only the 'National' government as their own, but the whole dominion of England, Englishness, Empire, and Constitution too.[132]

For the first time in his life the Tories dominated without let or hindrance. There was perhaps more for Orwell in this Conservative interwar Englishness than has been recognized, but in a party-political sense Labour did not, and the Conservative party could not, interest him. He had been a mere schoolboy when the Lib-Lab-Irish alliance was in full swing (1909–16), so he did not know how exciting, how radical, and how decisive electoral politics could be. The Liberals took power in 1906 with a 350-seat majority. In 1914 Home Rule was finally passed for Ireland. In 1926 Orwell had been in a policeman's uniform for the General Strike and lock-out: wrong side, and he did not see Britain's finest corps of labour in battle. He had been cut off in school as a child and exiled in Burma as a young man, only to be beckoned into a suburban middle-class existence on his return, during a period when suburban England was reckoned by its finest observer, C. F. G. Masterman, to be somehow 'lacking'—so lacking that he found it difficult to say what it lacked.[133] If there was ever a chance that Orwell was going to break out in search of political adventure, it was certain that for a man like him, at a time like this, it was not going to be in the direction of the three big parties. These closures nudged him onto the margins of small left magazines and movements but, as we have seen, by 1936—maybe as early as 1935—something had gone fundamentally wrong in Orwell's relationship with these groups. He was never in their inner circles, but he knew people, and wrote for people, and shared flats with people, and occasionally slept with people who, like him, were on the London left.

All through his life Orwell pretty generally refrained from attacking right-wing intellectuals—largely because he said there weren't any.[134] This was not true, as it happened. As for the left, time and again he said he belonged, but time and again he hardly had a good word to say for it. Whenever Orwell sees a worker struggling with a left-wing intellectual, you know he is instinctively on the worker's side. At the same time, his view of what constituted a left-wing intellectual was hopelessly narrow. The second part of *The Road to Wigan Pier* is more a manifesto than a story, and does not name names. For a man who liked to get to the bottom of things, Orwell is strangely reticent on his personal dealings with these people.

A representative sample of what Orwell disliked in the comrades during the 1930s probably can be found in his publisher's own editorial committee. The men who selected Left Book Club books were John Strachey, whose father had once owned the *Spectator*; Harold Laski, son of a wealthy Manchester cotton merchant; and Victor Gollancz, son of an upper-crust London jeweller. All three had gone to expensive schools. All three had gone to Oxford, where Gollancz and Laski had been contemporaries at New College. None of them had served in the war, though eligible (Strachey only just). All three were close to the Communist party, if not actually members, and sympathetic to the USSR, if not actually resident.[135] Strachey wrote popularizations of Marxism, and finally joined the Communist party in May 1936.[136] Laski the academic was a master apologist for the Soviet Union, at least up to 1939.[137] Gollancz was well connected with the King Street party headquarters, where he allowed party officials to vet and organize Left Book Club activities.[138] When Orwell joked that left intellectuals did not understand the military virtues, took their opinions from Moscow, and their cooking from Paris, he might well have been thinking of Strachey, Laski, and Gollancz.[139] *The Road to Wigan Pier* is a flat rejection of everything Orwell believed men like these stood for, but as an attack on left intellectuals in general it is ludicrous. Where, for instance, is John Maynard Keynes? Keynes was without peer in 1937: an intellectual power-house with real political influence, he was too technical, too interesting, and too elite to draw Orwell's attention.[140]

With 57,000 members by 1939, the Left Book Club was the Communist party's 'best-supported auxiliary organization': better-supported, for instance, than the National Unemployed Workers' Movement, at around 20,000 members in 1932, and far better-supported than the party itself, with 12,500 members in 1937.[141] Although it had something of a life of its own in the branches, the Club was the perfect front for a party that had built its strategy on front organizations. Given that strategy, and given the sympathies and provenances of the men behind it, it is difficult to see why the Left Book Club published Orwell's *The Road to Wigan Pier* with its notorious attack on the left. The only explanation is either that they did not see it for what it was, which is unlikely, or that that they did see it for what it was and regarded it as a contribution to the Communist International's 'Popular Front' policy, which is also unlikely. All Communists were under orders from Moscow to make friends with other parties of the left— broadly defined. In Britain, this meant befriending the Labour party with a view to joining it. Familiar figures on its higher slopes, Gollancz and his friends were well placed to pursue the Popular Front line, even if it meant wooing Lansbury, or publishing Attlee, or even publishing Orwell.[142] For his part, brooding over Spain, Orwell must have felt deceived by his involvement with what turned out to be little more than a Communist front. And not only the Left Book Club, but the National Unemployed Workers' Movement, and those journals and editors who would not publish his Spanish polemics.[143] It all seemed quite plain to see. George Orwell, outspoken anti-Communist, was published in a series that not only defended the show trials in Moscow but praised them. Two British Communist lawyers testified to that. One said he would have executed a few more.[144]

The truth was that although Orwell never recanted his view that left-wing intellectuals gave him 'the creeps', made him 'sick', flogged 'dead horses', were wilfully ignorant, 'spiritually inadequate', spouted 'tripe', were guilty of 'frightful intellectual dishonesty', 'hypocrisy and self righteousness', told lies, performed 'grotesque spectacles', pushed 'dope', sent him 'rot' and 'bloody rubbish', had 'strong tendencies to totalitarianism', distortion, exaggeration, 'humbug', 'cant', irrelevance, and countless other 'one eyed' deceptions—he offered himself as one

of their number. Auden and Spender were 'fashionable pansies' or innocent schoolboys; H. G. Wells ('the usual rigmarole') was stupid, impotent,
not worth taking seriously; J.-P. Sartre was ridiculous, a 'bag of wind'; the
BBC pious; and Pacifists, when the war came, were not only objectively
supporting Hitler, they were at a loss to understand ordinary emotions or
make the simplest calculations.[145] The trouble with people like them,
Orwell never stopped opining, lay in their opinions.[146]

Anti-intellectualism in England was not confined to him, even though
in him it was remarkably aggressive and long-lived.[147] It may have been
planted in him at Eton.[148] It may have survived in him by not going to
university (though equally, it might have done better by going). It may
have grown tall in Burma, where a police station was possibly not the
best place to be without it. Given the job he had to do (regardless of his
views on doing it), intellectualizing against the Empire from the safety
of a London armchair would have not gone well with the young policeman either. As for home-grown Burmese intellectuals, he was not
impressed. It is a fair supposition, then, after five years in Burma with a
lot of time for reading on his hands he brought a flourishing if slightly
exotic anti-intellectualism home with him to an England that already
had its fair share of the cheaper stuff, and that his subsequent time in
Paris at the moment of Benda's *Le Trahison des clercs* intensified his taste
for it even more. *Down and Out in Paris and London* might be characterized
as an account of unstable (but quite intellectual) French and foreign
down-and-outs, contrasted with sturdy (but thoughtless) British and
Irish ones. Orwell said he had come back from Burma 'conscious of an
immense weight of guilt' he had 'got to expiate'. Being curious, in a
vague socialist way, about tramps might have seemed a reasonable place
to start, but at that point Orwell did not know anything about England.[149]
In the event, he engaged with his predicament, and the tramps' predicament, and that, more or less, was how his politics stayed until Wigan
and Barcelona—engagement, mainly literary, across a gulf. Of course
he had his principles, but after Spain he wanted what books could
not give:

> For the flyblown words that make me spew
> Still in his ears were holy.
> And he was born knowing what I had learned
> Out of my books and slowly...

Your name and your deeds were forgotten
Before your bones were dry
And the lie that slew you is buried
Under a deeper lie;

But the thing that I saw in your face
No power can disinherit:
No bomb that ever burst
Shatters the crystal spirit.[150]

Inside England

When the Blairs got home to Wallington, life was quieter. They had seen Utopia and preferred Hertfordshire. Even British standards of secret policing were less intrusive.[151]

Orwell's homage to Catalonia bore directly on his appreciation of England. He now began to get into the habit of seeing Spanish lessons as English lessons; a habit that would persist well into 1940. Yes, he was convinced at last that the working class could stand and fight. No, he was not convinced that the English would. War and Fascism were on their way. The English were asleep. Murder was afoot.

As the European crisis worsened through 1938 and 1939, and dictatorships came to prevail not only in Germany and Italy and the Soviet Union but also in other countries holding themselves tense in anticipation of being attacked, Orwell began to translate the sleep of the English into the sleep of a people who, if they were not all that good, were not all that bad either.[152] (He kept to the English, whom he thought he knew best; but much of what he said applied to the British as well, though he knew better than most that differences looked for could be found.) He reasoned that the English had been insulated from continental invasions and revolutions since God knows when, which had made them insensitive to European virtues and vices alike. Defended by their navy, they were a people who could tolerate things done abroad, even by their own hand, which they could not tolerate at home. As for snobbery and class prejudice, they were famous for it. For all that, Orwell knew that life for most people was getting dramatically better, even during the Depression, and a new indeterminate class was making its impact.[153] Above all, looking back on their considerable history, Orwell saw the English as a free people who were foolish enough to believe that England belonged to them, and who had managed to live with each other with very little inclination to kill each other in the name of some avowed Utopia, either of the left or the right. In a world of false intellectuals and mass-murderers, this, at least, was something. It was true that the British may have ruled one-quarter of the earth at the end of a bayonet, but it was also true that they had built a politics that worked. Deceived they may have been; knaves and fools they were not.

Orwell's great reconciliation with England, his England, began in 1936 and was complete by 1940. It started out in working-class Wigan, gained ground in revolutionary Barcelona, and came home to him when war was declared in 1939. But first we must journey up the Thames to Henley—in fictional episodes from the life of a middle-class Londoner called George.

4

Mr Bowling Sees It Through

Massing of Arses

Orwell was diagnosed with TB in 1938. In September, the Blairs went to Marrakech, so that he might recover his health.[1] There he wrote *Coming Up For Air*, the story of George Bowling, who lives with his wife and two children in 'West Bletchley', known as 'Metroland' to its railway developers, taking in the new west London suburbs of Wembley, Harrow, Ruislip, Northwood, and Uxbridge.

Every morning George catches the 8.21 up to town, where he works in insurance. In a mildly irritating life, he has to share his bathroom every morning with those who want *to go somewhere*: ' "Dadda! I wanna come in!" "Well, you can't. Clear out!" '

They live in Ellesmere Road. Which is not inspiring. Some might say it is semi-detached:

> You know how these streets fester all over the inner-outer suburbs. Always the same. Long, long rows of little semi-detached houses—the numbers in Ellesmere Road run to 212 and ours is 191—as much like council houses and generally uglier. The stucco front, the creosoted gate, the privet hedge, the green front door. The Laurels, The Myrtles, The Hawthorns, Mon Abri, Mon Repos, Belle Vue... 'Five to ten quid a week', you'd say as soon as you saw me. Economically and socially I'm about at the average level of Ellesmere Road.[2]

On the day he was due to get his new false teeth George is walking down the Strand, enjoying the morning off, when suddenly he is back nearly forty years before, lost in another world, remembering his boyhood. He had been particularly reflective that morning—about life, about war, about what he'd spend his £17 winnings on the horses on (a woman probably)—when all of a sudden the past is with him, in him, suffusing him, analeptic, and making him matter again:

The past is a curious thing. It's with you all the time, I suppose an hour never passes without your thinking of things that happened ten or twenty years ago, and yet most of the time it's got no reality, it's just a set of facts that you've learned, like a lot of stuff in a history book. Then some chance sight or sound or smell, especially smell, sets you going, and the past doesn't merely come back to you, you're actually *in* the past...

I was back in the parish church at Lower Binfield, and it was thirty eight years ago. To outward appearances, I suppose, I was still walking down the Strand, fat and forty-five, with false teeth and a bowler hat, but inside me I was Georgie Bowling, aged seven, younger son of Samuel Bowling, corn and seed merchant, of 57 High Street, Lower Binfield.[3]

This happens early in the novel. Much later, after a very long middle passage where he takes you deep into his boyhood, his war service, and how he found his way into insurance, and Hilda his wife, George resolves to go back to Lower Binfield. He never forgot that reverie in the Strand, and he is on the open road on his way to a job when he suddenly decides to stop and smell the air. It is a beautiful day. He leans on a gate and looks at a field of winter wheat in the pale yellow sunshine and, in spite of the usual Bowling soliloquy about mortality, money, middle age, and so on, he feels happy. 'I only want to be alive':

I shoved my foot down on the accelerator. The very thought...had done me good already. You know the feeling I had. Coming up for air! Like the big sea-turtles when they come paddling up to the surface, stick their noses out and fill their lungs...I kept my foot on the accelerator until the old car worked up to her maximum speed of nearly forty miles an hour. She was rattling like a tin tray full of crockery, and under the cover of the noise I nearly started singing.[4]

It is not entirely a successful trip. For one thing, the Royal Air Force accidentally drops a bomb on the town, but even before that the place had changed beyond recognition. Lower Binfield used to be an old market town, and West Bletchley had been built in a hurry on the edge of London, but in George's time the two places have grown into the same kind of conurbation, each sharing a common mass culture (cinema and football) and both bursting with traffic and newcomers: 'might as well have been at Margate...swollen into a kind of Dagenham...red brick everywhere.'[5] Lower Binfield has succumbed to the blandishments of modern life and expanded in all directions. So has Elsie, George's first sweetheart. The mighty carp in the secret pool of Binfield House is not what it was either; nor the pool. At the end of the trip, with Hilda on the warpath in West Bletchley and no fish, no pleasure, no woman, no peace of mind, and the money all spent, you might say that George returns home a wiser man. Only—and contrary to appearances—he was not exactly stupid in the first place.

He knows his limitations. With false teeth and a wife who doesn't trust him, we might say he is wise to do so. But the second best thing about George Bowling is that he does not take himself seriously. This has its advantages. He knows, for instance, that there are better men than him, but makes the best of who he is. He knows that there are better lives to be lived than his life, but applies the same stoicism. When he is told by the Cheerful Credit Building Society that he owns the house he lives in, he knows that it belongs to them. When he is told by the Flying Sala-mander Insurance Company that he is a salaried representative on commission, he knows as well as any navvy that he works for wages. 'Did you ever know a navvy who lay awake thinking about the sack?' 'The basic trouble with people like us is that we all imagine we've got something to lose.' The truth is, George Bowling prefers the truth even when it hurts. He has built his inner man on it. Whatever he is told by his superiors, he thinks twice. He knows, for instance, that war is just round the corner. *His corner.*

There had been a time when a man such as this would not have attracted Orwell's attention. He would have regarded him as too fat, too thin, too south, too soft, too white, too suburban, too mass—too close to the Money God for comfort. But George Bowling *also* spends a lot of his time being irritated by people like that. They have, after all, turned him into a stranger in his own home: 'Bloody interlopers! Twenty thousand gate crashers who don't even know my name.'[6] But he is an interloper too. He does not know them by name any more than they know him, though that is not to say he doesn't know who they are. The whole novel, indeed, is filled with George's line that he knows them like they know him like you know them both: 'You know the kind of place', 'You know the kind of thing', 'You know the way', 'You know the feeling', 'You know how it is', 'You remember the line of talk', and so on.[7] And when he is not assuring us that we do know, he is asking us if we do: 'Do you ever...?' 'Do you know...?' What do we know? We all know the masses. How do we know? Because we are them.

More ordinary than 'Orwell' and less intellectual than 'Blair', George Bowling is the masses, and a good deal of superior people's time and effort in the 1930s went into being superior to people like him. Orwell had done his share.[8] *Coming Up for Air*, however, represented a major turn in his point of view. He sees Bowling as more honest and more knowing than those who claim to know better. A gullible, 47-inch waist, 15-stone fat man on the outside, he is thin on the inside, and the very best thing about him is that he is not deceived.[9] For all his vanity, for all his vulgarity, and for all his mass, George knows the score, and *Coming Up for Air* trusts him with it. Bowling was hard for Orwell—harder than being on the side of downtrodden natives, or statuesque coalminers, or romantic revolutionaries. But in the end he helped Orwell reconcile with his class and his country. Loving The Revolution was easy. It is the masses who take some effort. *You know the type.*

Clashing of Clarsses[10]

As it happened, he did not know the type. Bowling is middle class, but not Orwell's middle class. Orwell knew a little about suburban semis from staying with his sister up in Leeds, but he did not know the details of white-collar insurance work and had to take advice.[11]

Being a salaried representative of the Flying Salamander Insurance Company is middle class in the sense that Bowling earns twice what a worker earns and, unlike most workers, he earns it every week. But it is not middle class in the sense of Marx's bourgeoisie, who owned capital rather than worked for it; and it is not middle class in the sense Orwell was used to it as an Old Etonian son of a middle-ranking civil servant. The huge expansion of Bowling's 'new' middle class—commercial, financial, technical, managerial, state—happened in the inter-war years. For the vast majority of Victorians, class division meant the simple but calloused difference between those who worked with their hands and those who did not, with up to a third of those who did living hand to mouth—as Charles Booth discovered.[12] But between Seebohm Rowntree's first social survey in 1899 and his second in 1936 the percentage of the population living in that kind of poverty fell by over one-half, and for the vast majority of the industrial working class who lived well above that level life had ceased to be such a daily struggle.[13] In fact life was generally more agreeable for everyone in the 1930s, except the long-term unemployed, while the expansion of non-manual occupations graded class relationships ever more finely according to when, where, and how one worked, and for how much.[14] *Coming Up for Air* is about a number of things, not least Orwell's reconciliation with his own England. But before he can do that, he has to deal with his own class.

In 1930s England even the finest class gradations carried powerful cultural connotations, connotations Bowling is only too aware of. For the working class, about 70 per cent of the population, the decisive difference in wages was between the skilled and the unskilled, and the decisive difference in cultural connotation was between the dependent and the independent. George Bowling is not in the least interested in working-class people of any type, except perhaps in harbouring a tinge of envy for the latter sort, who he suspects, wrongly, live a life free from care. For the middle class—about 20 per cent of the population—what kind of 'middle class' you were depended on how far you were from the life of a skilled and respectable worker at the bottom end of the income scale, and how near you were to the life of a gentleman at the top.[15] The whole picture was complicated by piecework, overtime, night shift, bonuses, expenses, dividends, rents, commission, tips and perks, and the like but, crudely put, class was a sliding scale which could get interesting if you had more money than manners at the top end, and more manners than money at the bottom. Clearly, one could be as poor as a church mouse (my dear), like the Blairs in their tiny Hertfordshire cottage. But *he* had gone to Eton you know, and *she* had gone to Oxford, and *he* did not appear to have any work to do: all of which was gentlemanly enough.[16] Bowling, on the other hand, made no secret of the fact that he had no such pretensions, was good at making money, and was not fooled by the system into thinking that either he (or it) was gentlemanly.

George Bowling therefore is almost classless, but not entirely so, and this is the part that makes him elusive. He rejects the old middle-class shibboleth that not being working class is the most important thing. He harbours no prejudice against the workers—'good luck to them', is his approach—and takes pride in his own ability to rough it when he has to. He may not have to work like a navvy, but he's tough and adaptable and says he would back himself in 'almost all circumstances'.[17] He has learnt, however, that being middle class is more than a matter of money. He knows that gentlemanliness is a bit of a performance, and when he steps back and observes his own performance, as all *flaneurs* must, he knows he doesn't quite cut it. In a nice summary of the wiles and wherefores of the more brazen members of his troupe, George picks his spot:

It was almost as if I could stand at a distance and watch myself coming down the road, with my fat red face and my false teeth and my vulgar clothes. A chap like me is incapable of looking like a gentleman. Even if you saw me at two hundred yards' distance you'd know immediately—not, perhaps that I was in the insurance business, but that I was some kind of tout or salesman. The clothes I was wearing were practically the uniform of the tribe. Grey herringbone suit a bit the worse for wear, blue overcoat costing fifty shillings, bowler hat and no gloves. And I've got the look that's peculiar to people who sell things on commission, a kind of coarse brazen look. At my best moments, when I've got a new suit or when I'm smoking a cigar, I might pass for a bookie or a publican, and when things are very bad I might be touting vacuum cleaners, but at ordinary times you'd place me correctly.[18]

When he was in the army he met Sir Joseph Cheam of the ASC. In a way, the tramp major meets the tramp again:

'You a gentleman?'
'No, Sir.'

Cheam, who was not a gentleman either, took George on. So Bowling, an officer now, saw out the war as OC Twelve Mile Dump, North Cornwall. He had been wounded late in 1916 as a private in the ranks, but in this sudden change of fortune he spends 1917–19 as an officer and a gentleman, with nothing to do but guard eleven tins of bully beef. (This is a lesson in war that is not lost on him.) He joins a lending library and reads everything. His education had not been special, but now that he has his pips he takes his chance.

If George's career ambitions are middle-of-the-road, so are his cultural ambitions. He reads H. G. Wells' *The History of Mr Polly* and loves it (as well he might), and he half enjoys D. H. Lawrence's *Sons and Lovers* (bit of a surprise), but in the main he does not want you to 'run away with the idea that I suddenly discovered Marcel Proust or Henry James or somebody. I wouldn't have read them even if I had.'[19] He reads indiscriminately. 'God knows I don't set up to be a high brow.' 'I'm not a fool, but I'm not high brow either.'

In 1932 J. B. Priestley had provoked a spat with Virginia Woolf and pals when he referred to her in the *Evening Standard* as the highbrow 'High Priestess of Bloomsbury'. Woolf was not amused, and gave as good as she got, depicting 'the great novelist' (Priestley) as a little man who was no more than *a journalist*. Woolf revealed much more than her reading habits when she defined a highbrow in contradistinction to this as a 'man or woman of thoroughbred intelligence who rides his mind at a gallop across country in pursuit of an idea'.[20] Not for the first time, or the last, we find Orwell shadowing Priestley. He wants George Bowling to be a man of the world: hack not thoroughbred, Ealing not Bloomsbury, *Daily Blah* not *Country Life*. Sitting atop Twelve Mile Dump, Orwell has him reading his way through a mountain of popular authors: Arnold Bennett, H. G. Wells, Oscar Wilde, Joseph Conrad, Rudyard Kipling, and John Galsworthy; but also Compton Mackenzie, Anthony Hope, Elinor Glyn, 'and even Silas Hocking and Gene Stratton Porter'.[21] By putting George firmly in the camp of the Philistines, but at the same time stressing his intelligence and eye for the truth, Orwell set out an interesting and unusual proposition.

Bowling, then, is not upper class, nor working class, nor middle class exactly. But he is not classless either. Culturally, he is ordinary; one might say 'middlebrow'. He likes fishing, and says he 'likes reading' in a way that a highbrow would never say he 'likes reading'. Socially, he's 'incapable of looking like a gentleman', as we have seen. Politically, he has no politics, except an indomitable cynicism. Personally, he goes his own way. Economically, he earns 'about seven quid a week. And properly speaking that's the end of my story.' If Orwell had wanted to make him *nouveau riche*, he would have made him an estate agent or a car salesman, not an insurance man.[22] Insurance was in the doldrums in the 1930s. According to the *old* connotations of class, therefore, George Bowling— defined almost entirely by what he is not, and not as brash and *nouveau* as he might have been—is almost invisible. He has no school, no college, no club, and no distinguished family or honourable profession to turn to or be proud of.[23] He does have a regiment, as it happens, even though he remembers it more than it remembers him. According to the *new* connotations of class, however, he doesn't quite fit either. He is not vulgar enough for an estate agent or a car salesman, not prosperous enough for a mortgage broker, and not technical enough for a draughtsman or an engineer. For someone who likes talking of 'types', what type is he? How do we spot this almost invisible man, lost between the class and the mass? Orwell gives us two clues: first, his mobility; and second, where he lives.

George bowls along. He wins his commission in the army age 23. He meets Hilda at the tennis club—another excellent place to learn yer manners. She comes from an old colonial family—poverty-stricken maybe, but still a step up for George. In 1929 they move to West Bletchley, another step in the right direction, though when he is promoted to inspector he has to be away a lot ('Of course I was unfaithful'). George's managerial position gives him a certain room for manoeuvre, which makes the story possible. But when he is not on the road and has to go to the office, he does it with millions of other Londoners who take the train in and take the train out, in and out, ebb and flow, five times a week, like breathing.[24] Commuters are assumed to be all the same because they all move in the same direction. But when they are on the loose, they are very self-conscious of it. George does that too. Orwell couldn't set his south of England in Southwold or anywhere like it, because it was too small and too old in its connotations. In order to make his reconciliation authentic and see Mr Bowling through, he needed the London masses.

Bowling's London is not the teeming, degenerating metropolis of a highbrow Oswald Spengler or Lewis Mumford, any more than it is the dark, foggy, unknowable, slightly spooky city of 1930s cinema.[25] On the contrary, Bowling's London is a flourishing, moving, intelligent world seemingly without end, and though George doesn't like it he does not want it to end either. It is the greatest nexus of knowledge in the world, and it flourishes because people like him live there.[26] And he lives there because—on the whole and taking all things into account, like an insurance agent must—it isn't too bad:

> Seems a pity somehow, I thought. I looked at the great sea of roofs stretching on and on. Miles and miles of streets, fried fish shops, tin chapels, picture houses, little printing-shops up back alleys, factories, blocks of flats, whelk stalls, dairies, power stations—on and on and on. Enormous! And the peacefulness of it! Like a great wilderness with no wild beasts. No guns firing, nobody chucking pineapples, nobody beating anybody else up with a rubber truncheon. If you come to think of it, in the whole of England at this moment there probably isn't a single bedroom window from which anyone's firing a machine-gun. But how about five years from now? Or two years? Or one year?[27]

Bowling works in a City of London business once thought gentlemanly.[28] It has to be said, however, that the City was not renowned for its acuity. No one ever accused the banks of running a meritocratic recruitment policy. Whatever the pros and cons of opting for financial orthodoxy in 1931, and coming off gold in 1932, a national unemployment rate of

22 per cent meant that the City's monetary policies were not in good repute.[29] Bowling deals with money, but he is not City as an insurance man, any more than he was Sandhurst as an army man. He goes out to evaluate claims. We must assume that this demands some judgement on his part, though he makes light of it. He leaves us in no doubt, however, that he makes good money on commission. His £364 a year is not on a par with brokers and bankers, it is true, but he manages to clear roughly the same as a middle-grade civil servant or a qualified teacher. He earns far more than a skilled worker, of course, but nowhere near a barrister.[30]

If he is not a worker, and is all but invisible as a salaried representative, he is not a toff either. If not the most prestigious or the best-paid, by common consent insurance was one of a number of new and growing middle-class occupations, especially in and around London, all of which required some sort of technical, chartered, or City and Guilds qualification. These occupations also required a secondary education, preferably grammar-school, where cap, tie, and blazer denoted the beginning of a long and winding road to examination success, while the playing-fields indicated the higher-educational riches also on offer.[31] Some of the new occupations called themselves professions, and included state-employed schoolteachers and civil servants, the new managerial and secretarial grades, surveyors and draughtsmen, dentists and laboratory workers, and the scientists, engineers, and technicians who would make the machines that would win the war.[32] Qualifying associations spread rapidly between 1910 and 1950, 'so that by mid-century a quarter of their total went to engineering, a tenth to management and administration, and a twelfth to accountancy'.[33] Orwell laughs at Cheam of the ASC as a bit of a bore, but David Edgerton tells us how in wartime the government looked to businessmen like him for ordnance and procurement.

It is hard to be precise about indeterminate categories, but it is likely that all or nearly all of these new middle-class people would fail the class test that George also failed. Not particularly cultured, or gentlemanly, or ladylike, or *de haut en bas*, or partisan; and not likely to be tied by old school tie to club or college or regiment; too many to be distinguished and too few to be mass, this class is best recognized, like George is best recognized, by its mobility. These are his main points of reference—'the ordinary chaps that I meet everywhere'—ranging from his friend the retired schoolmaster to clerks and typists and travelling salesmen in ladies' fashions. Shops selling radio-parts seem to figure strongly. After the war Lewis and Maude would conclude that the modern middle class had provided 'most of the nation's brains, leadership, and organizing ability'.[34] Bowling would never put it like this, of course. He is much too knowing. *You know the type.*

He is also defined (he defines himself) by where he lives. Priestley's *English Journey* (1934) made great play of places like West Bletchley, the third of his three Englands that began with the old England of 'Parson and Squire', still beautiful, but long since insolvent; followed by the industrial England of Coal and Cotton, once prosperous, but now with too many people living in places like Wigan; followed by the 'newest England', the classless, formless, and maddeningly indeterminate George Bowling England of 'arterial and by pass roads...filling stations and factories...giant cinemas and dance halls...bungalows with tiny garages'.[35] This is West Bletchley, more or less, and though George says he hates it and calls it a trap and a snare ('just a prison with the cells all in a row'), in truth this is Eric Blair speaking, not George Bowling.

Sneering at the suburbs was an old highbrow game, and in Eric Blair, left-intellectual and former resident of suburbia's 'plague centre' at Hampstead, it found an enthusiastic player.[36] Sneering at the suburbs, however, does not sound right for George Bowling. One would have imagined him going to the cinema at least at the national average of twice a week, maybe even with Hilda a few times. As for semi-detached villas, most home-owners were pleased with their well-trimmed privet, their French windows to lawn, their tidy little investment. At the very least, one could imagine George treating his house in a row much as he treated his books in a row, or his women in a row: indiscriminately, but open to hidden pleasures. It was Sir Patrick Geddes, impenetrable highbrow and founder of modern town-planning (not himself a commuter), who coined the words 'conurbation' and 'megalopolis' to express his disgust at the sprawl, and it was Sir Patrick Abercrombie, leading British planner in 1939 (and not himself a Do It Yourself type) who opined that the semi-detached villa is probably 'the least satisfactory building unit in the world'.[37] Quite against everything else we know about him, Bowling agrees.

Those who actually lived there would have not called them 'units' but homes—almost certainly the best they had ever had or were likely to have. The English middle classes used to live in tall town terraces and pay rent. Now they had more light, more sun, more space, more privacy, and, with bank rate at 2 per cent, more money. Orwell himself had been quick to enjoy the pleasures of his sister's semi, especially after the confinements of Wigan, and Bowling was a realist anyway who would have weighed the options. Central London he couldn't afford, unless it was a rented slum or a council dwelling: both unacceptable. Ellesmere Road he could afford. In the 1930s you needed an average income of £3. 8s. 9d. a week to afford a house such as this, and George Bowling earned twice that.[38] Money was tight, but with a steady income, falling prices, low interest, mortgage tax relief, and a fast train out in the morning, he could just about cope. He wasn't there that much anyway, while Hilda, who was, had far more reason to be anxious, or depressed, and Orwell signals that. Although George is not open to her concerns, on his own account he had reason to be happy with his plot.[39]

Suburban bungalows and semis led the first wave of owner occupation in inter-war Britain. Over 4 million houses, or 30 per cent of the housing stock in 1939, was built during this period, and the vast majority were private dwellings.[40] They were sold as a rural arcadia, but fears about their popularity ('sprawl') led to some of the first environmental legislation in the world—all with the problem of London and the south in mind.[41] The East Kent Regional Plan of 1925, the South Downs Preservation Bill of 1934, the Restriction of Ribbon Development Act of 1935, the Green Belt (London and Home Counties) Act of 1938, and the Barlow Commission on the Distribution of the Industrial Population in Great Britain from 1937 all paved the way for large-scale town-planning after the war.[42] The semis themselves were not significantly bigger or better-built than council houses of a similar type, but they did carry those touches—hall and parlour, bathroom and kitchen, slightly larger gardens—that people appreciated. *Chez* Bowling has a garden 10 by 5, a bathroom, and a dining-room with oak sideboard, two decanters, and the benefit of a wall-mounted gas fire. It went on the market for £550 leasehold. George took to it like a noose round his neck.

Daphne Patai argues that the real reason Orwell loathed suburbia was not for its class connotations but for its gender connotations. She argues that against all that soft furnishing and shopping power, Orwell idealized an austere masculine ideology of hard-left hardness. She sees

this as part of 'the Orwell mystique'.[43] There is truth in this, except that
in point of fact George Bowling is more integrated into the suburban
mystique than he likes to admit and, when openly confronted with the
masculine mystique, he absolutely rejects it.

He goes with Hilda and her friends to a local meeting of the Left Book
Club. 'We are the West Bletchley revolutionaries.'[44] There they hear Mr
So and So, 'the well known anti-Fascist'. Home-grown bona-fide British
Fascism hardly appears in the novel. Orwell seemed to understand
instinctively what was in fact the case: that Mosley was less important
than his stunts and speeches suggested.[45] At any rate, George doesn't like
what he hears at the meeting ('queer trade, anti-Fascism'), and right
there, in among what he hears, in among the Dialectical Materialism
and the Popular Frontism, is the masculine mystique. It certainly isn't an
argument. It *is* a mystique:

> I'd stopped listening to the actual words of the lecture. But there are
> more ways than one of listening...I saw the vision that he was seeing.
> And it wasn't at all the kind of vision that can be talked about. What he's
> *saying* is merely that Hitler's after us and we must all get together and
> have a good hate. Doesn't go into details. Leaves it all respectable. But
> what he's *seeing* is something quite different. It's a picture of himself
> smashing people's faces in with a spanner. Fascist faces, of course. I *know*
> that's what he was seeing. It was what I saw myself for the second or two
> that I was inside him. Smash! Right in the middle! The bones cave in like
> an eggshell...

At the end of the meeting, when they are getting up to go, an argument
breaks out among some of the younger men about whether it would be
right, if war started, to join the army. An ardent young man appeals to
George: wouldn't he want to smash Fascists for once and for all?
' "Wouldn't you fight? If you were young, I mean." ' George's answer is
unequivocal. *No.* ' "I went off the boil in 1916", I told him.' ' "If it comes
again, you keep out of it." '[46]

Having brushed off the youthful masculine mystique, he goes in
search of the more mature variety. 'Old Porteous', his cultivated friend,
lives in rooms. With his books and his cricket, his whisky and his soda,
the retired classics master is just as much a caricature of the old boy
south as George is of the new. Bowling could be just about anybody who
wears a tie to go to work. Porteous, on the other hand, could be Rupert
Brooke, aged about 60:

Old Porteous has got a way of strolling up and down, with that hand-some head of his, with the grey curls, held a little back, that makes you feel that all the while he's dreaming about some poem or other and isn't conscious of what's going on round him. You can't look at him without seeing the way he's lived written all over him. Public School, Oxford, and then back to his old school as a master. Whole life lived in an atmosphere of Latin, Greek and cricket.[47]

'"I'm part of the modern world myself",' says George, '"but I like to hear him talk."' Fair enough. But Porteous has got nothing to say. Harold Perkin called his class 'the forgotten middle class', and the old man does not disappoint. He puffs away on his pipe, foot on the fender, carefully considering his answers. 'Wonderfully learned, wonderfully good taste', and all that, but—

> 'Tell me, Porteous, what do you think of Hitler?'
> 'Hitler? This German person? My dear fellow! I *don't* think of him.'[48]

George leaves, knowing now for sure that Porteous is England's past and he, George Bowling of West Bletchley in the county of Middlesex, in some sort of ill-defined, sprawling, suburban way, is England's future.

Country

In *Coming Up for Air* one can see the beginning of Orwell's reconciliation with his class and his country. 'Lower Binfield' is Henley-on-Thames, Orwell's childhood home. It is striking that he depicts London and Henley—that is, West Bletchley and Lower Binfield—as effectively one place linked by a river. He ends *Homage to Catalonia* on that very note: London and its hinterland, one a garden, the other a wilderness, but one place all the same, and neither of them 'abroad'. Orwell had felt glad to get back home after Burma, and he would be glad to get back home after Morocco. But after Spain he was glad to be back in an Eng-lish south where peace was a way of life that browsed in meadows and swam in pools before making its way downstream:

> And then England—southern England, probably the sleekest landscape in the world. It is difficult when you pass that way, especially when you are peacefully recovering from sea-sickness with the plush cushions of a boat-train carriage under your bum, to believe that anything is really happening anywhere. Earth quakes in Japan, famines in China, revolutions in Mexico?

Don't worry, the milk will be on the doorstep tomorrow morning, the *New Statesman* will come out on Friday. The industrial towns were far away, a smudge of smoke and misery hidden by the curve of the earth's surface. Down here it was still the England I had known in my childhood: the railway cuttings smothered in wild flowers, the deep meadows where the great shining horses browse and meditate, the slow-moving streams bordered by willows, the green bosoms of the elms, the larkspurs in the cottage gardens; and then the huge peaceful wilderness of outer London, the barges on the miry river, the familiar streets, the posters telling of cricket matches and Royal weddings, the men in bowler hats, the pigeons in Trafalgar Square, the red buses, the blue policemen—all sleeping the deep, deep sleep of England...[49]

At the same time, *Coming Up for Air* represents London and the south as just another region. This was (and is) unusual.[50] English topography usually represented England as a country of regions *except* for London and the south, which was (and is) usually represented as England itself. London was central to this configuration, especially from the late nineteenth century when it was redeveloped as an imperial capital. In English topography the 'south' really means the 'south-east', comprising the so-called Home Counties round the capital, and those counties clustering around them up to a border point still somewhere far south but no longer to the east, now more to the west, or the 'West Country'. English history matched this topography, with Alfred of Wessex the founding figure, king of a southern kingdom stretching along the coast up to its indeterminate western limits. 'Wessex' took its name from the West Saxons, meaning west of London, but in time the kingdom took in all London, and all its environs, bellying out east and west to become England itself. A king described by Churchill as someone who had 'built up the strength of that mighty south which has ever since sustained much of the weight of Britain, and later of her Empire', Alfred is the only English monarch to be called Great.[51] Insofar as inter-war Englishness was concerned, the north of England was off limits. Insofar as George Orwell was concerned, the north of England ('a smudge of smoke and misery' far away) had shown him the real England, but he still had to come to terms with his own southern portion.

Underscored by its topography, and its history, and containing the country's greatest concentrations of wealth and population, with more middle-class households than the rest of the country put together, the south entered the twentieth century as an iconic land—a land of shaded greens, darkening cottages, and the River Thames making its imperial progress up to London, greatest city in the world.[52] This was deep England, seemingly unchanging and inward-looking, yet metropolitan and global and modern as well; the England foreigners think of; the southern view; the elite view, the high-cultural view of what it means to be English, musical score by Elgar.[53] And we can see this in Orwell too, for even oppositional writers still privileged London and the south over every other region. Hobson's *Imperialism* (1902), for instance, saw the southern region as simply the hinterland of London, paying tribute as part of a new feudal order.[54] So did William Morris's *News From Nowhere* (1890). Morris's hero makes his leisurely progress by barge up the Thames from London to Oxford, through Runnymede and Windsor, out by 'the lovely reaches of Wargrave and Shiplake' to Wallingford and Abingdon, wondering at the majesty of it all.[55] In 1933 Arthur Bryant vested the entire national character in a suburban world that could only be somewhere south of Watford:

> And how different the Englishman is when he closes the garden gate behind him and takes his ease in the Zion where he would be—that holy of holies in which the cherubim and seraphim are his wife and children and the fox-terrier who leaps for his hat as he enters the door, and the thrones, dominions and powers of the armchair, the wireless set…and the garden roller.[56]

Orwell does not quite see it this way. Bowling never came home to such a welcome. West Bletchley and Lower Binfield are linked by some sixty miles of Thames, it is true, and both stand for Bowling's England, it is also true, and the garden cities were a welcome experiment in social housing and the semi-detached suburbs were not all bad by any means—but it is also the case that Orwell has Bowling go by road, not by river, that his memory does not reach back to Alfred, that his meagre garden has a bald patch, and that he lives in a place where there is no rural idyll, not a garter leg to be seen, and not a trace of tradition anywhere in a land where, according to the Right Book Club at least, 'the works of generations of the people blend imperceptibly with those of nature'.[57] In other words, Bowling is Orwell's means of reconciling with mass, class, country, and the south of England, but he is not going to do it in the conventional way.

The south of England had been enjoying its middle-class moment of Englishness since the 1890s—a revival of national identity that liked to dream of a 'quiet, ordinary, evasive little England'. But Orwell was having none of it. There had been starvation in the south in his own time, and during the inter-war years the region was a battle-zone between developers and planners—between those who wanted to ramble and those who called ramblers trespassers; between those who wanted a room with a view and those who wanted to build council houses.[58] Orwell is right to see national identity and conservation as a difficult issue in the 1930s, and for his own part sets up the south's moment of conservation Englishness only to laugh at it. Old Porteous is no Mr Chips, while in 'Mr Edward Watkin' we have a fine young architect with 'such a feeling for the Tudor'. Watkin is designing a fake Englishy estate (with Pixie Glen) for highbrows at Upper Binfield.[59] That these are the people who have turned Bowling's secret pool into a rubbish-dump gives Orwell another excuse to say his piece about the sort of bourgeois bohemians who want to live in Merrie England.[60]

He may well have had Letchworth in mind. Founded just before the First World War as a 'garden city', and rich in local reputation as a place for cranks, Letchworth was just down the Baldock Road from where George and Eileen lived in Wallington. He had been encouraged in his *Wigan Pier* attack on middle-class cranks after attending an *Adelphi* conference in Langham. Now it was Letchworth's turn.[61] Not that he offers any thoughts on housing. If he isn't keen on West Bletchley, or Lower Binfield, or Upper Binfield, nowhere does Orwell give the case for new towns, town-planning, or any other kind of blueprint for national identity. He senses fraud in the very idea.[62] Or to put it another way, George Bowling is not the sort of bloke to linger by his garden gate and give thanks for his heritage. By now, you know the type.

Bowling does not need *faux* Englishness. If he is going to be tugged he has got to feel the rod tighten.[63] Orwell failed to recognize the first English folk revival, not just its socialist and working-class sympathies but also its deep significance to twentieth-century English life and letters. It certainly was not just a middle-class spasm, and it certainly was not just fake emotion. Edward Watkinses there may have been, but there was D. H. Lawrence and Vaughan Williams too, and no end of a lesson for English cultural criticism.[64] That apart, Orwell made a good point in the end. By making the Thames Valley a region, and only a region, Orwell makes it real enough, and provincial enough, and ordinary enough to be his own: 'all houses, houses—and what houses!' Same for London, which he renders just as flat and ordinary as any other

English city where, in Orwell's account anyway, there are no mighty offices of state, no horsey regiments, no wonders of the Constitution, no imperial glory.[65] Just mile upon mile of houses. Lower Binfield is no different, a place now where you could go for months without hearing a bishop's niece.[66] If this is the south, Orwell seems to be saying, old or new, then at least it was *my* south—a people's south of dusty white roads and sacks of grain, summer bluebottles and long walks with George Bowling trailing behind, a man who is more than he seems, a man from Priestley's third England who nevertheless retains a deep love for the first. It is myth of course, as sweet and heavy as lardy cake, but Orwell is acknowledging that there are times when being undeceived is not enough. You have got to belong, and belonging has its history or it is nothing: it is as much who you were as who you are. Orwell takes a scene from whom George was, and applies it to who George is; he takes a scene from the north, and applies it to the south:

> [after Sunday dinner] and Mother on one side of the fireplace, starting off to read the latest murder but gradually falling asleep with her mouth open, and Father on the other, in slippers and spectacles, working his way through yards of smudgy print. And the soft feeling of summer all around you, the geranium in the window, a starling cooing somewhere, and myself under the table with the *Boys' Own Paper* . . . [67]

Self

If you are going to belong to your country, you have got to believe in it. Bowling finds both stages difficult, because although he lives in the age of the masses, and he is one of the masses, he does not share their most distinguishing trait. He is not gullible. He is shrewd and individualistic. Orwell invests him with north regional qualities, a man whose 'independence, candour, sense of humour and democratic spirit' makes him see things as they are.[68] For all his brashness, George is a plain man. He does not like what he sees in the bathroom mirror every morning, but neither does he fool himself that what he sees is any younger, slimmer, or more handsome than it actually is. Well, just a little bit. He may live in West Bletchley or even Lower Binfield, but this does not prevent him from seeing these places as they are. 'God rot them and bust them!' He wants to belong, but will not be deceived into it. He is one of the masses, but he is not 'humbugged'.[69] He is middle class, but does not feel superior to the working class. He likes the rural life, but not the fake rural life.[70] He is a southerner, but shares a number of northern qualities, stubbornness for instance. He is his own man, in other words, shaped by Orwell to be quite unlike any representative Englishman of the period. He is clearly not a gentleman; he tells us that. He is not really one of the masses; he is too independent for that. Nor is he a Victorian; he is too modern for that. Though he loves the Edwardians, he is not one of their silent suburban multitude; he is too opinionated for that (though Masterman's observation that 'no one fears them', 'no one respects them', comes close to George's fatter side).[71] He does not like the bosses, but he is not one of José Ortega y Gasset's revolutionary masses either; he is much too self-critical for that.[72] Nor is he a jingo, or a patriot, or a nationalist, or a 'blood and soil' man, and though he likes women he is not the sort of scoundrel who would dream of talking about his country as if it was his mistress.[73] But this does not make him Sidney Strube's 'Little Man' or Graham Laidler's 'Average Englishman' either. He is much too forthright for them, and does not resemble G. J. Renier's 1931 reserved, almost secretive Englishman for the same reason.[74] He is common, but not commonplace. He is average, but rejects the mean. It is difficult to see him cooperating with the British Institute of Public Opinion, for instance.[75] He is not a modern gent, does not see himself as a world citizen, would not use words like 'communitarian', shows no interest in the unemployed, and would not dream of going anywhere, let alone north, to see how they were getting on.[76] What, then, is Orwell trying to do with this rebellious and least corporate of Englishmen?[77]

He is exploring the possibility of telling himself who *he* is without deception or self-deception. Bowling the fat man on the outside is not much like Orwell, except he is one of the masses who Orwell has willed himself to be. Bowling the thin man on the inside is much nearer the existential Orwell—the man who is trying to come to terms with himself, the man who wants to see it through. After Wigan, after Spain, after six months in a sanatorium and another six months in French Morocco, George Bowling is a calming influence on his creator. 'I only want to be alive', he says, and by writing him in the first person, Orwell puts responsibility for that onto his own self.[78] For a man in a novel whose first words tell you about his big idea and whose last words tell you that it was all his fault, where else could responsibility lie?

Though Bowling is responsible for himself, it is clear that he does not feel he belongs to himself alone, and wants to make it known to you, his confessor, in that chatty style of his, that he wants to stand with you.[79] This 'you' is 'us', the English people. In *The Road to Wigan Pier* Orwell let it be known that he was not prepared to change who he was, even if he could. In *Homage to Catalonia* he let it be known, finally, that England was home. In *Coming Up for Air* he declares his reconciliation with his class and his region, however much they have changed. We all change and stay the same. Why should a country be any different?

So, in the whale-like figure of George Bowling England finally comes up for air in Orwell's work. Orwell had always seen England best from abroad, from Burma or Barcelona, and from the margins, from Wigan or Wallington or Eton College. But in Bowling he gets close and takes a clear view. Early contact with Geoffrey Gorer and Malcolm Muggeridge might have given him the confidence to try; or they might have merely confirmed in him the idea. After reading *Burmese Days*, Gorer, an English anthropologist and writer, had put it to Orwell that one could know one's own country in ways that were right and proper and not by merely pandering to one's prejudices about it; that anthropology was not just about other people's lives, that it could be about your own as well.[80] Orwell wrote back warmly about 'trying to study our own customs from an anthropological point of view'. The two men stayed in touch, with various exchanges through to 1939 and after. If Gorer suggested a method, Muggeridge suggested a faith. He had been a leader-writer then a freelancer for the *Manchester Guardian*, and first came to Orwell's attention when, in a series of secret dispatches from the Ukraine, he had revealed the truth about famine in the Soviet Union. Reviewing his book *The Thirties* at the end of the decade, Orwell noted the *Guardian* man's taste for the truth. Beneath the hard-nosed reporting, however, he sensed Muggeridge's 'un-confessed fact' that he did, 'after all' believe in something. He believed in England.[81]

Orwell was ready for a change after Spain, and was probably heading Muggeridge's way even as he wrote *Coming Up for Air*. But the idea of England as anthropology and the idea of England as something to believe in, not just somewhere to come from, or go to, or criticize, made particular inroads on him in 1939 and established itself in the spring and summer of 1940. Wigan and Barcelona had taken him away from politics in the usual sense of the word. He no longer thought that politics was going to enter stage left and save them all. It was going to have to be something more visceral. Enter George Bowling. However, settling for England would prove more difficult than settling for Bowling. Orwell was going to have to introduce a more stoical, more pliable note in his writing.[82] Believing in a country, rather than in a point or a principle or a position or even a literature, meant that from now on he was going to have to take things as he found them—the good and the bad, the past and the present, the fat and the thin, the left and the right. In short, he was going to have to trust the people as they were and not as he would want them to be. Bowling was a good try-out for this; but more was to come.

So much in Orwell is about being recognized. For a writer so keen on the facts, Orwell would judge a person usually on the strength of little more than the catch of the eye. He tried to catch the eye in Wigan, but couldn't quite, except once—the eye of a young woman from the train, or so he said. He caught the eye almost immediately in Barcelona, and was elated, but in the end he left Spain trying to avoid the eyes of almost everyone he met.[83] *Coming Up for Air* is essentially about recognizing and being recognized. Bowling is always assuring us that we know the type, and even when he is not recognized, he expects to be.[84] And the 'us' that is invited to do the recognizing in modern Bletchley and modern Binfield is a very different 'us' from the 'them and us' of Orwell's Wigan, or Comstock's North London phantoms, or the prying eyes of Dorothy's Knype's Hill, or the lost souls of John Flory's club, or the un-named narrator drifting along la rue du Coq d'Or. Unlike these people, and for all his protestations, Bowling actually feels at home. 'I'm vulgar, I'm insensitive, and I fit in with my environment.'[85]

Orwell was later to admit that there was much of himself in George Bowling.[86] Bowling is a contemporary figure, but he also lives in the past, particularly through his emotions. 'I know that in a sense one never forgets anything.'[87] Although his boyhood world has gone, the memory of it brings him to life again—though in fact, of course, it is he who brings *himself* to life again by managing the relationship between who he was and what he has become. Note the subtle shift from past to present in this crucial remark: 'Is it gone forever? I'm not certain. But I tell you it was a good world to live in. I belong to it. So do you.'[88]

> You saw ghastly things happening sometimes. Small businesses sliding down the hill, solid tradesmen gradually turning into bankrupts, people

dying by inches of cancer and liver disease, drunken husbands...girls ruined...And yet, what was it that people had in those days? A feeling of security even when they weren't secure. More exactly, it was a feeling of continuity...things would go on as they'd known them.[89]

'Fatty' Bowling, in other words, for all his ego, understands that this is not just his story, that he is not alone in wanting to live in a way that will endure. Some generations have had to face the prospect of extinction while others have lived in societies that were just stable enough, and just peaceful enough, and common enough, to stay together and in touch. Bowling counts his parents among that number, but not himself. Not only has the modern world destroyed his childhood home, but war is coming ('they say it is booked for 1941') to destroy his adult life as well. With his past closed off and his future ready to shut down, it would appear that Bowling is pretty much on his own—except of course that he belongs to a country that is in the same predicament as him and, along with millions of other people, he is able to share what he knows. The English do not have to know each other personally or go to citizenship classes to do this. It is enough that they can share past and present. In Orwell's time it was called 'national character'—a living tradition that linked a country's history to its experience, and by so doing saved it from extinction. When the war came, G. M. Trevelyan's *English Social History* (1942–4) became an English best-seller, even though Trevelyan lacked any real feel for the people.[90] Orwell, on the other hand, at precisely the same time, was about to set off in another direction with a new and radical body of work which was not only in touch with the people but which was imaginatively and emotionally theirs almost even before he wrote it.

Who can you trust? At first, all Orwell's subjects were deceived—by others, by themselves, by the world they lived in. In 1939, a good year for deceptions, Orwell turned George Bowling into one of the non-deceived, and, because he was who he was, one of the masses, there were millions like him. There was no longer any need for despair in George Orwell. He had thought too much of himself. He had forgotten all that was around him.[91]

5

England the Whale

I, as far as I am concerned, am quite willing to trust to the talent, the justice, and the loyalty of the great mass of the people—I am quite willing to make common cause with them, to be one of them.

(William Cobbett, *Political Register*, 24 April 1819)

Getting in step

In his important essay 'Inside the Whale', written between 1939 and 1940, Orwell identified his generation of writers. First there were the English patriots, 1910–25, typified by those he called the 'nature poets', some genuinely attracted to country ways like Housman, and some middle-class rural weekenders like Brooke. Then there were the international transients, 1920–30, typified by Joyce, Eliot, Pound, and D. H. Lawrence. Great writers they may have been, but political they were not. 'What is noticeable about all these writers is that what "purpose" they have is very much up in the air.' Finally there were the young moderns, typified by Auden and Spender and the literary left in the 1930s. 'If the keynote of the writers of the twenties is "tragic sense of life", the keynote of the new writers is "serious purpose".'[1]

Orwell's march from innocent boys to unhappy wanderers to serious young men was a heroic version of his own story. By 1939 those phases of his life were all but over, but they account for a good deal of Orwell's discomfort with himself: a man who had turned from an innocent into a snob and then into a police bully, from a sponger and a tramp into a threadbare intellectual, and, apart from a couple of decent books, one of them virtually unread, a failure at all of them. Not only that, but now he had TB and had lost a year of a shorter life dealing with it. How hopeless. *How clichéd.* And what made him depressed with his own life, he transposed onto the lives of other writers: their wanton vagrancy, joyless politics, foolish distractions, minor talent. 'Inside the Whale' shows Orwell on the brink of abandoning all this failure in order to reach out into the lives of those who did not have opinions on whether their lives were failures or not—as he saw it, those who just put up with things.

He had been writing about ordinary and marginal people on and off since 1928, but it was Miller's *Tropic of Cancer* in 1935 which first alerted him to the possibility of writing about them not as down-and-outs, or have-nothings, or know-nothings, or people to be petted and pitied, or avoided, or lectured, or admired or loathed from afar, but as people to be taken just as they were, who got on with it, who were normal, who went with the world rather than seeking to avoid it, or change it, or interrupt it, or interpret it. Orwell called Miller a 'completely negative, unconstructive, amoral writer' who had edited a journal devoted to nothing.[2] Yet he was drawn to him for that very reason, and although he denied Miller the accolade of greatness, and never tried to imitate him, he affirmed that the American's refusal to sit in endless judgement on his fellow creatures was the only way forward for writers in times like theirs. Miller had told him to 'stop thinking and worrying about the external pattern', and in that Orwell felt he heard the '*real politik* of the inner mind talking', and wanted to feel it as a *physical* sensation, not an intellectual one, bringing that 'peculiar relief that comes not so much from understanding as from being understood':

> '[because] he is passive to experience, Miller is able to get nearer to the ordinary man than is possible to more purposive writers...
>
> Miller's own work could be described... [as] a voice from the crowd, from the underling, from the third-class carriage, from the ordinary, non-political, non-moral, passive man.[3]

Not for the first time, when writing about other people Orwell was actually writing about himself. His first published pieces, particularly *Down and Out in Paris in London*, had been written strongly, but passively.[4] He had described what it was like to live on six francs a day and concluded that it was complicated, so complicated that it left no time for any other kind of thought. 'You discover the boredom which is inseparable from poverty; the times when you have nothing to do and, being underfed, can interest yourself in nothing...You discover that a man who has gone even a week on bread and margarine is not a man any longer, only a belly with a few accessory organs.'[5] At the same time, and different from Miller, the person Orwell describes trying to live on six francs a day (himself) was a man who retained his old standards, a gentleman who can hardly afford to eat at all trying to hide the shame of not eating in a restaurant. This was not Miller's mad, meretricious world. While Orwell was in Paris dodging the baker's bill and keeping up appearances, Miller was in Paris sledging along the bottom, dealing equally with everything, as he put it, 'from dreams to faesces [*sic*]'.[6]

If *Down and Out* had no politics as such, in 1933 Orwell was on his way to seeing himself as a writer of the left. Having read Miller in 1935, however, and thinking about Miller while writing *Road to Wigan Pier*, and having gone back to him again in 1939 after severe personal and political defeats in Spain, Orwell's politics was on the turn. He was calmer now, taking the world as it was. Knowing he had TB might have contributed to that. He was also more accepting that if you cannot know everything equally well, you can know some things very well, usually from the inside, and that is where he would start. Orwell had already given up on intellectuals. Now he was on the point of giving up on the idea of progress too. 'Progress and reaction have turned out to be swindles', he mused, and war was coming.[7]

By the time of 'Inside the Whale' war had already arrived, and although not much was happening in a military way, yet, it was a war Orwell did not seek, did not want, and could not stop.[8] Unable to move forward, he thought he might observe, endure, stay dispassionate, ignore the war and attend to things as they happened in a third-person sort of life.[9] This was what the writers in the last war did, in all their 'helplessness and ignorance', and this is what he would do. Or might do. His war diaries, opened late 1939, might have been first drafts of dumb endurance or they might just be accounts of how many eggs his hens were laying. It's hard to tell.

You could call these musings a number of things. You could call them anti-imperialist. Why get killed in a war of empires? You could call them socialist. Why get killed on behalf of capitalists? You could call them pacifist. War is immoral. Keep out of it. You could call them quietist. What's it got to do with me? Or *us*? You could call them the musings of a conscientious objector, or a non-cooperator, a war-resister, a defeatist, or an appeaser. You could even call them the musings of a Keynesian—someone who recognized the economic consequences of the peace and wanted nothing to do with it.[10] But Orwell called them inside the whale. Taken from a passing reference in Miller to the advantages of being inside the belly of a whale (Jonah 1: 17), Orwell made the case that Miller's writing was inside the whale anyway—'a willing Jonah [who] feels no impulse to alter or control the process that he is undergoing. He has performed the essential Jonah act of allowing himself to be swallowed, remaining passive, *accepting*.'[11] There was more than a touch of this in Bowling, who just wanted a bit of peace and quiet, and now here it is in Orwell himself, reconsidering his options in a war that will give him so few:

> The very idea of sitting all day under a willow tree beside a quiet pool—and being able to find a quiet pool to sit beside—belongs to the time before the war, before the radio, before aeroplanes, before Hitler. There's a kind of peacefulness even in the names of English coarse fish. Roach, rudd, dace, bleak, barbell, bream, gudgeon, pike, chub, carp, tench. They're solid kind of names. The people who made them up hadn't heard of machine guns, they didn't live in terror of the sack or spend their time eating aspirins, going to the pictures and wondering how to keep out of the concentration camp. (Bowling 1939)[12]

> For as a writer, he [the creative writer] is a liberal and what is happening is the destruction of liberalism. It seems likely, therefore, that in the remaining years of free speech any novel worth reading will follow more or less along the lines that Miller has followed—I do not mean in technique or subject matter, but in implied outlook...Get inside the whale—or rather, admit that you are inside the whale (for you *are*, of course). Give yourself over to the world-process, stop fighting against it or pretending that you can control it; simply accept it, endure it, record it...A novel on more positive, 'constructive' lines, and not emotionally spurious, is at present very difficult to imagine. (Orwell 1940)[13]

He wanted to avoid war. Hitler had taken power in 1933, and although from the beginning Jews were persecuted and the Versailles Treaty forgotten, Britain and France held back. Hitler took back the Saarland region in January 1935 and ratified this by plebiscite (91 per cent)—as he was entitled to do under the Treaty. Then in March 1936 he moved 30,000 troops into the Rhineland—this time explicitly against the Treaty and against the French, but once more ratified by plebiscite (98 per cent). As in the case of the Saarland, he could hardly be accused of invading his own country. In 1935–6 he announced expansions of the German army and air-force (against the Treaty) and made military arrangements with Italy and Japan. But as he had made military arrangements with the British too, this time over relative naval strengths, and the British had been glad to make them, the case against him was compromised. In 1938 Hitler bullied and brokered union with Austria ('Anschluss') and German armoured columns went in yet again—to another rapturous reception, and yet another (apparently) overwhelming endorsement by plebiscite (99 per cent). Still the British and French held back.

That there were good reasons to hold back is beyond doubt. Nobody wanted war.[14] Hitler made his best speeches about the unfairness of Versailles. He said that he was only taking back what was rightly German. In 1936 even a politician as wily as Lloyd George could share this position, though after that date Chamberlain deftly set about preparing Britain for war just in case.[15] But when in September 1938 Hitler called for incorporation into the Reich of the ethnically German part of Czechoslovakia, Chamberlain got out his travel-bag, boarded an aeroplane for the first time in his life, and made three urgent trips (15, 22, 29 September) to Germany to meet the Führer and try to talk him into changing his mind. The most important trip was the third, when he and the French premier Daladier travelled to Munich to meet Hitler and Mussolini. The price of a little more peace, they believed, might have to be a little less Czechoslovakia.

At this point, unlike the vast majority of his fellow countrymen, Orwell seems to have had difficulty telling the difference between a 70-year-old English Conservative prime minister in a winged collar with a preference for housing policy, and two bullish dictators in uniform who said they believed in war as a test of national will.[16] Orwell had already explained in June 1938 that he had joined the Independent Labour Party because it was the only party that would take a principled stand against a war between rival empires, and warned moreover against 'the dope' that the British political class would push in its favour when the time came.[17] Three months later, at the time of Munich, he told Jack Common that the idea of war was 'pure nightmare' to him, and in that same month he put his name to a *New Leader* manifesto, 'If War Comes We Shall Resist', signed by forty-eight left intellectuals. The manifesto promised to end all War by building a just world.[18]

All through 1938 and 1939 Orwell maintained the ILP line of moral equivalence. If the Nazis were imperialists, then so were we. If Hitler was a warmonger, so had we been. If Germany had gone bad, the blame was ours, going back to Versailles.[19] At the same time, Orwell argued the old POUM case that preparation for war would only serve as a catalyst for Fascism in Britain. In September 1938 the ILP manifesto warned that war would lead to the 'destruction of the liberties of the people' and the 'imposition of totalitarian regimes' in Britain and elsewhere. In October 1938 Orwell berated the Labour party as 'bloody fools' for talking about getting ready for war. In January 1939 he favoured 'illegal anti-war activities' when the time came. In March 1939 he warned against a 'fascisizing process' within the British state, with 'sham war preparations designed to cover up other objects'. As late as July 1939 he challenged the integrity of a 'British governing class' intent on war but 'unconsciously treacherous' at the same time. And yet, in March 1939, having already taken the German Sudetenland and having forced the Czech president, Hacha, to sign the necessary papers ordering non-resistance, Hitler had rolled into the rest of Czechoslovakia and every-one but George Orwell and the ILP knew then, if they did not know before, that very soon Britain was going to war with Germany. Every Nazi expansion up to that one could, if one was determined enough, be interpreted as an act of German self-determination—in military arrangements, in the Saarland, in the Rhineland, in Austria, and even at a long stretch in the Czech Sudetenland. But this was different. This was the breaking of a state. And Orwell *still* opposed war with Germany. According to him, what the country needed in the summer of 1939 was not the RAF but the ILP—'a real mass party', 'whose first pledges are to refuse war and to right imperial justice'.[20]

Orwell did not want war. The ILP did not want war. Chamberlain did not want war (though he was stealthily preparing for it), and Eileen did not want war. She told Geoffrey Gorer from Marrakech in October 1938 that she was 'determined to be pleased with Chamberlain' because she wanted 'a rest'. She thought the Czechs and Slovaks ought to be pleased with him too because, either way, 'it seems geographically cer-tain that that country would be ravaged at the beginning of any war fought in its defence'. We have to assume her husband agreed with her. 'Eric is going to write to you & I shall leave him the crisis.' They did not disagree on politics, and if they had she surely would have mentioned it on a subject so profound. Eileen ended her letter with a characteristic Orwellian dig at the left. The Labour party's warmongering, she averred, was not only wrong, it was cowardly. 'But of course the English Left is always Spartan; they're fighting Franco to the last Spaniard too.'[21]

For a time what Eileen called her husband's 'extraordinary political simplicity' found common ground with the ILP's extraordinary political naivety.[22] But the Blairs were *not* naive. Barcelona had cured them of that. The result was a degree of political confusion rare in Orwell. He did not want war, but knew it was coming. He would not fight, but knew he might have to. He would go on resisting, up to a point. What point? The point at which his resistance to the British state would tip over into resistance to the Nazi state. What was the tipping-point? The tipping-point was that rather unlikely moment when it would be made absolutely clear to everyone (in an objective sense that had to involve military disaster of some kind) that of two equivalent imperialisms, Fascist or capitalist, that faced the British people, their own indigenous capitalist kind was the least worst, and they had better start fighting Nazis away while at the same time revolting against capitalists at home. Quite some strategy. Quite some people. In the meantime, the family back home talked of building air-raid shelters. Eileen offered her sister-in-law the Wallington cottage as somewhere 'more remote for the children'. 'It could be almost as safe as anywhere in England.' 'It's fantastic & horrifying to think that you may all be trying on gas masks at this moment.'[23]

Coming Up for Air, published 12 June 1939, was written in this dread spirit, a spirit which had already been aired in public with H. G. Wells's *The Shape of Things to Come* in 1936 (made into a movie in 1939), and Nevil Shute's *What Happened to the Corbetts*, also published in 1939.[24] Orwell admitted later that George Bowling was autobiographical. An anti-Fascist who does not want war. This is 'what he calls the voice of the people', said Eileen. But it was left to her to finish the thought:

> Eric, who retains an extraordinary political simplicity in spite of everything, wants to hear what he calls the voice of the people. He thinks this might stop a war, but I'm sure that the voice would also say that it didn't want a war but of course would have to fight if the government declared war.[25]

In the end, this is what he did. He resisted right up to the last possible minute, then when the balloon went up he tried to join the forces. This does not explain, or excuse, his doublethink that you could fight a war by not preparing for it (an argument he visited on appeasers and pacifists later), and even though it does not add up, it is what he thought, and it is what he argued, in spite of everything. In the meantime, already behind public opinion when it was published in the summer of 1939, *Coming Up for Air* tried to have it both ways. Bowling is sure that war is coming. He is equally clear that the people should keep out. 'Why should you get your body plugged full of lead?' Orwell told his agent that the novel's 'general tendency is pacifist'. Equally, Bowling is a survivor, though it has to be said that if this is a story of survival, it is not a story of survival by fighting for it.[26]

As late as September 1939 Orwell was still criticizing 'left-wing jingoes' who did not see that 'every increase in the strength of the military machine means more power for the forces of reaction'.[27] Quite incredibly, so late in the day, when he said this he was thinking of the British military machine, not the German. For all useful purposes, in other words, Orwell was still stuck in Spain. Having come to the opinion in the summer of 1937 that under pressure of war the Spanish Republic had moved from bourgeois democratic to anti-fascist Fascist, he thought the same thing was happening in Britain through 1938–9. He was still loyal to his old POUM comrades. For it was their point of view that when dealing with rival imperialisms (one Nazi Fascist, the other British Imperialist-nudging-into-Fascist), and rival capitalisms ('Fascism and Bourgeois "democracy" are Tweedledum and Tweedledee'),[28] the only hope of defeating one and the other was to fight both at the same time. Although he ditched this argument in the end, it remained in his imagination well past 1939 into 1940. In his essay 'My Country Right or Left', published autumn 1940, Orwell revealed himself as the best and worst political commentator on the scene. On the one hand he understood better than anybody how national identity worked, and how it had moved aggressively left and patriotic at the same time. On the other hand he still seemed to think that this would involve bloody revolution on the streets: 'I dare say the London gutters will have to run with blood...when the Red Militias are billeted at The Ritz.'[29] He imagines such things, but one can't help asking if he meant them. What sort of movement did he think would lead the revolution? One led by Victor Gollancz? Hardly. One led by Fenner Brockway and the ILP? Surely not. Not even Orwell thought that. What about Harry Pollitt and friends? God forbid, and not likely in the wake of Stalin's non-aggression pact with Hitler (a surprise to everyone, not least King Street). How about the Red Militias of the Labour party? The Labour party did not have red militias. Major Attlee would not have approved of armed men in The Ritz. As for the people themselves, many British people, not least Orwell's own parents, lived on dividends and pensions. They were not going to billet themselves anywhere they couldn't afford. What about the workers? Doubtful. Circumstances change, it is true, but Orwell's big discovery in 1940 was that the working class was patriotic. It was a long time since London's gutters had run with blood, and the people were not going to fight Nazis in Newham by slaughtering schoolboys in South Ken. Orwell's war strategy made some sort of sense in Barcelona. But in Britain it was preposterous.

In those dog-day afternoons of 1938–9—bed-ridden in a sanatorium, holed up in Marrakech—POUM double-helix Fascism had mixed with George Bowling cynicism and Henry Miller passivism to give Orwell the strangest anti-war position. This, in fact, was the end of ideology for Orwell. It had boxed him into an impossible corner. Damned if he does, damned if he doesn't, and saved only if he fights on two revolutionary fronts at the same time in a country showing no sign of wanting to fight a revolution on either—no wonder Orwell contemplated life inside the whale.

Late in August 1939, with Czechoslovakia dead and buried and Poland next, Germany and Russia signed a non-aggression pact. They invaded Poland on 1 and 17 September repectively, and on 3 September, under protocols which had been hurriedly agreed with the Poles over the previous March and August, France and Britain found themselves at war with Germany to protect a country they could not reach. Orwell was horrified. Whatever residual strategies he still harboured in his Spanish breast, six days after war was declared he made his services available to the (in his eyes, proto-Fascist) British state—an act which precipitated his immediate departure from the ILP. Most of the anti-war left came round. Sir John Reith of the BBC told the Ministry of Information policy review committee in March 1940 that they could expect their most creative propaganda contributions from those of a 'left-wing tendency'.[30] Appeasement had allowed the British an extra year to prepare for war. The Emergency Powers (Defence) Act of 24 August 1939 delivered to the state an astonishing range of powers to possess and control the country's resources—but nobody really believed they were Fascist powers. Everyone did believe, however, that the bomber always gets through (a strong theme in *Coming Up for Air*), and without that extra year which Chamberlain (and the Czechs) had bought so expensively the RAF would have started the war without the Hurricane fighter or radar.

Over the coming months Orwell witnessed the left politicization of the British people in their own defence. At first there was the 'phoney war' from September 1939, with very little to show for it. Then in the 'high political crisis' of May 1940, which according to Ross McKibbin overthrew 'or at least immediately weakened, suddenly and unpredicted, the predominant Conservatism of the 1930s',[31] Churchill came to office to express the national mood (call it what you will) more confidently and more eloquently than the rest. With Norway lost, France and the Low Countries about to be overrun, the British army in retreat, and the policy of appeasement (call it what you will) utterly vanquished, Churchill understood what the people understood—the very unpolitical and therefore revolutionary position that this was now a straight fight, them and us, up and down, no room for doubters.[32] And because the political class was in no position to manipulate anyone into anything after the failure of appeasement, it could never have been anything other than a People's War, and Churchill saw that first. He had been warning about Hitler since 1934, and now that he was prime minister, with Labour and the labour movement at his back, he bent policy to the general will. Conscription, the most demanding of any combatant country, went through without hesitation.[33] There was immediate and substantial volunteering. It was a moment of popular left politicization that was to last ten years. 'To the historian the second half of 1940 is a different world from September 1939.' In a letter to his wife, the film-maker Humphrey Jennings noted the transition:

> Some of the damage in London is pretty heart-breaking but what an effect it has had on the people! What warmth. What courage! What determination. People sternly encouraging each other...People in the north singing in public shelters...WVS girls serving hot drinks...Everybody absolutely determined: secretly delighted with the privilege of holding up Hitler. Certain of beating him...a curious kind of unselfishness is developing...We have found ourselves on the right side and on the right track at last![34]

Much to its own surprise, Labour suddenly found itself standing for the nation as a whole—the first time it had done so. 'Very fast', 'extraordinarily sudden', 'a crisis within the political elite', 'English politics simply shifted left', 'across the spectrum': McKibbin thinks that Labour could have won any general election from July 1940 up until the end of the war, when of course it did win, by a landslide.[35]

Orwell declared for his country, moved ground, got into position, and took aim. Quite astonishingly, first in his sights were those 'boiled rabbits of the Left' who did not understand 'the spiritual need for patriotism and the military virtues'.[36] Paradoxically, the security service rejected him (25 May 1940), as did the army (medical 'C' grade, 28 June 1940) and the RAF (3 April 1941).[37] So he made do with the Local Defence Volunteers (Home Guard). Another small platoon. No one was more delighted than he to get his uniform in August. Only a year ago he had been warning that the entire British standard of living depended on a hundred-thousand imperial bayonets holding down an empire.[38] Now he had a little imperial bayonet of his own.

He remained a self-contradictory and rebellious Englishman. In April 1940 he was claiming that *if* he thought 'a victory in the present war would mean nothing beyond a new lease of life for British imperialism' he would be inclined 'to side with Russia and Germany'—a ridiculous thing to say, even by his recent standards. He said it knowing that Nazism was a monstrous, brainless, and enslaving empire led by a maniac—but he said it all the same.[39] Later in the same piece, and not more than a few months since saying the very opposite, he accused pacifists of helping Hitler, and swore that he would sooner side 'with the older imperialisms' such as the French and the British which, though 'decadent', were not 'completely merciless'. In June 1940, a terrible month, he expressed his complete exasperation at the ILP's continuing call for workers' resistance to invasion while at the same time calling for sabotage of the arms factories: 'these people live almost entirely in a masturbation fantasy conditioned by the fact that nothing they say or do will ever influence events.'[40] In October 1941 he overturned his Tweedledum and Tweedledee nonsense about Fascism and bourgeois democracy being the same thing—much to the discomfort of pacifists.[41] In July 1942 he said that those who called this an imperialist war 'have got their heads screwed on backwards'; that you could not beat Hitler by resisting the war; that it was a lie to say that 'those who fight against Fascism go Fascist themselves'; that pacifism was a 'bourgeois illusion' that depended on British sailors risking their lives to feed it, and that above all else pacifists were 'objectively pro-Fascist' anyway: a complete reversal of his reasons for joining the ILP in

1938 and staying in it right up to the last breath of appeasement in September 1939.[42] Orwell was at his best taking salients he himself had so recently commanded.[43] To call pacifists 'objectively pro-Fascist' was particularly unpleasant because this was largely the argument that the Spanish Communists had used against the POUM: that they were 'objectively' pro-Fascist because they were 'objectively' anti-war or, to put it another way, the POUM did not see the war in the same way that the Spanish Communists saw it. Orwell admitted the dishonesty of his argument three years later, but by then the pressure was off and he could afford to be generous.[44] The greater point, surely, was that Orwell was not kidding. He was fighting for survival and not taking prisoners. Deserters he shot on sight.[45]

Getting inside

Late in May 1940 Orwell closed the Wallington cottage and joined Eileen in London. Not fit for the forces and possibly not thought reliable enough for intelligence work, he had to make do with the Home Guard. By night he did theatre reviews, unwillingly. By day he pondered on what he saw and heard, watched the drama unfold, and turned his diary into a war diary.

The first entry is characteristically uncompromising. With the British army in full retreat, his brother-in-law among them, Orwell confided that, 'horrible though it is', he would sooner it was 'cut to pieces...than capitulate'.[46] But he could not sense any strong war feelings around him. He watches 'fearful tripe' at the theatre. The barmaid refuses to have the nine o' clock news on the wireless. There are not many men in uniform around the place, and Sunday crowds loiter with no 'indication in any face or in anything that one can hear that these people grasp that they are likely to be invaded within a few weeks'.[47] We find him moping about the lack of turbulence in the people again—just as he had done at the ladies' social in Wigan in 1936. Orwell was desperate for a sign of fight. Only a year before he was asking what was the use of a national identity.[48] Now he was hungry to find one.

He was not averse to epiphanies of the people. He had had one in Wigan, and he had had one in Barcelona, and he had had one recently, or so he said, in a dream. Given his problem with intellectuals, it had to be in a dream—from himself to himself, as it were—but the message was clear. The night before the Russo-German non-aggression pact (signed 23 August 1939) he said he knew in a dream that he would not resist the war effort, that he 'would not sabotage or act against' his own side, that he would support it and 'fight in it if possible', and he knew in his bones 'that once England was in a serious jam' he could do no other. 'What I knew in my dream that night was that the long drilling in patriotism which the middle classes go through had done its work.'[49]

War was made known to him in a dream, but it was only the following May, with the politicization of the British people, that he was convinced that it could be won. He is roaming the railway stations looking for his brother-in-law. Captain Laurence O' Shaughnessy of the Royal Army Medical Corps never arrives, but in the waiting and the watching Orwell takes heart. Having so recently been in favour of persuading the British people not to fight, it came upon him that they would fight, 'if only they [were] told what to do', and that there were powerful institutions in the country which could do that, if in the right hands. And so it was that this sworn enemy of the British Empire found his heart leaping at the sight of a squad of Royal Marines square-bashing their way across Victoria station.

> The refugees were greeted in silence but all sailors of any description enthusiastically cheered...Saw a company of marines marching through the station to entrain for Chatham. Was amazed by their splendid physique and bearing, the tremendous stamp of boots and the superb carriage of the officers, all taking me back to 1914, when all soldiers seemed like giants to me.[50]

Long ago, in 1936, at a social in the Cooperative Hall, Wigan, Orwell had said the English people lacked turbulence. One part of the evening included a silly song with the chorus: 'For you can't do that there 'ere.' Orwell didn't like the singing and said so. In 1944 he took the same song, claimed he heard it in a northern pub, not a ladies' social, and used it to make exactly the opposite point, that the English people were a force to be reckoned with.[51] His story goes that it is 1936 and the Germans have just that morning occupied the Rhineland. He tries to draw the saloon bar's attention to the fact that 'The German army has crossed the Rhine', but all he gets back is the old soldier's chorus: '*Parly-voo.*' Although it was an event that 'quite obviously meant war', nobody turned a hair or seemed to care. So much for the English sober. But later that evening, or so the story goes, back in the selfsame pub, they sing their silly song, 'For you can't do that there 'ere', and, even though it is still banal, he says he knew, that they knew, that it was a song of defiance. Which is to say, Orwell's people go from passive to turbulent in the words of a single song. Fascism might do in Other Countries, *but it won't do 'ere'*. And *'ere* suddenly means everything. 'It struck me that perhaps this was the English answer to fascism.' So much for the English drunk:

> For you can't do that there 'ere,
> No, you can't do that there 'ere;
> Anywhere else you can do that there,
> But you can't do that there 'ere!'

And now that *he* could feel the most ordinary emotions about his country, intellectuals, it seems, could not:

> I grew up in an atmosphere tinged with militarism, and afterwards I spent five boring years within the sound of bugles. To this day it gives me a faint feeling of sacrilege not to stand to attention during 'God Save the King'. That is childish, of course, but I would sooner have had that kind of upbringing than be like the left-wing intellectuals who are so 'enlightened' that they cannot understand the most ordinary emotions. It is exactly the people whose hearts have never leapt at the sight of a Union Jack who will flinch from revolution when the moment comes.[52]

This least corporate of men was now an Englishman through and through. He had indeed got inside the whale, only the whale was England. Henry Miller he once described as giving himself up to a 'world process'. Orwell could never have given himself up to something so abstract. He was a political animal, but showed no interest in thinking about politics as politics. He was a libertarian, but showed no interest in weighing up the two types of liberty.[53] He was socialist, but showed no interest in imagining any life but the one people had now, only better.[54] Like Cobbett, he wanted nothing brand new. Like Chesterton, he trusted to the people as they were. He was only ever interested in communities which he knew already or knew themselves: like the hop-pickers, like the miners or the militias, like 'Astonishing sights in the Tube stations' with families asleep, the children pink-cheeked like wax dolls, while people stepped over them.[55] This is not to suggest that England was actually existing socialism in 1940—only that it was actually existing. Unable to get on with his life, tired of ratiocination, frustrated by his failure to mark a position on the left but suspicious of the comrades and hostile to the Blimps[56]—England the whale saved him from all this fretting and delivered him from himself, 'now that we are in this bloody war'.[57] If his new patriotism was unthinking, it was nothing to do with devotion to Crown, Empire, Church, Eton, Parliament, Blues and Royals, BBC, and all the usual stuff. It was low-key rather than top-drawer: about knowing that not everything was open to rational intervention, still less rational outcome; that there were such things in life as fate and circumstance; that human nature still had to be accounted for; that direct experience was a more reliable guide than books; that national mythologies may not be true, but can be real, and that what was important about a nation was not its objectivity but its ability to recognize itself.

So Orwell climbed inside England the whale and, once he had swallowed her whole, she provided him with all that he desired—protection from the storm, 'a womb', 'a dark cushioned space', an intimate world.[58] But what a whale. A killer-whale one minute, 'wallowing among surface waves', small and quick with tremendous global range—a giant whale the next, 'shooting down into the blackness of the middle seas (a mile deep, according to Herman Melville)' before coming up spouting tremendous resources, unfathomable money, serious bulk. Orwell never said that England was his whale, but given how easily he slipped from Miller's elemental inner cushion into a dream of elemental inner emotion, the analogy commends itself. Loyalty to England past and present, right or left, drunk or sober, hardly gave him anywhere else to move:

> It was one of those dreams which, whatever Freudian inner meaning they may have, do sometimes reveal to you the real state of your feelings. It taught me two things, first, that I should be simply relieved when the long-dreaded war started, secondly that I was patriotic at heart...Patriotism has nothing to do with conservatism. It is devotion to something that is changing but is felt to be mystically the same.[59]

Britain was a first-class power. Far more militarily capable than appeasers had tried to claim, as David Edgerton has shown, once she got into the middle seas of the war she was a powerful adversary. Not only could she trade with the world and draw on her vast imperial resources, she could make war on a scale that outperformed Germany in little over a year. Even as the British Expeditionary Force was staggering back to the coast at Dunkirk, the British war machine was gearing up.[60] In the meantime, it was necessary to hold out a few months longer. Orwell stood with the people because, not for the first time, they had been there when he had only been thinking about it. He knew he could not stand with them without pretending to be unmoved, as they were unmoved, by the country's intellectual elites.[61] At the same time, there were other intellectuals and other elites too, particularly technical and scientific elites, who could make victory possible.[62]

Churchill had swept into office with the People at his back. 'The people should be told this is a civilians' war, or a People's War', the Ministry of Information told the Home Office.[63] Labour dealt with the unions, and Ernest Bevin, Minister of Labour, dealt with Churchill. No one ever doubted that the country would work (and queue) to the end. As for the middle class, along with the Ministry of Information, Broadcasting House, the Crown Film Unit, the Women's Institute, the Church of England, the Army Bureau of Current Affairs, the Political and Planning Group, and all local notables, from Rotarians to Former Pupils, the government played this white-collar version of the 'People' for all it was worth.[64] Orwell had been interested in transmuted identities ever since Spain. What he had seen there in former public school-boys at war with Franco, he saw now in the English middle class at war with Hitler. Suddenly he and they were among the ranks of the People again, and for once he was determined to fit in. Not interested in parliamentary politics or elite institutions, never one for high-cultural events or formal pronouncements, formerly of the upper middle class but more recently of the lower middle class, in salary at least, but beginning to make some money at last (Penguin published 55,000 copies of *Down and Out* in December 1940) and confident in his own competence and intelligence, never living anywhere other than in the busy streets of N1 and NW8, Orwell took his place, alongside Eileen, in the People's War.[65]

Orwell's Local Defence Volunteers (later the 'Home Guard') was C Company, 5th London Battalion, St John's Wood. He did his turn. In June 1941 he joined the BBC Empire Service Indian Section as a talks producer—his first proper job since the Imperial Police, and just as well paid.[66] In 1942 Eileen, still suffering from depression after the death of her brother, moved from the Ministry of Information to the Ministry of

Food, where she produced cookery programmes for radio. In a busy life, Orwell was well liked at the BBC, winning the respect of his colleagues and managers.[67] After two years, however, he reckoned he was not finding enough time to write, and did not think anyone in India was listening anyway.[68] He left 200 Oxford Street in November 1943 to join the left Labour weekly *Tribune* as its part-time literary editor. This gave him more time to write and more time to swan around before moving on again, this time to the *Observer* in February 1945 as an official war correspondent.

During these years Orwell moved into a number of circles, all talented, some famous. Family members came and went for 'frugal late night suppers punctuated by the thump of bombs'.[69] One of the Blairs' homes, 10 Mortimer Crescent in Kilburn, was hit by a V1 flying bomb, but they were over at the O'Shaughnessys that night. At the BBC Orwell was one of a new intake which included Louis MacNeice, Roy Campbell, and Dylan Thomas. When he described life there as 'a mixture of whore shop and lunatic asylum', we can assume he had his moments.[70] Then there was *Tribune* as a community of readers, which brought a more relaxed tone, and writers and literary types in an ever-widening circle of friends and fixers, including Anthony Powell, David Astor, Malcolm Muggeridge, Julian Symons, Rayner Heppenstall, Arthur Koestler, Stevie Smith, Lydia Jackson, Tosco Fyvel, William Empson, David Sylvester, Paul Potts, Margaret Crossland, Ivor Brown, Victor Gollancz (now forgiven),[71] Fred Warburg, and others. Occasionally he would be invited to meet special people: H. G. Wells, E. M. Forster, Evelyn Waugh. He was in correspondence with George Bernard Shaw and Graham Greene. To a student of English literature, Orwell's address book would look impressive, although being at the BBC helped. On 16 October 1942 we find him writing to T. S. Eliot ('Dear Eliot'), asking him to read on the air.

One senses a sea-change in his expectations. He spoke to the Oxford University Democratic Social Club in May 1941 and to the Fabian Society in London in November 1941. Famous, but not very, sometime in 1942 he was asked to read his work to the Oxford University English Club. A young Philip Larkin was the treasurer. 'We took Dylan Thomas to the Randolph and George Orwell to the not-so-good hotel. I suppose it was my first essay in practical criticism.'[72] Once he had joined *Tribune*, in the Strand, he was mixing with serious politicians of the left including Nye Bevan, its editor, and young tyros like Richard Crossman,

George Strauss, and Michael Foot. No boiled rabbits here.[73] He was writing for a wider range of publications too, including Cyril Connolly's *Horizon*, David Astor's *Observer*, Kingsley Martin's *New Statesman* (also forgiven), John Beavan's *Manchester Evening News*, Michael Foot's *Evening Standard*, and Philip Rahv's left American periodical *Partisan Review*. There were Old Etonians to lunch: Connolly, Lehmann, Rees, Powell, and Astor. David Astor, like Connolly and Rees, would prove a special friend—patron, helpmate, confidante, best man, pall bearer. There were Adelphians for a drink, Southwoldians to catch up on, old friends, new friends, a baby, Richard Horatio, their adopted son, brought to them in October 1944. Many of these people either knew each other or knew others who did, and Orwell liked to mix with them in the pubs and cafes of Soho and Fitzrovia. He could afford it. The BBC paid well (about £12 per week), and *Tribune* nearly as well (£10), and of course this was a man-about-town sort of life, an open-and-shut sort of life, a man's life, not short of young and liberated women. He met Sonia Brownell at the offices of *Horizon*, and her biographer says he was 'electrified'.[74] Along with life at the BBC, compared to what he had been used to in Wallington, this was heady stuff, perfect for a public-school satirist.[75]

To be sure, the war years started badly. He was marooned in a cottage that was and always had been 'bloody awful'.[76] The shop didn't make any money. He couldn't join up. He couldn't decide what to do next. He was too tired to get on with his next book.[77] True, Eileen was working to ease their money troubles, but they only met on alternate weekends. Her physical health was not good. His was chronically bad. They were both heavy smokers. London was exhausting, the air-raids shattering, their futures temporary, and their accommodation the same.[78] It might have been that they were hoping for a family.[79] Orwell had no roots—a parlous position for one who distrusted people who had no roots.[80] One can see how Miller's whale wished itself upon them. But gradually the war took its hold. Life gathered meaning. They, or at any rate *he*, saw himself as at the centre of the world. He was known and getting known, and all common sense pointed to a better future. In June 1944 they found a comfortable four-bedroom flat off the Essex Road. The old nightmare world of imperial hangmen, sad-faced lads, gaunt school-masters, and Spanish jailors must have seemed like a dark age away. The war yielded his finest work.

The surge

Orwell started to solve the riddle of Englishness in 1940. He writes about England because that was where the battle raged, and he turns to the essay, the great republican form, because of its flexibility for attack or defence, as necessary. He begins to write about the English people without restraint or apology—an unusual thing in itself, reckoned Bernard Crick, but vital to where Orwell wanted to stand.[81] 'ARM THE PEOPLE', he tells *Time and Tide* readers in 1940—unusual in a man who was about to celebrate English gentleness. Echoing Cobbett, he tells *Evening Standard* readers to hold on to their weapons. 'A rifle leaning on the wall of the working-class flat or labourers' cottage is the symbol of democracy. It is our job to see that it stops there.'[82]

For once in his life Orwell is pleased with his public-school education. He mocks those who do not know the right end of a gun. He is buoyed by the London Home Guard, on parade in Regent's Park.[83] He finds honour in the military virtues and wants an English militia to defend the homeland and force the revolution. Yet these were also the months when he sees the significance of a softer Englishness, and sets about merging the orthodoxies of hard and soft to the point where it is difficult to tell them apart: a right little tight little island punching above its weight on the one hand; a gentle people, an undulating land, an 'emotional unity' on the other. Above all, and in spite of its deep and unremitting class divisions, Orwell responds to the country's idea of itself as one nation. Only Blimps and highbrows get in the way: one 'with his bull neck and diminutive brain'; the other with his 'stalk' neck and 'domed head'.[84]

He went on to redefine Englishness almost in an afternoon. Not without help, it must be said. The 1930s had seen a long, slow release of national identity—'a modern English renaissance', says Alexandra Harris—that seemed to incorporate at one time or another almost every English (and some non-English) artist and writer in the land. To name, as they say, but a few: W. H. Auden, Cecil Beaton, Vanessa Bell, Bill Brandt, Roger Fry, Duncan Grant, John Nash, John Piper, Stanley Spencer, Evelyn Waugh, Vita Sackville-West, Vaughan Williams...and on and on, all contributing to a new cultural collage, all reacting against Modernism and the 'International Style', a 'form of liberty that involved the abolition of roots'.[85] But in spite of their search for roots all these people remained moderns, and one can see the same in Orwell.

First, a substantial patriotic essay, or book (as the adverts had it), called *The Lion and the Unicorn* (1941). He writes in defence of the British nation-state as an old and not entirely dishonourable form of political life. Second, a short essay on seaside postcards called 'The Art of Donald McGill' (1941). From an ephemeral but popular source, Orwell identifies a central aspect of Englishness. Third, a general essay, 'Politics and the English Language' (1946)—a postscript to the Englishness he had set out earlier. Fourth, another long meditation on an ephemeral source, this time cheap comics, 'Boys' Weeklies' (1940), where he ventures into the reactionary England he knew before and during the Great War. Fifth, 'Charles Dickens' (1940), another essay from the inside out, as much about himself as about Dickens, with adjacent essays on Kipling (1942) and Wodehouse (1945) where the same applies. And finally, all that followed up to 1946, including another substantial essay, *The English People* (1943, but not published till 1947), a brilliant short allegory, *Animal Farm* (1945), and a spate of small features and reviews, where he showed there was no detail of Englishness which he could not turn to account.

Changing and staying the same is the driving-force behind *The Lion and the Unicorn*, written in the summer and autumn of 1940 and published by Secker & Warburg in February 1941.[86] It was preceded by the much shorter 'My Country Right or Left', published in the autumn, which may or may not have been originally part of the longer pieces, 'Our Opportunity', published in *Left News* in January 1941, and 'Fascism and Democracy', published in the same journal in February 1941. All three linking pieces made the same points as *The Lion and the Unicorn*: that England had to fight or die; that the common people were patriotic though they might have to be patriotic *and* revolutionary to win the war; that only 'apologists of totalitarianism' argued that ' "bourgeois" Democracy' was a fraud.[87] He had held these ideas for a year or more. In fact, as we have seen, he held these ideas when talking to some people, Gollancz for example, while at the same time holding other ideas, anti-war ideas, when writing to other people.[88] But in this book he had more than mere strategy on his mind. He told Gorer in January 1940 that he was incubating 'an enormous novel', a 'family saga sort of thing' about England, and although the novel did not happen, one can see in the *The Lion and the Unicorn* the same emotional unity that such a project would demand.[89] It has the same confessional tone, the same family likenesses. In this war we have to fight to survive, he says, but in order to have a chance of winning and at the same time staying together, we will have to write some family members out of the will. He assures us that whatever happens England will still be England.

The Lion and the Unicorn sets out to describe just what sort of country England is.[90] Because he tries to interpret a whole country, and its whole history, from a whole nation point of view, and because he tries to do so plurally, not from a single perspective, and because he tries to do so rationally, without resort to abstraction or mysticism, he has to resort to extraordinary measures. In the event, he delivers a straight defence of the English people—though it is a well-observed feature of his writing that when Orwell refers to 'England' he is referring either to an English-ness many of whose features were shared by the other nations who made up the United Kingdom of Great Britain and Northern Ireland, or he is referring simply to the machinery of the British state. It is hard to know why Orwell consistently excluded the Scots, Welsh, and Irish any more than why he included some of the English but not all of them.[91] It could have been on grounds of weight of numbers, but it was most likely on grounds of argument: England's relationship with the Celts would have complicated an argument he wanted to simplify, just as the English people's relationship with the 'uppers' and their grip on the constitution would have complicated a shape he wanted, for the time being at least, to keep natural—what he calls the country's 'native gen-ius' and 'real shape'.[92] Thus, he lives through the Abdication Bill of December 1936 without a word. He even misses the prime minister's reference to Edward VIII as Hamlet.[93] There is no time for philander-ing royals in Orwell's life.[94] In *The Lion and the Unicorn* he does the same, confiscating Englishness from its aristocratic owners and putting it in the hands of the people—half England indeed, the proletarian half, the 85 per-cent half, the half that counts. This he does without compunction.

The Lion and the Unicorn carries the tropes and arguments of a life-time. He opens with the best few hundred words on English national identity ever written—a defence of why it mattered at that moment. He proceeds by affirming the significance of the nation-state in the modern world ('there is nothing to set beside it'), and goes on to make the relative case for the power for good of England in that world—a civilization built on the instincts and experiences of the people as a whole. This is the Englishness he found in Wigan and Barnsley, writ large. The English are not, he says, patriots in any conventional sense. They are not given to flag-waving or jingoism. They may have built the biggest empire the world has seen, but they are gentle-minded. Red-coats may have fought and pillaged their way across three centuries, but 'the only enemy they ever named was the sergeant major'. The English may be gamblers, drunkards, and exceptionally foul-mouthed, but they are also a highly moral lot who prize the domestic virtues. Orwell never wavered in his contention that the English were a gentle and law-abiding people, even though in 1941 they were intent on turning their country into a military airstrip.[95] Their most important trait, he argued, was their 'respect for constitutionalism and legality'.

Even so, he requests that they ditch it for revolution. The constitutionalism and legality of the old must be overturned in order to secure the constitutionalism and legality of the new—which is revolution by any other name. When it comes to the preservation of the English, therefore, Orwell argues that respect for the law and respect for revolution are not just inseparable, they stem from the same source: 'it is only by revolution that the native genius of the English people can be set free'; 'by revolution we become more ourselves, not less'.[96] In *Coming Up for Air* Orwell had nearly 250 pages' worth of practice in the dialectics of England-changed and England-still-the-same, and in *The Lion and the Unicorn* he used it.

The Leavises had spent ten years warning from their Cambridge bully pulpit that the English had suffered a terrible breach in their culture and could not be saved.[97] Orwell said the opposite: they had changed and stayed the same, and only by so doing could save themselves.

Changed and stayed the same? Was this not just a mite contradictory?

No. The very idea was inscribed in the textbook of English constitutionalism. Walter Bagehot's *The English Constitution* (1867) argued that in order to secure democratic change the political system had to pretend that nothing had changed. Thus, in the wake of the Reform Acts of 1832 and 1867 the bourgeoisie (though very dull) had been left to run the country, while the aristocracy (though very stupid) only pretended to. Bagehot's England, therefore, was rule by the secret of change (bourgeois power) and no change (aristocratic show).[98] Orwell was right. Nations *do* change and *do* stay the same, but only if they can stay together well enough and long enough to contrive a critical mass of connecting myths and stories that are historically as well as aesthetically convincing.[99]

The older and more aware the nation, the older and more resourceful the contrivance, and because the contrivance is human, the process is natural. The English had endured twists in their history that matched anything Orwell asked of them in *The Lion and the Unicorn*. They had had their Glorious Revolution in 1688 and 1689. They had had political revolutions in 1832, 1867, 1884, 1918, and 1928. They had had their Industrial Revolution all through. Yet here they were, in the midst of the latest crisis, never more aware of themselves and never closer to the state as an expression of their general will. Even more important than getting your history right or wrong was keeping it connected.[100]

But first, Orwell says, we have to recognize that the situation is urgent. Second, we have to recognize that the ruling class is too degenerate to save us. Third, that the intellectual class is too alienated to know us. Fourth, 'they' (by which he meant 'we', by which he meant sympathetic intellectuals like himself and the new middle class, whom he is actually addressing) must become conscious of themselves as the articulate nation. Fifth, once having realized their moment, that class must align with the old working class, win the revolution, and win the war. Enter the new English, in other words, held up by Orwell as men and women of revolutionary potential who hold the chance to make England new again.[101] These are the 'wholly necessary people', 'the rather restless, culture-less' suburban people, the airmen and mechanics, the scientists and technicians, the chemists and teachers and journalists of 'the naked democracy of the swimming pools', of 'Slough, Dagenham, Barnet, Letchworth and Hayes'—the very places at which Orwell had once turned his nose up, heartlands now of a country which, in order to save itself from extinction, has willed itself to life in the great politicization of 1939–40. They were new but, remember, Orwell wanted nothing new.

> In tastes, habits, manners and outlook the working class and the middle class are drawing together. The unjust distinctions remain, but the real differences diminish. The old-style 'proletarian'—collarless, unshaven and with muscle warped by heavy labour—still exists, but he is constantly decreasing in numbers; he only predominates in the heavy-industry areas of the north of England...
>
> This war, unless we are defeated, will wipe out most of the existing class privileges. There are every day fewer people who wish them to continue. Nor need we fear that as the pattern changes life in England will

lose its peculiar flavour. The new red cities of Greater London are crude enough, but these things are only the rash that accompanies a change. In whatever shape England emerges from the war it will be deeply tinged with the characteristics that I have spoken of earlier....

The Stock Exchange will be pulled down, the horse plough will give way to the tractor, the country houses will be turned into children's holiday camps, the Eton and Harrow match will be forgotten, but England will still be England, an everlasting animal stretching into the future and the past, and, like all living things, having the power to change out of recognition and yet remain the same.

What can England of 1940 have in common with the England of 1840? But then, what have you in common with the child of five whose photograph your mother keeps on the mantel piece? [102]

Part Two, 'Shopkeepers at War', confirms the urgency of the situation ('we are in the soup full fathom five'); identifies fifth-columnists and fellow-travellers (Blackshirts, Communists, Pacifists); and famously affirms that 'England is a family with the wrong members in control'. Private capitalism has been shown not to work. Only socialism—by which Orwell means national unity plus state direction of the economy—will deliver victory.

Part Three, 'The English Revolution', comes down a register by talking plausibly about revolution as a gradual and non-violent process. It is an English revolution after all, and bound to be exceptional. Orwell says that it started before the war, picked up speed in the summer of 1940, and is now apparent in the general public feeling that something is radically wrong and needs to be radically changed. 'The initiative will have to come from below', he claims, and offers his most generous evidence for the revolution yet in Noel Coward's *Cavalcade*, Tom Hopkinson's *Picture Post*, Frank Owen's *Evening Standard*, and J. B. Priestley's 'Postscript' broadcasts for the BBC.[103]

If this is a revolution it is a very cultural revolution, and Orwell adds his own thoughts to the mix with a six-point programme of basic socialist measures, the nearest he ever got to an ordinary political prospectus. It says a lot about the kind of socialism he envisaged that two of his measures—alliance with countries attacked by the Fascist powers, and educational reform—were achieved under Churchill's administration, and three of them—nationalization of basic industries, progressive income tax, and independence for India—were achieved without uproar under Attlee's. Mr Attlee did not, however, nationalize the land or fill the ancient universities with bright working-class children, which Orwell called for. It says even more about Orwell's socialism that, for one who knew something about being hard-up and who suffered from chronic health problems, his six-point plan did not mention social insurance or a national health service—policies which would form the centrepiece of Labour's welfare state after 1945. He assures us that these six points 'could be printed on the front page of the *Daily Mirror*', but *Picture Post* had already run its 'Plan for Britain' months before. Beveridge's Report of the Inter-Departmental Committee on Social Insurance and Allied Services was published in December 1942.[104]

Orwell proposed that through measures such as these 'the common people... [will] feel, as they cannot feel now, that *the state is themselves*'—a proposition, or at any rate a rhetoric, that Churchill's government appeared to accept. The Ministry of Information and the Crown Film Unit were putting out books and films that confirmed it scene by scene, line by line. The London fire-brigades, for instance, were represented as democratic fighting-crews who enjoyed the trust and intelligence of local people because they were local people.[105] And not only the state, but Orwell's people had also grown into the nation as well, and not only the nation now, but the nation before:

> The heirs of Nelson and Cromwell are not in the House of Lords. They are in the fields and the streets, in the factories and the armed forces, in the four ale bar and the suburban back garden...Compared with the task of bringing the real England to the surface, even the winning of the war, necessary though it is, is secondary. By revolution we become more ourselves, not less. There is no question of stopping short, striking a compromise, salvaging 'democracy', standing still. Nothing ever stands still. We must add to our heritage or lose it, we must grow greater or grow less, we must go forward or backward. I believe in England, and I believe that we shall go forward.[106]

Orwell calls upon his people to wake up to their own defence nine months after they had done it anyway.[107] A late call, no doubt, but as usual he had his reasons even if he did not always find it in him to admit they came late. *The Lion and the Unicorn*, however, was built to last. Though specific to its time and place, it remains a high point in English political writing.[108]

In 'The Art of Donald McGill', written in 1941 but not published until February 1942, Orwell changes his palette and adds local colour.

Not entirely plebeian, not middle class, and certainly not 'art' as it was appreciated in the art colleges and galleries, but equally, something which everyone would know and understand, the art of Donald McGill is the English dirty postcard. It is what George Bowling might have sent to his pals, if not to his mother-in-law. Orwell picks out McGill as the most prolific and original of a small school of comic artists who specialized in the smutty-humorous cartoon. So accomplished was this school, and so familiar its conventions, it would have been easier for Orwell to show a McGill rather than write about it. But he wants us to take it seriously as art in a tradition of English vulgarity, and he wants, moreover, to write the catalogue: a collection of red-nosed drunks, pop-eyed officials, neck-stretching young men, impossibly voluptuous young women and impossibly upholstered older ones. The colours are gaudy, the jokes awful, the humour visual (or *double entendre*), the situations illegitimate (babies, seductions, states of undress), or physical (breasts and bottoms), or both. In every last bead of sweat Orwell sees the best traditions of English bad taste as exemplified by Mr Max Miller at the Holborn Empire. *He says to her:*

> 'I like seeing experienced girls home.'
> 'But I'm not experienced!'
> 'You're not home yet!'

What has this got to do with the riddle of Englishness?

Orwell argued that these are the people as the people like to be seen on their day off. There is no sign of it in *The Road to Wigan Pier*, and it was positively alien to Comstock and his kind, but ever since Miller (Henry, not Max) it had been on Orwell's mind—a low-grade everything-you-can-buy-in-Woolworths sort of Englishness with its Wall's ice creams, celanese stockings, cheap smokes, sweet toffees, *and* the art of Donald McGill. The postcards are as sharp as salt and vinegar. Most likely to be found on the beach, in a deckchair, McGill's old English give life to the new.[109] They have been there since the beginning of time. It would take a crane to lift them:

> It will not do to condemn them on the ground that they are vulgar and ugly. That is exactly what they are meant to be. Their whole meaning and virtue is their unredeemed lowness, not only in the sense of obscenity, but lowness of outlook in every direction...They stand for the worm's-eye view of life, for the music-hall world where marriage is a

> dirty joke or a comic disaster, where the rent is always behind and the
> clothes are always up the spout...they are a sort of saturnalia...

Lions and unicorns are all very well but these are people with bags of
bottom. Whatever the state could and could not do for them, and whatever intellectuals wanted out of them, they were not going anywhere
they did not want to go. It was not just the army or the navy Hitler had
to get past.[110] They called him 'Corporal Schicklgruber'. He had never
been a corporal or a Schicklgruber, but as an upstart and a twerp they
called him that anyway. They tried saying 'Heil Schicklgruber!' They
said he was puny and monorchic.[111] They would brush him away with
one sweep of the arm, as they had with Bonaparte. John Gillray's 'Little
Boney', also known as 'The Corsican Caesar' or 'The Corsican Fairy',
had known their wrath too: 'Dam ye, you blackhearted treacherous
Corsican, if you were not such a little bit of a fellow, in spite of your
large cocked hat, I'd crack your skull...(seizes him by the Nose).'[112]
Hitler, Orwell seems to be saying, will not move this lot, and a Bolshevik
would be foolish to try. Not an engineer of the human soul in sight,
changing them is nigh-on impossible. 'The slightest hint of higher influence would ruin them utterly':

> I never read the proclamation of generals before battle, the speeches of
> *fuhrers* and prime ministers, the solidarity songs of public schools and left-
> wing political parties, national anthems, Temperance tracts, papal encyc-
> licals and sermons against gambling and contraception, without seeming
> to hear in the background a chorus of raspberries from all the millions of
> common men to whom these high sentiments make no appeal.[113]

Orwell is writing now about the people not as they ought to be but as
what they were already, in a way, at least in caricature, and his 1946
essay 'Politics and the English Language' is remarkable for how it too
puts what the people ought to have alongside what they have already.
This essay was not part of Orwell's first English surge, but it fits *The Lion
and the Unicorn* and 'The Art of Donald McGill' in its devotion to a
politics of actually existing ordinariness.

Having established the underlying strength of the state, and the lowbrow
weight of those who keep it down to earth, 'Politics and the English
Language' addresses the possibilities of corruption in high places. Our
politics and our language are in decline, he says, and this is dangerous
because, just as they mutually depend on each other, our life and liberties

mutually depend on them. Orwell understands that mere vigilance is not enough; that the language used to express vigilance is a system like any other system, and open to corruption in just the same way. He prefers his language as he prefers other things in his Englishness (such as socialism, or the art of Donald McGill) which is to say: directly intelligible, personal, and accountable; which is to say, not over-intellectualized, not generalized, and definitely not complicated or hidden. If there are clearer alternatives to hand, Orwell tells his readers to use them.[114]

But it was not just a question of clarity. The more language was removed from everyday life, he argued, the more abstract and untestable it became. And the more abstract and untestable it became, he argued, the more likely it would come to serve ideological purposes. For ideology·served power, not truth, and modern intellectuals, caught in a web of words and unusually keen to change the world, were especially prone to offering their services. All of Europe attested to this. Franco had his Carlists, his Jesuits, and his Falangistes. Hitler too had his politics and his language. Stalin had whole schools of creative writing to do the job. For his part, Orwell recognized a scribbler when he saw one: 'Sometimes I look at a Socialist . . . the intellectual tract writing type of Socialist, with his pullover, his fuzzy hair, and his Marxian quotation— and wonder what the devil his motive really is.'[115]

'Politics and the English Language', then, is a manual of honest political dealing. He takes you round the scrapyard of politico-linguistic swindles (clapped-out metaphors, verbal false parts, foreign duds, prefabricated sentences) pointing out some old friends along the way—a Communist pamphlet here ('frantic Fascist captains'), a letter to *Tribune* there ('the British lion's roar at present is like that of Bottom'), and Professor Harold Laski, late of the Left Book Club ('I am not, indeed, sure whether it is not true to say', 'In a sense, I am not quite certain that this note of mine is not really superfluous'). Laski had opened his review of *The Road to Wigan Pier* in great and pointless form, and Orwell remembered.[116]

His answer to bad political writing was not more university degrees in English or Politics. The answer lay not in the lecture halls but on the streets, where you learned how to make yourself understood. 'Good prose is like a window pane', he said, not because he thought it could be transparent, and not because he thought it could be neutral, but because he wanted a way of writing that did not seek to draw attention to itself.[117] Orwell's guide to the regeneration of the language, then, was that it should be practical, sensible, active, and short. This is not to say that he thought it was easy. 'All writers are vain, selfish and lazy.' 'Writing a book is a horrible, exhausting struggle.' Nor did he think that language should not try to be beautiful and evocative—but he is talking about politics, and for him above all else politics should be ordinary. One might say Orwell believed in the ordinariness of good language in the same way that generations of English constitutionalists had believed in the ordinariness of good law.

He had already confirmed that England's major trait was its belief in the rule of law. He was now very close to saying that the essence of Englishness was the rule of ordinary law and the ordinariness of the language as expressed in ordinary sense in ordinary places, by ordinary persons in ordinary cases. Such an ordinariness, or what Keynes called 'a prosaic sanity free from sentiment or metaphysic', framed the thinking of what Keynes also called 'the High Intelligentsia of England'.[118] Compared to centralized legal systems, which always found their codes confounded by the details of actual cases or top-down judgements; or compared to abstract philosophies, which always reasoned from the idea rather than the practice; English common law and its philosophic tradition were based on actual cases and exchanges naturalized into a rational system. That is to say, they were based on common exchange—and taught the same way, orally, by a system of moots, wranglings, and pupillage. The greatest interpreter of the common law, Sir William Blackstone, like Orwell, was known for his capacity to outline 'a rational system' and then work it into 'a natural method'.[119] Orwell showed no interest in the English folk revival of his youth, but on closer inspection his theory of common law and common language was not unlike the English folk revivalists' theory of common lore and common folk.[120] In effect, Orwell argued the folk revivalists' case that authentic Englishness did not come from the top down but from the bottom up; that it had been guarded and kept secret by the people over centuries of high-cultural and political domination; that it was never designed to be 'Englishness' any more than common practice had been designed to be 'the Law', but somehow over the centuries it had grown into that.[121] The national culture, in other words, like the common law itself, was familiar, known by ancient rules. Orwell had been drawn to James Joyce and Henry Miller not because their worlds were strange but because they were familiar. Or, as the English constitutional lawyer Sir John Davies put it in 1612: the nation had made itself like the silkworm, 'that formeth all her web out of her self onely'.[122]

Orwell embraced the idea of real Englishness going on in ordinary lives. Some part of this, there can be no doubt, he learned, even if he did not acknowledge it, from his old 'Popular Front' connections.[123] I will return to the politics later, but for now it is helpful to see Orwell's 1940–1 writing surge as personal in the sense that this most deracinated of intellectuals (India–Henley–St Cyprian's–Eton–Burma–London–Wigan–Wallington–Spain–hospitalized–Marrakech–back to London again) was trying to write himself back into the lives of the people, as indeed he was trying to restore the authenticity of those lives by rescuing them from the condescension of intellectuals. Like all the achievements of the folk, or indeed the market, common law was bottom-up, true to experience, passed on, and real.[124] Or so it was said.[125] In the end, the common law lost its pre-eminence because its practitioners found it too ordinary for their gentlemanly ambitions.[126] But before that happened Orwell would have stood with Sir Matthew Hale in his judgement that respect for the law (like respect for the language) stood with 'the Disposition of the English Nation...by long Experience and Use', and with Lord Mansfield's judgement that laws built on subtleties, niceties, and pretensions compared unfavourably with 'rules easily learned and easily retained, because they are the dictates of common sense, drawn from the truth of the case'.[127]

What was the truth of the case? In 'Boys' Weeklies' Orwell found the truth of one case at least at the local newsagents. The *Gem* and the *Magnet*, along with the *Triumph* and *Champion* and *Rover* and *Skipper* and half-a-dozen other boys' comic weeklies, had been keeping English boys amused for nearly forty years:

'Oh cwumbs!'
'Oh gum!'
'Oooogh!'
'Urrggh!'[128]

Going back for point of origin to Thomas Hughes's *Tom Brown's Schooldays* (1857) and possibly Kipling's *Stalky & Co* (1899), but with all the adult sermonizing taken out and inflated to boyish bursting-point, Orwell saw these boys' comic stories as essentially the same, all following the same well-worn path of grey stones, ivy walls, ancient quad, upper remove, and yet another day in the life of Bunter and his pals. It was Orwell's contention that every English boy, no matter how poor, knew this world, and just to add Marxist spice, he offered the thought that because the stories followed a formula they must have been written, just as they were published, by a business syndicate. He sets out to shows how a seemingly innocent comic culture teaches boys how to love their rulers, and how from 12 to 18 years and after (sometimes a long time after) every boy learned every corner of the old school yard and more: how to sing the old-school song, guy the masters, call a fag, beat a bully, hit a six, eat a muffin, bang a mug, and not miss lock-up. He admits that these stories are all pernicious nonsense, of course, not at all like the world as it really is or even as it really was, but given the state of that world, he is forced in the end to make the entirely *un*-Marxist point that all boys would prefer the nonsense to the reality. What boy would rather read about starving in Paris than dining out on sausage and cake in front of the fire at St Jim's? What boy would not like to know these boys (he does, of course) and their wonderfully free, innocent, lives?[129]

Orwell once remarked in a letter that his son Richard 'gets a horrible low-class comic paper every week from Dundee and likes to have it read to him'. Horrible and low the *Beano* might have been, but it is hard to believe that Orwell found reading it a chore. It is hard to believe, too, that he wrote a passage such as this not for his own guilty pleasure:

> The mental world of the *Gem* and *Magnet*, therefore, is something like this. The year is 1910—or 1940, but it is all the same. You are at Greyfriars, a rosy cheeked boy of 14 in posh tailor-made clothes, sitting down to tea in your study on the Remove passage after an exciting game of football which was won by an odd goal in the last half minute. There's a cosy fire in the study, and outside the wind is whistling. The ivy clusters thickly round the old grey stones. The king is on his throne and the pound is worth a pound. Over in Europe the comic foreigners are jabbering and gesticulating, but the grim grey battleships of the British Fleet are steaming up the Channel and at the outposts of the Empire the monocled Englishmen are holding the niggers at bay. Lord Mauleverer has just got another fiver and we are all settling down to a tremendous tea of sausages, sardines, crumpets, potted meat, jam and doughnuts. After tea we shall sit round the study fire having a good laugh at Billy Bunter and discussing the team for next week's match against Rookwood. Everything will be the same for ever and ever.[130]

As well as pretending to be appalled by these publications, Orwell tried to give his position left-credence by pretending that some boys—maybe all boys—might have enjoyed a little more left literary realism. He says that boys' weeklies are 'sodden in the worst illusions of 1910', and imagines a spot of 'political development' in the storyline to make it right. But whatever his head may have said, his heart was not in it.[131] It is clear from the writing that, like it or lump it and hard cheese to you, he far more believed in the comic world of Greyfriars than any progressive line he may have wanted to wish on it. Who ever heard of Bunter sending his hamper to Oxfam? Who would believe Lord Mauleverer giving his fiver to the NUWM? Orwell is clearly more than a little chuffed to see his old chums Merry and Cherry once again, and glad to be back in the ruck. Truth would come later, but just for now he is among old friends.

In 1938 a bunch of them sent him a signed copy of the 'Eton Collegers' Dinner Plan' from the Park Lane Hotel. They knew he had been to Spain, they knew he was a Commie, and they knew that he was ill, and even if he wasn't he would be unlikely to join them anyway. Yet he was still one of boys, and they wanted to tell him so. Scribbled in pencil in a bold hand right across the six courses and the three toasts, seven Old Etonians signed themselves: '*Homage to Blair*. Greetings and regrets you are not here.'[132]

Orwell never really left Eton. His essay on boys' comics is about the *essential* truth of the case.[133] Terrifically out of date, frightfully snobbish, awfully silly, and quite unbelievable, Orwell knows that 'the outlook inculcated by all these papers is that of a rather exceptionally stupid member of the Navy League in the year 1910'. But his criticism does not match his evocation, any more than his not turning up to Park Lane meant he was not a Colleger. False in consciousness Bunter may be, but false in feeling he is not:

> Groan!
> 'Shut up, Bunter!'
> Groan!
> Shutting up was not really in Billy Bunter's line. He seldom shut up, though often requested to do so. On the present awful occasion the fat Owl of Greyfriars was less inclined than ever to shut up. And he did not shut up! He groaned, and groaned, and went on groaning.
> Even groaning did not fully express Bunter's feelings. His feelings, in fact, were inexpressible.

'Charles Dickens' is Orwell's finest essay in literary criticism, and in the way he constructed a whole English world it is very close to 'Boys' Weeklies' and 'The Art of Donald McGill'. He starts by correcting some misconceptions. Dickens was not proletarian, though it has often been claimed that he was. He is sorry for the poor, but he is not one of them and never could be. He is not ignorant of their condition, and they are always labouring away in the background to his stories, but because he was not really interested in their work he could not really appreciate their life. Stephen Blackpool in *Hard Times* and the Plomishes in *Little Dorritt* are genuine proletarians, for sure, but the only ones. There are few factories or mines, strikes or trade unions in Dickens and those there are are nearly all crammed into one novel. None are convincing. His best proletarian characters, Bill Sikes, Sam Weller, and Mrs Gamp—a burglar, a servant, and a nurse—Orwell dismisses as unrepresentative of the working class. Orwell is wrong on Weller in fact (domestic service was a leading sector of the labour force throughout the nineteenth century),[134] but he doesn't want to talk about servants. Neither does Dickens. He is far happier writing novels about his own class, which, as it happens, is the same class as Orwell's.

Orwell argues that Dickens is not a revolutionary writer either. In *A Tale of Two Cities* he is alert to the aristocracy as a class who dug their own graves, as he is alert to the Jacobins as a class who dug other people's. The guillotine may have been an enlightened and altogether superior severing instrument, but Dickens has five hundred people dancing in its shadow like demons while their creator 'broods over their frenzies with a curious imaginative intensity'. Orwell knows the great man's faults ('imagination overwhelms everything like a kind of weed'), but he sees in Dickens' Jacobins his own day's Bolsheviks. However they tried, it was not possible for Jacobins or Bolsheviks to straighten human nature without injuring human beings. He quotes from *A Tale of Two Cities*:

> All the devouring and insatiate Monsters since imagination could record itself are fused in the one realisation, Guillotine. And yet there is not in France, with its rich variety of soil and climate, a blade, a leaf, a root, a sprig, a peppercorn, which will grow to maturity under conditions more certain than those that have produced this horror. Crush humanity out of shape once more, under similar hammers, and it will twist itself into the same tortured forms.

'Again and again', we are told, Dickens insists upon 'the meaningless horrors of revolution—the mass-butcheries, the injustice, the ever present terror of spies, the frightful blood-lust of the mob...He even credits some of these wretches with a taste for guillotining children.'[135]

Not a proletarian or a revolutionary writer, Orwell argues that Dickens was not even a political writer. He is not interested in detailed schemes or grand plans, does not feel close to the state, and is at his mad comic best when dealing with that vast and expensive class of blimps and bureaucrats who infest it. At this point, enjoying the ride, Orwell begins to gallop. Dickens may be middle class and 'a south of England man' at that, but that is not to say he is pro-business, still less a free-market liberal, and of course he is by no means landed gentry. This frees him from class ideology but narrows his capacity for being political 'in the accepted sense'. In the absence of ideology or politics, therefore, it is time for Orwell to get his exclamation-marks out:

> Dickens' attitude is never irresponsible, still less does he take the money-grubbing Smilesian line; but at the back of his mind there is usually a half-belief that the whole apparatus of government is unnecessary. Parliament is simply Lord Coodle and Sir Thomas Doodle, the Empire is simply Major Bagstock and his Indian servant, the army is simply Colonel Chowser and Doctor Slammer, the public services are simply Bumble and the Circumlocution Office...
>
> And of course this narrowness of vision is in one way a great advantage to him, because it is fatal for a caricaturist to see too much. From Dickens' point of view 'good' society is simply a collection of village idiots. What a crew! Lady Tippins! Mrs Gowan! Lord Verisopht! The honourable Bob Stables! Mrs Sparsit (whose husband was a Powler)! The Tite Barnacles! Nupkins! It is practically a case book in lunacy.[136]

Or 'cranks', as he might have put it.

So, Dickens 'attacked English institutions with a ferocity that has never since been approached' as a subversive and a radical, but not as a revolutionary or a prole and, funnily enough, not as a political man 'in the accepted sense' either.[137] The thrust of his attack comes in his depiction of the problem-makers, not in his identification of the system. He is 'all fragments, all details'. Insofar as he addresses what is to be done, it is always in the gift of men—usually good rich men—to do the right thing by behaving more decently. Orwell sniffs out an unpleasant streak of what he calls the 'class-sex' theme in Dickens here—that is, the rights of all women to be 'above' all men, existing alongside the rights of all rich men to be nearer the womanly ideal than all poor men.[138] Good rich men have rights to the kind of woman poor men dare not dream of. But this is a sideshow in the essay, worth an essay in itself perhaps, but not affecting Orwell's general intention to reveal in Dickens a man who strives to make his England good without so much as a theoretical footnote about how it got to be bad or a practical suggestion about how to make it better. Dickens' novels hardly have plots, let alone a social structure. He simply calls upon decent men to act more decently in order to make the world more decent, and that, kind sirs, is as far as he gets. Orwell starts by calling this a platitude, but ends by saying that it is 'not necessarily so shallow as it sounds'.[139] Given Orwell's own recent reluctance to indulge in theory or approach the wilder shores of revolutionary politics, we can take this as tantamount to a recommendation.

Dickens, then, according to Orwell, is a not a proletarian writer, or a revolutionary writer, or a political writer, or hardly even a social writer. He is an English cultural writer, and in his young men one can see new moral heroes, just as in his happy bourgeois families one can see all the wealth and liberty a country defended by its navy could expect. Dickens is unmoved by the army, plays no sport, has no land, invokes no obvious patriotism, shows no interest in party politics, is kind on the poor, benevolent to foreigners, and sees no virtue in Empire. In this, as in every other mark of Dickens fingered by Orwell, we see the face of the man he would like to be:

> It is the face of a man of about forty...It is the face of a man who is always fighting against something, but who fights in the open and is not frightened, the face of a man who is *generously angry*—in other words, of a nineteenth century liberal, a free intelligence, a type hated with equal hatred by all the smelly little orthodoxies which are now contending for our souls.[140]

Orwell took up two other unfashionable national writers during the surge. In 1942 he wrote a short essay in defence of Rudyard Kipling, and in 1945 he wrote in defence of P. G. Wodehouse.[141]

He starts 'Rudyard Kipling' by admitting the bad ('Kipling *is* a jingo-imperialist, he *is* morally insensitive and aesthetically disgusting') and then working his way back to the good, which looks, lo and behold, a bit like Orwell himself. Kipling, we are told, is old-fashioned but he is a survivor: he may be good for a smirk in more enlightened circles, but he is as alive to his own times (1885–1902) as Dickens was to his (1832–68), with an equal ability to surprise his friends and confound his enemies. He is better than his fame—writing things his admirers could not possibly admire and believing things they could not possibly believe.[142] We can see Orwell warming to Kipling in *Burmese Days*, when he describes the 'Kipling-haunted little Clubs' ('whisky to the right of you, Pink 'un to the left of you') with the same gentlemanly relish he described 'Boys' Weeklies'.[143]

Like Dickens, like Orwell, Kipling was a great public moralist whose friends and supporters were not, on the whole, intellectuals; a writer who 'was just about coarse enough to be able to exist and keep his mouth shut in clubs and regimental messes'; an Englishman who did not trust the political class but was not entirely comfortable with its opponents either; and an imperialist who lived the first part of his life in its glory days, only to discover in the second part that the glory, and the virtue, had disappeared. Orwell loves Kipling's depiction of a old British world, how he recounts in detail the 'old pre-machine gun army' with the oats and horse-piss we have smelled before in the barracks at Barcelona, with the workhouse deaths we find in Richard Jefferies' Hodge,[144] with bloody skirmishes straight out of *Gem* and *Magnet*, and the heat and concubines straight out of *Burmese Days*. Orwell ruminates on a redcoat British army in India or the Med which is very different but the same as the khaki one which will soon to be put once more into the breach in France:

> ... the sweltering barracks in Gibraltar or Lucknow, the red coats, the pipe clayed belts and the pillbox hats, the beer, the fights, the floggings, hangings and crucifixions, the bugle calls, the smell of oats and horse piss, the bellowing sergeants with foot long moustaches, the bloody skirmishes, invariably mismanaged, the crowded troopships, the cholera-stricken camps, the 'native' concubines, the ultimate death in the workhouse.[145]

Kipling was a Tory, and there were aspects of Dickens that were Tory too—particularly his taste for good order and a hard hand when the occasion demanded it. According to Orwell, this injected a sense of political responsibility in both men. The same could not be said of P. G. Wodehouse, however. Before he was captured by the Germans at his French country villa in the summer of 1940, Wodehouse had thought he was not in danger. When he was released after a year's internment he was taken to Berlin, where he agreed to make some broadcasts and give an interview to the American CBS network. Wodehouse's remarks were unhelpful and irresponsible, but on reflection, four years later and in very different circumstances, Orwell's 'In Defence of P. G. Wodehouse' picked up on their irony. He had told his Nazi interlocutors that in return for a loaf of bread and the man on the gate with the 'musket' looking the other way, he was 'prepared to hand over India, an autographed set of my books, and to reveal the secret process of cooking sliced potatoes on a radiator'. He told them that 'this offer holds good till Tuesday week'.[146]

Wodehouse, or 'Plum' to his friends, was a political innocent who had not understood his captors. Given that he too had created a whole English idiom, it is significant that Orwell strove to make cultural connections between Wodehouse, Dickens, and Kipling, and between them, Englishness, and himself. All three lived in worlds that were pre-Fascist and not conventionally (or even unconventionally, in Wodehouse's case) political. All three were too popular to be favoured by intellectuals and other superior types. All three understood Englishness from the inside in ways that their critics (and in Wodehouse's case, England's enemies) did not. There is reason to see Kipling as more of a Greater Briton than a Little Englander, but Dickens, Wodehouse, and Orwell were all certainly Englishmen, if 'hardly aware of it'.[147] Wodehouse (like Orwell up to 1939) might have understood the situation better than he did, but it was not all his fault. As Orwell argued in Plum's defence, and maybe his own, things change. Up to May 1940 interest in the war was tepid. After that point it was a matter of life or death. At any rate, Wodehouse was grateful to Orwell, to the point of offering him a 'Grade A lunch' in a city where all the restaurants were closed.[148]

In 1943 Orwell started putting these strands together for a composite essay, *The English People*.[149] This was completed to book-length in 1944 and attended by a second surge of writing on Englishness—including short features on open fires, home cooking, village cricket, solid junk, common toads, moral conventions, ideal pubs (friendly barmaids, no radio), a nice cup of tea (eleven steps to Englishness), and all the joys of imagining what was hard to find in a strictly rationed country—from smoked kippers and hot muffins to treacle tarts and apple dumplings. He always had a taste for what he saw in Charles Reade as his 'penny encyclopaedic knowledge'.[150] We have seen already how some part of Orwell's appreciation of Dickens involved clutter, and some part of his appreciation of Kipling involved detail, and some part of his appreciation of boys' weeklies and seaside postcards involved local colour and example. This is how whole worlds are made up, or at least how Orwell made them up. To him, James Joyce's *Ulysses* ignored the war in order to produce a work comprised almost entirely of detail.[151] Trench life in Spain was another world, with hardly anything to report except the mess and the clutter and the thick vest, flannel shirt, and two pullovers that the lanky English corporal wore to keep out the cold.[152] And what was a sanatorium but a white whale where people were kind and one had to lie still? Later on Orwell would feel horribly exposed in Paris, where he did a stint as war correspondent for the *Observer*. Amidst the ceaseless movement and his own anonymity, he felt he was going to be assassinated. After the war, he escaped with his young son Richard to the island of Jura in the Hebrides—another kind of whale. Difficult to get in, difficult to get out, 'in abt [*sic*] 10–20 years & this country will be blown off the map whatever else happens. The only hope is to have a home with a few animals in some place not worth a bomb.'[153]

In the surge of 1940–1 Orwell had created a little England made for war. In the surge of 1944–6, amidst dreams of soft creams and pastries, in pieces on Sunday roasts (potatoes under the meat), Stilton cheese, and Cox's orange pippins, he created a little England settling down for peace.[154] His essay for the British Council on 'British Cookery' is grossly upper-middle-class, not to say corpulent. He has the British eating their breakfasts at nine in the morning and finishing their lunch with a piece of cheese and a cup of coffee. Some hope. Thankfully, his patrons turned it down.[155] 'The Case for the Open Fire', written in December 1945, has Orwell warming his hands in every new post-war home and using fireside family pageants in ways he had done before—'a comely pattern'. 'Moon Under Water', written in February 1946, has him describing his favourite pub, only it doesn't exist. 'Bad Climates Are Best', written in the same month, looks forward to March winds, August bathing, and a soft red winter solstice. 'Decline of the English Murder', also written in February 1946, sees him in familiar fettle, settling down in front of the Sunday fire again, spectacles on his nose, the wife asleep already. All he needs now is the *News of the World*, a bit of peace, and a nice murderer.[156] What we get instead is a disquisition on the English taste for restraint (compared to the American talent for violence).[157] These short, sentimental pieces are not important in themselves.

When taken together, however, and fed into Orwell's earlier pieces on the regenerative powers of ordinary people and his liking for whole literary worlds, they have their place.

The English People pulls all these threads together. Orwell lost interest in it once the war was over.[158] Nevertheless, Collins managed to produce a beautiful book, in modernist green with fine colour plates and black-and-white illustrations that were made to match Orwell's picture of a civilized people.[159] He starts by laying down the ground-rules for national identity. In 1940 these rules were self-evident. The people had stayed in touch with their myths. They had changed but stayed the same. They knew who they were. Although class distinctions still prevailed ('the most striking difference of all is in language and accent'), class had not prevented them from seeing themselves as one people.[160]

The English people of this book are not particularly intellectual, philosophic, artistic, cosmopolitan, or morally consistent. But they are more mature, and understand themselves better than—well, people in Most Other Countries.[161] In this modest celebration of ordinary Englishness, Orwell was not in accord with Dr Temple, the socialist archbishop of Canterbury. One may say that neither man's point of view was open to testing, but Orwell's attempt to align himself with the regenerative powers of 'ordinary, useful and unspectacular people' was far more attractive than Dr Temple's conventional moral homilies.[162] Orwell thought the English could do better, it is true, but all things considered, he thought their 'outstanding and—by contemporary standards—highly original quality... of not killing one another' ought to be commended.[163] The revolution will continue, with more equality, education, and so on, but Orwell thought that even though nearly all English people loved their country, they had to learn to love it more intelligently.[164] He offered some advice on what this might involve, including devolution and a more questing sense of regional identity,[165] but it is on the question of the people's intelligence that we must attend.

On the face of it *Animal Farm* has very little to do with Englishness. It is a one-off political satire that owes far more to Orwell's Spanish period than to his English. Orwell had lived to see Stalin turn into 'Uncle Joe'. After the entry of the Soviet Union into the war, following the German invasion of June 1941, everyone understood the scale of the Eastern

Front and the suffering of the Russian people. Some praised Stalin for his leadership in the Great Patriotic War. Not Orwell, however, who remembered the Spanish terror, who was certain that life inside the Soviet Union was brutal, and not just at Nazi hands, and who wanted to make it all known to his own country—a country that had no experience of such horrors.[166]

Animal Farm is the story of what happens on a badly run English farm when a lot of gentle-minded English animals try to be free of the farmer and his men. Orwell knew his *Gulliver's Travels*, and how the Houyhnhnms (who were horses) had the Yahoos (who were human-like) working for them. He also knew the history of the Russian Revolution and Trotsky's *The Revolution Betrayed* (1937). *Animal Farm*, then, is a fable of 'Communism' as 'Animalism', but like all fables, there is virtually no explanation in it. Why did the pigs act badly? Because pigs act badly. Could you ever imagine them acting well? Why did the revolution go wrong? Because revolutions go wrong. It would be impossible to tell the story of a revolution that went right. Orwell said *Animal Farm* was a satire on the Russian Revolution, but it is also against revolutions in general.[167]

Conceived and written sometime between November 1943 and February 1944, just prior to his writing of *The English People*, which was finished in May 1944, *Animal Farm* was not published until August 1945. It was late because at first Orwell could not find a publisher.[168] Gollancz refused it because the story was bitterly anti-Soviet and badly timed. Jonathan Cape refused it for the same reason. An official from the Ministry of Information briefed him against it.[169] Faber also refused. T. S. Eliot wrote to Orwell on behalf of the company congratulating him on a masterpiece; suggesting that he might have considered the impossible (that the pigs act well); but finally explaining that 'its meaning is not acceptable at this moment'.[170] This was the second time that Eliot had turned him down. He had refused *Down and Out in Paris and London* too—though the two of them remained cordial. Collins refused it because at 30,000 words they said it was too short. At a time of paper shortages, this was an odd decision. In the end, Martin Secker and Frederic Warburg took it, with an initial print-run of 4,500 copies. In 1946 the American publishers Harcourt & Brace published 50,000. It was made American Book of the Month (540,000 copies) soon after. Orwell was a well-known author now, and free from money worries.

The jacket flap to *The English People* said: 'The Author of Animal Farm...should need no introduction to English readers.'

With one or two exceptions, the farm animals are a cross between English workers and Russian serfs. There is not much sign of the free-born English down on this farm. No technically minded middle class either. No dirty postcards. No bold Bob Cherry (though possibly a Bunter). No free-spirited Dickens. No folk memory. No military tradition. No aggression. No bull. On the other hand, one can argue over the details, but the main producers, those who are the source of all value that the farm lives by, the eggs and the beef and the wool and the milk and the mutton, including those who provide the power and drive, Boxer and Clover, carthorses of immense strength and gentleness, are close to the people Orwell first met in *The Road to Wigan Pier*, first brought into political focus in *The Lion and the Unicorn*, and first made natural in *The English People*. They are 'The Beasts of England', and in that ordinary 'moral quality which must be vaguely described as decency', they are Orwell's English.[171] The animals make their move on Midsummer Eve. They read *Tit Bits* and the *Daily Mirror*. They drink beer and their leader eats off Crown Derby. At the same time, the animals are oppressed by the pigs, and pigs are animals too. Marx, or 'Old Major', is a prize boar exhibited as 'Willingdon Beauty', while Stalin, or 'Napoleon' (no friend of the English), is a Berkshire.

However, it has to be said, if animal decency is working-class decency, what of animal slowness? Like the Houyhnhnms, the workers are 'dreary beasts' really, and Orwell could not bring himself to give them an independent life in this fable any more than he could in his other works. The animals *need* the pigs. And if they need them, they cannot do without them. But why are the animals (for pigs are animals) deceived by another animal, a prize animal at that? Is it that, although the pigs look like animals—as Yahoos look like humans—they are not animals, not in their outlook, for when the time comes they betray the animals and slaughter them. But if they are not animals (workers), what are they? They are certainly not humans (capitalists), and though they are clever, they are not really intellectual either. Does this make them Orwell's new middle class (origin uncertain)? And if it does, T. S. Eliot was right after all: all the farm needed was more public spirited middle-class pigs to run the show. All metaphors break down under scrutiny, Orwell's not excepted.[172]

Insofar as *Animal Farm* was a story, it was a fairy story. Insofar as it was an allegory, it was a clever match and a great success. But it had no impact on attitudes to the Soviet Union in Britain in 1945.[173] It did, however, signal a turn in the road for Orwell: an English farm turned into a Soviet Gulag? A good intention turned out bad? A socialist turning not quite Tory?

6

Not Quite Tory

Labour man

The last five years of Orwell's life was also the period of Attlee's great reforming Labour government. Elected by a large majority in July 1945, Labour took into public ownership the key industries, including coal and rail, sustained economic growth and full employment, granted independence to India and Pakistan, and introduced the world's first fully comprehensive, publicly funded, national health service. In spite of many domestic problems—huge debts and deficits, low reserves, worn-out industries, imperial overstretch—this was Orwell's revolution made real.[1] At the same time, Labour's foreign secretary Ernest Bevin was encouraging the Americans to put dollar life into the European economy (Marshall Aid), had used British troops against Communists (in Greece), and was the key figure in setting up a new military alliance (the North Atlantic Treaty Organization) that would keep Russian tanks off the North German plain. In 1947 Labour introduced peacetime conscription, the first British government to do so. In 1950 it was obliged to go to war in Korea. It introduced these measures and made these interventions without losing popularity or threatening civil liberties.[2]

Orwell defended this government on almost every count—welfare and public ownership at home, tough-minded anti-Communism abroad—as well he might, for under the circumstances it was just about the best he could hope for. He did not endorse Herbert Morrison's dictum that socialism was as Labour does, but he certainly understood what the home secretary was getting at. In 1949 he assisted the security services with a list of names of writers and other Soviet sympathizers who could 'not be trusted as propagandists' to write well of Britain. His contact reported to her superiors that he had 'expressed his whole-hearted and enthusiastic approval of our aims', but was too ill to write himself. In the event, the Foreign Office found some talented social democrats to do the writing, but (strangely) did not take up Orwell's suggestion that they pay the 2,000 Deutschmarks necessary to translate *Animal Farm* into Russian.[3] Apart from that, there is nothing here that is surprising. Orwell was not alone in giving this government his unflinching support. The whole labour movement went against its instincts and did the same: the TUC, who did not rock the boat; the party conference, who followed its leader; the national executive committee, who did the same; and the 157 standing committees, 306 ad hoc committees, 259 new MPs, and the 1,000 new Labour councillors, who all saw in this administration a government they could trust. That a few Communists were expelled or not allowed to join raised not a ripple of concern.[4] Orwell knew all about 'fifth columnists' from his time in Spain, and indeed had been one himself, it would seem, in his mind at least, in Burma. But when it came to telling the truth as he saw it, he was deadly serious. He liked the BBC because it never tried to censor him, and left it without disagreement or grievance. At the same time, and not entirely in accord with his liking for the truth, he had told the assistant controller in his interview that he understood 'absolutely the need for propaganda ... and stressed his view that in war time discipline in the execution of government policy is essential'—and took the same view in 1949.[5]

Orwell named the highly respected J. B. Priestley as someone the government should not invite to write on its behalf. Although it is difficult to imagine Priestley knowingly writing against his own country in favour of another, it remains the case that his anti-capitalist play *An Inspector Calls* had premiered in Moscow in 1945, and that his immensely incurious *Russian Journey*, published by the 'Writers' Group of the Society for Cultural Relations with the USSR' the following year, had managed to squeeze more political naivety into forty pages than Orwell had managed in a lifetime. Russia is war-weary, but Priestley has never seen such merriment. Russia is hungry, but his table groans with food. The train is late, but the welcoming party waits into the dead of night with flowers and speeches and yet more food ('huge tuck-ins'). He admits there is censorship, but the foreign correspondents had brought it upon themselves. He admits there are restrictions, but Mr and Mrs Priestley go where they please on a tour of Potemkin villages and magic tablecloths. 'These are fine people and I will never willingly say a word to hurt them or the way of life they are creating.'[6] Three years later John

Steinbeck's *Russian Journal* told the same story.[7] No grapes of wrath in Russia. All through the war there had been plenty more lies and distortions in the well-stocked pages of *Soviet News* and *Russia Today*. Through VOKS, the Society for Cultural Ties Abroad, the Soviets had long experience in bringing over, and winning over, well-known progressives from Europe and the United States.[8] As Priestley and Steinbeck ate their way through Russia's regional food reserve, the people had never been so reliant on potatoes.[9] As Priestley and Steinbeck expressed their love of Soviet theatre, the Soviet intelligentsia was being traumatized and the bodies of officials of the Society for Cultural Ties were not long cold.

For all he could sense these horrors, and knew how naive the left could be, Orwell never wavered in his claim that he was a socialist. Socialism was what Labour said it believed in.[10] Socialism was what he said he worked for, why he wrote for *Tribune*, why he was friends with Aneurin Bevan, why he doorstepped for Attlee, and why he supported Labour in government through thick and thin (there was a lot of thin.)[11] But did he *belong* to the left? That is another question. Alongside his lifelong support for socialism there was also his lifelong criticism of socialists, and in this sense at least, Orwell's claim that he was a socialist, in the face of so much evidence that he was not, is as convincing as his protestation that he did not like intellectuals, in the face of so much evidence that he was one himself.[12]

He believed in the inherent equality of people, and the intervention of the state in promoting it.[13] There again, he feared arbitrary, ignorant, and catastrophic interventions in people's lives. In the case of the British Empire or Soviet Union, say, this was clear for all to see—though they were not equivalent interventions.[14] He was a liberal in the sense that he was gratified by the extent to which the British people had been spared the worst abuses of the central state and had been able to retain their own forms of civil life. It is a fact that he was sometimes ignorant of the true nature of their achievement, and did not seem to be aware of its part in an alternative tradition of non-statist English socialism, as he was also seemingly unaware of the degree to which workers themselves were wary of major state interventions. They trusted what worked, and they trusted best their own ways of making it work.[15] Nevertheless, after 1940, and in accord with English liberal traditions in the wide sense, the war taught Orwell, as it taught the labour movement generally, that major state interventions could work. He agreed with Arthur Koestler that all animals are equal and all revolutions are failures, but he added: 'they are not all the same failures.'[16]

After a brief flirtation, as we have seen, with the Independent Labour Party, he supported the Labour party for the rest of his life. Indeed, only days after receiving his ILP membership card he declared, in 'Why I Join the ILP', that his 'most earnest hope' was 'that the Labour Party will win a clear majority in the next General Election'.[17] Yet in the same article he managed to damn Labour for its 'temptation to fling every principle overboard in order to prepare for an imperialist war', just as he managed to write *The Road to Wigan Pier* with hardly a mention of the party at all or of the trade unions, just as he managed to make almost nothing of party policy on foreign or domestic affairs until *The Lion and the Unicorn* in 1941—and then only fleetingly. But once war began and he became immediately hostile to views he held only yesterday, Labour grew increasingly real to him. Partly this was a matter of policy. Labour promised The English Road to Socialism. But Orwell was never one for too much policy. In one of his rare forays into what he called 'realizable policy' he had once managed to propose a narrowing of incomes that was in fact a widening.[18] Nor did he ever find it in his heart to write at length about the National Health Service or the National Coal Board— no matter how hard Bevan had to wheedle and (miners' leader) Will Lawther had to bellow to get these institutions built.[19] For Orwell, the true importance of Labour was its instincts and connections rather than its plans—more about what it knew best than what it could mark on a board.

From its foundation in 1900, the thick organic cord of the trade unions had saved Labour intellectuals and careerists from outright disassociation from the lives of the people.[20] Some of these unions not only paid the piper, they called the tune.[21] At the Labour party conference at Scarborough in 1947 the National Union of Mineworkers treated government ministers to a day out at Billy Butlin's holiday camp. Hugh Gaitskell recalled how everybody in the party said they liked it, but 'everybody agreed they would not go...' on their own account.[22] In other words, this was a party where ministers and MPs were answerable to those they represented in a relationship that was not so much democratic as fraternal. The old industrial working class—or at least its male half—had organized itself into tightly bound circles that connected trade with trade union, trade union with club and lodge, club and lodge with Friday night and Saturday morning, and Saturday night and Sunday morning with beer and skittles and football. To enter this world you did not need a vote (though once inside you would be given many), you needed a skill, a job, and a union card. It was a diminishing world (as a proportion of the total work-force the industrial working class had fallen from 75 per cent in 1911 to 65 per cent in 1951) but the war had made it stronger, and after the war full employment, female second incomes, rising trade-union membership, and universal state welfare provision was about to ensure that this was a world that had never had it so good, *or* so proletarian.

In the 1950s sociologists would come and look and declare the workers 'affluent'; that they were becoming *embourgeoisified*. But becoming *bourgeois* had nothing to do with it. This generation of workers did not want to get out of the working class but, having grown up in the insecurity of the 1930s, and having defeated Fascism in the 1940s, they wanted some security in a system they knew to be inherently unstable. They wanted steady work, better health, a clean home, a good suit, paid annual leave, children who had the chance to 'get on', and a society that respected who they were and what they needed. Their wives wanted roughly the same, plus less dirt. For them, socialism was not a theory but a way of life. They had tamed an Industrial Revolution and learned to live with free markets. They knew each other because they were obliged to know each other. When the women mustered to take control of the streets, they had knowledge of those streets. When the men's branch meeting broke up they declared themselves 'Upstanding Worthy Brothers' not just because they knew each other, and each other's fathers, but because the rule-book said they were. Labour MPs, if they were going to be Labour MPs, had to pay attention to this world and pretend to be part of it. Sometimes, while at party conferences, this involved spending precious time at holiday camps. There was even a chance, though an ever slimmer chance, that in this party the minister and the worker could be the same person. Ernest Bevin, Nye Bevan, and Herbert Morrison, all key figures in the cabinet, all came from working-class homes. Though they were the only ones who did.[23]

Labour in government was the best Orwell could hope for—a socially minded party with *mass* support and local ties. Margaret Cole estimated in 1945 that 150 out of 394 Labour MPs were working-class, including eight housewives and twenty-three Cooperative and

119 trade-union-sponsored members. But working-class support did not necessarily imply equal support for central planning and widespread state interventionism. The poet Stephen Spender looked forward in 1945 to a new patriotism built on small neighbourhoods. The home secretary agreed, or said he did.[24] It was true that Attlee (deputy prime minister), Bevin (minister of labour), Morrison (home secretary), and Dalton (Board of Trade) had all served effectively on the Cabinet Reconstruction Committee. It was also true that planning was thought necessary in 1945 in a way that had not been thought necessary in 1935. But planning, if it was going to be popular, had to stay in touch with the trade unions' inalienable right, as they saw it, to free collective bargaining.[25] As such, we can hardly assume that planning (however defined)[26] won easy votes. By 1947 it was deemed impossible anyway. The same was true of all forms of political collectivism. Collectivist systems had been practised all through the war, but it is impossible to say to what extent evacuation, rationing, rationalization, queuing, conscription, army education, and all the rest helped Labour in any direct way. When it came to winning votes, the collectivist experience can be argued both ways.[27]

Orwell's support for Labour was to do with what it stood for, which was plain enough, and what it did, which could only be judged going forward. Indian independence, full employment, public ownership, and the making of what people began to call a welfare state by national insurance would have been huge achievements by any government's standards, let alone a bankrupt one.[28] Bevin's undeceived anti-Communist foreign policy, too, suited Orwell. He had his criticisms though. In spite of a huge popular mandate, the government made no move on the constitution, the public schools, the universities, the very rich, the Established Church, or the Monarchy—and Orwell thought it should have done.[29] All things considered, though, he saw that these institutions had offered Labour no ostensible obstruction, and he knew that Labour people valued their traditions and that too much interference with what might be seen, however misguidedly, as the expression of those traditions could lose the government their trust. In the event they held that trust. Most people who voted Labour in 1945 did so again in 1950. The swing against them was only 3 per cent. If Labour had fought on the same constituency boundaries it had fought on in 1945 it would have won with a majority of sixty seats. The left politicization of the British people that had started in 1940 lasted at least ten years.

Orwell was a Labour man, then, first because he saw it as a responsible party, attuned to real lives rather than ideological postures, and second because it was a party of workers and intellectuals where the workers carried more weight. Herbert Morrison might have gone about the Festival of Britain site 'with his customary clutch of middle-class progressive intellectuals' calling for a modern aesthetic,[30] but back at the coal-face Labour had a country to run, and priorities to make. Above all, it had to prove itself better than the Conservatives—better indeed than epochs of upper-class rulers. In a weird reversal of history, the health secretary told the Durham Miners' Gala in 1948 that, as *they* were the ruling class now, they had to work harder. Orwell agreed. Political responsibility was the test of true socialism.[31] No one can doubt Bevan's and Orwell's commitment to working-class people, but the call for them to be more responsible was the definitive middle-class call too.[32]

Orwell could find a man like Bevan only in the Labour party. Both men were mavericks interested in more than politics, and contrarians who liked to squeeze the other side just to see how hard it would squeal. But they had been brought up in different worlds. Bevan was chairman of the biggest miners' lodge in South Wales at the same age as Orwell was playing the fool at Eton. In Orwell's eyes the Welshman had all the virtues of a socialist politician. He was a worker and an intellectual. He was a democrat but not a populist. He was a flashing left-winger but not a Communist. He fought the class war but was not embittered by it. And as the whole country knew from his sharp parliamentary exchanges with Churchill, for all his humour 'Nye' had that bit of maleficence in him which every leader must have. But he was practical and responsible too, and cultured. What more could Orwell want from a politician? In his profile of Bevan for the *Observer*, note the last point:

> Bevan thinks and feels as a working man. He knows how the scales are
> weighted against anyone with less than £5 a week...But he is remarkably
> free—some of his adversaries would say dangerously free—from any feeling
> of personal grievance against society... [and] he does not have the suspicion
> of 'cleverness' and anaesthesia to the arts which are generally regarded as
> the mark of a practical man. Those who have worked with him [and
> Orwell had] in a journalistic capacity have remarked with pleasure and

astonishment that here at last is a politician who knows that literature exists and will even hold up work for five minutes to discuss a point of style.[33]

Orwell supported Labour in office. At the same time, he stayed wary of policy pedants, well-bred socialists, utopian cranks, and state rationalists—Fabian, Wellsian, Marxist, technocratic, or ministerial, and especially those few who found their home in the Labour party but who owed their allegiance elsewhere.[34] He was not fussy who he huffed. In 1941 he went before the Fabians, of all people, to tell them how stupid intellectuals could be. He said they were people who made a career out of discontent.[35] In 1944 he picked on H. G. Wells's concept of world government as banal. 'It is startling to be told in 1944 the "the world is now one". One might as well say that the world is now flat.'[36] In 1948 his 'Writers and Leviathan' essay delivered a long warning blast against the foggy dangers of socialism, arguing that it was not good at seeing the world as it was.[37]

By the time he completed *Nineteen Eighty-Four* in December 1948 Orwell had spent three years being impressed by ideas that were intended to operate as a check on socialist ideas—not all of them anti-socialist ideas exactly, but certainly ideas which, if driven hard enough, could be seen that way. Among the writers receiving Orwell's attention in these years were five European dissident conservatives: Friedrich von Hayek, Joseph Conrad, John Plamenatz, Arthur Koestler, and Victor Serge; one former American Trotskyite turned conservative, James Burnham; and E. I. Zamyatin (1884–1937), a Russian who had written *We*, an early science-fiction novel on the surveillance state.[38] Orwell did not agree with them all, as such, but he saw their objections to socialism as not just 'family' differences rather than fundamental challenges to the central socialist idea that who informs the party controls the state, and who controls the state controls the property that controls the people. Hayek and his fellow exiles (Mises, Schumpeter, Popper, Drucker) took the argument one step further by arguing that all this control would inevitably fail, and that failure would lead to Fascism, as it had in their native Austria. Always alive to the threat of totalitarianism, late in 1945 Orwell wrote a retrospect on Jack London as a visionary of iron heels and dictators.[39]

At the same time as he was being impressed by liberal conservatives, there were the socialists and semi-socialists whom Orwell checked hard

(J. D. Bernal, Jean-Paul Sartre, and Oscar Wilde), and anti-socialists he perhaps did not check hard enough, including a very equivocal review of T. S. Eliot's *Notes Towards the Definition of Culture*, a very positive review of Churchill's *Finest Hour*, and a very affectionate review of George Gissing.[40] We find in his papers a set of notes towards a critical but ultimately warm and considerate (if unfinished) review of the novels of Evelyn Waugh. As always, it was the little worlds Orwell liked best. He used to not like the semicolon; but here it is listing Waugh's kindest reveries.

> ... the 'wet, bird-haunted lawns' and the walled garden with its crucified pear trees; the large untidy porch with its litter of raincoats, waders, landing nets and croquet mallets; the plastery smell of the flagged passage leading to the gun room; the estate map on the library wall; the case of stuffed birds over the stair case.[41]

Orwell was beginning to forgive the right more than the left. His literary notebook for 1949 contains a long quotation from Waugh summing up his political philosophy which begins: 'I believe that man is, by nature, an exile ... and will never be self-sufficient or complete on this earth,' followed by all sorts of reasons why governments must not overreach themselves in changing a human nature that is implacably unchangeable and a human society that is invariably unequal. We cannot know how Orwell, lying in his sanatorium bed, intended to deal with this. Waugh was a Roman Catholic who approved of capitalism. They should have been on clean different sides, but Orwell, ever the rebel, shifts the meaning of the sides: 'It is nonsense to pretend, for instance, that at this date there is something daring and original in proclaiming yourself an anarchist, an atheist, a pacifist [or a homosexual, he says later] ... The daring thing, or at any rate the unfashionable thing, is to believe in God or to approve of the capitalist system.' More predictable perhaps was a big thumbs-up for Robert Tressell's *The Ragged Trousered Philanthropists*, the classic socialist novel published in 1914, and a big thumbs-down for Ezra Pound, even though a panel of distinguished American intellectuals had awarded him a literary prize.[42] Orwell's 1945 'Notes on Nationalism' suggested that nationalists shared the same intellectual obsessions as doctrinaire Communists and Catholics, and 'if one follows up this train of thought, one is in danger of being led into a species of Conservatism, or political quietism'.[43] Not that Orwell did intend following this train of thought,

PLATE I Orwell in imperial mode, well wrapped up, Easton Cliff, Reydon, Suffolk, 1934. He spent a good part of that year at his parents' home in Southwold recuperating from pneumonia—where he wrote *A Clergyman's Daughter*.

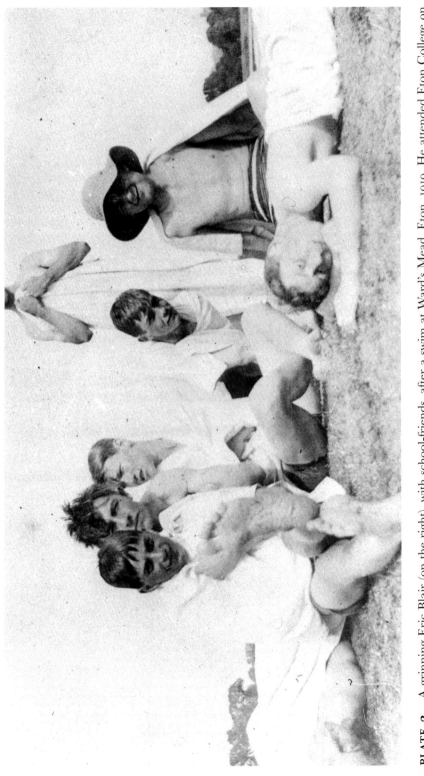

PLATE 2 A grinning Eric Blair (on the right), with school-friends, after a swim at Ward's Mead, Eton, 1919. He attended Eton College on a scholarship from May 1917 to December 1921. On finding a role for himself as a rebel and intellectual in a caste of rebels and intellectuals, Orwell was happier at Eton than he had been at prep school.

PLATE 3 Eric having fun on South Green, Southwold, in the summer of 1922—just before going to Burma.

PLATE 4   Thin khaki line: third from the left, back row, Blair in training at the Police Academy, Mandalay, Burma, 1923. He served in the Indian Imperial Police from October 1922 to December 1927.

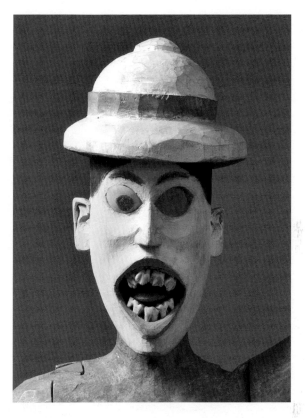

PLATE 5 Doll's head, nineteenth-century. We know a great deal of what British colonists thought of colonized people, but here is an example of what the Nikobar Islanders, Indonesia, thought of the colonists. Orwell remarked that out 'East' the white man grows an imperial mask to hide his face, and save it.

PLATE 6 Book Lover's Corner, 1, South End Road, Hampstead, where Orwell worked as a part-time assistant from October 1934 to January 1936. During this period he found a circle of like-minded friends and wrote *Keep the Aspidistra Flying*.

PLATE 7   Eileen Blair (née O'Shaughnessy), travel-visa photograph, French Morocco, 1938. She met Orwell at a party in Hampstead in March 1935 and married him in June 1936.

PLATE 8　Miner at work: Ashington Coal Company official photograph, 1930.

PLATE 9   The miner's view of the miner at work: Oliver Kilbourn, *Coal Face Drawers* (1950), oil on fibreboard.

PLATE 10 The Wigan Orwell did not show: a young cotton worker pleased to have her picture taken, Eckersley's Mill (*Picture Post*, 11 November 1939).

PLATE 11 Second anniversary of the Catalonian Revolution, Barcelona, 6 October 1936—200,000 people take to the streets to celebrate the 1934 proclamation of a Catalan state, including the the Partido Obrero de Unificacion Marxista (POUM).

PLATE 12   POUM militiamen on the Aragon front—Orwell second from the left, 1937.

PLATE 13   Ilford, Essex, April 1936: the raw suburban world of George Bowling, anti-hero of *Coming Up for Air* (1939).

PLATE 14 Eileen holding her nephew Laurence, London 1939. She was particularly close to her brother, Capt. Laurence O' Shaughnessy, killed with the Royal Army Medical Corps, Dunkirk, June 1940.

PLATE 15 Orwell looking relaxed with comrades of the St John's Wood Company of the Home Guard, May 1940–November 1943. He is back row on the right.

PLATE 16 & 17 (*opposite*)
London at war and London in peace—
Dig For Victory, or Allotments in the Park (1941)
and *Victory Day, Richmond Park* (1945), two
paintings by Mary Kent Harrison, oil on
canvas; a version of the second was well
chosen for Orwell's *The English People* (1947).

PLATE 17

PLATE 18   Sonia Orwell, 1950.

of course. In 1947 he completed his school memoir 'Such, Such Were the Joys', which had nothing to say about socialist education but plenty to say about class inequality (against the right) and total institutions (against the left). Least of St Cyprian's iniquities, it seems, was its worship of money. Far worse was its abuse of power, where little boys were so crushed they loved their abusers.[44]

In 1948, coming to the end of a post-war period where Orwell the Labour man seemed to find more to rue than to hope for, we find him critical of Britain's left-wing newspapers, and in a very low-key assessment of 'The Labour Government After Three Years' his message to Attlee was that the worst was yet to come. It might seem to some that the worst had already been. The year 1946–7 had been terrible. The worst winter on record had turned into a coal crisis, the coal crisis into a political crisis, and all capped by a full-blown sterling crisis in the summer. With Britain's industry worn out and her independence compromised, the best Orwell could do was to advise that the best Labour could do was find a third way between capitalism and Communism and hang on.[45] Which was not very different from saying that the best Labour could do was hang on. In August 1949 the decision was taken to devalue the currency. In the face of all this, only *Tribune* won Orwell's plaudits. The rest of the left-wing press he blamed for their lack of imagination and pro-Soviet opportunism: *The Daily Herald* ('dull'), *Reynold's News* ('strong Communist influence'), the *New Statesman and Nation* ('uncritically Russophile'), and the *Daily Worker* ('propaganda sheet').[46] He hardly noticed that Labour ministers were increasingly looking west, not east. Relations with Washington were warm and about to get warmer. Without dollar aid, Labour's welfare programme could not have been carried out. *With* dollar aid, Britain was expected to toe the American line on foreign policy.[47] But Orwell was even less interested in relations with American politicians than he was in relations with American dime novelists. He was a literature and liberty man at heart—and he believed most of that resided in England.

After *Animal Farm* it is hard to ignore Fred Warburg's judgement on *Nineteen Eighty-Four* as an attack on 'Socialism and socialist parties in general'—'a final breach'. Orwell was a Labour man not because of public ownership, which he hardly mentioned,[48] but because Labour enjoyed an organic connection with the British working class. The ruling party of *Nineteen Eighty-Four*, by contrast, is called *Ingsoc*, or 'English

Socialism', and they have no organic connection with anybody, not even with themselves. It is possible to see in Ingsoc not only Lenin's and Stalin's Russian road to socialism, but also something of Sidney and Beatrice Webb's English road as well.[49] The Fabians called their administrative socialist elite 'brainworkers'. In *Animal Farm* Orwell called them pigs.

Godless Protestant

He continued to see himself as someone who belonged to the left. He was involved in the Freedom Defence Committee from its foundation in 1945—a left forum ranging in membership from Bertrand Russell to Benjamin Britten. At the more vital end of the range of Orwell's immediate post-war duties, it is no surprise to see young Richard, his adopted son and dearest responsibility, parked with the Whiteways Anarchist Commune at Cranham in Gloucestershire when he was taken there to visit his father in the sanatorium in June 1949. Nevertheless, whatever his personal tastes, in his writing Orwell certainly over-identified intellectuals with the left, the left with London, London with the middle class, and the middle-class London left with the suburban fringe, the political fringe, the cranky fringe, the state-worshipping, foreign tastes, and French-restaurant fringe ... and so on. He was not fair and did not always get it right. It turns out they preferred Italian.[50]

On the other hand, insofar as he identified socialism with democracy, with improving ordinary lives, with the land and landscape, with useful labour, with telling the truth and defending what works and husbanding social capital to make it work, and with gentleness and civilization and Woolworth's roses for *all* the people, not just the few, then he was on safer ground.[51] The British had spent the war seeing themselves at the pictures, and the way Humphrey Jennings and Harry Watt, Sidney Gilliat and Frank Launder, Noel Coward and David Lean had shown them was in little bands—fire-crews, destroyer crews, ambulance stations, shop-floors, and parish councils.[52] The hard formulaic language of the political left—its short-cut talk of 'power' and 'process', 'substructure' and 'superstructure', 'mass' and 'movement'—was impersonal, unpeopled, and heading nowhere anyone wanted to be.[53]

In 1940–1 Orwell too tried to reach out to the English people as they actually were, closer to the British nation-state as it actually functioned.

He averred that if it ever came to it, an English revolution would stay in touch with England's history and identity. The judges, in other words, would keep their wigs on. He allowed that income differentials would have to be drastically reduced, major industries nationalized, the Empire dismantled, the public schools thrown open, and government organized in the interests of the majority, but that this new regime, for all its search for fairness, would 'still bear all over it the unmistakable marks' of the old.[54] He restated his commitment to this in 1946 by writing against Jonathan Swift's 'inability to believe that...ordinary life on the solid earth...could be made worth living'. Later, as we have seen, he criticized Labour for not making its revolution sweeping enough by not making it ordinary enough.[55]

This was as close to the liberal view of English history as a Labour man was likely to get. All talk of bloody revolution aside, Orwell took the view that not only were the law and the constitution central to English liberty, and liberty to Englishness, but that it was unfolding all the time, a condition which he saw—and liberal constitutionalists saw—as a settled condition on the one hand and a progressive movement towards more self-realization on the other.[56] Old liberalism had once regarded every portion of power taken away from the state as a portion of liberty gained by the nation. The whole of English progress, therefore, could be measured out in portions of the state rolled back, and portions of the people rolled out, and although this was liberalism, not anarchism, it was unusual compared to other nations in that it was a mainstream politics that tied itself to the state *while remaining sceptical of it.*[57] In this account, even English climate and geography were liberal, which is to say, temperate and low-lying, not centralized, open to all the people. England had often been seen as a garden and its mood as the weather—changeable, or to put it another way, diverse.[58] English history, meanwhile, was a liberal pageant. Magna Carta, Simon de Montfort, Common Law, Tudor Reformation, Civil War, Glorious Revolution, Whig Liberty, Great Reform Act, Free Trade, Cheap Bread, Nonconformist Conscience, Mother of Parliaments, Women's Suffrage—all were seen as milestones on the march towards liberty, against the state, towards the people. New Liberalism, on the other hand, forming at around the time young Eric Blair was at prep school, recognized, as Orwell came to recognize, that state power could not only coerce you, it could also free you. As Hobhouse put it in 1911, for liberals the 'first point of attack is arbitrary government' and the second is inequality—for 'liberty without equality is a name of noble sound and squalid result'.[59]

Orwell went with this, alongside just about every sensible little liberal, labour, and tory supporter in the land, as a particularly English political position: how to capture the state and make it work for you in expanding your liberty, but at the same time not for a minute believing that your liberty depended on it. He went with this as someone liberal by profession,[60] as he went with it in the associated idea that England had the liberal, civil traditions that had allowed it all to happen. In an 1883 critique of the American socialist Henry George, Arnold Toynbee made the case for English liberalism. To the student of Orwell, Toynbee's arguments are entirely familiar.[61] The English people enjoy free institutions. The ruling class is not entirely corrupt. Class war has been avoided. National unity must be recovered. We must fight for our liberty. England will prevail. 'Do remember of what nation you are speaking in the case of England', Toynbee reminded the American.

Liberalism, then, advocated progress at the same time as it celebrated actually existing Englishness. As Stubbs famously said in his *Constitutional History* (for all good liberals, constitutional history *was* English history), no matter what the changes, 'the continuity of life...never fails'.[62] Ernest Barker's 1948 description of an ordinary English urban crowd captured this perfectly. The irrational crowd had been seen as a dark and threatening aspect of the rise of the modern city. But Barker assured the most urban nation in the world that this was not the case. For in England we have the crowd that governs itself:

> its members are not lost in the mass: they polish, through constant attrition, new facets of individuality. The English urban crowd, in particular, may justly be said to have developed from its own experience and its own good sense, a species of self-discipline and a tactic of 'fitting in' neatly on a little space. You seldom feel unsafe in a London crowd: you know in your heart that it is experienced...A new situation will find a new response: queues will form...there will be some bad manners and a little thrusting, but the institution (for the queue is of that order) will be made to work.[63]

Those who start out recognizing a country as it is before considering how it might grow into more of the same presume a living tradition. In Orwell's own time, Herbert Butterfield, eminent Professor of Modern History at Cambridge, went from attacking the living tradition as it applied in peace (*The Whig Interpretation of History*, 1931) to praising it as it applied in war (*The Englishman and his History*, 1944). England, Butter-field said, had '*resumed* contact with her traditions', because 'in time of danger it was a good thing not to lose touch with the rest of the convoy'.[64] For him, this was a living tradition so liberal that it denied the Tories an Englishness of their own. They had been forced to find their story abroad in the British Empire instead, but even there they found them-selves sitting in a pool of liberal myths brought to the brim with the prospect of imperial liberty too: 'Now, however, even this [imperial] structure of the history of England is a Tory alternative no more... only in the shock of 1940 did we realize to what degree the British Empire had become an organization for the purpose of liberty.'[65]

There was some of this in Orwell, but not too much. For all his belief in a living tradition, and for all his commitment to law, liberty, free speech, and the like, Orwell was not really a liberal. He admitted that all independent writers required free speech. Like the great liberal histo-rian J. R. Green, author of the best-selling (half-a-million copies) *Short History of the English People* (1874), he also believed that common liberty demanded a common tongue, and sought to write in that tongue.[66] But he was not deceived by any loose talk on liberty. He had seen coolies kicked in India and tramps leaning on the rope in London. He had seen the rich gorge themselves at the Ritz, and he knew what a 'death stop-page' was in Wigan. He knew, in other words, that liberty without equal-ity was meagre fare, showed no interest in its philosophical forms or its constitutional history, and kept his knowledge of liberal economics to rudimentary levels. PPE, for him, was a practical subject, not an Oxford one. He well understood what Arnold Toynbee meant when he apolo-gized to the industrial working class for all that had been inflicted on them, and shared some of that 'class consciousness of sin' that suffused Toynbee's generation.[67] But this was what Chesterton had called his 'ordinary disgust'; no need for self-mortification. Orwell was not inter-ested in the Whitechapel curate and his New Liberal dons. T. H. Green, Bernard Bosanquet, and L. T. Hobhouse all passed him by; so did a future generation of New Liberals led by John Maynard Keynes. Nor does he seem to have noticed the Hammonds' brilliant New Liberal histories until very late in the day.[68] In 1945, along with half of the country, he agreed that markets should be regulated, fiscal policies should be redistributive, and major industries should be brought into public control, but apart from calling Dickens a freethinking liberal and thinking of himself when he said so, Orwell made no pretence at being liberal or a Liberal or a New Liberal. He reviewed Hayek's *The Road to Serfdom* in 1944 without mentioning the price mechanism.[69] It is true he did not trust the central state. His message was the same as Acton's— 'power tends to corrupt and absolute power corrupts absolutely'. But he did not trust *laissez faire* capitalism either. Individuals he believed in. Individualism he did not. Reason he believed in. Rationalism he did not. He was more interested in deeper collective experiences.[70] None of Orwell's political beliefs were incompatible with being a liberal.[71] But that did not make him one.

Except, that is, in his enduring belief in a sort of godless Protestantism. Orwell was baptized, confirmed, married, married again, and remembered and buried according to the rites of the Church of England. His wife had been head girl at an Anglican girls' school. There had been clergymen in the family. He knew he had TB for sure from 1938 onwards, so in his case the clock was always ticking. Yet he was patchy on religion. Ardent at times, indifferent at other times, he never gave it his sustained attention.[72] We might say that he was a Protestant like Jane Eyre was a Protestant. That is, he was a Protestant in his belief that as an individual he had 'as much soul as you, and full as much heart', and in the knowledge that it is not through custom or convention that she speaks, but freely, through the spirit: 'it is my spirit that addresses your spirit.'[73]

Orwell was a Protestant *positively* in the way he praised its influence on the novel ('practically a Protestant form of art...product of the free mind, the autonomous individual')[74] and in his natural talent for wrangling with all tests and corporations. He nursed a high regard for old English Dissent and admired the seventeenth-century pamphleteers for their 'one-man show' against the state. He started each of his novels in a dissident spirit and ended them having searched for new life in a way Protestants called salvation. Orwell's protagonists ask what should they do to be saved.[75]

He was a Protestant *negatively* in his vendetta against Catholic intellectuals, and in the way he worked his way back against Calvinist precepts of salvation in order to conclude that it is not a person's inner beliefs that matter but how they live together in the faith. Theology is a subject without a fact and not, therefore, the sort of subject to catch Orwell's attention. At the same time, the Church of England was a grand fact for all to see and hear. *Hymns Ancient and Modern* outsold every Dickens and all Tennyson. Adam Bede goes to work singing hymns, not folk-songs.[76] Dorothy Hare in *A Clergyman's Daughter* lives her days in torment over whether she does or does not believe, but in the end, like nearly all the world's believers, she comes to see that her unbelief is a small thing in comparison with the broad religious tradition that flows beneath her—the pastoral, communal, ritual, meditational, and confessional aspects of belonging to the church. Evelyn Waugh would speak seriously to Orwell about the falsity of a faith without a theology, but for Dorothy it is more an everyday question of small things—of having to share a communion cup with old ladies, for instance—not a once-and-for-all question of big things.[77] At least it saves Dorothy from the pointlessness of worrying whether there is a God or not. Orwell invokes a living religious tradition in order to save the clergyman's daughter from her individuated self. She is not alone. All members of the Anglican Communion are the same under the skin, he says, whatever they think:

> Beliefs change, thoughts change, but there is some inner part of the soul that does not change. Faith vanishes, but the need for faith remains the same as before . . . that faith and no faith are very much the same provided that one is doing what is customary, useful and acceptable. She could not formulate these thoughts as yet, she could only live them. Much later, perhaps, she would formulate them and draw comfort from them.[78]

Orwell did not go to church or believe in God, but, without going so far as Parson Thwackum,[79] he liked the Church of England through family ties and friendships; knew its Bible, hymnody, and Book of Common Prayer from school and college and personal affection; saw the Reformation in general as a war against privilege and ignorance; admired the Puritans as dissenting English, and published some of their literature; and was very quick to spot the passing of Protestant England in his own day and the problems that would stem from that—not least the demise of the freethinking individual.[80] One can hold Protestantism responsible for the demise of the confessional state and the rise of the freethinking individual—even the freethinking, non-believing individual.[81] But the harder part, Orwell thought, was how to remain religious if you do not believe in God. Harder still, he wondered, was how to prevent the religious deficit from being turned to account in institutions and ideologies far more dangerous and ill-willed than the Church. On occasion we find

Orwell describing this as 'the real problem' of his age.[82] Whether it was or not, it was certainly characteristic of him to turn his own freethinking to face the dangers of freethinking. Rather than see a godless universe as a problem for the godly, Orwell turned it into a problem for the godless.[83]

He was, then, an intellectual who did not like intellectuals, a socialist who did not trust the state, a writer of the left who found it easier to forgive writers of the right, a liberal who was against free markets, a Protestant who did not believe in God even if he believed in religion, and a dissenter who believed in Dissent even if it was only to enjoy the right to dissent from it. What was he *really*? Was he a Tory?

Not quite Tory

Not quite, but nearly. There are some strong arguments to be made for Orwell's conservatism. First, as we have seen, he liked to let it be known that he was a 'Tory Anarchist', particularly if he thought there were people around who might be upset by the idea.[84] Second, there are those who credit him with the invention of some powerful conservative myths about the stability and traditions of post-war England.[85] Third, there are those who see him as an out-and-out 1950s Cold War warrior—and when it is pointed out that Orwell died before the Cold War really began, there are others who blame him not only for his persistent anti-Communism but for the fact that he meant it.[86] Fourth, and most perceptively perhaps, there are those who see him as the sworn enemy of most socialisms, especially those of Eastern Europe and the Soviet Union.[87] Fifth, it is not difficult to make links with Orwell and what some scholars have called 'conservative modernity'. For instance, he is close to Alison Light's inter-war conservative feminists in his preference for 'an Englishness at once less imperial and…more domestic and private'.[88] It is true he was always committed, in his own way, to the Empire (and far more interested in it than the Constitution),[89] but in his lexicon the British Empire is always a knowable corner, a village or a club or a custom, and never that sudden, uncontrollable high-idealistic wind that one found in the jingoistic books and pamphlets of his day. In his taste for the familar and everyday, there are ways in which Orwell's writing reflects not only conservative tastes but also the documentary movement in film and literature, and Post-Impressionism's desire to make 'a new and definite reality' out of art.[90]

Many writers could come under some or all of these conservative outlooks. But while official Conservative party supporters wrote ponderously and ideologically in favour of things that were not supposed to be ponderous or ideological, Orwell wrote swiftly and originally; and while Conservatives wrote blankly in favour of the known and the familiar, Orwell wrote with colour and tone. The essay form helped. Dr Johnson's *Dictionary* called 'the essay' 'a loose sally of the mind', and Orwell sallied forth as he pleased.[91] For all that, you can thrust your arm into any bran-tub of Conservative Party Central Office thinking from the 1930s onwards and come out with some of Orwell's key political principles.[92] He too was against ideology and dogma; he too preferred to think in terms of dispositions rather than theories; he too liked to mix his thinking, not minding contradiction; he too believed in England for all its faults, and on occasion wrote about Socialism as the enemy.[93] In *The Lion and the Unicorn* Orwell had argued in favour of revolution as part of the national identity. But so had Mosley and the Liberal party for that matter.[94] Of course, he had many sharp differences with the Conservative party. He was not interested in national institutions, for instance, or sport or business, or his own career, and he wanted to stand with the people, not just talk down to them. He could never have written a book called *I Lived in a Slum,* or a sentence that read 'after my stay...as a slum-dweller I returned to the neighbourhood as myself'.[95] Even so, it is difficult to overlook the fact that those who knew him best, as a man and a writer, were convinced that he was possessed of a conservative temperament underlying a radicalism which could be described as Tory. Richard Rees knew him from Eton and from his first days at *The Adelphi.* They stayed friends all Orwell's life, and good enough friends at that to survive Orwell's depiction of Rees as Ravelston in *Keep the Aspidistra Flying.* Rees showed that Orwell was not only instinctively anti-authority and anti-orthodox, but for three years he was an anarchist. All this is just by way of Rees saying how radical Tories could be when driven to it. Nineteenth-century English Radicals knew one of the most famous Tories of them all, William Blackstone, off by heart.[96]

Rees starts by quoting Orwell on Swift ('driven into a sort of perverse Toryism by the follies of the progressive party') and then, in a century of what he calls 'insane theories', reveals a deeply conflicted man suspicious of extremes, searching for balance, believing in duty, and willing to upend all of these tendencies in order to save any one of them. One can sum Rees's Orwell up in a single quotation from Burke—'It is ordained in the eternal constitution of things that men of intemperate minds cannot be free. Their passions forge their fetters.'[97] 'Orwell' resembled Burke in defence of old England from French invaders, just as he resembled him in defence of old Ireland from English invaders: the pluralism of national cultures is to be respected. After Burke, any number of counter-revolutionary radicals can be found in an English tradition of defending the lives of the poor from their Industrial Revolutionary masters—including Wordsworth, Southey, Ruskin, and not least Richard Oastler ('King of the Factory Children'), Charlotte Brontë ('I approve nothing utopian. Look Life in its iron face'), and William Cobbett. Orwell had given up on seeing socialism as a set of correlates and had come to see it as the life of the people as applied to the life of the nation. Such was his taste for life over politics, Rees declared him 'meta-political'—'not a political writer at all'.[98] Orwell's enemy is never some dim equation about 'the capitalist system', or those across the floor of the House of Commons. It is more Cobbett's 'Old Corruption', a spider's web of moneygrubbers and nepotists spinning lies off the backs of the people.[99] With Orwell, as with the radical Tory tradition as a whole, the real party is the country party, which for him was Labour, not the court party, and real politics lies not with Whig politicians (however defined) but the people. The final aim, of course, is the representation of the English people free from mediators and, according to Milton as quoted by Orwell, free 'by *the known* rules of ancient liberty'.[100]

George Woodcock's *The Crystal Spirit* was published in 1967. He too had been a close friend, and he too recalled Orwell's temperament more readily than he recalled his politics—a flat stuffed with things, a man and his likes, a man on the bus, a man sitting down to tea, a man rolling his own cigarettes, a man in ordinary conversation one week only to turn it into literature the next. Woodcock noticed Orwell's avoidance of grand plans and holy saints.[101] He sought out instead what was small or ephemeral (books, conversations, neighbourhoods, firesides, cosy snugs, bits of the past), including the smaller, cultural understanding of things which he felt he knew well—the significance of people with dirty hands, for instance, or 'nancy' poets, or tobacconists in their kiosks.[102] Orwell's 1945 *Observer* articles attest to this. He writes about war-torn Europe well enough, but without conviction.[103] He was happiest not writing to order, and he was at his best writing about what he knew already, or had taken pains to find out, and of course he was without peer in the art of synecdoche. England was always the place he came back to. After Burma ('one sniff of English air decided me'); after Spain ('And then England...'); after Marrakech ('the beer is bitterer, the coins are heavier'); after Europe and after anywhere, in fact—back to where the ordinary patterns of life applied: the common decencies, the quick marks of recognition.[104] 'In all but name', Woodcock said, 'this point of view is of course conservative, more truly conservative, indeed, than the policies of most Conservative parties.'[105]

In the beginning Orwell did not have much of an Englishness to believe in. In the 1940s, however, he redefined Englishness for a generation, turning English socialism from something you lived under into something that underpinned how you lived. Against those who were ashamed of England, and on behalf of those whose opinions were never canvassed anyway, Orwell advocated an Englishness that was *socialist* in that it defended the poor, *liberal* in that it looked for liberty, and *Tory* in that it could take in the other two and believe in Englishness just the same. Socialists had universal truth and justice on their side. Liberals had universal truth and liberty. Tories had the British nation-state: not universal, not especially open to comparison, and not even always admirable, but very particular, and very accountable.[106]

Above all, Orwell turned his face against political universalism (including Roman Catholicism) and put his trust in the English people, whom he saw as conservative in their custody of a way of life they themselves had made. He may have been right. In his own day, in a life marked by insecurity, the British worker was revealed as a realist, someone who distrusted ideas that did not accord with his own local powers or experience. In the period following Orwell's death the British industrial working class would be provoked into expending all their powers, and testing all their experience, in trying to defend that life from annihilation. That they fought not in the name of revolution, still less in the name of Communism or any other political ideology, accorded with Orwell's view. So did their essentially conservative (and non-party) battle to defend what they understood, and had made—what a later generation of left scholars would call their 'material culture' and a generation of right ones would see as their 'manner of living'.

Orwell would have called it belly-to-earth. It was certainly pluralistic, or even anarchistic. In certain respects, his interest in material culture over philosophy, and his preference for thinking about 'governmental-ity' rather than governance (how people are rendered governable rather than how they are rhetorically addressed), are all features of Orwell's English Toryism that put him closer to Foucault's French structuralism than to any comparable theorist of his own time and place.[107] Above all, at the heart of English working-class life in the 1950s was not 'patriot-ism' as a rhetorical address, but 'patriotism' as a living tradition of the sort that Orwell had put at the centre of national identity. Ferdynand Zweig reported on *The British Worker* in 1952:

> You would imagine, as most economists and rationalists do, that everyone uses his leisure and his money under the regulating control of reason, reviewing his needs, wishes, and means, so as to get the maximum satis-faction; but this is simply not true. In fact every man has his particular bent which has been turned into a habit at a given period of life and followed nearly blindly.
>
> In my inquiries I came to realize that the past is something still alive and potent, carried on into the present by the habits and customs it engen-dered. It is handed down from one generation to the next just as myths and folklore are handed down ... and even more powerfully it lingers on in our subconscious mind, its image vague ... emotional more than rational.[108]

Orwell was capable of drawing on any or all of these political tags—labour, socialist, liberal, Tory, *Marxisant*, demotic—as any writer in search of a 'national' position must.[109] But in his advocacy of Englishness, and in his lifelong criticisms of socialists (less often socialism), and in the people he was interested in and the ways in which he was interested in them, we can conclude that beyond party politics he was more Tory Radical than anything else. As in the works of those other like-minded Englishmen, J. M. W. Turner, John Clare, and William Cobbett, his figures people the foreground, small and busy and occasionally difficult to handle.[110]

Orwell starts Part Two of *The Road to Wigan Pier* by saying that the upper middle class are 'done for'. He modifies this by explaining how the lower end of this class, that is, those on less than £400 a year as opposed to more than £2,000, had always lived much closer to the mar-gins of proletarian insecurity than they were prepared to admit, and for that reason, and because gentility was more important to them than money, they loathed the proles more, not less. He admits he was no dif-ferent himself, harbouring all sorts of prejudices about the 'Lower Orders' (smelly, violent, lazy, and so on) until he met them, and once he met them he had a cup of tea with them and that was that: he was on their side. 'It was a kind of baptism.' So he became a thinking socialist and against 'class', but like intellectual socialists in general he did not really mean it, *could not really mean it*, because to be against 'class' and all that was to be against oneself, and that was not possible, not honestly possible anyway, unless one wanted to go round hating oneself (and Orwell had done enough of that already). In this way, his own ills and the ills of intellectuals on the left in general he pronounced 'incurable'. His answer to these imponderables comes in the final pages of *Wigan Pier*, and has remained relatively unnoticed because the book is wrongly seen as a book about the working class and socialism rather than about the middle class and Orwell. Socialism as he saw it had nothing to do with his personal life.[111] Rather, for him at least it was a form of upper-middle-class charity for the poor, because whatever one might say about poverty and desperation, nobody on £400 per year in 1937 was poor or desperate, and whatever one might say about getting rid of the middle class, no middle-class person wanted to get rid of their own self. The nearest Orwell gets to describing the sort of socialism he wants lies in liberty and justice, which everyone could agree on, and more help for the unemployed, which, whatever their privations (children running barefoot in Hampstead and so on), did not generally apply to those on £8 per week. In *The Lion and the Unicorn* Orwell's socialist programme is about what 'it' will do for capitalism's victims, not what 'it' will do for everybody, and certainly not what 'it' will do for the salaried classes. Except, that is, provide general help when called upon to do so, because Orwell understood from his own life, as well as from that of his family,[112] that occasionally people do fall on hard times, and when that happens and a nastier life beckons, everybody needs it.[113] This is the final message of *The Road to Wigan Pier*. For Orwell, socialism is largesse for the working class that is also there for the middle class—when they need it (and pray they never need it).

Other than that, plus a qualified belief in liberty, it is hard to find a consistent political voice in Orwell. English Toryism never gave itself to consistent political philosophizing. That was Orwell's politics too—what George Santayana called 'the weather in the Englishman's soul', his 'mass of dumb instincts and allegiances'.[114] Politics fell like shadows across his face. It is recognizably him, however, no matter how long it takes to trace his features: on the nation-state (really belongs to the peo-

ple); on politics and the English language (really belong to the people);
on English culture (really belongs to the people); on the English people
(really belong); on intellectuals (no roots); on English poetry (make it
ordinary); on free speech (make it ordinary); on the BBC (make it ordinary); on English cricket (village is best); on English cooking (home is
best); on English morality ('a set of reflexes'); on English murder (the
same); on English postcards (highly conventional); on boys' weeklies
(highly conventional); on Charles Dickens (hero: went against the grain);
on Jonathan Swift (hero: went against the grain); on P. G. Wodehouse
(deserves a second chance); on Rudyard Kipling (deserves a second
look); on a good English pub (how to think of one); on a nice cup of tea
(how to make one); on the English people (a family); on an abiding but
evolving national culture (build a socialist on a Blimp); on a nation that
can change beyond compare and still be the same (build a gentleman on
a sailor): 'compare the brawny sailors with their buttocks bursting out
of their white trousers...with the gentle-mannered, undemonstrative,
law-abiding English of today'.[115]

Case by case, Orwell built his politics out of his nation.[116] What sort
of nation? The philosopher and political theorist Michael Oakeshott
would come to describe conservatism as characteristically a frame of
mind rather than a consistent position, a preference more than a theory: 'familiar relationships and loyalties will be preferred to the allure
of more profitable attachments.'[117] At the heart of Orwell's Englishness was a preference for trying to see the people as they were, and not
thinking too far beyond that. Sets of national characteristics were a poor
guide.[118] Party attachments were no guide. Nor were values.[119] Even the
past was no guide, if not used aright. Only the people were the guide,
and this sense of taking the people as they were, and trusting to what
they had built, involuntarily, between them, in this place, over time,
made him temperamentally rooted. To express it, he preferred informal
and personal forms of literature—the diary, the journal, the memoir,
the essay, the conversation and the squib over the textbook, the mono-
graph, the theory, the speech, the lecture, and the sermon. As a child
Orwell used to talk to himself in the third person, but he taught himself to write by adopting the first person.[120] Like taking a walk or learning a language or playing jazz saxophone, first person got you started
right near your subject and allowed any number of improvisations
along the way.

But he could be impulsive too, was impatient for justice, had no time for the political right, and polished his essays into very sharp republican instruments indeed. If he regarded the Conservative party at all it is doubtful that he would have regarded it as conservative, because whatever it was conserving for itself it certainly was not conserving for others. He refused to speak on Conservative party platforms or write for Conservative outlets. He said the Conservative party was pointless and bankrupt of ideas, like Eton College. But he also said that Eton was 'tolerant and civilized', his best friends were old Etonians, he enjoyed regular lunch-dates with one or two Tory grandees, and admitted to the Duchess of Atholl that she spoke the truth on Russia.[121] Orwell knew full well that the new techno-classes—the lords of Magneto and Radar—were not natural Conservatives, but he never took less than a pragmatic view of them as practical people who knew their business. They were triers and testers too, and Orwell trusted to that.

Richard Rees, George Woodcock, Michael Sayers, and Stephen Spender all noticed the Tory Radical in Orwell. He told Spender that he hated writing about partisan politics, and much preferred writing about his own experiences.[122] The truth is, this most famous of political writers did not have a consistent—let alone a symmetrical—politics, and the strain of trying to be true to the situation as he found it, and true to the natural justice as he believed it in the situation as he found it, there and then and thereafter, sometimes long after when he decided finally to write about it, produced in him a sort of 'doublethink' almost from the start. He put his belief in the people, and that may indeed have been a strange thing to do. He put his belief in socialism, less strange no doubt—and then tried to align it with his belief in the people, which came first. Then he put up his belief in the British nation-state, and tried to align it with his belief in socialism and the people—something that was easier to do after 1940 than before it, but increasingly difficult to do after 1945 as global power blocs took a new shape. He was a writer in the end, and went where he pleased. He did not write to order or according to some ideological position. His 'godless Protestantism' had taught him to be wary of such things. His politics, in other words, came primarily out of particular predicaments or, as Oakeshott put it, out of a 'custody' and an 'exploration' 'of a manner of living'.[123]

Starting in Wigan, but finding new spirit in Barcelona and commitment in war-torn London, Orwell switched from thinking about politics to thinking about country—a move that allowed him all the emotional satisfaction of a place without any of the drawbacks of a philosophy.[124] Given his antipathy to intellectuals, it was unlikely that he was ever going to choose philosophy anyway. In this sense his writing had to be artless and able to live with inconsistency.[125] But in another sense it had to be *artful*, about the things he knew well, and could draw with his own eyes, and could fit together to make a case. Orwell's could not be a politics of abstraction. It could not be a politics made by no one in particular for no one in particular. It could not even be settled, mind made up, impervious to his life as he lived it. It could only be a politics of time and place and conviction. Only in this sense can we talk about an 'Orwellian' point of view.

7

Last of England

Eileen

Eileen Blair once complained of her husband that he never accepted he was ill, even when he was, and in this as in so much else she and Orwell were alike.[1] Eileen died in Newcastle upon Tyne of cardiac arrest on 29 March 1945 while being operated on for the removal of uterine tumours. In a letter to a friend six days before, she had made it clear that her Newcastle surgeons were less fussy than the London ones about preparing her properly for the operation and would do the job a lot quicker. 'Apart from its other advantages this will save money, a lot of money. And that is as well.'[2] Orwell came home, arranged her funeral, and went straight back to Paris where he was working as a war correspondent. He returned again at the end of May to organize Richard's care before plunging back into the London scene. Over the next twelve months he filed 130 pieces—more than one every three days.

His wife had been a loving, clever, and witty woman who knew how to manage him.[3] They first met in March 1935 at a party in Hampstead. She was 29 and studying for an MA at University College in educational psychology. He was 31 and still working in the bookshop. They married on 9 June 1936 in the village church at Wallington—just over from where he rented a cottage. Their wedding menu was splendidly English: Roast Aylesbury Duckling and Sherry Cream Trifle. In 1938 they submitted photographs to the British Consulate prior to their trip to Marrakech. He looks handsome and she looks pretty, both in an English film-star sort of way. Eileen was tall and slim and cultured.[4] In this first flush of love and marriage Orwell went from the failure and loathing of *A Clergyman's Daughter* (1935) and *Keep the Aspidistra Flying* (1936) to the high tempo and attack of *The Road to Wigan Pier* (1937) and *Homage to Catalonia* (1938).[5]

Of course, it is not possible to measure Eileen's impact on Orwell's writing any more than it is possible to measure her 'impact' on any other aspect of his life. He made no allusions—which might have been because he assumed it to be the case.[6] According to her friend Lydia Jackson, Eileen helped transform his writing into something that could carry conviction. She would 'pounce' on his lazy generalizations, apparently, and force him to be logical.[7] Orwell did tell two American correspondents for a writers' directory that 'My wife's tastes fit in almost perfectly with my own'.[8] Whether or not this was a touch of blindness on his part, it is quite true that in her eye for detail she wrote like him, and in her relish for challenge and understatement and story she thought like him. In Spain, when he is shot in the neck and survives against all the laws of ballistics, and necks, her telegram home reads: 'Eric slightly wounded progress excellent sends love no need for anxiety.'[9] And when she lives through the bombardment of Barcelona she tells her brother she found it 'quite interesting'. And while she says that the ILP men sit in the Spanish trenches dreaming of Lee & Perrin's, she is not one to miss the contrast with her own mad social round ('Every night I mean to go home early...'), where the mere flash of a Dunhill is enough to make her yearn. '*Si, si, es bien, es Ingles.*' She notices how the waiter puts the lighter in her hand, 'thinking I should like to caress it a little'. She sends droll observations of a Spanish doctor home to a family of doctors, but nothing puts her off:

> But the doctor is quite ignorant and incredibly dirty. They have a tiny hospital...in which he dresses the villagers' cut fingers etc & does emergency work on any war wounds that do occur. Used dressings are thrown out of the window unless the window happens to be shut, when they rebound to the floor... I <u>thoroughly</u> enjoyed being at the front. If the doctor had been a good doctor I should have moved heaven and earth to stay (indeed before seeing the doctor I had already pushed heaven and earth a little) as a nurse...[letter ends abruptly] but you may as well have a letter written from a real fighting line.[10]

At the same time, Eileen had the humorous, whimsical flicks which her husband did not have, and they were nowhere better flicked than in his direction. So we learn that the Spanish government has *especially* arranged it that Eric does not sleep 'at all'. Thus we learn that in the meantime he has built an air-raid shelter that falls on everyone's head, 'not under any kind of bombardment but just from the force of gravity'.[11]

She makes the road to Marrakech sound like *The Road to Morocco*: bulging suitcases, twenty newspapers, mosquitoes everywhere, a hotel that 'was obviously a brothel', and a porter 3' 6" tall. On the boat out she describes Eric taking a pill for seasickness before proceeding to walk round the deck inspecting the sick, as she says, 'with a seraphic smile'.[12] At the time of Munich, Eileen says in a letter that she is happy to leave the big stuff to her husband like any good wife should—but at the same time she warns her sister-in-law Marjorie that her brother's 'specialities are concentration camps and famine. He buried some potatoes and they might have been very useful if they hadn't gone mouldy.'[13] In 1941 there were a few people who were beginning to see the author of *The Lion and the Unicorn* as a great national writer, but no man is a hero to his valet or to his wife. As usual Eileen cut through to the essentials. 'George has written a little book', she reported, 'explaining how to be a Socialist though Tory.'[14]

It was not all irony and understatement, however, though for a man who took the world seriously her wit probably saved him from taking himself the same.[15] She shared his outlook but she had difficulty with his notions of fidelity. The biographers make Orwell's clandestine sexual liaisons a key theme. Bowker in particular leaves no woman unturned.[16] But it is not possible to know the true nature of Orwell's private life. He had his opinions, of course, as he had his intimacies and, being a writer, he sort of wrote about them. But it is unclear where his cordial invitations ended and his sexual affairs began or, for that matter, where his affairs began and his imagination began. Nor is it possible to know whether he was more or less sexually experienced than other men of his class and coterie. At the same time, although it is said that Eileen had her flings, if she did they seem not to have been nearly so numerous nor so speculative as his.[17] We know from a long, loving letter ('Dearest') written from her sister in law's house only days before her death that, although she was depressed and had been for some time, there was no question of a break-up between them, and that young Richard, the baby they had recently adopted, carried all sorts of bright possibilities for the future. 'RICHARD HAS SIX TEETH.'[18] The letter is full of the baby (blankets, playpen, welfare foods, drinking-mug), with lots of looking forward. 'I'll be home Greystones on Friday afternoon.' But she came from a medical family and knew the operation was serious. The letter also deals with arrangements for baby Richard in the event of their death, and she wrote her will on the same day. Orwell knew she had been miserable. She wrote to him intimately on 21 March 1945, eight days before the operation, expressing her trust in him but also her unhappiness. 'It's odd—we have had nothing to discuss for months but the moment you leave the country there are dozens of things.' Their life in the capital seems to have been a particular source of disagreement and distress. London went less well for Eileen. She lost her brother in 1940, her mother died in 1941, and Orwell, it seemed, proved unfaithful. She confessed to profound depression in 1941, may have had a breakdown of some sort in 1942 and continued to be in poor health through to 1945. She was increasingly at a loss. 'I don't like even the things that you do.' 'From my point of view I would infinitely rather live in the country on £200 than in London on any money at all. I don't think you understand what a nightmare the London life is to me.'[19] All the same, she was talking to him right to the end. She reported being 'enema'd, injected…cleaned & packed up like a precious image in cotton wool'. She told him 'This is a nice room'—virtually her last words.[20]

When she died Orwell told Lydia Jackson 'very bad news. Eileen is dead' and then went straight into the practical details. He went round the houses saying she had been 'a good old stick'.[21] Which was less than some of his friends found it in their heart to say about her.[22] It could even be seen as unworthy of him, if one puts aside Orwell's (apparent) reluctance to express anything much in his personal relationships. Anything more might seem unmanly. Anything unmanly, for his generation at least, might be unseemly. One had got one's duties after all. So Eileen was buried, and Richard was cared for, and Eric carried on with the writing, and everything personal stayed personal.[23] There are almost no surviving letters from him to her.[24]

There was a dark side. There *is* sexual sadism in *Nineteen Eighty-Four*: not very much, and not very serious, but odd. It might have been that the darker side of Orwell's personality helped him imagine the worst excesses of the human personality. Or it might have just been an aberration, or an insight into Winston, not Orwell. His brother-in-law said he was a prude who did not like smut.[25] Various explanations are possible because all texts are unstable.

It is true that Orwell is not at his best when writing about women, and feminists have had their say in this respect.[26] When they are in positions of authority (Flip in 'Such, Such were the Joys', for example, or Mrs Creevy in *A Clergyman's Daughter*, or Elizabeth in *Burmese Days*), they are destructive. When they are not in positions of authority, they are weak (Dorothy Hare), or gullible (Hilda in *Coming Up for Air*). It is true that he was just as hard on his male characters as his female characters—including an unfortunate habit of attaching physical marks to personal failings—but it is his men who are self-aware, not his women, and when the clergyman's daughter finally does stumble into self-knowledge, at the end, it is her hope and her charity that brings her there, not her intellect or will. Orwell always associated suburbia, the Church, and the softer parts of the bourgeois progressive brain with women; and Wigan, Barnsley, Barcelona, and hard bodies of truth with the men. That said, Orwell's best hope is a woman, and his England begins to look increasingly feminine after 1940. Being inside a whale (and what a whale) is like being inside a womb.[27]

Last Man in Europe

In February 1945 Orwell donned the captain's uniform of a war correspondent of the *Observer* and went to Paris, where we can be sure he did not abide by Foreign Office's *Instructions*.[28] There he mixed with army-intelligence people and met André Malraux and on a separate occasion Ernest Hemingway (Camus failed to turn up), before travelling east to Cologne, and then south to Stuttgart and Nuremburg. Moving through the German countryside a day behind the advancing French, he saw for himself the true cost of war. No room for *Schadenfreude* here. Just another beaten people.

He was a Labour man, but Labour's manifest success in foreign and domestic policy did not prevent a gathering depression in his post-war outlook. The war had ground to a halt right in the middle of Europe with terrible devastation on both sides. There was no clear winner and a rapidly forming geopolitical divide. To the east he saw a new Russian barbarism. Allied conferences at Tehran (1943) and Yalta (1945) had given notice of Soviet bad faith, and Berlin in 1945 was a city of 3 million starving people, 2 million of them women hiding from the Red Army. In Orwell's eyes, Soviet atrocities in Poland, the Crimea, and Germany all had the look of terror, cover-up, and collusion (some of the collusion British). In the west, meanwhile, he saw a resurgent American capitalism and a Marshall Aid programme which, no matter how generous in the short term, was not going to save Europe in the way that Europe needed saving in the long. Only a united Europe could do that. But only a democratic Europe could be united, and only a socialist Europe could be truly democratic, and Orwell was not sanguine on either count. In August 1947 he told *Partisan Review* that 'a socialist United States of Europe' was 'the only worthwhile political objective today'.[29] But it also seemed to him 'a very unlikely event'.[30] The Russians would want to bully it, the Americans would want to get their way whatever it called itself, and the Catholic bishops would be intransigent on all counts. As for the *ancien régime*, he believed the old colonial right would not go quietly and the old revolutionary left would not go at all.

Whose future did this Europe follow? Certainly not Hitler's, buried now under ten square miles of rubble called Berlin. Nor Stalin's, though the Soviets had got what they wanted: no Germany and no guarantees. The future was not President Truman's to give either. He had wanted to get out of the European theatre almost as soon as his armies stopped at the Elbe. General de Gaulle's vision was more to do with the rehabilitation of France. In fact, with the British out of it and everyone looking for a plan, paradoxically the new Western European way forward grew to be German: declare *Stunde null*; acknowledge your shame; deny your national identity, or avoid it, or forget it; and start all over again.[31] For Chancellor Adenauer, it is difficult to see how he could offer anything else. Germany was the complete nadir of a nation-state. Divided and shamed, Germans had no other way to go but to shut down the past. In East Germany, Berlin's Karl Marx Allee showed the road ahead: wide and straight and well surveyed: one *Volk*, one *Kunst*, one *Kultur*. In West Germany, engineering replaced ideology: apply the rules, make it run, make it run better. In May 1950 West Germany and France founded the European Coal and Steel Community. It had clear rules and, to English ears at least, a Gilbert-and-Sullivan sounding 'High Authority'.[32] This and other steps towards federal union had been encouraged by Churchill and other senior British politicians. They wanted Europeans to unite in order to save themselves—but what they did had nothing to do with being British.

After the publication of *Animal Farm* in August 1945 Orwell had a little bit of fame and for the first time in his life a lot of financial security.[33] But the war years had taken a terrible personal toll.[34] His father had died in 1939. His brother-in-law was killed in action in 1940. His mother died in 1943, Eileen in 1945, his eldest sister Marjorie in 1946, and his own health took a turn for the worse in 1947. From this year on, he is a dying man. In letters to friends he feels increasingly obliged to report on his own wretched health in contrast to his son's. 'Richard is offensively well & full of violence. He went through whooping cough without noticing he had it.'[35]

In the writing, too, there is a turn. Englishness abates. He begins to consider global struggles and the prospect of atomic war. For the first time in a life filled with war he is able to envisage one that could wipe out everyone and everything in a couple of hours.

In May 1946 he and Richard, and Susan Watson the nanny, left for Barnhill, on the Scottish island of Jura in the Inner Hebrides. Almost as far on the edge of Europe as it is possible to get, and said to be good for the lungs, Jura was another whale—another place to hide and be free. With his younger sister Avril and her husband Bill Dunn, who joined them, Orwell set about restoring Barnhill's house and garden. They worked hard to make the place comfortable and productive. He loved the moody sea and shifting skies. He went fishing, did the garden, pot-shot rabbits, and rumbled around with Richard. He also had a book on his mind.

From April to December 1947, in a tiny upstairs room with a paraffin heater, a table, a typewriter, and a cigarette jutting from the mouth, Orwell rattled out the first draft of a book which he called 'The Last Man in Europe'. In this lonely faraway place, hard to get to even on a good day, he must have felt that he was that man. Published in June 1949 as *Nineteen Eighty-Four*, the novel was an immediate best-seller and critical success—a rare combination. *Animal Farm* had been a late outcrop of his 1930s thinking. *Nineteen Eighty-Four*, on the other hand, was Orwell imagining a future.

Suddenly world-famous, he lived for only another seven months. Much of the novel had been drafted and redrafted in a sickbed. In and out of sanatoria since completing the first draft in Christmas 1947, he was finally admitted to University College Hospital in London in September 1949, where he could be near to a gathering clan: his doctor, his agent, his publisher, his lawyer, his accountant, his literary pals, and his girlfriend. He died there, alone, in the early hours of Saturday, 21 January 1950. The death certificate gave cause of death 'pulmonary tuberculosis', but the immediate cause was a haemorrhaging of the lung. He left behind a new will, signed 18 January; Richard, now aged 5, to be brought up by Avril and Bill; and a new wife, Sonia.

Sonia

Sonia Brownell was fifteen years younger than her husband. Born in Bihar, India, in 1918, she was the daughter of a freight broker who died soon after her birth, obliging his wife and young family to go back to London and face harder times. As a very young woman Sonia earned a reputation among the London art set as a sitter, but at the outbreak of war she found her way into small-magazine publishing, joining Connolly's *Horizon* in November 1940, where she 'freelanced energetically' between jobs and boyfriends.[36] Sonia seems to have had a Ritzy sort of war.

She met Orwell at *Horizon* sometime in 1940 or 1941. Her biographer says he was keen, and she was young, and they got on well together. There was another flurry of exchanges in 1945. Once installed on Jura, Orwell tried to persuade her to make the trip north. Not that he tried very hard. Everybody got the same sound advice Rayner Heppenstall, an old flatmate and BBC colleague of Orwell's, had received the year before, that the trip would take twenty-four hours and he'd have to walk the last five miles. Sonia was told the same and advised to bring a week's rations.[37] She did not make the trip. Nor did she visit him in his Glasgow sanatorium. She did visit him, however, in his Gloucestershire sanatorium—five months after admission, in May 1949.[38] He transferred to University College Hospital on 3 September 1949, and they got married on 13 October. Orwell sat up in bed wearing his new smoking-jacket. After a short ceremony, Sonia and friends set off for the Ritz where they went French (if not Dutch).[39]

Sonia probably came too late to be an influence on Orwell's intellectual life, though we can never be sure. Some critics say she is Julia, heroine of *Nineteen Eighty-Four*. She knew the London literary scene, and in some respects her prejudices were his prejudices, though it is difficult to reconcile her marriage to Orwell with her very recent and very involved affair with Maurice Merleau-Ponty, a Stalinist.[40] Although there appear to be gaps in their nine-year relationship, she and Orwell were sexually experienced, all biographers attest to their intimacy in one form or another, and, given Orwell's predilection for secret liaisons, it is not impossible that they knew each other better than we can sense from the letters and memoirs. She was a modern woman who worked for herself and went where she liked. He was attracted. In the end, with Orwell desperately ill but with an international publishing success on his hands, they appear to have married in the hope that with her companionship, his money, and a mutual love of books and ideas he could attain the life of what his doctor called 'a good chronic' while she ran around London managing his career.[41]

This was not an implausible future, but it was not to be. Sonia's main role in her husband's intellectual biography came after. In a stormy life, she tried to promote his work and defend its integrity. With Ian Angus, she set up the Orwell Archive at University College London in 1961. Also with Angus, in 1968 she edited the four-volume Penguin edition of Orwell's collected essays, letters, and journalism—which this author for one has used over and over again. She also commissioned what turned out to be an outstanding biography of her husband, by Bernard Crick, published in 1980, and she finally won her legal battle with George Orwell Productions, thereby securing Richard his inheritance.

It has to be said that Sonia's influence was not appreciated by all Orwell's friends at the time and has not been appreciated by all Orwell's biographers since. Meyers, Shelden, and Bowker have all had their say, and certainly Sonia did not come cheap. But she had her day in biographical court in 2002, and it won't be long before nobody will be interested anyway.[42] She married again in 1958, and left £289,000 at her death in 1980.

England without Englishness

Nineteen Eighty-Four envisages the end of England ('Airstrip One') by the wiping out of its identity, the brutalization of its people, and the manipulation of its language, truth, and logic.[43] Winston Smith is the last of the non-deceived. He and Julia want to be free again, but they cannot understand what that might mean. Winston seems to think he can remember a time when England was free and together, like a family even.[44] In his Spanish War poem in praise of the Italian militiaman Orwell averred that no bomb could burst his 'crystal spirit'. In *Nineteen Eighty-Four* Winston Smith, lover of beautiful old objects, sees his crystal paperweight shattered by the police when they come to arrest him. Between *The Lion and the Unicorn* and *Nineteen Eighty-Four* Orwell's England had turned from a family whose natural instincts were socialist into a concentration camp whose most powerful inmates, the English Socialist Party, were busy eradicating natural instincts. He and Julia are found out as conspirators and tortured up to the point where execution is preferable.

Orwell's England was not an unmixed blessing. But Europe was far worse. A war zone for virtually the whole of his life, in Fascist Italy and Nazi Germany, in Franco's Spain and Stalin's Russia, and in all the little totalitarian satellites before the war and after it, the death camps lay in wait. In France and Britain there were gross inequalities and hard-handed empires. Imperial service gave Orwell a broadly misanthropic view of his country. But he was incrementally reconciled to it after 1936 and contributed towards its common culture after 1939 in works which, no less than the tank or the aeroplane, were designed as instruments of war. After 1945 he supported Labour's programme of welfare and public ownership, though he had surprisingly little to say about it. His thoughts were turning elsewhere.

A clever young man, he might have gone to Cambridge and joined the Apostles to ask 'Is I Me?'[45] Instead, he skipped this kind of thing and took a direct step into the Empire, only to re-emerge five years later as a writer with a taste for the ethnographic over the philosophic. After Burma he moved in among the marginal poor in Paris and London, the working class in Wigan and Barnsley, and the Spanish peasantry and urban poor in Catalonia, before finally, and brilliantly, dealing with his own country during the war. Orwell listened to England. His refusal to adopt ideological positions was based on a longstanding English liberal suspicion of the 'state', made real by his experiences in Spain and bolstered by a very privileged education which gave him the confidence to resist authority. He would speak as he found. Someone less public-school (or more grammar-) might have been more inclined to work with ideological set-squares and equations. But Orwell was that very rare figure—a public moralist with a middle-class upbringing and an upper-class education who mixed confidence in his own powers with a deep feeling that liberty lay with the people, not with the state or some higher intellectual caste. His Englishness was not typical of the 1930s (no cricket, no foolishness about country cottages, definitely not quiescent). It was the product of a free mind with the maverick touch under pressure of war.

He believed in the people. This was the top and bottom of it. This was the Englishness of George Orwell, so hard fought. But in *Nineteen Eighty-Four* he abandoned this, to see what England felt like without it. The book is not so much a prophecy as a deduction. He starts with a premise, and sees what follows.

All is to begin again

We know at once that the London of 1984 is not quite right. Winston Smith goes into Victory Mansions on a 'bright cold day in April', but the clock strikes *thirteen*. Who would be called 'Winston Smith' in England in 1949? Maybe a recently arrived West Indian, or a blitz baby (John Winston Lennon, for instance), but the name is not typical, slightly discordant. As for 'Victory Mansions', there was nowhere called that in post-war London. It is unlikely that any British war memorial would ever be called 'Victory' anything—it is not the way. That the hall smelled of boiled cabbage and old mats was all too possible, but 'Winston Smith' letting himself into 'Victory Mansions' and checking his watch at 'thirteen' is not. The next paragraph tells us about 'Hate Week' and shows political posters inside residential flats. Paragraph three has Winston wearing blue party overalls. This may be England, but it is not any England we know.

Yet the novel is filled with evidences of the England people did know: patched windows and sagging roofs, ration-books and dried-out tobacco, black markets and bombed buildings. O'Brien, party intellectual and key figure in the government, is strangely familiar too. It's that man again. Apart from his inner-party black overalls, it could be Ernie Bevin: '[a] burly man with a thick neck and a coarse, humorous, brutal face. In spite of his formidable appearance he had a certain charm of manner. He had a trick of resettling his spectacles on his nose which was curiously disarming—in some indefinable way, curiously civilized.'[46]

London is capital city of Airstrip One and the third most populous province of Oceania. Orwell touches down on what we know before taking us immediately away from it. The book is littered with references to his other works—shock posters, foul tortures, death row, explosions in the brain, and so on—but only in the most incongruous contexts. For example, the language is English, but the dialogue can be strictly Hollywood B movie; not at all how the people spoke (which Orwell could do so well). Compare 'she started kicking up a fuss and shouting they didn't oughter of showed it not in front of the kids they didn't it ain't right not in front of the kids it ain't', with 'And now, I am afraid, it is time for you to go. But wait. You had better let me give you one of these tablets.'[47]

If this is an England that does not always look right, or sound right, it is also a land without laws or liberties. It is not just that the police can pick you up and beat you up and kill you without record, but the Party is engaged in the systematic destruction of all record of all civil society— all the little platoons, wherever they may be, civil and familial and personal. With his insidious 'community centre', Winston's neighbour Parsons leads the destruction at a local level ('I mean to say there is a war on'),[48] while Winston's colleague Syme spends his days clearing society of the common language on which all transactions depend. It is impossible for party members to know how many party members have a private life, but we know in Winston's case that all that Orwell valued in a writer (in a life)—your own thoughts, private notes, intimate liaisons, spontaneous ideas, factual documents, ordinary language, a personal diary—has been eradicated.

This is an England then, without a history or an identity, without law and with a language it is trying to kill. All the resources of the state are engaged in wiping out the past through 'continuous alteration'. Winston works in the Records Department of the Ministry of Truth. He rectifies old figures by making them tally with new figures until the new ones become old ones, to do it again and again until no one knows or has the means of knowing the figure in the first place. Winston cannot remember his parents. As with the numbers, there is no means of remembering them because there are no facts that can be checked. Did his parents live in England? 'England—was its name, he thought, or Britain.' What happened to them? 'The two of them must evidently have been swallowed up in one of the first great purges of the fifties', if it was the fifties. If England's past is a palimpsest of deliberate and hideous complexity, Winston's past is a dream time where everything he thinks did happen only might have happened. Nothing can be verified or falsified. Nothing can be brought to judgement. Winston and Julia are tortured for wanting what they think (England) might have been. They can feel it in their bones, but they have no access to it because they live without history and therefore they live without identity. Indeed, they live as they die, and when the time comes they will be written off, extinguished, annihilated, vapourized, all without record. One day, they are told, they will be 'lifted clean out from the stream of history'.[49]

Once upon a time, in *The Lion and the Unicorn* and *The English People*, Orwell had written in praise of an England that knew who it was because it had stayed in touch with who it used to be, whose 'all important trait' was its respect for law and the constitution, and whose most marked characteristic was its 'extreme gentleness'. In Winston and Julia's England it is becoming impossible even to think these things because, assuming you can conceive of them in the first place, they are unverifiable. England has no historians because it has no records, and it has no history because it has no historians. By breaking with its past it has broken with itself, and it goes on breaking with itself, again and again, as a matter of course:

> And this hall, with its fifty workers or thereabouts, was only one sub-section, a single cell, as it were, in the huge complexity of the Records Department. Beyond, above, below, were other swarms of workers engaged in an unimaginable multitude of jobs. There were the huge printing shops with their sub-editors, their typography experts, and their elaborately equipped studios for the faking of photographs. There was the tele-programmes section with its engineers, its producers, and its teams of actors specially chosen for their skill in imitating voices. There were the armies of reference clerks whose job was simply to draw up lists of books and periodicals which were due for recall. There were the vast repositories where the corrected documents were stored and the hidden furnaces where the original copies were destroyed. And somewhere or other, quite anonymous, there were the directing brains who co-ordinated the whole effort and laid down the lines of policy which made it necessary that this fragment of the past should be preserved, that one falsified, and the other rubbed out of existence.[50]

Or as Edmund Burke put it at the time of the French Revolution: 'When men, therefore, break up the original compact or agreement which gives its corporate form and capacity to a state, they are no longer a people; they have no longer a corporate existence...They are a number of vague, loose individuals, and nothing more. With them all is to begin again.'[51] And in Winston's England all had begun again, sometime in the forties, with an atom bomb dropped on Colchester.[52]

Bad thinking drives out good. For O'Brien, all political crime (the only sort that really interests him) starts as 'thought crime', and all thought crime starts the moment it is put into words that mean something political. The state's plan is to make new words and fewer words: new words that conceive the thoughts the Party wants to be conceived, and fewer words so that the thoughts the Party does not want to be conceived are less conceivable. The new language is called Newspeak, a great national project of salvation. For those who are already saved, it reduces their ability to think but also increases their ability to be free (but only in the way the state wants them to be free). For those who are too late to be saved, there are lobotomies, electric shocks, and extinction. In 'Politics and the English Language' (1946) Orwell spoke in praise of good prose as a window on the truth. He characterized the English language's propensity to do this by its uncommonly large vocabulary and its simple and commonly understood grammar. In *Nineteen Eighty-Four* it is the state's intention to use the language to make truth unthinkable and freedom unknowable by decimating its vocabulary and simplifying its grammatical rules to nullity. No doubt Orwell remembered his early days in Paris, and 'Uncle' Eugene, the Universalist Marxist Esperantist:

> 'You haven't a real appreciation of Newspeak, Winston', he said...'You don't grasp the beauty of the destruction of words. Do you know that Newspeak is the only language in the world whose vocabulary gets smaller every year?...Don't you see that the whole aim of Newspeak is to narrow the range of thought? In the end we shall make thoughtcrime literally impossible, because there will be no words in which to express it. Every concept that can ever be needed will be expressed by exactly *one* word, with its meaning rigidly defined and all its subsidiary meanings rubbed out and forgotten. Already, in the Eleventh Edition, we're not far from that point...The whole climate of thought will be different. In fact there will *be* no thought, as we understand it now. Orthodoxy means not thinking—not needing to think. Orthodoxy is unconsciousness.'
>
> One of these days, thought Winston with sudden deep conviction, Syme will be vaporized. He is too intelligent. He sees too clearly and speaks too plainly. The Party does not like such people. One day he will disappear. It is written in his face.[53]

All their interventions in the way human beings perceived the world had persuaded English Socialism, Ingsoc, the Party, that the world could be anything they wanted it to be. Along with respect for the law and the constitution, the connectedness of English history and its living tradition, and the beauty and force of the language and the gentleness of their civil life, Orwell takes the English tendency to be non-intellectual—that is, to have a 'horror of abstract thought' and a strong liking for facts and common experience—and crushes it like a ball of paper. In other words, Orwell takes a long-standing tradition of English scientific empiricism and replaces it with its opposite: idealist solipsistic nonsense.

O'Brien tells Winston that the party not only remakes the soul, it remakes the laws of Nature, and to think otherwise is 'thoughtcrime'. 'We control matter because we control the mind.' 'Reality is inside the skull.' 'There is nothing that we could not do.' Winston replies that the universe came first; that mind followed matter. O'Brien counters that 'outside man there is nothing'.[54] Winston objects that man is tiny. O'Brien counters that 'nothing exists except through human consciousness'.

In *Language, Truth and Logic* A. J. Ayer made the case for common-sense empiricism by resting the means of knowing what we know on the possibility of verifying (or not verifying) the 'sense content' of our experience of the world. We know what we know by how we encounter the material world. Does that mean that if we only know what we know by our senses, our senses are all that we know? Ayer rejected this by arguing that although it is true that 'a man's sense-experiences are private to himself inasmuch as each of them contains an organic sense-content which belongs to his body and no other', it is also true that we have good grounds for supposing that other persons, persons like us, have the same sort of sense histories and they too must be taken into account when deciding what the world is like.[55] Which is to say that, according to Ayer, O'Brien's claims are absurd. When he says that the stars are merely bits of fire only a few kilometres distant, because that is what the Party wants them to be, he is not taking into account all those others (in the world) whose sense histories, properly constituted knowledge, and practical experience tells them different. Except that, for O'Brien solipsism is not a private affair. It is a mass affair or, as he puts it, a collective affair; which is not the same as solipsism.

The Party is actively creating a world where everyone's sense histories are not only dulled but talked into being the same, and no one has the means of expressing or even thinking otherwise. So, when the aeroplane fails to reach the stars because the stars are *not* only a few kilometres away, and when the geologist's hammer finds that mankind is *not* the same age as the rocks and fossils, and when the astronomer's calculations shows that the Sun does *not* travel around the Earth and anyway it is nonsense for O'Brien to reject the laws of physics on the grounds that 'outside man there is nothing' because planes fly and stars are untouchable and fossils exist regardless of what the party thinks, O'Brien has immediate recourse to a second-level rejection of empiricism called *doublethink*, or 'the power of holding two contradictory beliefs in one's mind simultaneously'. Orwell called the Marxist concept of Dialectical Materialism the 'old pea and thimble trick' of the infinite mutability of things, whereby everything is in the process of becoming something else and everything therefore must be, in potential at least, two (opposite) things at once. In his 1978 essay 'The Peculiarities of the English', E. P. Thompson called this a theory of 'co-existent opposed possibilities'. Even the idea of a revolutionary class is to some extent a species of doublethink, whereby a class perfectly formed has to contemplate itself as a class perfectly destroyed. In the second part of *The Road to Wigan Pier* Orwell agonized over what that would mean for him in person.

In *Nineteen Eighty-Four* party intellectuals are at the heart of all this deception because they know (they must know) that it is a deception, and therefore they must deceive (and not deceive) themselves in order to do it. Winston learns that the central tenet of Ingsoc is the mutability of intellectuals:

> Doublethink means the power of holding two contradictory beliefs in one's mind simultaneously, and accepting both of them. The Party intellectual knows in which direction his memories must be altered; he therefore knows that he is playing tricks with reality; but by the exercise of doublethink he also satisfies himself that reality is not violated. The process has to be conscious, or it would not be carried out with sufficient precision, but it also has to be unconscious, or it would bring with it a feeling of falsity and hence of guilt...[56]

'The Party told you to reject the evidence of your own eyes and ears.' In the pain of having his humanity put on the rack and twisted out of shape, Winston holds on by remembering simple things he knows to be true. However, his simple calculation that two and two make four, not five, even if the Party wanted it to be five, was not a good choice on Orwell's part. Because they follow logically from the axioms, all mathematical statements are tautologies. That two and two makes four is a restatement of the axioms, only in more acute form. If the party redefined the axioms and by collective solipsism could have persuaded the world that two and two made five, then it could be axiomatic that two and two made five. It would have been better for Winston's case had he stuck with a law based on scientific experiment. Here the numbers would have been meaningful statements about the world (subject to measurement error) and Winston would have had something solid and real to hold on to. The problem with Ingsoc, or Marxism, or any ideology that tries to reduce the world to its own axioms, is that the axioms are not well defined and certainly not quantitative. Even when they are defined, they are not operationally defined. Ingsoc does not care about this because it has abandoned science and embarked on an epistemological programme of advancing human knowledge by torturing people. The Communist party, on the other hand, *did* care about this and spent an inordinate amount of time trying to alter the axioms and widen the margin for measurement error (i.e. for getting it wrong).

There can be no doubt that Oceania is a Marxist state and Big Brother is Joseph Stalin. The Party manages the means of production, distribution, and exchange through the state. Nazis make a brief erotic appearance in the novel (in chapter 1 of Part 3), but after that it is Communists all the way—'a style at once military and pedantic, and, because of a trick of asking questions and promptly answering them ("What lessons do we learn from this fact comrades?") easy to imitate'.[57] O'Brien likens Oceania to Nazi and Communist systems and says it is superior to both. But given his theory of knowledge, he is never going to know.

Orwell's faith in Englishness began in the north of England. He saw the miners as guardians of an authentic England that had been driven down only to survive in ways that the official England did its best to disable or ignore. This is essentially a Victorian idea of the folk. The folk might be appallingly ignorant and out of date, but they are also appallingly right and important as well. In *Nineteen Eighty-Four* it was the 'proles' who sang popular songs, watched pornography, had sex, and bore children pretty much as they pleased. 'Only the proles used scent.'[58] They were also the only ones who had private property, worked with their hands, suffered poor health, showed blind indifference to all that was good for them, and otherwise enjoyed all the other aspects (football, beer, gambling, and petty crime) of a vile and counter-revolutionary capitalism. If it was true that all hope lay with them, as Winston thought, it was only because they were the 85 per cent of the population who lived beneath civilization. The proles lived without English Socialism just as English Socialism lived without them. One day they would meet their final reckoning from the men in black, but for now Winston can think of no one else he can turn to.

One evening after work he ventures into the slums north of St Pancras station—an old Victorian philanthropic hunting-ground. As he walks by, the locals go quiet (Orwell knew all about slum-visiting). He follows an old man into a pub. Like thousands of English folklorists before him, Winston tries to enter into conversation with this decayed old guardian of Englishness.[59] This time, however, it is hopeless. Although the proles live according to their own 'ancestral pattern', they do not understand it—a classic criticism of the labouring poor since Adam Smith's time and a key aspect of ethnological theory in Orwell's.[60] The old man recalls a few random facts from the past—top hats, lords and ladies, boat races, and so on, but it is all 'a rubbish heap of details'. 'It was no use going on.' The intellectual life of the English working class, insofar as they had one, is no more. They are epigones and suddenly we are back to Wigan and black beetles again: 'They remembered a million useless things...They were like the ant, which can see small objects but not large ones.'[61] The prole woman Winston sees from the upstairs window, the woman with strong arms and a fertile belly, the woman who looked as strong as a Norman pillar, the woman he imagined as a schoolboy smacking down the reign of science, '*had no mind*'.[62]

Worst of all, this is a state devoted to the murder of its own people. The object of power is power and the object of murder is murder. Towards the end of his interrogation Winston takes off his clothes, looks in the mirror, and walks forward:

> A bowed grey-coloured skeleton-like thing was coming towards him. Its actual appearance was frightening, and not merely the fact that he knew it to be himself...bent carriage...nobby forehead...bald scalp...crooked nose...cheekbones above which the eyes were fierce and watchful...barrel of the ribs...knees thicker than the thighs...curvature of the spine...cavity of the chest...scraggy neck...bending double under the weight of the skull.[63]

We are all Jews now.

Nineteen Eighty-Four was Orwell's most exacting work, unlike anything else he ever did. Winston, Julia, and the rest play out their roles in a massive conceit. The story is hugely upsetting, but only as an idea, not because anyone feels they know Julia or cares about Winston. Hans Fallada's *Alone in Berlin*,[64] first published in German in 1947, is the novel Orwell would surely have preferred to have written, and might have written, had he stuck with realism. Years before, in 'A Hanging', he showed how he might have been able to get as close. But *Nineteen Eighty-Four* is not that work. It is an experiment in telling the truth, not a truthful story.

And the truth is: if there is hope, it lies in Julia, because she is not an intellectual. Winston is the intellectual, a man who believes that truth is to be found in books, and in this case the man who believes that all truth resides in one book—Emmanuel Goldstein's *Theory and Practice of Oligarchical Collectivism*. This is a book as ugly in its title as in the revolutionary cadre it has—or has not (such is the capacity of intellectuals for deceit, we cannot be sure)—given rise to. Goldstein's book accounts for the long history of betrayal of Party intellectuals by Party intellectuals. But Goldstein *is* a party intellectual, and the Brotherhood he leads is only a parody of the Big Brother they oppose. Julia and Winston join the Brotherhood, and promise to do such disgusting things in the name of one side that they cross over into the territory of the other. We know at this point that, as the man who cannot save them even if he is who he says he is (which we canot be sure of), Goldstein is the ultimate left intellectual.

Hope lies with Julia, but who is she? It is hard to know. We do not know anything about her other than who she says she is and what she actually does with Winston. It is hard to see what she sees in him as a sexual partner, and she is certainly not interested in him as a conversationalist. There is always the possibility that she is a Party plant, or started out as such. At the same time (and Orwell is never an easy writer), if there is hope it lies in her because in her we see what sort of person, if any, is going to win in the end.

Winston reads to her from Goldstein's book. Worse! It is at least four books in one, taking in Malthus, Marx, Spengler, and James Burnham, and she falls asleep.[65] She might be the girl from the fiction department, but she does not read books, not books like this anyhow.

Winston trusts the book like all intellectuals must. Julia does not. What she knows about the Party she has not learned there. She is a 26-year-old mechanic—a technical woman, one of the new middle class that Orwell had reached out to in the late 1930s—smart, young, self-aware, unsnobbish, and competent in all the ways Winston is not. She does as she pleases. She is practical. She is instinctual. She is effective. She gives him hope. She shows him how. She tells him where. She stalks him and risks everything in the same way she stalks the Party and risks everything. She does not seek to understand her opponents. She seeks to outwit them. Nature, not intellect, is the driving force in Julia, and *through her* it is Winston's mission to recover himself by tracing back to his natural self. In short, he seeks to translate his humanity back into nature—the role of philosophy through the ages. He is not the first lover she has chosen, nor will he be the last. The Party is against sex between Party members, not because it is against sex any more than she is for it, but because it is against any form of human liaison that creates bonds stronger than those it imposes itself. When she and Winston embrace, therefore, it is 'a political act'. She adores 'it', and 'that was above all what he wanted to hear': 'not merely the love of one person but the animal instinct.'[66]

Orwell spent his life trying to get away from empty abstraction and closer to the world as it was. Julia is a belly-to-earth, below-the-waist sort of person not because she is stupid but because she is clever. The most important words in the book have nothing to do with the proles, or Big Brothers, or Room 101:

'We are the dead', he said.
'We're not dead yet', said Julia prosaically.[67]

8

Death in the Family

He was buried on a cold, rainy day on Thursday, 26 January 1950 at All Saints Church in the village of Sutton Courtenay, Berkshire. David Astor and Sonia Orwell accompanied the body down from London, where there had been the memorial service he had expressly requested should not happen.[1] The gravestone says: 'Here Lies Eric Arthur Blair.' Not 'George Orwell'.

He spent the last year of his life in bed reading books—144 volumes in all, twenty-seven of which he had read before. In his last full month, December 1949, fretting over whether he could get a good cup of tea once Sonia had got him to Switzerland, he read four Conrads, Huxley's *Soviet Genetics*, Malcolm Muggeridge's new novel, *Affairs of the Heart*, and E. H. Carr's *The Romantic Exiles*—a story of the nineteenth-century Russian revolutionary anarchist left which ends in death and futility.[2]

In the event he never made it to Switzerland, never enjoyed the pleasures of sun on an open balcony, never tasted tea in a low-pressure environment, never knew what it was like to have Sonia and the sputum flask by his side.[3] He got buried instead—buried in a village he had never visited, next to a prime minister (Asquith) he had never mentioned, according to the rites of an institution he did not attend. It was his choice all the same, as requested in the will. Muggeridge, who over the past few months had charted Orwell's decline from 'pretty wretched' to 'he's got an idea he's had it', remembered reading the obituaries and thinking how legends are made.[4]

Had Orwell gone abroad, and mended, and had he and Sonia pushed on together through 1950s London with a bath-chair between them, it is interesting to speculate how he would have survived. There is one thing we can be sure of. *If* his health had held out, *and* he was able to write, *and* Sonia managed to provide the love and support which she promised, then he would have flourished in a country where people were better off and more free than at any time in their history. The National Health Service and Isoniazid might have been able to save his lung. Television would most certainly have gilded his reputation. There would have been no shortage of opportunities for George Orwell Productions. Grand old man of English letters would not have suited him, but he would have enjoyed the platform. We can see television producers coming up the hill and Sonia making them march down again. Face to face with Daniel Farson in a darkened studio, or side by side with World in Action wheezing up a Wigan slag-heap—Orwell in battered tweeds with stick pointing right or left and face to camera. One can see him being interviewed by Betjeman on this and that. One can imagine his old pal Muggeridge inviting him down to Falmer to meet the Slightly Christian Movement. Back in Barnsley to sniff the air of affluence, back in Burma and Barcelona to sniff the air of democracy, or back to Jura just to sniff the air, the worst that Orwell imagined could happen did not happen. The middle class did not slide into the abyss. The working class did not billet their militias at the Ritz. The Atomic Bomb was not dropped on London. The Rolling Stones did the job instead. Fascists died out. Imperialists shut up. Communists gave up. Cameras surveyed every high street, but nobody seemed to mind. Europe found some measure of common purpose. But if the worst he could imagine did not happen, that which he could not imagine did. If he had lived to extreme old age he would have seen the exposure of finance capitalism as a conspiracy and the destruction of British manual workers as a class. According to the Chichele Professor of Economic History at the University of Oxford, British workers were humbled into being seen as consumers rather than producers (or citizens) and left the century relatively less educated, less rewarded, less united, less numerous, and less coherent. Deserted by the Labour party (though not the Labour party by them), and exposed under New Labour to heavy migrant competition for jobs and resources, this was the death of a culture that Orwell had committed to in the winter of 1936.[5]

Yet it is impossible to predict how he would have reacted, because his belly-to-earth Englishness always insisted on the terrain first and the politics second. Who knows what he would have made of a second trip to Agnes Terrace? Who knows what he would said about the life of a supermarket shelf-stacker? As for post-Christian England, it is possible that growing secularization and materialism would have bothered him into a more sustained treatment of it. It is possible too that he would have supported European unity, if not for the United Kingdom, and if he had lived to see the UK's membership there is a good chance that he would have ended his days taking a look at how a Commission could ruin a language and a politics in so short a time.[6] Certainly his days as a roving journalist were over. It is unlikely he would have got to Washington, DC to see Senator Joseph McCarthy's un-American activities, or to the Congo to see how not to leave a colony. He would not have made it to Cape Town or over to Memphis. The signs are he would have been a Cold War warrior, but how far that would have taken him it is difficult to estimate. US politics would not have been to his taste, Republican *or* Democrat. He would have been interested in Khrushchev's criticisms of Stalin at the Twentieth Party Congress. Suez and Hungary would have caused him to look both ways in horror. Mutually assured nuclear destruction would have terrified him as an abstract as well as an absolute. The war in Vietnam would have brought Burmese memories back to life. That said, one wonders just how far he would have taken his suspicion of left intellectuals. Against the Campaign for Nuclear Disarmament in the 1950s? Against the students in the 1960s? The carworkers in the 1970s? The miners in the 1980s? Surely not.

Maybe.

The odds are he would have stuck with the Labour party, primarily because there was nowhere else to go, and also because only Labour was capable of saying it was against the big things he most opposed (Communism, Fascism, Poverty, Imperialism, Racism, Inequality, and so on) while equivocating on the little things that really mattered (cruise missiles, redistributing wealth, improving schools, saving industry, opening up the constitution and so on). After 1979 Mrs Thatcher would surely have brought his deepest hostilities to the surface. That she was female would not have blunted his attack, unless of course the Iron Lady had made him OM first. What he would have made of New Labour we do not have to consider, because by then he most surely would have been dead.

As it was, he died in 1950. If only he had lived another couple of years he could have visited the Festival of Britain. We can see Sonia now pushing him away from Skylon up to a wooden kiosk in Battersea Park, where he buys six ounces of Player's tobacco and pronounces all tobacconists Fascists.

Life after Death

A Bibliographical Essay

On the other hand

Orwell spent the first half of his life being mainly *against* things.[1] According to A. L. Rowse, he wasn't just anti-prep school, anti-public school, anti-women, anti-Empire, anti-class, anti-intellectual, and anti-society: he was 'anti-*la condition humaine*'.[2]

His first great loathing was the British Empire—five years of his life which he remembered as 'wretched prisoners...reeking cages...scarred buttocks'.[3] After he died, a new post-colonial age found his anti-imperialism increasingly attractive, not to say *de rigeur*. The same cannot be said of the other things he was said to have been against, which drew increasingly mordant criticism. His references to 'Jews' or 'The Jew', for instance, descriptions which even some politicians of his day tried to avoid, were harder to bear for a post-war generation who knew about Auschwitz. Here he is in the year of Hitler's coming to power saying how it 'would have been a pleasure' 'to flatten the Jew's nose, if only he could have afforded it'.[4] It is unfortunate that Orwell's 'Jew' in question is a moneygrubbing pawnbroker in the rue de la Montagne St-Genevieve. A few months later and Orwell's Jew turns out to be 'gangs' of them, no less, 'Jews and Scotchmen', making fortunes out of coolies in the Empire. In 1940, after seven years' vile persecution of the Jewish population of Germany, we find him saying there is something appealing about Hitler and taking himself off to investigate rumours that a disproportionate number of Jews are sheltering in the London Underground. 'What is bad about Jews is...'[5]

On the other hand (and one soon learns with Orwell that he is two-handed), one might say that his reputation suffered from inflation in the number of people capable of being offended by racial categories, and that his Jewish pawnbroker, one of a gallery of rogues and vagabonds in *Down and Out*, is not uniquely a figure of evil as opposed to good.[6] More to the point perhaps, Orwell enjoyed the friendship of a number of Jewish men, all of them men of the world who knew how to tell their friends from their enemies. Tosco Fyvel, for instance, met him in January 1940 at the St John's Wood home of Hans Lothar, German-Jewish former editor of the *Frankfurter Zeitung*.[7] Together with Fred Warburg, Orwell's publisher, they founded Searchlight Books, an anti-Nazi venture which Orwell led off in 1941 with his *The Lion and the Unicorn*. He was friends with Arthur Koestler, certainly not one to be deceived. There again, if Orwell was not anti-Semitic, he was certainly anti-Zionist, his language about Jews never softened, and it has been said by one of his grittiest defenders that he completely missed the scale and significance of the Holocaust.[8] *There again*, there were those who carried Orwell's early minor indiscretions forward in order to show, in the end, a truly great writer who saw the Holocaust's uniquely horrible meaning. Bertrand Russell reckoned that Orwell went through Buchenwald imaginatively so that other writers would not have to.[9]

He is also seen as being against women. His most accomplished critic in this regard is Daphne Patai, whose *The Orwell Mystique* (1984) marked the turning of the feminist tide against him. According to her, Orwell was at the heart of a male conspiracy that united him and his readers in a hatred of women. She saw this as the main reason not only for his critical acclaim (by men), but also for his final despair in the brutal and pointless androcentrism of *Nineteen Eighty-Four*. We recall that Julia is betrayed by the unusual intimacy of two men.[10] Beatrix Campbell also saw Orwell as a male conspirator, and she too charged him with misogyny.[11] So did Anne Mellor. So did Urmila Seshagiri, though in her eyes he was an 'anti-imperialist misogynist'—which is, I suppose, something. To Ana Moya and Jenny Taylor, however, Orwell was an anti-imperialist proto-feminist, while Erika Gottlieb exonerated him from all charges of anti-Semitism *and* anti-feminism by drawing attention to the newsreel scene in *Nineteen Eighty-Four*.[12]

Those who knew Orwell personally did not remember someone uncomfortable with women, and the biographer most interested in his personal life did not find in his female companions the sort of women who would put up with a misogynist.[13] Not that those who knew him well always spoke well of him. Rayner Heppenstall, for instance, drew attention to what he saw as Orwell's sadism.[14] Orwell's second wife, Sonia, reckoned that if his male friends united at all in their regard for her husband, they did so as silly schoolboys, not foul conspirators.[15]

Most of Orwell's male friends were intellectuals. If he did have a flagrant prejudice it was directed against men like them. Anthony Burgess noted Orwell's bias against left intellectuals especially: not difficult to spot.[16] E. P. Thompson noted the same bias, but in doing so kept to Orwell's own script for reasons for not liking left intellectuals, which rather destroyed his point—somewhat borne out in his 'Open Letter' to the hapless Professor Kołakowski.[17] While Stefan Collini mistrusted Orwell's intellectual anti-intellectualism, and John Rodden tried to explain it, Sue Lonoff showed how Orwell's most loathsome example of it, O'Brien in *Nineteen Eighty-Four*, was born not of woman but of two words: one Latin, the other French.[18]

Not that Orwell thought intellectuals had nothing to say—or if he did, he spent an awful lot of time reading them.[19] Even here, his reputation for plain speaking in the face of their reputation for deceit is not quite what it seems. Rather, his ability to persuade readers that they are seeing what he saw, and that what he saw was real, was not so much plain speaking as a highly developed rhetoric.[20] There have been various interpretations of this, all centring on Orwell's art of pretending to be artless.[21] Simon Dentith drew attention to it by comparing Orwell with lesser left writers. Richard Filloy found clues to it in Aristotle. Daniel Kies found it in Orwell's manipulation of the active and passive voice. Lynette Hunter explained how Orwell worked through layers and layers of analogy.[22] The very idea of an instinctive rebel as an artful rhetorician seems wrong, yet he was the man, in 'Politics and the English Language', who advised that using the very simplest English was the best and most sincere way to write, and the man who took that same simple English in *Nineteen Eighty-Four* and reduced it to showing the worst and least sincere way to write.

In *Down and Out*, Bozo says 'I'm a free man in *here*', and taps his forehead to prove it. But he proves nothing because men are not only made free by the mind but held captive by it too. Reading the mind is never far from Orwell's politics. *Nineteen Eighty-Four* has been noted for a number of strong Freudian resonances, including sexual repression, libidinal rebellion, the power of memory and suggestion, maternal identification, Oedipal and sadomasochistic themes, and so on.[23] Some commentators have seen that novel as Freudian with 'a Trotskyesque tinge', some as Freudian with a Marxist bent.[24] Others say it is 'anti-Freudian', or 'pro-Adlerian', or 'psycho-historically therapeutic'. Some have noted Orwell's obsessions—with smells for instance, or rats. Wikipedia speculates that Orwell suffered from Asperger Syndrome. An early comment in the *Manchester Guardian* thought it obvious that 'Big Brother' should have been called 'Big Father'.[25]

In *The Lion and the Unicorn*, subtitled 'Socialism and the English Genius', Orwell has the English people sleepwalking their way to socialism. This was not the first time Orwell invoked unconscious conditions in order to resolve whatever intellectual difficulties he was having in seeing his way through an argument. Certainly he reckoned he was some sort of socialist, but there is no consensus on what sort. In 1941 Hendon Labour party asked him to stand for Hampstead Garden Suburb, but, as he told Tosco Fyvel, socialist writers were 'dull empty windbags'. Kay Ekevall remembered herself and Orwell in the 1930s as part of a group of friends who went round calling themselves socialists without knowing what they meant, and when his brother-in-law was asked point-blank by the BBC 'Was Orwell a socialist?' his answer was an unhesitating '*No*'. His publisher agreed. He was definitely not a socialist.[26] Yet, according to another old friend, himself a socialist, rather a famous one in his time, Orwell *was* a socialist—far more than most people who called themselves that.[27]

Orwell is never an easy subject, even on the easy subjects. If we go to *Orwell for Beginners*, we find he was 'passionately pro-socialist'.[28]

We know for sure that he saw himself as a socialist. His position shifted from North London-soft to Barcelona-hard somewhere between 1936 and 1937, but as his interest in the English matured so did his socialism turn again. By the time he had started working for *Tribune* in 1943 he had turned into a pretty straightforward supporter of the Labour party, someone who thought life could be made better for more people more of the time by the intelligent interventions of the state.[29] That he believed Attlee's government more or less represented such a state, and that it was a socialist state and ought to be defended as such, explains why he was hated by the Communist party. But that did not make him a Trotskyite, and he needed no lessons from Isaac Deutscher or Tony Cliff on how to be one.[30]

Those who understood him least saw him as a reactionary.[31] Those who understood him best saw him as a conservative. His friend George Woodcock said the smartest thing anyone ever did about his politics when he noted that Orwell's socialism could only 'be built on what was

there already'.[32] It was fear of amputating a living tradition that provoked in him profound misgivings about the sense in which he belonged
to the left.

Richard Rees, George Woodcock, Jack Common, Arthur Koestler,
David Astor, and Malcolm Muggeridge all understood that Orwell
wanted to be a socialist, said he was a socialist, tried to look the part of
a socialist, and never wavered in his belief that he was a socialist. But
they understood too that he could not hide his Tory upbringing, his old-
school sensibilities, his gentlemanly drawl, and the way in which he took
his bearings from a natural and moral universe.[33] 'Anti-intellectualism',
after all, began as a reaction of the right against the posturings, as they
saw it, of the left, and has stayed that way, more or less, since 1898.[34]
When Orwell claimed there were no right-wing intellectuals, or very
few, he was only repeating left-wing common sense. That he should
have feinted to the left only to cross with the right comes as no surprise.
Considering his interest in the cultural, Orwell knew what all conservatives from Burke and Burckhardt to Taine and de Tocqueville knew:
that the rational order is only rational, and indeed only orderly, insofar
as it works through conventions (practices, meanings, understandings)
that provide the repetitions that make it understood.[35] Even in his most
ardent moments, these were the things that interested him most. He
never mentions the Report of the Burma Police Enquiry (1924). He is
more interested in how a man is hanged, in a yard, according to convention. He shows no interest in the two Royal Commissions on the coal
industry, Sankey (1919) and Samuel (1926). He is more interested in
how miners squat to eat their bait, or scamper to the coal-face, according to convention. He hardly addresses the politics of the Spanish
Republic, saving himself instead for the little platoons at the front.
Orwell did not attend to conventions just because they were there (some
were not there for long), but because he understood that without them
there would be no culture and without culture nothing would be social,
let alone socialist. His final story is the story of Airstrip One: a country
without a name, let alone a tradition or an identity. In a century intent
on wiping everything out and starting all over again, the real enemy was
not those who wanted too little change but those who wanted too much.
Orwell spent his life fighting those who wanted to 'control life' and
'entirely refashion people' 'with an absolute authority which penetrates
into a man's innermost being'.[36]

Louis Menand therefore is wrong to claim that Orwell identified too much with ideas and too little with everything else that makes us up.[37] In truth, Orwell cannot hold an idea in his head without holding another idea in his head about the 'everything else' that holds it up. This inclined towards a conservatism of mind, if not opinion. True, there is another, more politically opinionated interpretation of his conservatism which says he was a *neo*-conservative, but the neo-conservative case is entirely speculative, and has to be weighed against speculations about other pat-terns in his thought—his liberalism for instance, or his anti-liberalism,[38] or his humanism,[39] or his modernism, or his anti-modernism.[40]

Orwell was a good debater, but no philosopher.[41] Of a famous phi-losopher, he told a BBC colleague that he 'did once start one of his books but I found he was discussing whether people exist or not' (which did for him).[42] Orwell often ruminated on the deeper implications of things, particularly words, and the passage of time, but not in any sys-tematic way.[43] In open debate he could quickly abandon ring-craft for hard punching, and the occasional low blow. After all, this is the man who claimed in *Homage to Catalonia* that prostitution declined by 75 per cent in the early part of the revolution. Indeed, it is an established fact understood by every sensible person who has ever thought about it properly that one could construct the world's most banal speech from Orwell's rash guesses and slippery generalizations.[44]

His Christian credentials do not look any more promising, unless you start from an existential rather than a theological point of view. He was a man in search of his honestly aware self or, if you prefer, his soul. He did not have much time for the philosophical existentialists of his day— Sartre in particular—but it is clear that his fictional characters are peo-ple responding to big questions about their existence. All his novels begin with people in trouble, seeking renunciation.[45] They are not alone in this, however, for the world is not of their own making. And because they have come to believe that God is dead, they are going to have to find their own way through. In his journalism Orwell went in search of the authentic encounter, not the agency one.[46] He did not believe in authentic encounters with God, but not believing is not the same as not looking. Hollis, for example, finds in him a man looking for his self in God, while Sandison finds in him a man looking for God in his self— 'the quite conscious inheritor' of a Protestant religious tradition.[47] In any case, it is not always best to take Orwell at his word. He was a classicist, but a subversive classicist.[48] He was worldly, but other-worldly.[49] He believed there was no God, but no end to the need for God either. Reilly calls him 'Feuerbachian'.[50]

Everybody has a view. The intrinsic difficulty of agreeing on Orwell can be seen by comparing not the first and last appreciations of his work, but the first and second. Tom Hopkinson's 1953 appreciation is narrow, and lacks judgement. John Atkins's 1954 appreciation, by contrast, anticipates many future themes.[51] Both men had limited access to Orwell's works and, compared to now, very little available commentary. But they disagreed anyway. Hopkinson makes hardly any reference to Orwell's Englishness. Atkins starts and ends with it. And so it goes. Communists accused Orwell of wilfully distorting their history. Apologists for snobby little prep schools in Sussex did the same. Some saw in him an unusual moral integrity, as a kind of saint— a reputation that appears to have begun at the BBC. Others compared him to Winston Churchill.[52] Nor does it help by rolling him up into one complete 'Orwell' who always speaks the same, or reducing him down to one essential 'Orwell' who always speaks the truth. To say that he was *essentially* against the abuse of power, for instance, does not quite cut it.[53] Moreover, it is hard to know enough. We can get him wrong. Jeffrey Meyers knows more than most. He can explain Orwell's clipped moustache at one end of the knowledge spectrum, and he can take Orwell's biographers to task as unoriginal, flat, graceless, derivative, and careless at the other. But even he does not know it all.[54]

Orwell could be unoriginal, flat, graceless, and so on himself. It is easy to mistake sheer aggression in him for moral rectitude, and moral rectitude for consistency. He is not consistent. Not long before his own famous argument in praise of English gentleness (as set out in *The Lion and the Unicorn*), he attacked Wyndham Lewis's *The Mysterious Mr Bull* for making exactly the same case: inviting Orwell's most severe rectitudinous criticism. Gentle? Did Mr Lewis not know that for a hundred years these English had 'exploited their fellow creatures with a callous selfishness unparalleled in history?' Did he think he was writing a leader for the *Daily Telegraph*?[55] Later, Orwell would become bosom friends with a man who did just that (Malcom Muggeridge).

He was, then, a difficult writer who spread his long limbs across many intellectual traditions, to invite mixed reviews. He might be an 'icon', but he is never going to be found at rest. For his every last word, we can find new ones beginning to form. He always seems to be storing up ideas for future use, or others are storing them up for him. Repression is not forgetting.[56] One day someone may come up with a complete and final 'Orwell', 'mythical and monumental',[57] but it will still be an argument, not an audit, and it will be a biographical argument at that. Mark Rawlinson is right. It is best to move viscerally and fleetingly, with life as it came at him.[58]

He was not really well known until his last year. His books had always drawn national reviews, but not enough to sustain a national reputation. Just occasionally he found himself in distinguished company, usually on printed cards, or signed manifestos, or contents pages. Because *Down and Out* was known on the left, and *Wigan Pier* enjoyed large sales through the Left Book Club, he was known in the 1930s as the man who dealt with poverty.[59] By the mid-1940s, after stints at the BBC and *Tribune*, he was known across a wider literary spectrum and among the London intelligentsia. But it was not until *Animal Farm* and *Nineteen Eighty-Four* that he became well known, almost a celebrity. He received a letter from the prime minister shortly before he died. Had someone tipped off the Cabinet Office? His memorial service warranted a paragraph in *The Times*. His name had already begun to creep into the late-night schedules of the BBC. Even so, he was not famous outside of London. For the *Manchester Guardian*, 'George Orwell' remained a subject for its London gossip column.[60]

In the long run, he became a world figure and his posthumous reputation had to deal with a different world and different ways of seeing the world. In a post-colonial, post-industrial, post-modern, pro-feminist, deconstructionist age, he was brought back in for questioning on a number of counts. Charges range from alleged anti-Semitism to imperialism, misogyny, and grand cultural larceny. Bloomsbury and Cambridge always felt cultural criticism belonged to them. He was supposed to have been against telephone surveillance, but there is not a single phone call in *Nineteen Eighty-Four*.

In the short run—that is, in the years immediately after his death running up to the generation born in the 1940s but going intellectually live in the 1960s—Orwell's reputation was caught up in arguments largely about class and war. These were, and to some extent still are, arguments between those who felt near enough to be his inheritors.

Inheritors

Orwell said he belonged to the left. He may have protested too much the fact. Nevertheless, apart from the Communists, who demonized him, this is how he was seen in his lifetime. Orwell the rebel, Orwell the common man, Orwell the good and virtuous man, Orwell the honest man, Orwell the conscience of the left. These characterizations, and mixtures of them, started in the 1950s and still prevail.[61]

Among those who thought about such (admittedly arcane) matters of where Orwell stood on the left, the Bevan wing of the Labour left kept faith with him as one of its own. So did the London literary intelligentsia, left to right, including those who had been his friends. V. S. Pritchett wrote a very fine obituary, but his elegant phrases turned out to be hares let loose on his reputation—Orwell as 'the wintry conscience of his generation', Orwell as 'a lone hand', Orwell as a man 'gone native in his own country', Orwell, in other words, as 'Orwellian'.[62] Stephen Spender also got to the point early, judging Orwell guilty of sainthood.[63] The BBC signalled his national importance in 1954 by televising *Nineteen Eighty-Four*, adaptation by Nigel Keane, but avoided the big question whether Airstrip One was a totalitarianism of the left or the right by making it a totalitarianism of English high camp.

There were other 1950s appropriations of Orwell by a small but increasingly influential band of young writers who also saw in him something of the man they wished to be. Kingsley Amis, Robert Conquest, Donald Davie, D. J. Enright, Philip Larkin, John Wain, and a few others in 'the Movement', so called, started by seeing Orwell as someone who was not deceived by Communism or indeed by any other -ism. They concentrated their fire, therefore, more on what he did not believe rather than on what he did. Which matched his own approach.[64] But as they grew older, and the good causes with them, these (quite irritable) young men found it harder to keep left. The striking car-workers of Dagenham looked less inspiring than the unemployed miners of Wigan, somehow, and in Cuba and North Vietnam they found it impossible to support bad regimes even for the right reasons.[65] So the Movement shuffled from fed-up literary left to fed-up literary right, and had Orwell lived long enough he might have shuffled with them.

There were similar claims on him by small but significant schools of American intellectuals, who were also shuffling left to right. Orwell's

Critical Essays were published in the United States in 1946, but he had started writing for the New York-based *Partisan Review* much earlier, in January 1941, and the men around that hard-left publication like Irving Howe, Dwight Macdonald, and Lewis Coser stayed close to the Englishman in his life, and even closer after his death. Macdonald remembered Orwell as, 'more than any other English intellectual of our age', embodying 'the values of personal independence and a fiercely democratic radicalism'.[66] Howe saw in him 'the greatest moral force' of the age and 'a revolutionary personality'.[67] Later, both men gave up on the left but still stuck hard by Orwell—sometimes uncomfortably so. Howe, for instance, found himself talking about Orwell and Appeasement as a way of talking to 1960s student ultras about America and Vietnam.[68] Orwell also had influential admirers among elite American liberals, as he had among dissident East European ones—both sides looking for shelter from the Cold War storm before forming 'neo-conservative' foreign-policy positions in the 1970s.[69] He remains a subject for academics on both sides of the Atlantic, but it is hard to judge his living political influence. Art Spiegelman's Pulitzer Prize-winning anthropomorphic cartoon depiction of the Holocaust, *Maus* (1986), did not draw on his Englishness or *Animal Farm* for any kind of inspiration, and of all the animals that he could have selected to represent the wartime British, Spiegelman chose fish. 'I decided to give the Brits a walk-on part... I thought about fish and chips, an island culture, fish out of water...'[70] A walk-on part? *Fish?*

In Britain, many post-war intellectuals found in Orwell a way of being left and being English at the same time. John Braine's *Room at the Top* was published in 1957, Alan Sillitoe's *Saturday Night and Sunday Morning* in 1958. Orwell would have had a field-day with these novels. One can see a long generic essay from him on 'Kitchen Sinks in Keighley'. Foremost among what Orwell called 'semi sociological' studies of literature was Richard Hoggart's *The Uses of Literacy*, a landmark study of working-class life in the Leeds district of Hunslet.[71] Like Orwell, Hoggart saw working-class people as refined. Unlike Orwell, Hoggart really knew what he was talking about. Other investigations happened—including Mogey's St Ebbes, Oxford (1956), Dennis, Henriques, and Slaughter's Featherstone (1956), Willmott and Young's Bethnal Green (1957), Kerr's Ship Street, Liverpool (1958), Tunstall's Hull fishermen (1962), Marsden and Jackson's Huddersfield schoolchildren (1962), and

Goldthorpe and Lockwood's Luton car-workers (1969). In these studies there were shocks in store for those who had fixed ideas about class. It appeared, for instance, that according to the axioms of the left those who should have been conscious of class struggle were not, and those who were were not conscious in the right way.[72] Orwell would have had no problems with that. He would have enjoyed these adventures in work and community.[73] He would not have enjoyed, however, what came after. By the 1990s the very conditions of stable community and family life were in abeyance.[74] It is true he had defended love on the dole and babies on the means test, but only in the context of love and marriage generally.[75] What he would have made of inter-generational welfare dependency, or the Commission for Racial Equality's call for special measures to assist 'the white working class', is altogether another question.[76]

Meanwhile, the 1950s saw metropolitan excitements that owed something (impossible to tell how much) to Orwell's forays into popular culture. English theatre, cinema, and paperback fiction became defined by a new wave of writers and directors, actors and actresses, some from the north, some from the north by way of a RADA accent, who were intent on taking politics to ordinary life—just as Orwell had done. They were anti-theatrical theatricals, just as Orwell had been an anti-political political. This made it easier for them to reject the patricians. It also made it easier for them to confuse being 'anti' for being 'pro'—in this case, being anti-theatrical for being pro-socialist: ' "*Look Back in Anger*", one prominent university left-winger shouted at me recently, his voice almost shaking with passion, "is a more important political document than anything the Labour party has said since 1951".'[77]

There were other, less plausible inheritors of the cultural left. Orwell may have taken cultural criticism away from the Leavises, but what followed—'Cultural Studies' in the 1970s—was highly theoretical, all-but unreadable, tied almost exclusively to the universities, and certainly not in the business of recognizing Englishness as anything special, or indeed as anything at all.[78] 'Subaltern Studies' he would have found interesting, if horribly ideological, and when it came to 'Trans-Culturalism' ('a phenomenon of the contact zone') we find he had been doing it all the time.[79] Benedict Anderson picked up on Orwell's interest in national identities and mass communications in his highly influential text, *Imagined Communities*.[80] As for movements of sexual liberation, Orwell was never happy when writing about women, and, to say the least, had nothing helpful to offer queer theory. No inheritors on these fronts. He did, however, share with the best female writers of his generation a personal conservatism when writing about England.[81]

The 'new' left began to distance itself from Orwell almost from the moment it began to distance itself from the Communist party. Here the inheritance gets complicated, because this distancing was in one part connected to simultaneous appropriations of Orwell by the American right, and in other parts connected to the way in which his *former* left supporters were increasingly embroiled in Cold War arguments with old and new left alike. In these circumstances, made all the more interesting with the publication of Orwell's *Collected Essays, Journalism and Letters* in 1968, which widened the scope for debate, the new left could find no place for him. E. P. Thompson gave the impression that Orwell had betrayed somebody or something, for not seeing NATO and the Warsaw Pact as equivalent alliances. Raymond Williams went in for sly wordplay, charging Orwell's *Nineteen Eighty-Four* with having 'communicated', 'actualized', 'popularized', and otherwise having 'created the conditions for' bad things in the world—a heavy burden for a book to bear.[82] The old left could never forgive Orwell for being so wrong, and the new left could never forgive him for being so right.[83] There is a history here yet to be written, all the more so when one considers how much the new left owed him.[84] Not that everyone had a label, and not that everyone's politics were as 'new' as their new-left label suggested.[85] The difference was probably more to do with rival generations than philosophies.

Orwell was not entirely disinherited by the young during these years. The *Collected Essays* found a younger readership, and he was taken up by a new generation of scholars and writers such as Christopher Hitchens, Martin Amis, and Ian McEwan—some with a student-left background. Like the Movement before them, they used Orwell as a stick to beat those they believed to have been deceived in ways that he, and they, had not. Hitchens called his bullies the 'No Bullshit Brigade', and in his and Amis's hands the war on bullshit made for some brilliant journalism— though it has to be said, much of it written in and for the United States. After 9/11 it tended to share, though not in easy or convenient ways, the State Department point of view.[86] Between the American foreign-policy right and the British social-policy left, 'Hitch' pitched camp and put up his own sign saying: 'Orwell's Victory'.[87]

It is easy to see how Orwell got picked up by the populist right, especially in the United States. The FBI and CIA played a part in this, but it is no secret that many Americans spontaneously claimed *Animal Farm* and *Nineteen Eighty-Four* as their own, and some Americans saw in their own neo-conservatism the makings of neo-conservativism in him.[88] It is undeniably true that in the Cold War years this belligerent anti-Communist, a man who never let an idea go by without grabbing it by the neck, would have had to decide whose side he was on. It is also true that had he lived long enough to see the apotheosis of Boris Yeltsin and Vladimir Putin, he would have had to decide who looked the most porcine.

At the height of the war in Vietnam Mary McCarthy said she could 'hear him angrily arguing that to oppose the Americans... is to be objectively pro-totalitarian'.[89] 'Objectively' was not one of Orwell's better lines—he had used it unfairly against pacifists—but Norman Podhoretz, editor of the formerly liberal Jewish journal *Commentary*, took it further in 1983 when he argued that had Orwell lived he would have seen great things in the West (decolonization, affluence, mass education, civil rights, welfare), and that these grand facts could not have failed, objectively speaking, to put him in the neo-conservative camp when it came to it, as it most certainly did come to it in Korea, Hungary, and Czechoslovakia, and in Cuba and Vietnam.[90]

It is just as possible that Orwell would have been repelled by Western affluence and welfare—that he would have looked upon a rich First World and a dollar-a-day Third World to find his way back to Marxism through the 1960s new-left theories of Herbert Marcuse. Thirty years before Orwell had argued that the Empire allowed the British—*all* the British, not just the rich—to live off the backs of blacks and Asians; that capitalism was neither ahead of nor apart from the undeveloped world, but in its midst.[91] But after some pleasantries with the American, maybe on his nice Californian campus, Orwell might have found Professor Marcuse's theories of 'repressive tolerance' faintly hilarious. There are arguments to be made against Podhoretz's neo-conservative case—including Orwell's hostility to free markets and his ability to recognize a black underclass when he saw one—but debating-points apart, in the end the neo-con case works best for neo-cons.[92]

Orwell's adoption by the right must be seen as the price paid by the left for losing sight of his work in some cases,[93] and handing it over so cheaply in others. Some famous figures on the left could never support Orwell because, in the last analysis and under cover of language, they endorsed the Soviet Union. Astonishingly, E. P. Thompson's open letter to Kołakowski berated the Pole for not keeping faith with the Soviet occupation of his country.[94] As late as 1987 British Communist historians were still referring to purges, terrors, and liquidations as part of the 'anti-Communist *presentation*', rather than the real thing.[95]

Orwell always tried to stay close to ordinary things. In this regard he hardly needed a political model, let alone a model politics. Needless to say, he was indifferent to Westminster party intrigue. He was careless of party politics, wherever it happened. He responded best to peoples and places as he came across them and, in Catalonia as in England, in Burma as in Barnsley, in London as in Paris, he came across them as a commitment. It is always a mistake to see patriotism as the stock-in-trade of the right. During the Second World War a new social democratic narrative replaced liberalism as the dominant national identity. Not for the first time, Conservatives had to face the fact that it was they who had proved least adept at lighting up the nation. Baldwin's Englishness was too village-green, Churchill's too bulldog-breed. Only Orwell's left knew how to include everybody, including those generations who had been and those yet to come.

Benchmark

Two great histories of post-war Britain, one by McKibbin and the other by Harrison, take Orwell as their benchmark.[96] However, very quickly, within a couple of generations, there was hardly any of Orwell's Britain left to mark. Only finance capitalism remained in a way that he would have recognize. The Empire had gone. The Industrial Revolution had gone. The ships and the regiments had gone. India had gone. The manufacturing had gone, more or less. Class had gone—as a political discourse at least. And as left and right distinctions faded, even Orwell's most fundamental subject, 'character', was being erased from a world system that increasingly preferred conditions of permanent impermanence. We live today in a world where 'we' are on our way out, and 'weak ties syndrome' is on its way in.[97] At the Festival of Britain in 1951 the British knew who they were. Fifty years later, wondering what to put in the Millennium Dome, they did not.[98]

The war against Hitler had been 'the first war in which all of the people were constantly bombarded with intimate descriptions of what they themselves were like'.[99] When the war ended, Englishness became more private but more relaxed too, less on show. 'Teenagers' Orwell never knew, but for a while popular culture looked more democratic than democracy itself. In the 1980s the British found themselves caught between their own historic nationalism (briefly made manifest by their ejection of Argentine armed forces from the Falkland Islands) and the beginning of trans-national ways of trading and thinking that weakened their sense of who they were as a distinctive people. There were many reasons for this, ranging from Britain's membership of the European Union to multiculturalism, de-industrialization, and the economic advance of multinational capitalism known as 'globalization'. Whatever the reason, there was a decline of confidence in Englishness among the population as a whole, and a growing taste among intellectuals for seeing the state as merely instrumental. The interventionist left saw the state as repressive, yet still wanted more. The free-market right saw the state as ignorant, and imagined the market could survive without it.

It was in this context that Englishness made a new and surprising return to academic circles.[100] More theoretical and accusatory than the old liberal and social-democratic version, the new Englishness was (is) more interested in discovering 'contradictions' than expressing its personal commitment or point of view.[101] At least there are still recognizable arguments over the north–south divide. The new Englishness still finds the north as strange as he did, though he would have struggled with the thought that it existed as a 'discourse' more than a place and that he had gone there in the role of the 'privileged rational master subject'.[102]

All this would have sparked some great polemic from the old man, but sadly it would have been seen as the great polemic of a grumpy old man. Get rid of Englishness as something personal and Orwell has few places left to go. Even so, in recent years his name has become England's favourite way of talking about itself. As his biographer remarked, Orwell is a 'moral force', 'a light glinting in the darkness',[103] and it is certainly the case that his presence could be felt in Danny Boyle's opening ceremony for the 2012 London Olympiad. No one expected this late celebration of left patriotism—a new national identity that had reached its high point ten years before Boyle was born.

Which is to say, in 2012, at a time when the conditions of Orwell's politics had become most scarce—at a time, in other words, when the kind of country he wanted was least likely to exist and increasingly difficult to imagine—Orwell seemed to matter more than ever. Boyle's tribute to the British people could have been scripted by Minister of Culture Blair and opened by Prime Minister Bevan to a sea of people's choirs. And yet that Britain, their Britain, benchmark Britain, has disappeared. Correct your maps. Britain is Peru.

It is not only that Orwell's country has disappeared and he has been dead for over sixty years: the more he is invoked, the more we define his absence; the greater our trust in him, the smaller our trust in ourselves. For he is The Less Deceived, The Crystal Spirit, The Fugitive from the Camp of Victory, The Age's Adversary, The Wintry Conscience of a Generation. He is a saint, a knight, a champion, a hero, a victor, a mystic, a patriot, a plain speaker, a great writer, a moral force, an unflinching patriot, a good and virtuous man. He is also a Society, a Trust, a Fund, and a Memorial Prize. Simon Heffer thinks he was 'as straight as an arrow', Julian Barnes thinks he has become a National Treasure.[104] In 2012, in the absence of a successor, he nearly became a statue.[105] Not that there has been a shortage of candidates for his position.[106] Calling for a second Orwell, indeed, is one of the great political clichés of our time.[107] Terry Eagleton blessed his name as a bloody-minded 'independent leftist and idiosyncratic Englishman', who was

> as adept at ruffling the feathers of his fellow socialists as at outraging the opposition. As he grew older, this cussedness became more pronounced, until his hatred of benighted autocratic states led him in the eyes of many to betray his left-wing views altogether. Such, no doubt, is how Christopher Hitchens will be remembered.[108]

Today the major exponent of prime Orwell political writing (albeit with a touch of Oakeshott and Buddhism) is John Gray. Like Orwell, Gray has no home on the right and few friends on the left. I will refrain from calling him 'an Orwell for our times'.[109]

Notes

Introduction

1. *Manchester Guardian*, 5 July 1935, review of *Burmese Days*.
2. John Rodden, *The Politics of Literary Reputation: The Making and Claiming of 'St George' Orwell* (New York, 1989).
3. MLA *International Bibliography 1960–2012*, 101–50: online accessed 26 Feb. 2012.
4. John Rodden (ed.), *The Cambridge Companion to George Orwell* (Cambridge, 2007), pp. x–xi. Certainly things have changed since 1974 when Donald Crompton could say that Orwell 'has had too little serious attention as a writer': 'False Maps of the World—George Orwell's Autobiographical Writings', *Critical Quarterly*, 16: 2 (1974), 149.
5. Two of her three references to him are wrong and the third is a quote: Alexandra Harris, *Romantic Moderns: English Writers, Artists and the Imagination from Virginia Woolf to John Piper* (London, 2010), 11, 175, 218.
6. D. J. Taylor remarks on life abroad as a 'creative counterpoint' to Orwell's sense of national identity: *Orwell: The Life* (London, 2003), 80.
7. 'The Tale of John Flory', Orwell Archive, University College London [henceforth Orwell Archive], A/1/U, ms drafts, and published in Peter Davison (ed.), *The Complete Works of George Orwell*, 20 vols. (London, 1986–98) [henceforth *CW*], x. 96; 'The Quick and the Dead', Orwell Archive, B/1.
8. Letters, Miller to Orwell, Paris, Aug. 1936, 5 Oct. 1936, 7 Nov. 1937, 20 Apr. 1938, Orwell Archive, letters to Orwell I, 1928–37, Appendix 2; Lionel Trilling, 'Orwell on the Future', *New Yorker*, 18 June 1949. See also Stephen Starek, 'Damning Praise: George Orwell Confronts the Works of Henry Miller', *Nexus*, 1: 1 (2004), 99.
9. John Atkins, *George Orwell: A Literary Study* (London, 1954), 1, 330; Stefan Schimanski (ed.), 'George Orwell. Unpublished Notebooks', *World Review*, 16 June 1950—other contributions by Russell, Fyvel, Muggeridge, Beavan, Spender, Hopkinson, and Read.
10. Raymond Williams, *Culture and Society 1780–1950* (1958; Harmondsworth, 1968), ch. 6; George Woodcock, *The Crystal Spirit* (London, 1967), part 3; Jenni Calder, *Chronicles of Conscience: A Study of George Orwell and Arthur Koestler* (London, 1968), chs. 8, 9.
11. Raymond Williams, *Orwell* (London, 1971), 9.
12. Bernard Crick, *George Orwell: A Life* (Harmondsworth, 1980), 137, 15–29; Julian Barnes, 'Such, Such Was Eric Blair', *New York Review of Books*, 12 Mar. 2009.
13. Collins's blurb-writer said Orwell was 'typically English' in his 'capacity to look with critical eyes upon his fellow citizens': book-jacket flap, *The English People* (London, 1947).
14. Gordon Bowker, *George Orwell* (London, 2003), p. xiv.
15. Trilling appeared to change his mind, seeing Orwell in 1952 much more as a world figure than an English one: 'Introduction', *Homage to Catalonia* (New York, 1952). Michael Walzer's 'George Orwell's England' is to be found in Graham Holderness *et al.* (eds.), *George Orwell* (Basingstoke, 1998). Starting with his decision

to trust in the people, Walzer regards national populism as Orwell's 'remedy for intellectual pride and vanguard presumption' (p. 194). For the rest, Atkins, *Orwell*, 330, 334; Martin Green, *A Mirror for Anglo Saxons* (1957; London, 1961), 157; Richard Rees (1970), in A. Coppard and B. Crick (eds.), *Orwell Remembered* (London, 1984), 124—'he set enormous value on [it]'; Crick, *Orwell*, and again in the *Oxford Dictionary of National Biography* (2004, henceforth *ODNB*)—Richard Rees's short 1959 *DNB* entry made no mention; J. R. Hammond, *A George Orwell Companion* (London, 1982), 27; Rodden, *Politics of Literary Reputation*, 185, 130; Malcolm Bradbury, *The Modern British Novel* (1993; London, 2001), 227—'interwoven by a European and internationalist view'; David Gervais, *Literary Englands* (Cambridge 1993), 175; Taylor, *Orwell*, 461, John Brannigan, *Orwell to the Present. Literature in England 1945–2000* (Basingstoke, 2003), 2; Christopher Hitchens, *Orwell's Victory* (London, 2003), 98—' "English" in the sense that Thomas Rainsborough and Tom Paine were English…intended for universal consumption'; Ben Clarke, 'Orwell and Englishness', *Review of English Studies*, 57 (2006), 86, and *Orwell in Context* (2007), 173. There were also forays by Christine Berberich, 'Orwell in Defence of Old England', in A Lazaro, *Road to George Orwell* (Bern 2001); and Jonathan Rose, 'Englands his Englands', and John Rossi, 'Orwell's Patriotism', in Rodden, *Companion to Orwell*; and Ian Williams ('bit of an old fogey'), in John Rodden, *Every Intellectual's Big Brother: George Orwell's Literary Siblings* (Austin, Tex., 2006), 138; and Peter Lowe, 'Englishness in a Time of Crisis', *Cambridge Quarterly*, 38: 3 (2009).

16. For the man of his time, acting English as the incarnation of English middle-class ordinariness and reserve in times of war, see: Gill Plain, *John Mills and British Cinema: Masculinity, Identity and Nation* (Edinburgh, 2006), Introduction: 'Acting English'.

17. On the guardians of the constitution: Robert Colls, 'After Bagehot: Rethinking the Constitution', *Political Quarterly*, 78: 4 (2007), and 'The Constitution of the English', *History Workshop Journal*, 46 (1998).

18. T. R. Fyvel, *George Orwell: A Personal Memoir* (London, 1982), 9; John Bright-Holmes, *Like It Was: The Diaries of Malcolm Muggeridge* (London, 1981), entries for 27 Sept. 1949, 21 Jan. 1950, pp. 353, 375. On various approaches to his literary biography, see Roger Averill, 'A Consideration of the Authorized Versions of George Orwell', *Clio* (Fall, 2001), 31, i.

Chapter 1

1. 'Night Attack on the Aragon Front', *The New Leader*, 30 Apr. 1937, *CW* xi. 19. The story was based on extracts from letters from the men involved, though there is no sign of anything from Orwell.

2. Or as Stefan Collini would have it, a 'public moralist': *Public Moralists* (Oxford, 1991), 16, 31. On the need for patrons in how a young left-wing public moralist went about his business in 1937, see K. O. Morgan, *Michael Foot: A Life* (London, 2007), 41–64.

3. 'The years between the world wars were the heyday of the idea of English national character': Peter Mandler, *The English National Character* (London, 2006), 143.

4. 'What I have most wanted to do throughout the past ten years is to make political writing into an art': 'Why I Write', *Gangrel*, 4 (1946), *CW* xviii. 319; 'Toward European Unity', *Partisan Review* (July–Aug. 1947), *CW* xix. 163–7.

5. '…a mistaken theory, but the natural result of being one of the oppressors yourself': George Orwell, *The Road to Wigan Pier* (1937; Harmondsworth, 1967), 129–30.

6. Dietmar Rothermund, 'Asian Peasants in the Great Depression 1930–39', in H. V. Harold James (ed.), *The Inter War Depression in an International Context* (Munich, 2002), 19.
7. Darkened Chinese opium dens in Limehouse set the scene: Andrew Blake, 'Britain, Asia and the Opium Trade', in Bill Schwarz (ed.), *The Expansion of England* (London, 1996), 258.
8. *Wigan Pier*, 112.
9. 'This was snobbish, if you like, but it was also necessary, for middle-class people cannot afford to let their children grow up with vulgar accents': ibid. 110.
10. Orwell came to this judgement over thirty years later when writing his school memoir, 'Such, Such Were the Joys' (*Partisan Review*, Sept.–Oct. 1952). The memoir appears to have been started in 1938 and finally completed to his satisfaction in 1948: *CW* xix. 353–6.
11. His father had been a medium-ranking civil servant in the Indian Civil Service. It would have been impossible for him to afford full fee instead of what he did pay, which was 10 guineas per year tuition and 10 guineas per year into the school fund. Full fee was about £100 per year, roughly equivalent in 1900 to what a skilled man in regular employment could expect to earn in the same period: A. Clutton-Brock, *Eton* (London, 1900), 170.
12. Which included fagging and flogging: ibid. 176–7.
13. Ibid. 201.
14. Warre was remembered as 'the largest and the loudest': Percy Lubbock, *Shades of Eton* (London, 1932), 10–12.
15. Lyttelton had to resign in April 1916 after suggesting that Britain give up Gibraltar as a sign of good intent before proceeding to a negotiated peace with Germany: Richard Ollard, *An English Education: A Perspective of Eton* (London, 1982), 90. It says something about Orwell that he made nothing of this in later life. All the same, 5,687 Old Etonians served in the armed forces between 1914 and 1918, nearly one-fifth were killed, a quarter were wounded, and thirteen won the Victoria Cross.
16. Noel Annan, *Roxburgh of Stowe* (London, 1965), 10.
17. 'But we'll still swing together | And swear by the best of schools': 'The Eton Boating Song' (1862: words by William Johnson). See Ch. 3, nn. 124–5.
18. 'The Sporting Spirit', *Tribune*, 14 Dec. 1945, *CW* xvii. 441. On the public-school games ethic, which Orwell experienced in its heyday, see Mark Girouard, *The Return to Camelot: Chivalry and the English Gentleman* (New Haven, 1981), ch. 15.
19. A 'fag' is English public-school slang for a young boy who performs menial tasks for an older boy. It was also used as a verb.
20. 'There are no rules on these subjects as far as masters are concerned...but there is an etiquette...the public opinion of the school has nearly always been extraordinarily sound': L. S. R. Byrne and E. L. Churchill, *Changing Eton* (London, 1940), 214.
21. 'The Man and the Maid' (1916–18), and 'The Adventures of the Lost Meat Card', 'The Slack Bob', and 'A Peep into the Future' (*The Election Times*, 4, 3 June 1918) Orwell Archive, A/1 b), c) and *CW* x. 31–50.
22. He described his time at Eton as 'five years in a luke-warm bath of snobbery': 'Inside the Whale', in *Inside the Whale and Other Essays* (London, 1940), *CW* xii. 104. He also remembered anti-war attitudes at Eton towards the end of the war— slackness on parade, sniggering at masters who had returned, and so on: 'My Country Right or Left', *Folios of New Writing*, 2 (1940), *CW* xii. 270. English public-school iconoclasm is supposed to have started in 1917 with Alec Waugh's account of his time at Sherborne: 'sooner or later pain grows into a custom': *The Loom of Youth* (London, 1984), 28.

23. As recalled by Tom Hopkinson, 'George Orwell', *Cornhill Magazine* (Summer 1953), 83. Eton's view of boy character comes from R. S. Chattock's *Sketches of Eton* (London, 1874), 50.

24. Patrick Joyce. *The State of Freedom* (Cambridge, 2013), ch.7. Unfortunately Joyce mistakes St Cyprian's for Eton (278). George Orwell, 'For Ever Eton', *Observer*, 1 Aug. 1948, in *Orwell: The Observer Years* (London, 2004), 226. See Francis Hope, 'Schooldays', in Miriam Gross (ed.), *The World of George Orwell* (London, 1971), and school memories of Cyril Connolly, Christopher Hollis, Denys King-Farlow, and Steven Runciman in Coppard and Crick, *Orwell Remembered*.

25. 'The Empire...leaves me cold...': A. C. Benson, Diary, 1917, quoted in Ronald Hyam, 'The British Empire in the Edwardian Era', in Judith M. Brown and W. Roger Louis (eds.), *The Oxford History of the British Empire* (henceforth *OHBE*), vol. 4: *The Twentieth Century* (Oxford, 1999), 47.

26. Jacintha Buddicom, *Eric & Us* (1974; Chichester, 2006), 119. Orwell's father had been one of twelve children, had not gone to public school or to university, and had been obliged to join one of the more lowly parts of the Indian Civil Service. Orwell's paternal grandfather, vicar of Milborne St Andrew, Dorset, had begun his career in the Church of England in Calcutta.

27. After 1856 twenty-four out of forty-eight King's College Scholarships were reserved for Etonians; the first non-Etonian King's Fellow was not elected until 1873: Revd Austen Leigh, *King's College* (London, 1899), 279.

28. Forster was writing *A Passage to India* (1924) at the time Orwell would have gone. Keynes was busy saving economics. For Keynes at Kings see Robert Skidelsky, *John Maynard Keynes: The Economist as Saviour 1920–1937* (London, 1992), 3–9 and *passim*.

29. 'I was both a snob and a revolutionary...I could agonize over their [working-class] sufferings, but I still hated them': *Wigan Pier*, 122.

30. Burma was indicated on the strength of 'have had relatives there': Indian Police Force Application (7 Apr. 1922) and Appointments (23 Nov. 1922), Orwell Archive, unreferenced in J catalogue. No Indian or Burmese records survive of his time there: see letters of 1961 from Indian government officials in the same file.

31. John Darwin, *The Empire Project: The Rise and Fall of the British World System 1830–1970* (Cambridge, 2009), 9–10.

32. Mahatma Gandhi, *My Appeal to the British*, 5 July 1942 (New York, 1942), 55. On British views of Indian history: Bernard S Cohen, 'African Models and Indian Histories', in Cohen, *An Anthropologist among the Historians and Other Essays* (Delhi 1996), 208–22.

33. Orwell could smell a vegetarian pacifist crank in India long before he could sniff them out in England: George Orwell, 'Reflections on Gandhi', *Partisan Review* (Jan. 1949), *CW* xx. 5–6. Gandhi's partial biography was first published in instalments in Gujarati in the journal *Navijan* and in English in the newspaper *Young India* (1925–9). Orwell does not say which he read.

34. 'I was part of the actual machinery of despotism...in the police you see the dirty work of Empire at close quarters': *Wigan Pier*, 127; District Officer's court: G. W. Stevens, *In India* (London, 1899), 165.

35. 'In Moulmein, in Lower Burma, I was hated by large numbers of people...': George Orwell, 'Shooting an Elephant', *New Writing*, 2 (1936), *CW* x. 501. Late nineteenth-century imperialism changed the way most British thought about being British as the Empire increasingly operated as a sort of fifth dimension to national identity: John M. Mackenzie, *Propaganda and Empire: The Manipulation of British Public Opinion 1880–1960* (Manchester, 1985), 2; Arthur Engel, 'Political Education in Oxford 1823–1914', *History of Education Quarterly*, 20: 3 (1980), 257.

36. George Orwell, *Burmese Days* (1934; London, 1989), 38. Richard Blair finished his career as Sub-Deputy Opium Agent, 4th grade. The British had nationalized the traditional drug trade with China; all revenue went to the Indian Treasury: Joshua Rowntree, *The Imperial Drug Trade* (London, 1905).

37. J. F. Cady, *A History of Modern Burma* (New York, 1958), 156–86.

38. Charles Joppen, *Historical Atlas of India* (Bombay, 1926), 33.

39. See e.g. C. A. Bayly, *Indian Society and the Making of the British Empire* (Cambridge, 1985), 194, and P. B. Rich, *Race and Empire in British Politics* (Cambridge, 1986), ch. 3.

40. Peter Burroughs, 'Imperial Institutions and the Government of the Empire', in Andrew Porter (ed.), *OHBE*, vol. 3: *The Nineteenth Century* (Oxford, 1999), 181–2.

41. Raleigh Trevelyan, *The Golden Oriole: Childhood, Family and Friends in India* (Oxford, 1988), 257. Servants were kept in the compound, not the bungalow: Thomas Metcalf, *Ideologies of the Raj* (Cambridge, 1997), 178.

42. Ibid. 183.

43. 'Our life in India, our very work more or less, rests on illusion': Sir Walter Lawrence, *The India We Served* (London, 1928), 43; Anthony Clayton, *The British Empire as a Superpower 1919–39* (Basingstoke, 1986), 11.

44. Quoted by Perry Anderson, 'Gandhi Centre Stage', *London Review of Books*, 5 July 2012.

45. And so the imperial experience of being Indian reflected back on the British view of being British. The British had seen Bengalis as unmanly almost from the start, but it had begun to change by Orwell's time: John Rosselli, 'The Self Image of Effeteness: Physical Education and Nationalism in 19th century Bengal', *Past and Present*, 86 (Feb. 1990), 123. In 1975 J. G. A. Pocock famously called for a new British history that recognized these complex imperial interconnections: 'British History: A Plan for a New Subject', *Journal of Modern History*, 47: 4 (Dec. 1975).

46. In his novel *Kim* Rudyard Kipling has the English curator of Lahore Museum give the Tibetan monk a *babu* kit of five sharpened pencils, a book of paper, and a pair of spectacles: *Kim* (1901; Harmondsworth, 1994), 21.

47. 'Land of shit and filth and wogs | Gonnorhoea, syphilis, clap, and pox | Memsahib's paradox, soldier's hell | India fare thee fuckin' well'—said to be a song of the 1st Cameron Highlanders, though it sounds more like officers' mess to me: L. James, *Raj* (London, 1997), 597. There were various attempts to teach the British about their Empire: the Great Exhibition in 1851, the Colonial and Indian Exhibition in 1886, the Imperial Institute in 1887, the British Empire exhibitions of 1924 and 1938, 'Colonial Month' in 1949, and of course huge encounters during both world wars. Yet a public-opinion poll in 1948 showed that over half those interviewed could not name a single British colony: *The Times*, 22 June 1949.

48. Report of the Burma Police Enquiry Committee (Rangoon, Office of the Superintendant 1924): British Library, India Office Records, V/26/150/4, p. 28.

49. On the principle of 'indirect rule' and political management, see Brown and Louis, *OHBE* iv. 233–48.

50. Orwell, 'Shooting an Elephant', 504.

51. Mary Louise Pratt, *Imperial Eyes* (London, 1992), 7. For early representations of these peoples, almost a prehistory, see M Daunton and R Halpern (eds.), *Empire and Others: British Encounters with Indigenous People 1600–1850* (London, 1999).

52. D. G. E. Hall, *Burma* (New York, 1950), 156.

53. Michael W. Charney, *A History of Modern Burma* (Cambridge, 2009), 23–5.

54. Claude Lévi-Strauss, 'Crowds', *New Left Review*, 15 (1962), 4–5. See also John Le Roy Christian, *Modern Burma* (Berkeley, 1942), 174.

55. 'When I said "irrigation", they replied "malaria". When I mentioned railways, they countered with the export of wheat': G. Lowes Dickinson talked to some Indian graduates of Oxford and Cambridge (*Manchester Guardian*, 18 Feb. 1913). They also observed that the English acted differently in England than in India.

56. As much a reflection of their own history as India's: Clive Dewey, 'Images of the Village Community: A Study in Anglo Indian Thought', *Modern Asian Studies*, 6 (1972), 294.

57. Crick, *Orwell*, 151.

58. Clive Dewey, *Anglo-Indian Attitudes: The Mind of the Indian Civil Service* (London, 1993), ch. 7.

59. An empire governed 'with astonishing small units': Ronald Hyam, *Britain's Declining Empire* (Cambridge, 2006), 10.

60. Virtually no one who did not have private means was promoted to leading positions in colonial administration; those who were, struggled. Empire professionals were the dominant group, but 'harsh climates, tropical disease, poor pay and diverse conditions of employment' made it difficult to recruit the right men. Applications fell off alarmingly from the early 1920s: Andrew Thompson, *The Empire Strikes Back? The Impact of Imperialism on Britain from the mid 19th Century* (Harlow, 2005), 19.

61. Colonial Office instructions banned 'concubinage' in 1909 in order to encourage British female emigration. White women 'became in turn the focus of tension and challenge': R. O'Hanlon, 'Gender in the British Empire', in Brown and Louis, *OHBE* iv. 393.

62. Charles Allen, *Raj: A Scrapbook of British India* (London, 1977), 23.

63. Orwell, *Burmese Days*, 14–15. Denis Kincaid describes this clubby world, through 'a faint and murky glow [that] came from the direction of the teeming city [where] few of them had ever driven': *British Social Life in India* (London, 1938), 234.

64. Against Gandhi's dictum that 'no contribution made to a conqueror can be truly described as voluntary': *My Appeal to the British* (New York, 1942), 24 May 1942, p. 17.

65. *Burmese Days*, 36–8. More likely to please Veraswami than Flory, Congress politicians had called for a self-governing India as a dominion in 'the Great Confederacy of Free States, English in their origins, English in their character, English in their institutions, rejoicing in their permanent and indissoluble union with England': Surendrenath Banerjee (1895), quoted in Darwin, *Empire Project*, 201.

66. See D. G. E. Hall, *Imperialism in Modern History* (Rangoon, Standing Committee on the Imperial Idea, 1923), 70.

67. Orwell claimed that British living standards would plummet without the imperial economy. In fact, although the volume of imperial trade increased in the nineteenth century, the Empire had accounted for a much greater proportion of British trade before 1776 than after it. Between 1854 and 1913 it accounted for 31.9 per cent British exports, and 23.6 per cent British imports, and 'was not great enough for Imperial considerations to dominate British international economic policy': P. J. Cain, 'Economics and Empire', in Porter, *OHBE* iii. 35, 43, 31. Even John Flory's timber was a falling commodity—the Empire accounting for 16.2 per cent British timber imports in 1913 compared to 55.2 per cent in 1854 (p. 43).

68. P. K. O'Brien, 'The Costs and Benefits of British Imperialism 1846–1914', *Past and Present*, 120 (1988), 181. See also L. E. Davis and R. A. Huttenback, *Mammon and the Pursuit of Empire 1860–1912* (Cambridge, 1986).

69. 'Britain's economic position was neither substantially improved nor materially weakened by the possession of an overseas empire'; financial gains from imperial

investments were 'not significantly greater than those to be made from investing in the UK or other markets overseas': Thompson, *Empire Strikes Back*, 156, 162.

70. For the promoters, Anandi Ramamurthy, *Imperial Persuaders: Images of Africa and Asia in British Advertising* (Manchester, 2003), 4–8, and David Meredith, 'Imperial Images: The Empire Marketing Board 1926–32', *History Today*, 37: 1 (Jan. 1987), 32. It was one of Orwell's frequent jibes at left intellectuals that 'those of us who are "enlightened" all maintain that those coolies ought to be set free; but our standard of living, and hence our "enlightenment", demands that the robbery shall continue': 'Rudyard Kipling', *Horizon* (Feb. 1942), *CW* xiii. 153.

71. Caroline Elkins insinuates genocide in 'a murderous campaign' by the British against the Mau Mau 'to eliminate Kikuyu people'—and carefully picks her words and makes her calculations accordingly. Her choice of the word 'gulag' seems particularly odd: *Britain's Gulag: The Brutal End of Empire in Kenya* (London, 2005), pp. xiv, 366.

72. Darwin, *Empire Project*, 54, 20, 12–14.

73. On the other side, the censuses from 1881 onwards helped shape Indian politics and religious and ethnic identity too: Ian Talbot, *India and Pakistan: Inventing the Nation* (London, 2000), 14.

74. As for the whole, the *Oxford History of the British Empire* avoids judgement. 'Can the lasting impact of British rule ultimately be judged as beneficial or harmful? The book as a whole adopts a pluralistic approach…': Brown and Louis, *OHBE* iv, p. xii. Linda Colley concurs: 'we all need to stop approaching empire in simple "good" or "bad" thing terms, and instead think intelligently and enquiringly about its many and intrinsic paradoxes': 'Into the Belly of the Beast', *Guardian*, 18 Jan. 2003.

75. J. A. Hobson, *Imperialism: A Study* (1902; London, 1961), 5–12. Hobson had begun by exploring the psychological dimensions of empire in his *The Psychology of Jingoism* (London, 1901). Avner Offer ends his economic case by making the psychological case in his 'The British Empire 1870–1914: A Waste of Money?', *Economic History Review*, 46: 2 (1993), 232–4.

76. Sidney Webb (Lord Passfield), was Secretary of State for the Dominions and Colonies 1929–31: Hyam, *Declining Empire*, 47. Burma became independent in January 1948 and opted not to remain in the Commonwealth.

77. 'it…seemed axiomatic that, in one form or another, with more local freedom or less, the bond of empire would hold and the system would endure': Darwin, *Empire Project*, 19.

78. On otherness as the vestige of a 'primordial, dark and instinctual past which their own society had left behind': Benita Parry, *Delusions and Discoveries: Studies on India in the British Imagination 1880–1930* (London, 1972), 3; on sexuality and land: R. K. Ray, *Exploring Emotional History: Gender, Mentality in the Indian Awakening* (New Delhi, 2001), 121; on the use of force as almost a definition of a lower colonial grade: Charles Townshend, 'Martial Law: Legal and Administrative Problems of Civil Emergency in Britain and the Empire 1800–1940', *Historical Journal*, 25: 1 (March 1982), 168–72.

79. O. Mannoni, *Prospero and Caliban: The Psychology of Colonization* (1950; London, 1956).

80. Paul Rich, *Race and Empire in British Politics* (Cambridge, 1986), 90–1.

81. Thus 'the Empire made no great material demands on most people, at least none that they were aware of, and did not need support or even interest': Bernard Porter, *The Absent Minded Imperialists* (Oxford, 2004), 307. For a more positive assessment: Daniel Gorman, *Imperial Citizenship: Empire and the Question of Belonging*

(Manchester 2010). Darwin reviews the historiography to show an Empire portrayed as either a British accident or a British conspiracy: John Darwin, 'Imperialism and the Victorians', *English Historical Review*, 112 (1997), 630.

82. Review of the *The Heart of the Matter*, *New Yorker*, 17 July 1948, *CW* xix. 405.
83. 'Marrakech', *New Writing*, 3 (Christmas 1939), *CW* xi. 420.
84. 'I was in the Indian Police five years and by the end of that time I hated the imperialism I was serving with a bitterness which I probably cannot make clear': Orwell, *Wigan Pier*, 126.
85. Ibid. 130.
86. In London (Booth 1889); in York (Rowntree 1901 and 1936); in Bolton, Northampton, Reading, Stanley, and Warrington (Bowley 1914, and 1924); in London (Llewelyn Smith 1935); on Merseyside (Caradog Jones 1930); and in Southampton (Ford 1931): see C. A. and C. L. Linsley, 'Booth, Rowntree and Llewelyn Smith: A Re-assessment of Interwar Poverty', *Economic History Review*, 46 (1993), 88–90 and table 7.
87. Most Liberal voters preferred the Conservatives over Labour as a second choice, and Labour never managed to collect more than half the working-class vote. Both facts left them struggling to find a combative politics: Ross Mckibbin, *Parties and People: England 1914–1951* (Oxford, 2010), 73, 63.
88. 'Why I Write', *Gangrel*, 4 (Summer 1946), *CW* xviii. 316.
89. 'He wrote like a cow with a musket', recalled Ruth Pitter (Crick, Orwell, *ODNB*), but by September 1929 he had had five articles published in professional journals, earning £20 the lot.
90. Orwell, 'How the Poor Die', *Now*, 6 (Nov. 1946), *CW* xviii. 459–67.
91. He got this generally right. On gradual upper-class withdrawal from government and administration, left with only their wealth and ceremonial duties, see: F. M. L. Thompson, 'English Landed Society in the 20th Century', *Transactions of the Royal Historical Society*, 16 Nov. 1990 and 20 Nov. 1992.
92. Revd Andrew Mearns, *The Bitter Cry of Outcast London: An Inquiry into the Condition of the Abject Poor* (London, 1883), one penny each or 6s. per hundred: Introduction by A. S. Wohl (Leicester, 1970).
93. Maude F. Davies, *Life in an English Village* (London, 1909), 285; G. K. Chesterton, 'Why I am not a Socialist', *The New Age*, 4 January 1908.
94. Davies (W. H.) reviewed Orwell's *Down and Out in Paris and London* for the *New Statesman and Nation*, 18 Mar. 1933.
95. Chaplin's tramp character, rather like Orwell's, was a gentleman of refined sensibilities down on his luck. Unlike Orwell, however, Chaplin (born 1889) knew the asylums and workhouses of South London at first hand.
96. Orwell was more a reader than a filmgoer, but there was no shortage of exemplars in the documentary film movement, all minor masterpieces made by people whose politics and aesthetics, for a while, converged with his—including John Grierson's *Drifters* (1929), Robert Flaherty's *Industrial Britain* (1931), Paul Rotha's *Shipyard* (1935) and *People of Britain* (1936), Arthur Elton's *Housing Problems* (1935), and Ruby Grierson's *Today We Live* (1937). If they had been made into films, the second part of *Down and Out in Paris and London* and the first part of *The Road to Wigan Pier* would have not looked out of place: British Film Institute, *Land of Promise: The British Documentary Movement 1930–1950* (London, 2007).
97. Mayhew reported how on one night 2,431 people preferred the dirt, noise, and cost of the cheap lodging-house compared to the 849 tramps who preferred the workhouse casual ward: *Morning Chronicle*, 25 Jan. 1850, in *Morning Chronicle Survey of Labour and the Poor* (Horsham, 1981), 46–9; George Orwell, *Down and Out in Paris and London* (1933; Harmondsworth, 1971), 186–8, and 'The Spike' (*The Adelphi*,

Apr. 1931), *CW* x. 197–203. See also Jack London, *The People of the Abyss* (London, 1903), ch. 9, 'The Spike'. In reference to later corners of Orwell's writing—his pea-and-thimble analogy with the Marxist dialectic for instance, or O'Brien's musings on astrophysics in *Nineteen Eighty-Four*, or the time he was sent from the hotel looking for a peach in the middle of the night, one can find in Mayhew the 'Thimble riggers and their 3 thimbles and a pea trick', the coster who considered the sun and stars to be no more than bits of fire in the sky, and the coster who got peaches for the Prince of Naples 'not far from here': Henry Mayhew, *London Labour and the London Poor* (1861–2; Oxford, 2010), 453, 146, 29–30.

98. E. A. Blair, 'La Censure en Angleterre', *Monde*, 6 Oct. 1928, *CW* x. 117; 'Every paper of this kind ... is the enemy of free speech': E. A. Blair, 'A Farthing Newspaper', *GK's Weekly*, 29 Dec. 1928, *CW* x. 120. In 1926 Norman Angell attacked the power of the mass press to 'intensify and fix' and otherwise manipulate popular opinion with 'evils like nationalism and race hatred': *The Public Mind: Its Disorders; Its Exploitation* (London, 1926), 138.

99. For the tradition of middle-class men going in search of the poor and destitute, for all sorts of reasons, not all of them philanthropic, see Seth Kovan, *Slumming: Sexual and Social Politics in Victorian London* (Princeton, 2005).

100. Orwell, *Down and Out*, 5, 189.

101. Hospital records say M. Arthur Blair was admitted 7 March 'pour une grippe': letter, Groupe Hospitalier Cochin to Mde Sonia Orwell, 25 Nov. 1971, Orwell Archive, unreferenced in J catalogue.

102. 'How the Poor Die', *Now* (Nov. 1946), *CW* xviii. 459–66. See as well his Universal Hop Pickers' Account Book, Aug.–Sept. 1931: Orwell Archive, J/5.

103. The Local Government Act of 1929 abolished the Poor Law Unions, makers of the modern workhouse from 1834.

104. Orwell, *Down and Out*, 186.

105. 'The Spike', *The Adelphi*, Apr. 1931; 'A Hanging', *The Adelphi*, Aug. 1931; 'Shooting an Elephant', *New Writing*, 2 (Autumn 1936). Orwell always wrote for small magazines as well as big ones, enjoying their 'real time' rapid publishing schedule: Peter Marks, *George Orwell the Essayist: Literature, Politics and the Periodical Culture* (London, 2011), 5. At the same time, he sought the public sphere and never wished 'to retreat into the private and elite confines of coterie publication': Mark S. Morrisson, *The Public Face of Modernism: Little Magazines, Audiences and Reception 1905–1920* (Madison, Wisc., 2001), 10.

106. He taught in Hayes from April 1932 to July 1933. He taught in Uxbridge from August to December 1933. Fray's was a much bigger school, with 180 pupils and thirty boarders. Orwell lived in.

107. Leonard Moore of Christy and Moore. After rejections at Faber and Cape, unbeknown to Orwell, his *Down and Out* manuscript was sent to Moore by a Southwold friend, Mabel Fierz. Twice in the same letter Orwell told the man he was inviting to be his agent that he did not think it was a good piece of work: letter, Orwell to Moore, The Hawthorns, Station Road, Hayes, 26 Apr. 1932, *CW* x. 243. Moore stayed with Orwell until the writer's death in 1950.

108. His Aunt Nellie Limouzin introduced him to the Westropes, who owned the bookshop and the flat. They were Esperantists, pacificists, vegetarians, and committed members of the ILP: *CW* x. 354–5. Orwell loved books, and says he only left the bookshop when he lost the love: 'Bookshop Memories', *Fortnightly* (Nov. 1936), *CW* x. 513. All his biographers testify to a lifetime reading, particularly the English classics (Chaucer, Shakespeare, Smollett, Surtees, Marryat, Dickens, Thackeray, Trollope, Bennett, Lawrence), and Somerset Maugham and James Joyce (special

favourites), and continental and American writers including Conrad, Villon, Maupassant, Zola, Poe, Twain, and Zola. In his sickbed he was asking for books to review ('I prefer the sociological ones, or else literary criticism'): letter to Ivor Brown, from Ward 3, Hairmyres Hospital, East Kilbride, 31 Dec. 1947, *CW* xix. 239. He told an American Writers' Directory in 1940 that 'I believe the modern writer who has influenced me most is Somerset Maugham, whom I admire immensely for his power of telling a story straightforwardly': letter, from The Stores, Wallington, 17 Apr. 1940, *CW* xii. 148. Maugham's collection of very short stories, *On a Chinese Screen* (1922), includes 'The Vice Consul', the story of an execution (involving a very young man with very long legs and a small round face), which is not unlike Orwell's 1931 'A Hanging'.

109. Jeffrey Meyers (ed.), *George Orwell: The Critical Heritage* (London, 1975), 68–9, and Gordon Bowker, *George Orwell* (London, 2003), 161, 171–2.

110. He first discovered *Ulysses* in 1933: letter to Brenda Salkeld, from 36 High Street, Southwold, early Sept. 1934, *CW* x. 348. He is writing *A Clergyman's Daughter* to the sound of merry-go-round music from Southwold's annual fair, which goes on into the small hours. Salkeld was a clergyman's daughter. She was also the object of his infatuation for over twenty years and, it would appear, keen to keep him at a Joycean disadvantage.

111. 'Big-dipper' singing as described by Richard Hoggart in *The Uses of Literacy* (1957; Harmondsworth, 1966), 154–5. Hoggart improves upon Owell's phonetics: 'you are-er/the only one-er/for me-er.' George Orwell, *A Clergyman's Daughter* (1935; Harmondsworth, 1960), 105. Orwell never liked the book: 'I am so miserable, struggling in the entrails of that dreadful book, and never getting any further, and loathing the sight of what I have done': letter Orwell to Brenda Salkeld, from 36 High Street, Southwold, 27 July 1934, in *CW* x. 344; 'it is tripe [*barbouillage*]': letter Orwell to M. R. N. Raimbault, from 77 Parliament Hill, Hampstead NW3, 11 Mar. 1935, in Peter Davison (ed.), *The Lost Orwell* (London, 2006), 44.

112. George Orwell, *Keep The Aspidistra Flying* (1936; Harmondsworth, 1968), 33.

113. 'I think most of the people who knew him in those days felt that there was something of themselves in that book...a lot of the incidents were things that I recognized': Kate Ekevall, friend and girlfriend, BBC typescript 1984, in Coppard and Crick, *Orwell Remembered*, 101. For their high-cultural but left-leaning friendship group, see also the testimony of his flatmate Rayner Heppenstall (ibid. 109–10).

114. 'And let us now, as men condemned...', etc.: poem 'Sometimes in the middle autumn days': *The Adelphi* (Mar. 1933), *CW* x. 306.

115. His first review came from 'MH' (Muriel Harris) in the *Manchester Guardian*, 9 Jan. 1933. She thought he had 'much to say in that quiet level voice of his'. Other reviews included those in the *Evening Standard* (J. B. Priestley), the *Daily Mail* (Compton Mackenzie), the *New Clarion* (H. E. Bates), *The New Statesman and Nation* (W. H. Davies), *The Adelphi* (Cecil Day Lewis), the *Tatler* (Richard King), and, in the USA, the *Herald Tribune*, the *New Republic*, and the *New York Times*. All these and more shouldered the burden of reviewing Orwell's small print-runs until he was properly slightly famous or at any rate known, with the publication of over 50,000 copies of *The Road to Wigan Pier* in March 1937.

116. Peter Stansky and William Abrahams, *Orwell: The Transformation* (London, 1979), 65.

117. Orwell, *Aspidistra Flying*, 21.

118. 'Complete inertia...and being obliged to spit very frequently, and the spittle being curiously white and flocculent': *Down and Out*, 34.

119. Anthony Comstock (1844–1915) was an American campaigner for the suppression of vice, particularly famous for the 'Comstock Law' of 1873 passed by Congress to prohibit the transport or delivery of obscene materials, including contraceptives. George Bernard Shaw coined the term 'Comstockery' for a particularly foolish form of bigotry. Orwell's Comstock considers contraceptives to be a capitalist plot against the poor.
120. Extract, published in *The Adelphi* (Apr. 1934), *CW* x. 338.
121. Brenda Salkeld to Orwell, Southwold, early Sept. 1934, and Orwell to Salkeld, 2 Windsor St, London W9, Oct. 1931, *CW* x. 348, 236.
122. Letter, Orwell to Leonard Moore, from 'The Hawthorns', Church Road, Hayes, 19 Nov. 1932, *CW* x. 274. See Bowker, *Orwell*, ch. 8, 'The Invention of George Orwell'.
123. Review of 'Caliban Shrieks' by Jack Hilton for *The Adelphi* (Mar. 1935), *CW* x. 381–2. Previous reviews had been signed 'Eric A. Blair'.
124. Orwell's friend Sir Richard Rees gave Peter Stansky and William Abrahams the clue to their study of Orwell when they visited him in London in 1967. They were finding Orwell 'elusive', but at 'some point in that afternoon, [Rees] remarked in a characteristically diffident way, "But of course if you want to understand Orwell, you have to understand Blair"—his way of pronouncing the name was remarkable and cannot be reproduced; he seemed to lengthen it by at least a syllable—"and to understand Blair, well, there's your book"': *The Unknown Orwell* (London, 1972), p. x.
125. This is not to say that the two of them did not work in tandem. Michael Shelden drew attention to an annotated copy of *Down and Out in Paris and London* that Orwell gave to Brenda Salkeld where he, 'Blair', confirms the general veracity of what, he, 'Orwell' has written: *Orwell: The Authorized Biography* (London, 1991), 145–6. Tony Judt noted that Orwell thought in two ranges—detailed English or universal moral: *Thinking the Twentieth Century* (London, 2012), 188.
126. Walter Bagehot, *The English Constitution* (1867; London, 1963), 248; *Letters of Lord Chesterfield* (1774), in S. M. Brewer, *Design for a Gentleman: The Education of Philip Stanhope* (London, 1963), 197; Colls, 'Constitution of the English', 97–108.
127. George Orwell, 'Writers and Leviathan', *Politics and Letters* (Summer 1948), *CW* xix. 292.
128. Stefan Collini, *Absent Minds: Intellectuals in Britain* (Oxford, 2006), 369.
129. Collini writes generally about resistance to intellectuals in Britain in the 1930s, a country with an identity based on it: ibid., chs. 1–5. Out of twenty-nine surviving letters to his friend Lydia Jackson between 1939 and 1949, Peter Davison has counted that Orwell signed himself 'Eric' on eighteen occasions and 'George' on eleven, with 'no apparent pattern': *CW* xix. 341.
130. Pieces for *Le Progrès civique* (1928–9), *CW* x. 121–38. His first published piece appears to have been 'La Censure en Angleterre', *Le Monde*, 6 Oct. 1928, *CW* x. 117–19.
131. Letter, R. N. Raimbault to Orwell, 22 Nov. 1934, in Davison, *Lost Orwell*, 18.
132. Eric Blair, 'The Spike', *CW* x. 199–200.
133. Ibid. 198.
134. Eric Blair, 'A Hanging', *CW* x. 208.
135. Only fiction, though Gollancz delayed publication because he feared libel. Orwell changed the names.
136. Untitled play, 1927–8, *CW* x. 104.
137. George Orwell, *The Lion and the Unicorn: Socialism and the English Genius* (London, 1941), *CW* xii. 406.
138. George Orwell, review of Henry Miller, *Tropic of Cancer*, *New English Weekly*, 14 Nov. 1935, *CW* x. 405. He returned to Miller in his important essay 'Inside the Whale' in 1940. Miller also saw Paris as 'leprous': *Tropic of Cancer* (1934; London 1995), 48.
139. Letter to Henry Miller, from The Stores, Wallington, 26–7 Aug. 1936, *CW* x. 495–6.

Chapter 2

1. Orwell, *Wigan Pier*, 5.
2. Robert C. Allen, *The British Industrial Revolution in Global Perspective* (Cambridge, 2009), 275.
3. J. D. Tomlinson, Alan Booth, and Sean Glyn, 'Inter-war Unemployment: Two Views', *Journal of Contemporary History*, 17: 3 (1982), 547, 553.
4. R. H. Tawney made the case for public ownership in his *The Nationalization of the Coal Industry* (London, 1920). The year before, the Royal Commission on the Coal Industry had found in favour of nationalization—a recommendation the government chose to ignore and the miners chose to remember.
5. G. D. H. and M. I. Cole, *The Condition of Britain* (London, 1937), 219. Good narrative accounts of the period are to be found in A. J. P. Taylor, *English History 1914–45* (Oxford, 1965), Peter Clarke, *Land of Hope and Glory: Britain 1900–1990* (London, 1997), and Ross McKibbin, *Parties and People: England 1914–51* (Oxford, 2010). See also R. Page Arnot, *The Miners in Crisis and War* (London, 1961), 10–33.
6. The government introduced 'Special Areas' assistance in 1934, but not for Lancashire. Although British trade-union membership halved between 1920 and 1933, 1920 had been an unnatural high point and wages for those still in work held up comparatively well through the 1930s. National insurance contributions trebled in number, thus providing a wage-floor: D. H. Aldcroft and M. J. Oliver, *Trade Unions and the Economy 1770–2000* (Aldershot, 2000), 86; Chris Wrigley, *British Trade Unions since 1933* (Cambridge, 2002), 7–8.
7. Gollancz commissioned that kind of work as well: see the 63 tables and 12 diagrams of the Coles' *Condition of Britain*.
8. Many cotton-workers were women. In his *The Road to Wigan Pier* Orwell looked at the miners explicitly. In her *Wigan Pier Revisited* (London, 1984) Beatrice Campbell attacked Orwell for not seeing or choosing to see Wigan's considerable population of female spinners. Orwell did try to address the lives of working-class women in the housing sections of his book, which he must have seen as a natural reaction to his investigations underground and a not-unreasonable approach to the lives of working-class women as replicated, for instance, by the Hygiene Committee of the Women's Group on Public Welfare in their 1939–42 study, *Our Towns: A Close-Up* (Oxford, 1943). For a similar but closer study of the lives of working-class women at home, see Margaret Balfour and Joan Drury's *Motherhood in the Special Areas of Durham and Tyneside* (London, 1935).
9. *The Adelphi* had been founded as a monthly by John Middleton Murry in 1923. It was taken over as a quarterly in 1930 by Max Plowman and Richard Rees. Rees paid the bills. He is 'Ravelston' in Orwell's *Keep the Aspidistra Flying*.
10. Victor Gollancz, publisher (1893–1967): St Paul's and New College, Oxford. The call by the Comintern for 'popular fronts' of liberals, socialists, and Communists against Fascists was officially endorsed as Soviet foreign policy in August 1935. It had been preceded by the 'Third Period', so-called, of ultra-leftism, so-called, where all liberal and left-wing, non-Communist organizations were denoted 'Social-Fascist'. Popular Front alliances were most powerfully formed in France and Spain in the summer of 1935.
11. Not only Comstock: with no thought for his personal safety, the documentary film-maker John Grierson expressed his desire 'to travel dangerously into the jungles of Middlesbrough and the Clyde': Samantha Lay, *British Social Realism* (London, 2002), 42.

12. Davison estimates that the trade and paperback editions of *The Road to Wigan Pier* made £604 in royalties for Orwell and a small loss for Gollancz: Peter Davison (ed.), *Orwell's England* (London, 2001), 22–3, and *CW* x. 531. As for Orwell's intentions, he admitted that although the road from Mandalay to Wigan was long, his 'reasons for taking it [were] not immediately clear': *Wigan Pier*, 106. Peter Davison (ed.), *The Lost Orwell* (London 2006), 66.

13. Saturday, 11 Feb. 1905, 'Baby much better. Calling things "beastly"!!': Ida Blair, Orwell's mother, in Coppard and Crick, *Orwell Remembered*, 19.

14. In 1930 over half the leading fifty British companies had their headquarters in London: Christopher M. Law, *British Regional Development since World War One* (London, 1980), 159.

15. 'The industry and inventiveness of the town, the institutions of civic self-government, its social and cultural bodies all figured as expressions of what in retrospect now seems a quite astonishing optimism and confidence': Patrick Joyce, *Visions of the People: Industrial England and the Question of Class 1848–1914* (Cambridge, 1991), 180.

16. The Pilgrim Trust compared 'doomed' Crook and Rhondda with the suffering but not doomed Liverpool and Blackburn, and both pairs with the prosperous Leicester and Deptford: *Men Without Work* (London, 1938), 28–9. Ross McKibbin explains how the middle class assumed the role of 'public opinion' and Englishness itself—a national identity built on 'their very strong sense of not being working class': *Classes and Cultures: England 1918–1951* (Oxford, 1998), 45.

17. S. P. B. Mais, *This Unknown Island* (1932; London, 1936), p. xiv; *National Geographic Magazine*, May 1929, pp. lv, 5, 577; H. V. Morton, *In Search of England* (1927; London, 1936), 186–90; W. S. Shears, *This England: A Book of the Shires and Counties* (London, 1937), 638, 642; J. B. Priestley, *English Journey* (1934; Harmondsworth, 1977), 248; 'and let it revert to an agricultural condition'—Thomas Sharp, *A Derelict Area: A Study of the South West Durham Coalfield* (London, 1935), 44; Belsen analogy, James Lansdale Hodson, *The Way Things Are* (London, 1947), 282–3.

18. David Matless, *Landscape and Englishness* (London, 1998), 32–3 and chs. 1–3.

19. The regions were originally called 'depressed areas' in the Report of Investigations into the Industrial Conditions in Certain Depressed Areas (HMSO, 1934); which was followed by the 1934 Act for state intervention into what it called 'Special Areas'; which was followed by the 1937 Royal Commission (Barlow Commission) on the distribution of the 'Industrial Population', which reported in 1940. Classical economics did not deal with location, or space, as a factor: Duncan Maclennan and John B. Parry, *Regional Policy* (Oxford 1979), 207, 103.

20. Thomas Carlyle, 'Condition-of-England Question', in *Chartism* (London, 1840), 8; Arnold Toynbee, *The Industrial Revolution of the Eighteenth Century in England* (1884; London, 1923), 64.

21. Martin Bulmer (ed.), *Working-Class Images of Society* (London, 1975), 7.

22. *Road to Wigan Pier*, 16–17. He gives a different version of events in his *Wigan Diary*, 15 Feb. 1936, where he encounters her personally, not from a train, but his response is the same: *CW* x. 427.

23. *Wigan Observer*, 1 Feb. 1936. I am grateful to Joe Hayes for this reference.

24. Orwell, *Wigan Diary*, 12 Feb. 1936, *CW* x. 424.

25. Orwell, *Wigan Diary*, 19 Feb. 1936, *CW* x. 430.

26. Orwell, *Wigan Pier*, 18.

27. Letter, Orwell to Connolly, from 72 Warrington Lane, Wigan, 14 Feb. 1936, *CW* x. 426.

28. Orwell, *Wigan Pier*, 110.

29. See Edgar Anstey's thirteen-minute documentary film *Housing Problems* (1935), made with Arthur Elton for the British Gas, Coke and Light Company. They made *Enough to Eat?* the following year.

30. Orwell, *Wigan Pier*, 47, 49.

31.. Margaret Mitchell, 'The Effects of Unemployment on the Social Condition of Women and Children in the 1930s', *History Workshop*, 19 (Spring 1985), 115.

32. Orwell, *Wigan Pier*, 86.

33. Ernst Thälmann (1886–1944), leader of the German Communist Party 1925 to 1933, executed Buchenwald 1944. Orwell had heard Wal Hannington, general secretary of the NUWM, speak in the same hall the week before and considered his speech, and his accent, fake: 'Once again, though a Communist, entirely bourgeois': *Wigan Diary*, 11 Feb. 1936, *CW* x. 424. Of Barnsley marketplace he noted that 'the trouble with all these Communist speakers is that instead of using the popular idiom they employ immensely long sentences': *Wigan Diary*, 22 March 1936, *CW* x. 465. Reviewing Hannington's *The Problem of the Distressed Areas* the following year, to Hannington's credit Orwell concedes that he grasps the 'tragic failure of theoretical Socialism to make any contact with the normal working class', a central theme in *The Road to Wigan Pier*. *Time and Tide*, 27 Nov. 1937, *CW* xi. 99.

34. *Wigan Diary*, 19 Feb. 1936, *CW* x. 436.

35. Humphrey Dakin, in Coppard and Crick, *Orwell Remembered*, 128, and Orwell, *Wigan Diary*, 11 Mar. 1936, *CW* x. 452–3. See Ellen Ross, 'Survival Networks: Women's Neighbourhood Sharing', *History Workshop Journal*, 15 (1983).

36. John Beavan, *World Review*, 16 (June 1950), 49.

37. 'Class political consciousness can be brought to the workers only from without, that is, only from outside the economic struggle', 'trade unionism means the ideological enslavement of the workers by the bourgeoisie': V. I. Lenin, 'What Is To Be Done?', *Selected Works* (1902; Moscow, 1967), 163, 130.

38. Orwell liked to know how things worked, but less so institutions. He was quick to write off the CIU delegates, and criticize them as greedy in the same way that those impeccably bourgeois intellectuals Sidney and Beatrice Webb had criticized the Cooperative Wholesale Society chairman J. T. W. Mitchell and his delegates thirty years before: *CW* x. 431, 455; Stephen Yeo, *Who Was J. T. W. Mitchell?* (Manchester, 1995), 27. On aspects of the English labour movement that Orwell was ignorant of, see J. M. Baernreither, *English Associations of Working Men* (London, 1889), and Ross McKibbin, 'Why Was There No Marxism in Great Britain?', in *Ideologies of Class* (Oxford, 1990), ch. 1. On friendly societies: Simon Cordery, *British Friendly Societies 1750–1914* (Basingstoke, 2003), 68. On women's street-life: Robert Colls, 'When We Lived in Communities: Working-class Culture and its Critics', in R. Colls and R. Rodger (eds.), *Cities of Ideas* (Aldershot, 2004), ch. 12. On the importance of hobbies: Ross McKibbin, 'Work and Hobbies in Britain 1880–1', *Ideologies of Class*, ch. 5.

39. John Benson, 'The Thrift of English Coal-Miners', *Economic History Review*, 2nd series, 31: 3 (1978), 418.

40. *Wigan Observer*, 3 Mar. 1936.

41. George Orwell, 'Looking Back on the Spanish Civil War' (given as 1943 but more likely 1942), in *Homage to Catalonia* (1938; Harmondsworth, 1968), 239.

42. For the literary figures: Andy Croft, *Red Letter Days: British Fiction in the 1930s* (London, 1990), chs. 2, 3, 4.

43. When he saw an exhibition of their paintings: Julian Trevelyan, *Indigo Days* (London, 1957), 102; John Newsom, *Out of the Pit: A Challenge to the Comfortable*

(Oxford, 1936), 83–4. Lee Hall makes powerful drama out of these class and regional encounters in his play about the Ashington School, founded 1934: *The Pitmen Painters* (2009).

44. They promised on the cover 'to apply the technique of anthropology for the first time nearer home, on the savages of our own continent': Mass Observation, *Britain* (Harmondsworth, 1939).

45. Gorer had been impressed by *Burmese Days*. Letter, Orwell to Geoffrey Gorer, The Stores, Wallington, 23? May 1936, *CW* x. 482: 'What you say about trying to study our own customs from an anthropological point of view opens lots of fields...' Jeremy Mulford (ed.), *Worktown People: Photographs from Northern England 1937–8 by Humphrey Spender* (Bristol, 1982), 7.

46. *Wigan Pier*, 26.

47. Orwell, *Wigan Diary*, 24 Feb. (Wigan), 19 Mar. (Barnsley), 21 Mar. (Grimethorpe) 1936, *CW* x. 435, 461, 463; *Wigan Pier*, 26–7, 19, 31.

48. Letter to Rees, from 22 Darlington Street, Wigan, 29 Feb. 1936: *CW* x. 441. He translated it for Jack Common: 'I have been in these barbarous regions for about two months': letter from 4 Agnes Terrace, Barnsley, 17 Mar. 1936, ibid. 458.

49. Orwell, *Wigan Pier*, 29.

50. 'his slavery is more or less useless': *Down and Out*, 105.

51. 'You can always tell a miner by the blue tattooing of coal dust on the bridge of his nose. Some of the older men have their foreheads veined with it like Roquefort cheese': *Wigan Diary*, 11 Feb. 1936, *CW* x. 424.

52. Bowker, *Orwell*, 185.

53. Jan Gordon, 'How to Paint Miners Coming Back from Work in the Dark' (1934), quoted in William Feaver, *Pitmen Painters: The Ashington Group 1934–84* (London, 1988), 9. The Report made to the Pilgrim Trust was essentially interested in the moral 'atmosphere' of homes of the unemployed.

54. Campbell makes something spiteful of what she sees as homoeroticism in Orwell's descriptions of the men's nakedness: *Wigan Pier Revisited*, 99. Yet muscularity (and exhaustion) is the most powerful and obvious fact of heavy manual labour. It comprises only eight lines in *The Road to Wigan Pier*.

55. 'Labour is the active and initial force... and Labour is therefore the employer of capital': Henry George, *Progress and Poverty: An Inquiry into the Cause of Industrial Depressions* (London, 1883), 103.

56. In 1920 we find Barts Hospital asking the rich for 'urgently needed' funds for a new nurses' home and offering information on 'the sums necessary' to have a ward or a bed named after one 'in perpetuity'. St Thomas's meanwhile had beds 'for the Absolutely Poor' and beds 'for those who can pay a moderate amount': *Debrett's House of Commons and The Judicial Bench* (London, 1920), advertisements.

57. Kenneth O. Morgan, *Ages of Reform: Dawns and Downfalls of the British Left* (London, 2011), 'Seven Ages of Socialism'. For some of the intellectual traditions that preceded the Labour party, see Stephen Yeo, 'A New Life: The Religion of Socialism in Britain 1883–1896', *History Workshop Journal*, 4 (1977).

58. Which is how Stansky and Abrahams read it: *Orwell*, 173.

59. Orwell, *Wigan Pier*, 112.

60. Letter to Victor Gollancz, from The Stores, Wallington, 20 Aug. 1937, quoted in Crick, *Orwell*, 344. The charge came up again in a correspondence in *Tribune*, 29 June–27 July 1945—'Orwell and the Stinkers'. Various people have their say, and Orwell has the last word, which is unconvincing in its argument that there is a difference between saying working-class people smell for a good reason and a bad: *CW* xvii. 204.

61. *Wigan Pier Diary*, 16 Feb. 1936, *CW* x. 428.
62. He spent some days being shown round Sheffield by James Brown, an unemployed man who was malformed in the hand and foot. Brown was very kind, but his harping on about the bourgeoisie got Orwell down: 'a tiresome person to be with...too conscious of his Communist convictions' (*Wigan Diary*, 5 Mar. 1936, *CW* x. 448).
63. 'not real people...ever rehearsing the same futile rigmarole': Orwell, *Wigan Pier*, 15.
64. 'negative, querulous...carping...shallow...severed from the common culture of the country': *The Lion and the Unicorn*, *CW* xii. 406. 'Sometimes I look at a Socialist, the intellectual, tract-writing type...and wonder what the devil his motive really is. It is often difficult to believe that it is a love of anybody, especially of the working class, from whom he is of all people the furthest removed': *Wigan Pier*, 156. Orwell is careful to distinguish community from regional identity: ibid. 57, 62–3.
65. *Wigan Diary*, 16 Mar. 1936, *CW* x. 457.
66. Thomas Linehan, *Communism in Britain 1920–39* (Manchester, 2007), 140.
67. In August 1936 Orwell addressed John Middleton Murry's Adelphi Centre Summer School at The Oaks, Langham, Essex, on 'An Outsider Sees the Depressed Areas'. The School was a 'meeting and holiday place for several hundred believers in self-education and improvement', including pacifists, socialists, Christian Socialists, Communists, and all who gathered round Murry and his *Adelphi*: Stansky and Abrahams, *Orwell*, 170. He lampooned such people in *The Road to Wigan Pier*, but told Jack Common that he enjoyed his visit 'and met some interesting people and...wished [he] could have stayed longer': letter, 5 Oct. 1936, from The Stores, Wallington, *CW* x. 507. The following August Orwell addressed the ILP Summer School at Letchworth.
68. 'Socialism in its developed form is a theory confined entirely to the middle classes': *Wigan Pier*, 152.
69. Orwell, *Wigan Pier*, 160, 152–3.
70. Kingsley Martin's diary recorded a very young Orwell being 'bullied' by a very imperious Beatrice Webb at a Fabian summer school at Dunsford in February 1922. Orwell would have just been out of Eton: Jonathan Rose, 'Eric Blair's School Days', in Jonathan Rose (ed.), *The Revised Orwell* (East Lansing, Mich., 1992), 87.
71. Common, in Coppard and Crick, *Orwell Remembered*, 143.
72. Jack Common, 'Cure for Bourgeoiserie', *New Britain*, 11 Apr. 1934. Common kidded his readers with a history that 'began with the amoeba and ended with the English gentleman' (*Eleventh Hour*, 13 Mar. 1935): an evolution 'which seemed reasonable enough to all parties'.
73. Uncle Robin had books on 'what you'd expect perhaps', but 'all around and overlaying them...a weird assemblage' including books on 'the deadly effect of salt, sugar, meat, feather beds, starch and the alternative advocacy of raw food, grass or yeast': Jack Common, *Kiddar's Luck* (1951; Bath, 1971), 189–91; and in Coppard and Crick, *Orwell Remembered*, 139: 'My friendship with Eric began in disappointment and grew under mutual suspicion.' But it was never less than warm. In 1938 the Commons looked after the Blairs' cottage while they were in Morocco, and in that same year Orwell reviewed Common's *Freedom of the Streets* as 'the authentic voice of the ordinary man', a writer 'of proletarian origin, and much more than most writers of this kind he preserves his proletarian viewpoint': *New English Weekly*, 16 June 1938, *CW* xi. 163. See my essay on Common, 'Three Northern Writers in 1951', in K. D. M. Snell (ed.), *The Regional Novel in the British Isles and Ireland 1800–1900* (Cambridge, 1998).

74. 'Knowledge cannot undo the workings of fate; virtue gives no protection against disaster': Euripides, quoted in John Gray, *Al Qaeda: And What it Means to be Modern* (London, 2004), 115. Gray sees Positivism as a post-Enlightenment secular religion very close to Soviet Marxism.
75. *Wigan Pier*, 190.
76. Ibid. 155.
77. Ibid. 80–1.
78. Ibid. 183.
79. 'Real identification with the proletariat demands real incorporation with it' (Middleton Murry): Philip Bounds, *Orwell and Marxism: The Political and Cultural Thinking of George Orwell* (London, 2009), 19.
80. Letter, Orwell to Dennis Collings, from 1B Oakwood Rd., Golders Green, 16 Aug. 1931, *CW* x. 211.
81. In further discussions on the bourgeois socialist paradox, he tells Jack Common that one can write from a working-class point of view, 'but of course as literature it's bourgeois literature': letter from Jellicoe Pavilion, Preston Hall, Aylesford, Kent, 20 Apr. 1938, *CW* xi. 134. As for 'genuine' working-class writing, apart from Common and one or two others like Hilton who got their gold star, Orwell never held out any great hope of it: review of Jack Hilton, 'Caliban Shrieks', *The Adelphi* (Mar. 1935), *CW* x. 382. This was the first review to be signed 'George Orwell'.
82. P. Collier, 'Dreams of Revolutionary Culture', in E. Timms and P. Collier (eds.), *Visions and Blueprints* (Manchester, 1988), 45. The word 'intellectual' first found popular currency in England during the time of the Dreyfus Affair in France (1898–99). Partly as a reaction to that, British commentators did not like to think that Britain had an intellectual tradition. In his sensational *La Trahison des clercs* ('The Treason of the Intellectuals'), Julien Benda argued in 1928 that European culture was in crisis because its intellectuals had betrayed their role as disinterested commentators and teachers in favour of their own self-promotion in politics and ideologies. 'If you need proof, says Benda, pointing at inter-war Europe, look around yourself': Ernest Gellner, *Encounters with Nationalism* (Oxford, 1997), 51. I speculate that Orwell picked up these pejorative interpretations of intellectuals during his intermittent residency in Paris, 1928–30. Benda's core argument is reflected throughout his work.
83. Orwell, *Wigan Pier*, 145, 148. I have changed the ordering of the phrases.
84. Ibid. 204.
85. Orwell, *Wigan Diary*, 7 Mar. 1936, *CW* x. 449.
86. *Wigan Diary*, 13–14 Mar. 1936, *CW* x. 454. The Narodniks were a revolutionary movement of Russian intellectuals who idealized the life of the peasantry (*narod*, people).
87. Orwell noted that the men did 'not a handsturn' around the house ('except carpentering and gardening'): *Wigan Diary*, 5 Mar. 1936, *CW* x. 449.
88. Orwell, *Wigan Pier*, 104. As a child he saw very little of his father, who worked in India and came back to England to retire and then serve in the army while Orwell was at boarding school. Nevertheless, Orwell's wife Eileen told a friend that the Blairs were fun 'and they all adore Eric', and this is well corroborated: letter, Eileen Blair to Norah Miles, from 36 High Street, Southwold, 3 or 10? Nov. 1936, in Davison, *Lost Orwell*, 65.
89. 'The household is to be regarded as a self-contained unit and the requirements of each individual member are to be considered in relation to the household income': *Public Assistance Officers' Journal*, 20 May 1932. See David Vincent, *Poor Citizens* (London, 1991), 72–8.

90. *Picture Post*, however, turned up in Wigan in 1939 to take another look at the unemployed. Although its 'Life in Wigan' was much more positive than Orwell's, the town council and the Chief Constable were sensitive to the town's reputation and made it clear that the *Post* was not welcome, confiscating some of its photographs. It went ahead anyway and among photographs of unemployed men offered a women's keep-fit class, a scene from Eckersley's Mill, and a photograph of the non-existent pier—'Its name is a joke to millions': *Picture Post*, 11 Nov. 1939.
91. Orwell, *Wigan Pier*, 17.
92. Collini, *Absent Minds*, ch. 3.
93. The marchers left Jarrow on 5 October 1936 and arrived in London on 31 October in a blaze of publicity. It was the most famous of a number of inter-war marches to London to protest against unemployment in the regions. Led by their MP and council leaders, 200 Jarrow men broke the trope by making their way south in order to speak for themselves. Ellen Wilkinson, the town's MP, described it as 'a great folk movement', and so it was: Betty Vernon, *Ellen Wilkinson* (London, 1982), 142, and Ellen Wilkinson, *The Town That Was Murdered* (London, 1939), ch. 12.

Chapter 3

1. Second Spanish Republic 1931–9: after the electoral victory of the left-coalition 'Popular Front' parties in February 1936 sections of the army and police attempted a *putsch* in July. Some parts of the country accepted the new military authority, some welcomed it, others resisted, and the nation fell into civil war. By the time Orwell arrived Republican forces had just lost Malaga in the south but still held large portions of the country in the east and middle, including Madrid, Barcelona, and Valencia. Prime minister was the former Socialist minister of labour Largo Caballero.
2. The Independent Labour Party was founded at Bradford in 1893 and grew out of Keir Hardie's Scottish Labour Party (1888–93). An ideological sect more than an amalgamation of societies and organizations such as constituted the Labour party, the ILP disaffiliated from the Labour party in 1932, the same year that *The Adelphi* affiliated to the ILP. The POUM was founded in 1931 as a left-Communist breakaway from the Communist Party of Spain, itself a left Communist breakaway from the Socialist party of Spain. With strong traditions of regional autonomy, Catalan politics were different from Madrid. In September 1932, the Republic had granted Catalonia a 'Statute of Autonomy' and with it a highly devolved government, the Generalidad.
3. Orwell, *Homage*, 7.
4. Known as 'The Italian Soldier Shook My Hand': first and second stanzas, ibid., including 'Looking Back on the Spanish War', written in 1942, saying that he had written the poem in 1939 (p. 246).
5. 'I first learned the Spanish bugle-calls by listening to them outside the Fascist lines': ibid. 11.
6. Ibid. 15.
7. Letter, Orwell to Victor Gollancz about 'genuine revolutionaries', from Hotel Continental, Barcelona, 9 May 1937, *CW* xi. 23; Orwell, *Homage*, 15, 102–3.
8. Orwell, *Homage*, 8–9.
9. His commanding officer remembered him as 'absolutely fearless': S. Wadhams, *Remembering Orwell* (Ontario, 1984), 78.
10. Orwell, 'Looking Back', *Homage*, 225.

11. Ibid. 74, 31.

12. Eileen Blair, letter to her brother Laurence O'Shaughnessy, from 10 Rambla de los Estudios, Barcelona, 1 May 1937, *CW* xi. 21 and Orwell Archive K 21. She had come to Spain in mid-February to work in the ILP offices.

13. Raymond Carr, *The Spanish Tragedy* (London, 1977), 167.

14. The Comintern defined 'Anti-Fascism' as opposition to the product of late capitalist financial imperialism. The Polish Home Army abolished the term in 1944 when the Red Army decided that it too was Fascist: Gregor Dallas, *Poisoned Peace 1945: The War That Never Ended* (London, 2005), 236.

15. Orwell, *Homage*, 134.

16. The representative was Walter Tapsell, who reported to his Communist superiors at Abacete that Orwell was the 'leading personality and the most respected man in the contingent': Bowker, *Orwell*, 217.

17. 'To join the IB with George's history is strange but it is what he thought he was doing in the first place & it's the only way of getting to Madrid. So there it is': letter, Eileen Blair to Laurence O'Shaughnessy, 1 May 1937, *CW* xi. 21.

18. Orwell, *Homage*, 137.

19. George Orwell, 'Shooting an Elephant', 1936.

20. Orwell, *Homage*, 177.

21. A 'terrible moral blow' to Negrin's new Republican government, which was bracing itself to restore law and order: Gabriel Jackson, *The Spanish Republic and the Civil War* (Princeton, 1972), 404.

22. Documents issued 'a favour del camarada BLAIR': Orwell Archive, C/5 b), a).

23. The facts are not clear but see Tom Buchanan, 'The Death of Bob Smillie', *Historical Journal*, 40 (1997). Bob Smillie (1917–37), chemistry student at the University of Glasgow, grandson of the Scottish miners' leader Robert Smillie, and member of the ILP. Andres Nin (1892–1937), founding member of the Communist party of Spain (1921), and the POUM (1935), former political secretary to Trotsky. Georges Kopp (1902–51), born St Petersburg, eventful life, friend of Eric, suitor of Eileen, cool under fire: see Bowker, *Orwell*, 217. See nn. 27 and 88 below and p. 292 n. 17.

24. Stafford Cottman (1918–99), member of the ILP, wartime RAF, lifelong socialist and trade unionist. John McNair (1887–1968), 'Boy Orator of Tyneside' during the 1910 engineers' strike; émigré and leather merchant in Paris, 1911–36; General Secretary ILP, 1935–55; Barcelona office, 1936–7. McNair had been one of the first to arrive in Spain at the outbreak of civil war in July 1936, with £5,000-worth of medical supplies from France. He returned 18 June, with more money, to assist in the evacuation of volunteers who through the offices of the ILP had been attached to the POUM: *Newcastle Evening News*, 29 Apr. 1955.

25. Report to Tribunal for Espionage and High Treason, 13 July 1937 (Valencia in liaison with Albacete and Moscow): *CW* xi. 31. For the spying activities of Crook and Wicks, see Bowker, *Orwell*, 222–7.

26. The Glasgow campaign was supported by William McDougall, MP: Orwell Archive, C/2, C/4 d), C/4 a).

27. Georges Kopp to Laurence O'Shaughnessy, 7 July 1937; and Eileen Blair, 8 July 1937: Orwell Archive, UCL, K25c), K25d). Kopp announces his intention to go on hunger-strike after three weeks imprisonment without charge. He tells how he is in a cell 10 feet by 15 feet, containing eighteen prisoners subjected to arbitrary beatings. He is seeking ILP publicity for his protest, and tells Eileen that he has decided to kill 'with bare fists' the first guard to approach him. Kopp's ultimatum to Lt.-Col. Burillo, the Chief of Police (K25 b2), would have appealed to Orwell's sense of personal honour and the military virtues: 'It appears to me that a foreign

volunteer, an officer of the Belgian Army, who, after siding [with] the legal Government of Spain by secretly manufacturing munitions in his own country, comes
to enlist in the anti-fascist militia and fights at the front where he is successively
commander of a company, a battalion, and a regiment, does not merit this kind
of treatment. Nor is such treatment merited by the prisoners whom I have seen
here and who after weeks of imprisonment do not know why they have been
arrested...I have come to the end of the time when I could regard my experiences with good humour...'

28. Richard Keeble, 'Orwell as War Correspondent: A Re-assessment', *Journalism
    Studies*, 2: 3 (2001), 403.
29. Orwell, *Homage*, 212.
30. He did, however, have a taste for short-cuts. To take a selection from his *Observer*
    pieces: 'it is easy for even the most ignorant person to grasp that...' ('India Next',
    22 Feb. 1942); 'the British people are not envious as peoples go...' ('Mood of
    Moment', 19 Apr. 1942); 'few thinking men will disagree' ('Revolt in Urban
    Desert', 10 Oct. 1943); and so on: *Orwell: The Observer Years* (London, 2003).
31. Calder notices how he plays up his ability to be accurate by playing down his abil-
    ity to be objective: *Chronicles of Conscience: A Study of George Orwell and Arthur Koestler*
    (London, 1968), ch. 5.
32. 'He always tells the truth—as he sees it. He has remarkably few prejudices, the-
    ories or preconceived notions about anything. He simply observes and records
    according to the Evidence of his eyes and ears': Julian Symons, *Manchester Evening
    News*, 7 Aug. 1947, in Rodden, *Literary Reputation*, 307.
33. See the art and film-making of Humphrey Jennings and the photography of Bill
    Brandt: Erik Barnouw, *Documentary: A History of Non Fiction Film* (New York, 1974),
    144–8; and Bill Brandt, *Shadow of Light* (London, 1977). Examples of first-hand
    accounts of Spain are plentiful in Valentine Cunningham (ed.), *Spanish Front: Writ-
    ers on the Civil War* (Oxford, 1986).
34. Including cuttings from the *Daily Worker, Manchester Guardian, News Chronicle,
    Observer, Sunday Express, Time* magazine, *La Vigie marocaine, Le Populaire, La Flèche,
    New Leader, Workers' Free Press*: notebooks and cuttings July 1937–8, Orwell Archive,
    C/1, C/3, C/4.
35. Memories of John Kimche, Henry Swanzy, Jane Morgan, Richard Peters, Geof-
    frey Stevens, Jack Braithwaite, and others in Coppard and Crick, *Orwell Remem-
    bered*, 86, 92, and Wadhams, *Remembering Orwell*, 95, 124, 83.
36. Morgan, *Ages of Reform*, 60.
37. Walter Lippman, *Public Opinion* (1922; New York, 1934), 248; Norman Angell, *The
    Great Illusion* (London, 1914) and *The Public Mind: Its Disorders; Its Exploitation*
    (London, 1926), 141; Harold D. Lasswell, *Propaganda Technique in World War One*
    (London, 1927), 32. The new Marxist sociology of the 1930s would look to the
    Frankfurt School, in particular Theodor Adorno, Max Horkheimer, Jürgen Hab-
    ermas, and to Antonio Gramsci. William Randolph Hearst (1863–1951), US
    newspaper tycoon. Alfred Harmsworth, Lord Northcliffe (1865–1922), British
    newspaper tycoon. Northcliffe and Beaverbrook, another press tycoon, had been
    made ministers of British Propaganda and Information respectively in 1918.
38. Beaverbrook told the Royal Commission on the Press that he ran the *Daily Express*
    'purely for the purpose of making propaganda and with no other motive' (Report,
    Cmnd. 7700, HMSO 1949, p. 25). 'New Reportage' dated from the 1880s, when
    the big-circulation American dailies bought big-name reporters to put their names
    on the line. These were the men you could trust; the men you could not gag. On-
    the-spot war reporting was much older, dating in the American case from the

Mexican War of 1846–8 and in the British case from the Crimean War of 1854–6. Journalists not only filed their reports, they gave witness: most notably Russell of *The Times*, who told how he watched, 'with my own eyes', the charge of the Light Brigade on the morning of 14 November 1854.

39. Orwell, *Homage*, 8.

40. J. Stapleton, *England of G. K. Chesterton* (New York, 2009). Orwell mentions Hemingway, critically, in two asides in reviews of 1935 and 1936, and again, also critically ('would be tough'), in 'Inside the Whale' in 1940: *CW* x. 397, 534; xii. 104. As for the eyewitness tradition in American journalism, Orwell started writing occasionally for the New York-based *Partisan Review* in January 1941 and may have been aware of Philip Rahv's 'The Cult of Experience in American Writing', *Partisan Review*, 6 (1940).

41. Gellhorn was in Spain on her first war assignment with *Collier's*. Orwell probably had more in common with her than with 'Ernesto'. Her intellectual biographer refers to 'truth tropes' in her writing which also apply perfectly to Orwell's—that is to say, a style that mixed first-person verbatim account with statistical evidence, original sources, primary documents, and corroborative testimony: Kate McLoughlin, *Martha Gellhorn: The Writer in the Field and in the Text* (Manchester, 2007), 62.

42. Who does this sound like? 'His stance was always that of the primitively strong man of simple integrity who tries to hold to plain virtue and plain language while buffeted by attackers who change their masks and identities with shifting literary fashions': Robert O. Stephens, *Hemingway's Nonfiction: The Public Voice* (Chapel Hill, NC, 1968), 109.

43. Michael Sheldon, *Orwell* (London 1991), 410–11. Hemingway claimed he sold Orwell a snub-nosed pistol. For the growing story, see John Rodden, 'Did Papa Rescue St George?', in Rodden (ed.), *The Unexamined Orwell* (Austin, Tex., 2011), ch. 11.

44. F. W. Watt, *Steinbeck* (Edinburgh, 1962), 107; Jay Parini, *John Steinbeck: A Biography* (London, 1994), 204–20.

45. David Wyatt, *New Essays on 'The Grapes of Wrath'* (Cambridge, 1990), 13; Watt, *Steinbeck*, 107; Upton Sinclair, *The Jungle* (1906; London, 1946), 40–1.

46. There was a literary flight from New York into small towns in search of articles on the Depression. Edmund Wilson, John Dos Passos, Theo Dreiser, Waldo Frank, Malcolm Cowley, James Agee, and others all moved out in search of the unemployed. On Wilson—'There was nothing unusual in those days about an owl-eyed literary man from the landed gentry, Princeton '16, showing up in Virginia coal country': George Packer, 'Don't Look Down', *New Yorker*, 29 Apr. 2013. Wilson corresponded with Orwell from the offices of the *New Yorker* in January 1940: Orwell Archive, App. 2, letters to Orwell.

47. See John Carey's tour de force, *The Intellectuals and the Masses: Pride and Prejudice among the Literary Intelligentsia 1880–1939* (London, 1992).

48. A. B. White, *The New Propaganda* (London, 1939), 11.

49. He recognized differences of origin, but showed little interest in European Fascist movements. He constantly sniped at Chesterton and Belloc as Catholic hacks: e.g. 'Notes on Nationalism', *Polemic*, 1, 1945, *CW* xvii. 144.

50. It went against the *New Statesman*'s political policy, apparently. For details, see letter Orwell to Raymond Mortimer, from The Stores, Wallington, 5 Feb. 1938, *CW* xi. 116–18 and 50. The review was taken by *Time and Tide* (31 July 1937) instead—'By January...the Communists were using every possible method, fair and foul, to stamp out what was left of the revolution' (ibid. 51–2).

51. 'This is pure imagination...This is a lie...This is a direct lie...Two lies are contained here': *New Leader*, 24 Sept. 1937, *CW* xi. 84–5. The *Worker* called their correspondent 'Frankfort'.

52. See his review of the Duchess of Atholl's *Searchlight on Spain*, in *Time and Tide* (16 July 1938) and the *New English Weekly* (21 July 1938), *CW* xi. 178–9. The *Manchester Guardian* followed a strongly favourable review of *Homage to Catalonia* (14 June 1938) with a long letter (5 Aug. 1938) from Orwell on the POUM trials in Spain calling for open courts and no forced confessions.

53. George Orwell, 'Spilling the Spanish Beans', *CW* xi. 42.

54. In spite of which there was a Major Attlee Company of the British Battalion, which the Labour leader met on its homecoming at Victoria station in December 1938. Attlee replaced George Lansbury, a pacifist, as leader of the Labour party in 1935.

55. 'Eye-Witness in Barcelona', *CW* xi. 55.

56. Paul Preston, *Concise History of the Spanish Civil War* (London, 1996), 236.

57. Orwell, *Homage*, 63–4: 'I should like to make an exception of the *Manchester Guardian*.'

58. Most of the 2,000 or so British volunteers in the International Brigades were not intellectuals (in the sense Orwell meant it) but working-class Communists and Labour-party people violently opposed to Labour's wavering endorsement of Britain's non-interventionist policy: Tom Buchanan, *The Spanish Civil War and the British Labour Movement* (Cambridge, 1991), 39; Hywel Francis, *Miners Against Fascism: Wales and the Spanish Civil War* (London, 1984), 279–81; L. Mates, 'Durham and S. Wales Miners in the Spanish Civil War', *20th Century British History*, 17: 3 (2006). The Brigades were organized by the Comintern.

59. About 49,000 on the Republican side and 130,000 on the Nationalist: Paul Preston, *The Spanish Holocaust* (London, 2012), pp. xvii–xviv.

60. Anthony Beevor, *The Spanish Civil War* (London, 2002), ch. 3.

61. So badly that it 'greatly facilitated the work of the Republic's enemies': Stanley G. Payne, *Spain's First Democracy* (Madison, Wisc., 1993), 373, 384.

62. Helen Graham, *The Spanish Civil War* (Oxford, 2005), 65.

63. Helen Graham, 'The Premiership of Juan Negrin 1937–39', in Paul Preston and Ann L. Mackenzie (eds.), *The Republic Besieged* (Edinburgh, 1996), 192.

64. Raymond Carr, 'Orwell and the Spanish Civil War', in Gross, *World of George Orwell*, 69. For criticism of Anarchist strategy see Chris Ealham, 'The Contradictions of Individualism and Collectivism in Spanish Anarchism', in Preston and Mackenzie, *Republic Besieged*, 161.

65. 'Probably false' was his final opinion on the 'Trotskyist thesis that the war could have been won if the revolution had not been sabotaged': 'Looking Back on the Spanish War' (1942), in *Homage*, 241.

66. See letters from Fenner Brockway on 'critical developments' 'which effect the whole working class movement of the world', and which need to be 'discussed between us and before the whole working class': to the ILP and Communist members and branches, 23–6 June 1937: Orwell Archive, C/4 a) 1–10. The Orwell Archive has an ILP membership card in the name of Eric Blair issued 13 June 1938: Orwell Archive, C/5 f).

67. Orwell, *Homage*, 60. John Strachey, *What Are We To Do?* (London, 1938), 372; Dean E. McHenry, *The Labour Party in Transition* (London, 1938), 303–9.

68. 'Why I Join the ILP', *New Leader*, 24 June 1938, *CW* xi. 169.

69. Raymond Carr, *The Spanish Tragedy*, 190–5. Carr, who was not a romantic socialist, expressed his personal 'admiration for the man'.

70. Hugh Thomas, *The Spanish Civil War* (1961; London, 1990), 667.

71. There is considerable personal and political sympathy for Negrin in Graham, 'Premiership'; Thomas, *Spanish Civil War*, 667–70, 812–21; and Jackson, *Spanish Republic*, 393–407.

72. Graham, *Civil War*, 109; Carr is more cautious in his judgement: *Spanish Tragedy*, 198.

73. Preston, *Spanish Holocaust*, 403–20.

74. Bowker, *Orwell*, 105.

75. Orwell's Wartime *Diaries*, 8 June 1940, *CW* xii. 182; letter Orwell to Gollancz from 27B Canonbury Square, Islington, London, 25 Mar. 1947, *CW* xix. 90. Peter Davison confirms the difficulties: 'Orwell and Marxism', *American Communist History*, 9: 3 (2010), 336. His anti-Stalinism, however, from 1932 seems to have been at first instinctual. He said in his Preface to the Ukrainian edition of *Animal Farm* that he had no clear politics until 1936, *CW* xix. 87. Christopher Hitchens describes the outcome of this ingrained political instinct as 'Orwell's victory': 'He never underwent a Stalinoid phase, never had to be cured or purged by sudden disillusionment': *Orwell's Victory* (London, 2002), 41.

76. Lyons, *New English Weekly*, 9 June 1938, *CW* xi. 158–60; Borkenau, *New English Weekly*, 22 Sept. 1938, *CW* xi. 202–4.

77. Edward Crankshaw, 'Orwell and Communism', in Gross, *World of George Orwell*, 122–4.

78. Soviet publications in English offered a good supply of bad political writing as identified by Orwell in 1946. For two prolier-than-thou examples see, Revd Stanley Evans, *Religion in the USSR* (*Russia Today*, London, 1943) and A. T. D'Eye, *Russia Revisited: With the Dean of Canterbury through the USSR* (*Russia Today*, London, 1945). The lawyers did equally well with Ralph Miller's (Barrister at Law), *Soviet Justice: An Authoritative Survey of the Legal System in the USSR* (Haldane Society, London, 1943).

79. Orwell's review of James Burnham's *The Struggle for the World*, in *The New Leader*, 29 May 1947, *CW* xix. 100.

80. Orlando Figes, *The Whisperers: Private Life in Stalin's Russia* (London, 2007), 81; Wendy Z. Goldman, *Women, the State and Revolution: Soviet Family Policy and Social Life 1917–36* (Cambridge, 1993), 102–6.

81. Gellner, *Encounters with Nationalism*, 7.

82. On the crucial murder of Kirov, the Leningrad party boss, in 1934, see Amy Knight, 'Lone Gunman?', *Times Literary Supplement*, 20 May 2011. On terror tactics in general, see J. Arch Getty and O. V. Naumov, *The Road to Terror: Stalin and the Self-Destruction of the Bolsheviks 1932–39* (New Haven, 1999), 573–83.

83. Paul R. Gregory, *Terror by Quota: State Security from Lenin to Stalin; an Archival Study* (New Haven, 2009), 200; see table 6.4, The Fulfilment of Order No 00447, 1937–38 (p. 189).

84. Martin McCauley, *Stalin and Stalinism* (Harlow, 2008) p. 51; Gregory, *Terror by Quota*, 16; Figes, *Whisperers*, 81–105, xxxi, xxxvii.

85. Gregory, *Terror by Quota*, 157.

86. Davison, *CW* xi. 32.

87. Vladimir Antonov-Ovseenko, recalled June 1937: Davison, *CW* xi. 33.

88. See n. 27 above for details of the correspondence. Kopp was asking Eileen to alert the ILP to his hunger-strike but she did not receive his letter until 29 July: Eileen Blair to John McNair, Wallington, 29 July 1937, Orwell Archive, K 25a.

89. Based on claims by the Brigades' commander, the French Communist deputy André Marty, cited in Davison, *CW* xi. 35. Estimates of numbers in the five International Brigades vary from 30,000 to 40,000 and upwards: Buchanan, *Spanish Civil War*, 122–3. On British Brigade losses, Davison, *CW* xi. 34.

90. Gollancz published Hewlett Johnson's *The Socialist Sixth of the World* (1939), Pat Sloan's sycophantic *Soviet Democracy* (1937), and R. Page Arnot's *Short History of the*

Russian Revolution (1937). Johnson was Dean of Canterbury Cathedral. George Bernard Shaw visited the USSR in 1931 and remained a strong believer, as did Sydney and Beatrice Webb, who visited in 1932.

91. The Webbs' 'lack of curiosity about current Soviet propaganda was a disgrace of the intellect': Robert Service, *Comrades: A World History of Communism* (London, 2007), 203. The Webbs published their *Soviet Communism: A New Civilization?* (with question-mark) with Longman's Green in 1935, and the second edition (without question-mark) with Gollancz, in 1937. Their *The Truth About Soviet Russia* followed in 1942. Harry Pollitt, general secretary of the CPGB, had tragic personal reasons to know better (Service, *Comrades*, 200–1).

92. David Caute, *The Fellow Travellers: Intellectual Friends of Communism* (New Haven, 1988), 71.

93. 'Best selling fiction reflected and confirmed anti-Soviet opinion', and this included Richmal Crompton's fictional English schoolboy William Brown. In *William and the Outlaws* (1927) suburban Englishness clashed with the Communist party and won: Service, *Comrades*, 210. See also William Whyte's essay 'Richmal Crompton and Conservative Fiction', in Clare V. J. Griffiths, James J. Nott, and William Whyte (eds.), *Classes, Cultures and Politics* (Oxford, 2011).

94. Richmal Crompton, *William the Bad* (1930), quoted in Whyte, 'Richmal Crompton', 146.

95. Sheila Fitzpatrick, *Everyday Stalinism: Ordinary Life in Extraordinary Times. Soviet Russia in the 1930s* (Oxford, 1999), 2, 227.

96. Orwell made astute criticism of Christopher Hill's (ed.) *The English Revolution 1640* on these grounds, asking why do people have an ideological 'super-structure' such as religion when it only covers up their real and underlying interests? Why should they do that? Maybe it's another example of the deception of intellectuals? 'If no man is ever motivated by anything except class interests, why does every man constantly pretend that he is motivated by something else?': review in *New Statesman and Nation*, 24 Aug. 1940, *CW* xii. 244–5.

97. Tristram Hunt, *The Frock Coated Communist: The Revolutionary Life of Friedrich Engels* (London, 2010), 290–3. I am grateful for discussions with Andrew King and Gavin Kitching on these subjects.

98. Though some tried. See, for instance, H. M. Hyndman's *England For All* (London, 1881), ch. 2. Hyndman (1842–1921) was the founder of the first English Marxist party, the Democratic Federation. Marx's *Capital: A Critique of Political Economy*, vol. 1 (1867 and English translation 1887) showed the way with its 'Processes of the Production of Capital'. Marx averred that England was the classic case and chief illustration.

99. See e.g. Hyndman's 'The Railway Problem Solved', *Nineteenth Century and After* (Nov. 1916).

100. Francis Wheen, *Marx's Das Kapital* (London, 2006), 64.

101. Christopher Norris and friends tried to get at Orwell on empirical grounds in a Communist party-orchestrated attack on him called *Inside the Myth. Orwell: Views from the Left* (London, 1984). Alexander, the former International Brigadier, says Orwell did not know enough facts about Spain. Stradling, the professor, says Orwell knew no facts at all about 'the modern socialist dialectic'. Norris, the editor, invokes Frederic Jameson, in an example of what Orwell found laughable in political writing. According to Norris, it would appear that Orwell did not realize that 'A Marxist negative hermeneutic, a Marxist practice of ideological analysis proper, must in the practical work of reading and interpretation be exercised simultaneously with a Marxist positive hermeneutic, or a development of the

Utopian impulses of these same ideological cultural texts' (p. 9). Of course! So that's where Orwell went wrong. How could we have missed it?

102. J. Stalin, *Problems of Leninism* (1924), extract in McCauley, *Stalin*, appendix.

103. The Communist Party of Great Britain Historians' Group included Maurice Dobb, Rodney Hilton, Christopher Hill, E. J. Hobsbawm, and E. P. Thompson. Founded in 1946, the Group's best work came after 1956 when all but one (Hobsbawm) had left the party: Harvey J. Kaye, *The British Marxist Historians* (London, 1995), 10–20. Hobsbawm recalled how the modernists in particular felt constrained by party ideology (p. 134). For other, indigenous strands in the radical left tradition, including liberalism and Methodism, strands which Orwell also shared: Raphael Samuel, 'Sources of Marxist History', *New Left Review*, 120 (1980).

104. Eight million families or three-quarters of the British population owned property worth less that £100: John Stevenson, *British Society 1914–45* (London, 1984), 330.

105. Letter, Eileen Blair to Norah Myles, from The Stores, Wallington, 1 Jan. 1938, in Davison, *Lost Orwell*, 72.

106. On Orwell discussing Marx in 1934: Bowker, interview with Michael Sayers, Orwell's former flatmate, 23 Sept. 2000, *Orwell*, 174–5; and again in the summer of 1936 with, according to Richard Rees, 'breathtaking Marxist paradoxes and epigrams', at the *Adelphi* and ILP summer schools: ibid. 192. Spanish-war veterans remembered Orwell's knowledge of Marxism in 1937: Crick, *Orwell*, 254. Memories were mixed. Kate Ekevall thought their group of friends were 'all for the under dog' but not well versed in politics, except for Sayers (who thought Orwell was accomplished in the subject); Rayner Heppenstall, another flatmate, remembered him as 'satirically attached to everything traditionally English': Coppard and Crick, *Orwell Remembered*, 99, 110. David Caute shows how little authentic Marxism there was in British Marxism anyway. Most self-styled Marxists seemed to prefer variants of Benthamism, Positivism, and Owenism, mixed with criticisms of the Industrial Revolution: *Fellow Travellers*, ch. 6, 'Alternatives to Marx', and ch. 7, 'Postscript to the Enlightenment'.

107. It would appear that it was not delivered to anybody in the north of England. Orwell made sure Henry Miller and a few family and friends got a free copy, but, as far as we know, the men and women of Wigan, Barnsley, Sheffield, Liverpool, and Manchester who had helped him did not: letter, Eileen Blair to Leonard Moore, from 24 Croom's Hill, Greenwich, London, 11 Feb. 1937, *CW* xi. 11. To be fair, he and Eileen had no money and a lot on their plate.

108. Meyers, *Critical Heritage*, 99, 165, 103, 108.

109. Letter, Orwell to Gollancz, from Hotel Continental, Barcelona, 9 May 1937, *CW* xi. 22–3.

110. Crick, *Orwell*, 343. Gollancz was close to Pollitt in 1937, passing on Orwell's correspondence to him: Davison, *CW* xi. 74.

111. For all he said against left intellectuals, between 1934 and 1938 their interests reflected his interests: unemployment, Fascism, and class differences in language: Margot Heinemann, 'Left Review, New Writing and the Broad Alliance against Fascism', in Timms and Collier, *Visions and Blueprints*, 117, 123–4.

112. W. H. Auden (1907–73), pre-eminent English poet; unreliable 1930s Marxist. 'Unlike most of the people who have written of the Spanish war, Mr Jellinek really knows Spain': Orwell, *New Leader*, 8 (July 1938), *CW* xi. 172–4. Orwell drew attention to his factual distortions but completely disregarded Jellinek's defence of the 'historical dialectic'.

113. 'Famous Poet to Drive Ambulance in Spain', *Daily Worker*, 12 Jan. 1937. 'What we really wanted him for was to go to the front, write some pieces saying hurrah for the Republic and then go away and write some poems, also saying hurrah for the Republic': Claud Cockburn, in Alex Zwerdling, *Orwell and the Left* (New Haven, 1974), 8.

114. *Spain*, published as a pamphlet by Faber in May 1937 and reprinted in Nancy Cunard's *Poems for Spain* (London 1939), before appearing, with changes to the offending lines, as 'Spain 1937' in Auden's 1940 collection *Another Time*.

115. Orwell's 'Political Reflections on the Crisis', *The Adelphi* (Dec. 1938), referred, most unfairly, to an alliance of 'the gangster and the pansy'. Auden's friends made no secret of their Communism or their sexual preferences. Shortly before he left for Spain, Auden had stayed with Louis MacNeice's friend Anthony Blunt at Trinity College, Cambridge: Humphrey Carpenter, *W. H. Auden: A Biography* (London, 1981), 207.

116. Orwell, 'Political Reflections on the Crisis', *The Adelphi* (Dec. 1938), *CW* xi. 244.

117. Orwell,'Inside the Whale', *CW* xii. 103–4. This essay is not just about Auden; it is about the direction of post-1918 literature and sensibility in England, and appears to be influenced by the same source that influenced Auden's poem—Christopher Caudwell's *Illusion and Reality* (London, 1937), which called on poets to move decisively away from modernism in the direction of political commitment. Auden reviewed Caudwell, and Orwell certainly knew about Caudwell's book in 1940, even if he didn't mention it by name in 'Inside the Whale': Patrick Deane, 'Auden's England', in Stan Smith (ed.), *Cambridge Companion to W. H. Auden* (Cambridge, 2004), 34–5; and Orwell's mention of Caudwell in conversation with Desmond Hawkins, 'The Proletarian Writer', broadcast BBC Home Service, 6 Dec. 1940, *CW* xii. 297. Caudwell was killed at Jarama, 12 February 1937. It is possible that, for Orwell, Caudwell's death in battle stood as a kind of rebuke to Auden.

118. Orwell to Stephen Spender, from Preston Hall, Aylesford, Kent, 15? Apr. 1938, *CW* xi. 132.

119. Orwell, 'Inside the Whale', 103. He bunches left writers and intellectuals together as writers of boyish political cheer, with Auden chief scout, and Spender, Day-Lewis, MacNeice, Isherwood, Lehmann, Arthur Calder-Marshall, and the rest trooping along behind. Their erstwhile cult of Mother Russia and Holy Communism Orwell caricatures as 'the patriotism of the deracinated'. He had referred to 'Nancy poets' in another rash swipe at this branch of the posh left in *Wigan Pier*, 31.

120. Orwell, 'Looking Back on the Spanish Civil War', *Homage*, 228.

121. Richard Hoggart's observation that Auden's was the politics 'of the sensitive middle-class boy who has just discovered that the charwoman is a person' is one way into Orwell's Englishness: *Auden: An Introductory Essay* (1951; London, 1961), 114.

122. Auden explained, utterly fairly, in 1963 that he was 'only trying to say what, surely, every decent person thinks if he finds himself unable to adopt the absolute pacifist position': quoted in John Fuller, *W. H. Auden: A Commentary* (London, 1998), 286.

123. Frank Jellinek, *The Civil War in Spain* (London, 1938), 591, 19.

124. Being 'brilliant' and against the military was something that mattered at Eton, and Orwell elected not to be brilliant and not to be against the military and not to go to university either, the only one of his College 'election' who didn't. Those who were 'brilliant', on the other hand, included Harold Acton, Brian Howard, Oliver Messel, Cyril Connolly, and Henry Green: Martin Green, 'Orwell as an Old Etonian', *Modern Fiction Studies*, 21: 1 (1975), 4–10.

125. In 'Inside the Whale' he mocked the public-school games ethic for its 'atmosphere of uplift'—'rather like Kipling's *If* or Newbolt's "Play Up, Play Up and Play the Game"' (*CW* xii. 100). In 'My Country Right or Left', published that same year, Orwell invited readers to witness the matching atmosphere of uplift in John Cornford's *Before the Storming of Huesca* with Newbolt's 'Play Up', which he quotes this time as 'There's a breathless hush in the Close tonight', but is actually called *Vitai Lampada* (1897). Cornford was killed fighting with the XII International Brigade, and Orwell makes the point that his Communist beliefs did not stop him being 'public school to the core': *CW* xii. 272.

126. Orwell, 'Inside the Whale', 104.

127. He returns to young poets in 'My Country Right or Left' (1940), *CW* xii. 272. In addition to Cornford and Caudwell, another young public-school man and son of Bloomsbury, Julian Bell, was killed at the battle of Brunete, July 1937. Auden's poem referred to 'the young poets exploding like bombs'.

128. Morgan, *Ages of Reform*, ch. 8, 'Anglo-American Progressivism'.

129. Ross McKibbin, *The Evolution of the Labour Party 1910–24* (Oxford, 1974), pp. xiii–xv, 246.

130. Francis Williams, *Fifty Years March* (London, 1949), 353.

131. Jon Lawrence, 'The Transformation of British Public Politics after the First World War', *Past and Present* (Feb. 2006), 190, 214.

132. 'Aside from the mining seats, parts of Yorkshire, and bits of east and south London, there was nowhere in England they did not dominate. The cities, the suburbs, the industrial towns, the countryside, all were part of the Conservative family and few showed signs before 1939 of leaving it': McKibbin, *Parties and People*, 104.

133. C. F. G. Masterman, *The Condition of England* (London, 1909), 76.

134. 'It should be noted that there is now no intelligentsia that is not in some sense "Left". Perhaps the last right-wing intellectual was T. E. Lawrence.' He thinks the left can be found in a half-dozen weekly and monthly publications: *Lion and the Unicorn*, 405–6.

135. Victor Gollancz (1893–1967), H. J. Laski (1899–1956), John Evelyn St Loe Strachey (1901–63): all biographical information from the *ODNB*.

136. '…something which he had long been seeking': Andrew Thorpe, *The British Communist Party and Moscow 1920–43* (Manchester, 2000), 227.

137. 'a brilliant bird in perpetual migration': Caute, *Fellow Travellers*, 169.

138. John Callaghan, *Rajani Palme Dutt: A Study in British Stalinism* (London, 1993), 169.

139. Orwell, *Lion and the Unicorn*, 406.

140. '[since 1918] at or near the centre of the debate about British economic problems and the future of the world economy': Donald Winch, Introduction to John Maynard Keynes, *Essays in Biography* (1933; London, 2010), pp. xxi, xxx.

141. Matthew Worley, *Class against Class: The Communist Party in Britain between the Wars* (London, 2002), 314.

142. Thorpe explains the policy in full, a policy where 'sheltering behind non-party figures was to become fairly typical': *British Communist Party*, 228.

143. Callaghan tells us that the leading Communist ideologue Palme Dutt preferred to use non-Communist journals such as *Reynold's News*, the *News Chronicle*, and the *New Statesman and Nation* to pursue his vendettas: *Palme Dutt*, 169. As we have seen, in July 1937 Kingsley Martin at the *New Statesman and Nation* refused to publish Orwell's article on the POUM or his review of Franz Borkenau's *The Spanish Cockpit*, and Gollancz, who had published all Orwell's English-edition books to date, refused to publish *Homage to Catalonia* even before he had seen it: note by Davison

on reported conversation with Norman Collins, reported in turn to Orwell (*CW* xii. 37–8) and letter, Orwell to Leonard Moore from 24 Croom's Hill, Greenwich, SE 10, 8 July 1937, *CW* xii. 38.

144. The works in question are D. N. Pritt's *The Zinoviev Trial* (London, 1936) and Dudley Collard's *Soviet Justice and the Trial of Radek and Others* (London, 1937). See Caute, *Fellow Travellers*, 126–7, and Willie Thompson, *The Good Old Cause: British Communism 1920–91* (London, 1992), 60.

145. A mere selection: letters to Jack Common, from The Stores, Wallington, 16? Apr. 1936, *CW* x. 471, and from rue Edmond Doutte, Medinah, Marrakech, 12 Oct. 1938, *CW* xi. 223; and reviews in *Time and Tide*, 14 Sept. 1940, *CW* xii. 262; *New English Weekly*, 23 July, 12 and 19 Nov., 31 Dec. 1936, *CW* x. 490, 518, 533, and 29 July, 2 Sept. 1937, *CW* x. 41–2; review in *The Adelphi* (July 1939), *CW* xi. 360; article in the *New Leader*, 24 June 1938, *CW* xi. 168; unpublished response to Nancy Cunard, 'Authors Take Sides On The Spanish Civil War', 3–6 Aug. 1937, *CW* xi. 67; 'Writers and Leviathan', *CW* xix. 288; review in *The Adelphi* (Oct. 1941), *CW* xiii. 42; on Auden and Spender, response to Nancy Cunard (as above), and 'Inside the Whale', Mar. 1940, *CW* xii. 99; on Wells, 'Wells, Hitler and the World State', *Horizon* (Aug. 1941), *CW* xii. 537; on Sartre, letter to Fredric Warburg, from Barnhill, Isle of Jura, 22 Oct. 1948, *CW* xix. 457, and review in the *Observer*, 7 Nov. 1948, *CW* xix. 464–5; on pacifists, review of Alex Comfort, *The Adelphi* (Oct. 1941), *CW* xiii. 42–3; on BBC, first Orwell rude in letter to Common, 16? April, ibid., and then Orwell respectful in letter of resignation, having worked there as a Talks Assistant: Crick, *Orwell*, 421. He had no grievances with the Corporation and had had the time of his life mixing with writers and intellectuals. Yet he thought the work was useless. Andy Croft gives a more balanced view than Orwell of inter-war Left intellectualism in his *Red Letter Days*, while Meyers's *Critical Heritage* volume is particularly useful on what intellectuals said about him.

146. 'As if the whole world of socialist theory was composed either of official Marxists (the Communist Party) or provisional Marxists (the ILP). None the less he made deep and shrewd criticisms': Crick, *Orwell*, 343.

147. Collini, *Absent Minds*, 372.

148. 'I was against all authority': *Wigan Pier*, 122.

149. 'I knew nothing about working-class conditions', 'I had... no interest in Socialism', 'I wanted to get in contact': ibid. 129–31.

150. Third and final stanzas of a poem he claimed in 1942 he wrote in 1939: *Homage*, 246–7. See n. 4 above.

151. They certainly seemed less competent. His MI5 file is only a few lines long but contains a number of inaccuracies—his date of birth, his party membership, his army unit, and his previous career: National Archives, KV5/118, 'Eric Blair'. At least they got his name right. For a reflection of his political mood on coming home, see 'Aren't You Glad You Live in England?': *Daily Mirror* headline in reference to Spain, 5 Aug. 1936: quoted in Brian Shelmerdine, *British Representations of the Spanish Civil War* (Manchester, 2007), 173–4.

152. By 1940–1, with the whole country bound closer together, Orwell's emphasis on the English, and his reticence on the British, does not look incidental: Crick, *Orwell*, 260–3.

153. In his and his parents' lifetimes, crude death rates had fallen by 50 per cent, infant mortality by 80 per cent, and deaths at all ages due to infectious diseases by 90 per cent: J. M. Winter, 'The Decline of Mortality in Britain 1870–1950', in T. Barker and M. Drake (eds.), *Population and Society in Britain 1850–1980* (London, 1982), 100.

Chapter 4

1. Orwell's health had been shattered in Spain, and he had followed his tour there with a writing frenzy that saw him write four major articles, twelve reviews, and numerous letters intended for publication during the summer of 1937. By January 1938 he had completed *Homage to Catalonia*, but in March he was coughing up blood and was admitted to Preston Hall Sanatorium, Aylesford, Kent where, under the care of his brother-in-law, Laurence O'Shaughnessy, a heart specialist, he was diagnosed with TB. A patient at Preston Hall from 15 March to 1 September 1938, Orwell departed for French Morocco with Eileen the day after he got out. They returned 26 March 1939. Morocco was supposed to be better for his lungs and the stay was paid for (£300) by an anonymous donor, the novelist L. H. Myers.

2. George Orwell, *Coming Up for Air* (1939; London, 1990), 6, 9. See *Metro-Land: British Empire* (1924; London, 2004), introduction by Oliver Green.

3. *Coming Up*, 27–8.

4. Ibid. 172, 175, 177.

5. Orwell takes a conventional view of modern leisure excrescences: see Priestley, *English Journey*, 10, 26, 41.

6. *Coming Up*, 213, 222.

7. Ibid. 152, 198, 237, 177, 208, 215, 136.

8. Carey, *Intellectuals and the Masses*, 39–45.

9. 'Yond Cassius has a lean and hungry look; He thinks too much; such men are dangerous'... 'Let me have men about me that are fat': William Shakespeare, *Julius Caesar*, I. ii.

10. 'M is for Marx | and Movement of Masses | and Massing of Arses | and Clashing of Classes': Cyril Connolly, *The Condemned Playground: Essays 1927–44* (London, 1946), 151.

11. 'I have only very vague ideas as to what an insurance agent does', Orwell explained, a tad too modestly: letter to John Sceats, from Gueliz, Marrakech, 26 Oct. 1938, *CW* xi. 226–7.

12. Charles Booth (1840–1916), businessman, philanthropist, and social investigator, *Life and Labour in London* (1886–1903): LSE Online Archive.

13. Joanna Bourke, *Working Class Cultures in Britain 1890–1960* (London, 1994), Table 1.2; Seebohm Rowntree (1871–1954), businessman, philanthropist, and social investigator (*Poverty: A Study of Town Life*, 1901) used slightly different categories and procedures from Booth, but came to roughly the same conclusions. His second York study also slightly changed the procedures.

14. The number of non-manuals increased from 18.7 per cent of the occupied population in 1911 to 30.9 per cent in 1951, and the number working in the commercial, financial, and insurance sectors from 1,759,000 in 1921 to 2,213,000 in 1951: A. H. Halsey (ed.), *British Social Trends since 1900* (Basingstoke, 1988), Table 4.1 (a); B. R. Mitchell and P. Deane, *Abstract of British Historical Statistics* (Cambridge, 1962), Labour Force 1. Halsey grades the new middle class into four types and estimates their growth as a percentage of the labour force 1911–71: administrative (6.2 per cent to 13.2 per cent), technical (7.2 per cent to 16.3 per cent), supervisory (2 per cent to 5.7 per cent), and clerical (8.4 per cent to 24.1 per cent): *Change in British Society* (Oxford, 1978), 26.

15. 'The middle class began and the working class ended at £250 a year': McKibbin, *Classes and Cultures*, 44.

16. 'By education... by style of life, salary, dress and deportment, by social aspiration, by what was expected of them from parents, employers and society, these men and

women were middle class. And by that most crucial of social indicators, fertility': ibid. 45.

17. Orwell, *Coming Up*, 20.
18. Ibid. 10.
19. Ibid. 124.
20. John Baxendale, *Priestley's England: J B Priestley and English Culture* (Manchester, 2007), 23–9; Collini, *Absent Minds*, 117.
21. Orwell, *Coming Up*, 175.
22. Ibid. 135; on the flourishing housing market, Richard Dennis, 'Modern London', in M Daunton (ed.), *Cambridge Urban History of Britain*, vol. 3, *1840–1950* (Cambridge, 2000), 110.
23. Hobsbawm discusses how the new middle class had to find ways of recognizing itself in an initially alien suburban environment: 'Mass Producing Traditions: Europe 1870–1914', in E. J. Hobsbawm and T. Ranger, *The Invention of Tradition* (Cambridge, 1983). Bowling's genealogical interests, and an early interest in recreational tennis, accord.
24. Patrick Joyce ponders these questions in *The Rule of Freedom: Liberalism and the Modern City* (London, 2003). Let it be noted, however, that Bowling does not need maps and statistics to know his city so much as train timetables.
25. Oswald Spengler's *Decline of the West* (1918–22) and Lewis Mumford's *The Culture of Cities* (1938) were the great inter-war treatises on the city: Andrew Lees, 'The Metropolis and the Intellectual', in Anthony Sutcliffe (ed.), *Metropolis 1890–1940* (London, 1984), 85.
26. 'British cities were a complex balance between the diseconomies of pollution and disease, and the economies of information and knowledge': Daunton, 'Introduction', *Cambridge Urban History*, 48.
27. Orwell, *Coming Up*, 21.
28. P. J. Cain and A. G. Hopkins, 'Gentlemanly Capitalism and British Expansion Overseas II: New Imperialism 1850–1945', *Economic History Review*, 2nd ser., 40: 1 (1987).
29. David Kynaston, *The City of London*, vol. 3, *Illusions of Gold 1914–45* (London, 1999), 287, 368. The whole economic environment changed when sterling went off gold in 1931.
30. Executive officer, civil service ($£379$ p.a.), qualified schoolteacher ($£348$), draughtsman first class for the Post Office ($£343$), railway foreman ($£263$), coalminer ($£149$), barrister ($£1090$): Guy Routh, *Occupation and Pay in Great Britain 1906–60* (Cambridge, 1965), 64–70, 83, 88.
31. 'Exams were seen, not as burdens or barriers, but as merit's opportunity...' This sounds like the opinion of someone who was good at them: Brian Harrison, *Seeking a Role: The United Kingdom 1951–70* (Oxford, 2009), 51.
32. David Edgerton's *England and the Aeroplane* (Basingstoke, 1991) establishes the scale and technical ability of a 'militant and technological nation', while his *Warfare State: Britain 1920–70* (Cambridge, 2006) does the same but on a wider front.
33. Harrison, *Seeking a Role*, 22.
34. Roy Lewis and Angus Maude, *The English Middle Classes* (1949; London, 1953), 70.
35. Priestley, *English Journey*, 375.
36. Esme Wingfield-Stratford, *The History of English Patriotism* (London, 1913), ii. 598, 603. On 'plague centre' as coded anti-Semitism: Revd J. Basil Rust, 'East End Jewish Settlements', *The Times*, 6 Jan. 1912.
37. 'A specialized British product', according to Patrick Abercrombie (ed.), *The Book of the Modern House* (London, 1939), p. xix.

38. M. Swenarton and S. Taylor, 'The Scale and Nature of the Growth of Owner Occupation in Britain between the Wars', *Economic History Review*, 2nd ser., 38 (1985), 384.

39. For 'suburban neurosis', a syndrome coined by Dr Taylor in the *Lancet* in 1938, see A. M. Edwards, *The Design of Suburbia* (London, 1981), 127; and for George Bowling's reasons to be thankful, see Paul Oliver, Ian Davis, and Ian Bentley, *Dunroamin: The Suburban Semi and its Enemies* (London, 1982).

40. Julia Parker and Caroline Mirrlees, 'Housing', in Halsey, *Social Trends*, tables 10.30, 10.18.

41. London was always bursting its boundaries forcing new standards of local and metropolitan government: Dennis, 'Modern London', in Daunton, *Urban History*, 95–8; P. L. Garside, 'London and the Home Counties', in F. M. L. Thompson (ed.), *Cambridge Social History of Britain*, vol. 1, *1750–1950* (Cambridge, 1990), 494.

42. John Sheail, *Rural Conservation in Inter War Britain* (Oxford, 1991), chs. 2, 7, 8.

43. Daphne Patai, *The Orwell Mystique: A Study in Male Ideology* (Amherst, Mass., 1984), 184–8. She points out that 'Ellesmere' means 'She Mother', but there were five Ellesmere Roads in London in 1940, two in west London and one in Ealing, very like where the Bowlings live: *Bartholomew's Atlas of Greater London*, 7th edn. (Edinburgh, 1940), ref 60. E. Rather against Patai, or at any rate alongside her, Collini notes that ' "soggy", "soft", and cognate terms cluster around "intellectuals" in Orwell's writings': *Absent Minds*, 354.

44. Orwell, *Coming Up*, 154.

45. Nicholas Mosley, *Beyond the Pale: Sir Oswald Mosley 1933–80* (London, 1983), 64–5.

46. Orwell, *Coming Up*, p. 156, 159–60.

47. Ibid. 162. The grey curls might suggest Robert Graves.

48. 'And a curious thought struck me. *He's dead*. He's a ghost. All people like that are dead': ibid. 165, 168. Perkin's forgotten and 'curiously neglected' professional class included schoolmasters: *The Origins of Modern English Society* (London, 1978), 252–5.

49. Orwell, *Homage*, 220–1.

50. Orwell seems to have been intuitively in touch with the new regionalism led, under French influence, by a new generation of British geographers: see Arid Holt-Jensen, *Geography: History and Concepts* (London, 1988), 34–43. For an England of the regions the founding text is C. B. Fawcett, *Provinces of England* (London, 1919).

51. W. S. Churchill, *A History of the English Speaking Peoples*, vol. 1, *The Birth of Britain* (London, 1956), 100.

52. Colls, *Identity of England*, 241–3, 259–60, 312–16, 329–33.

53. Jeremy Crump, 'The Reception of Elgar 1898–1935', in Robert Colls and Philip Dodd (eds.), *Englishness: Politics and Letters 1880–1920* (London, 1986), and John Gardiner, 'The Reception of Sir Edward Elgar 1918–34', *Twentieth Century British History*, 9: 3 (1998), 382. 'The British middle classes—from which most elite group members were drawn—were disproportionately resident in London and the southeast', while 'the position of the north of England in the British elite structure had indeed become progressively less fortunate': W. D. Rubinstein, 'Education and the Social Origins of British Elites 1880–1970', *Past and Present*, 112 (1986), 200, 201, and table 19, 'Percentage of British middle-class income by region'.

54. 'parasitism...vast tribute...tame masses...new financial aristocracy...[the] south of England today [is] already reduced to this condition': Hobson, *Imperialism*, 314.

55. William Morris, *News From Nowhere or, An Epoch of Rest, being some chapters from A Utopian Romance* (1890; London, 1910), 183.

56. Arthur Bryant, *The National Character* (London, 1934), 15–16, originally broadcast on the BBC in 1933.

57. W. S. Shears claims they did in his Right Book Club volume, *This England: A Book of the Shires and the Counties* (London, 1937), 7.

58. Matless, *Landscape and Englishness*, chs. 1–4; on less than 'full physical efficiency' 'as late as 1910' among labouring families in the south: R. Floud and D. McCloskey, *Economic History of Britain since 1700* (Cambridge, 1994), ch. 6.

59. For the vesting of Englishness in the southern countryside, Alun Howkins, 'The Discovery of Rural England', in Colls and Dodd, *Englishness*, 80. Late nineteenth-century Englishness is central to Krishan Kumar's argument in *The Making of English National Identity* (London, 2003). In a possibly concealed joke of the 'Comstock' type, Orwell's *faux* Tudor Englishness architect shares a name with Sir Edward Watkin, driving force behind the Metropolitan Railway Company. Mr Chips was the eminently admirable and engaging public-schoolmaster in James Hilton's best-selling novel *Good-bye, Mr Chips*, first published in 1934 and made into a Hollywood movie in 1939. Porteous and Chips are almost opposites.

60. Orwell, *Coming Up*, 228. '...conjectural, nugatory, deluded, tedious rubbish' is how Jim Dixon reflects upon his 'Merrie England' lecture describing a certain type of English local history in Kingsley Amis's *Lucky Jim* (1954; London, 1961), 226.

61. Meacham quotes Linda Colley as to the garden city movement's progenitors: 'the very rich, the very cultivated, the deeply idealistic, the highly entrepreneurial and the downright eccentric.' There was no shortage of high-minded philanthropy in the garden city movement; nor was there any shortage of scepticism and ridicule: Standish Meacham, *Regaining Paradise: Englishness and the Early Garden City Movement* (New Haven, 1999), 64, 73–6, 128, 7. If it was Letchworth Orwell had in mind in his attacks on middle-class fads, he was certainly unfair on the town, its progenitor Ebenezer Howard, and its designers Barry Parker and Raymond Unwin. Nevertheless, that the garden city experiment was middle-class in practice and principle is undeniable.

62. 'Garden city reformers employed Englishness to institute an exclusionary hierarchy. They would use the garden city to define what was English and what was not': ibid. 7. For new towns as 'the epitome of planning': J. F. F. Robinson, 'New Towns and Ideology' (University of Durham Working Paper, 7, 1974), 4. For the high-handed and prescriptive: A. Beach and N. Tiratsoo, 'The Planners and the Public', in Daunton, *Cambridge Urban History*, 526–8.

63. Metaphor by Michael Carter, *George Orwell and the Problem of Authentic Existence* (London, 1985), 158.

64. Colls, *Identity of England*, chs. 12–16.

65. Orwell reverses expectations: Sidney Dark's *London* (London, 1924) has nothing ordinary or plain, while Dave Russell's north has little else: *Looking North: Northern England and the National Imagination* (Manchester, 2004), 243.

66. 'In a Lancashire cotton-town you could probably go for months on end without once hearing an "educated" accent, whereas there can hardly be a town in the South of England where you could throw a brick without hitting the niece of a bishop': Orwell, *Wigan Pier*, 102.

67. Orwell, *Coming Up*, 46. Raphael Samuel depicts northern rural qualities compared to southern rural qualities as energizers rather than tranquillizers, and that energy can be applied to Lower Binfield too: *Island Story: Unravelling Britain*, vol. 2 (London, 1998), ch. 9, 'Country Visiting'.

68. Jeffrey Richards, *Films and British National Identity* (Manchester, 1997), 255. Richards is talking of Lancashire and Yorkshire in general but Gracie Fields in particular.

69. Gideon Clark saw the classes as invariably snobbish and the masses as invariably 'humbugged': *Democracy in the Dock* (London, 1939), 174.

70. Paul Readman shows an 1895 cartoon by F. C. Gould depicting the 'Tory Village' as 'A Toy for Little Tories': 'No Other Cottages Allowed', 'Parish Pump: for key apply to Rector', 'School Room Not Available for Radical Meetings', 'To Allotments Grounds 5 Miles': 'The Edwardian Land Question', in M. Cragoe and P. Readman (eds.), *The Land Question in Britain 1750–1950* (Basingstoke, 2010), 191. In the 1876 Return 75 per cent of British acreage belonged to 5,000 people; 25 per cent of English to 710 (pp. 2–3).

71. C. F. G. Masterman (ed.), *The Heart of the Empire: Discussions of the Problem of Modern City Life in England* (London, 1901); and *Condition of England*, 68.

72. 'The mass man regards himself as perfect': José Ortega y Gasset, *The Revolt of the Masses* (1930; London, 1932), 49.

73. 'I have to love her': Ernest Raymond, in N. P. Macdonald's review of left/right establishment opinion: (ed.), *What Is Patriotism?* (London, 1935), 192.

74. 'Little Man' is Strube's 1930s long-suffering cartoon character in the *Daily Express*: Mandler, *English National Character*, 174. Graham Laidler drew for *Punch* as 'Pont': see his *The British Character Studied and Revealed* (London, 1938), with an Introduction by E M Delafield. Some aspects of Pont's average Englishman do sound very Bowling: for instance, his tendency to think 'That England is going to rack and ruin' as well as 'England is the finest country in the world', and the 'Importance of Not Being Intellectual' and 'A Tendency To Be Hearty'. G. J. Renier's Englishmen share some of these qualities too: *The English: Are They Human?* (1931; London, 1956).

75. The British Institute of Public Opinion (BIPO) was founded in 1937 and took the first 'opinion poll' in 1938 for the West Fulham by-election: Nick Moon, *Opinion Polls History* (Manchester, 1999), 6.

76. My references to the varieties of patriotism draw on the Macdonald volume. Lady Cynthia Asquith came closest to Orwell in her criticism of those who disparaged everything to do with England, 'its climate, its food, its codes, customs, language, art and manners' (*What Is Patriotism?*, 276).

77. On the deep-seated corporateness of modern Britain, and how long it took to break up, see Jon Lawrence, 'Paternalism, Class, and the British Path to Modernity', in Simon Gunn and James Vernon (eds.), *The Peculiarities of Liberal Modernity in Imperial Britain* (Berkeley, 2011). Because the gentleman was 'embedded in normative models of Englishness until the mid fifties', when he declined, it seems Bowling was ahead of the game: Marcus Collins, 'The Fall of the English Gentleman: The National Character in Decline 1918–1970', *Historical Research*, 75: 187 (Feb. 2002), 91.

78. Calder, *Chronicles of Conscience*, 163. Christopher Small says that in his search for God, Orwell/Bowling is going *down* to look for the likely places, and fails to find them, while the obvious truth is that he is coming up, up into the light and air, in order to find himself, and does so: *The Road to Miniluv: George Orwell, the State, and God* (London, 1975), ch. 3, 'Escaping Underground'.

79. Richard Filloy explains Orwell's use of Aristotle's concept of 'ethos' as a rhetorical device to persuade us that he is one of us: 'Orwell's Political Persuasion: A Rhetoric of Personality', Holderness *et al.*, *George Orwell*, 52.

80. Orwell to Geoffrey Gorer, from The Stores, Wallington, 23 May 1936, *CW* x. 482: Geoffrey Gorer (1905–85) reviewed *Burmese Days* for *Time and Tide*. For Gorer's

own failure to write a successful anthropology of the English, *Exploring English Character* (1955), see Peter Mandler, 'Being His Own Rabbit: Geoffrey Gorer and English Culture', in Griffiths *et al.*, *Classes, Cultures*.

81. Malcolm Muggeridge (1903–90), English journalist, writer, editor, television pundit, and Christian apologist, became quite close friends with Orwell after the war.

82. 'Inside the Whale' is important here; see next chapter. So are two linked pieces in *Time and Tide*, 'Notes on the Way', 30 Mar. and 6 Apr. 1940 (*CW* xii. 124–5), which invoked Muggeridge among others in order to argue the case for a decadent and flawed religious life (as in England or France) over an arrogant and merciless atheism (as in Germany or the USSR). This theme spills over into Orwell's revision of his views on the British Empire in 'Rudyard Kipling', *Horizon* (Feb. 1942), *CW* xiii. 150–62.

83. Julia will catch Winston's eye in *Nineteen Eighty-Four* and Winston will catch O'Brien's. For reasons best known to himself, Orwell's exchange with the Wigan girl moves from a direct encounter in the lane to a fleeting glance from a train: 'At that moment she looked up and caught my eye...': *Wigan Diary*, 15 Feb. 1936, *CW* x. 427; 'She looked up as the train passed and I was almost near enough to catch her eye...': *Wigan Pier*, 16.

84. Orwell, *Coming Up*, 152–3, 215, 155, 88.

85. Ibid. 20, 195.

86. 'Of course you are right about my own character constantly intruding on that of the narrator. I am not a real novelist anyway, and that particular vice is inherent in writing a novel in the first person which one should never do. One difficulty I have never solved is that one has masses of experience which one passionately wants to write about... and no way of using them up except by disguising them as a novel': letter, Orwell to Julian Symons, from Ward 3, Hairmyres Hospital, East Kilbride, 10 May 1948, *CW* xix. 336.

87. *Coming Up*, 128.

88. Ibid. 31.

89. Ibid. 110.

90. '...obviously a tale told by a toff': Stefan Collini, *English Pasts* (Oxford, 1999), 24.

91. In 1874 Eton College claimed to instil in each of its boys the will 'to save himself by his sole exertions': Chattock, *Eton*, 50.

Chapter 5

1. George Orwell, 'Inside the Whale', 97, 99. In addition to Auden and Spender, Orwell identified Cecil Day Lewis, Louis MacNeice, Christopher Isherwood, John Lehmann, Arthur Calder-Marshall, Edward Upward, Alec Brown, and Philip Henderson as leading lights.

2. *The Booster*—which declared itself 'non-political, non-educational, non-progressive, non-cooperative, non-ethical, non-literary, non-consistent, non-contemporary': 'Inside the Whale', 92.

3. Ibid. 91–2; Miller to Orwell, 20 Apr. 1938, Orwell Archive, Appendix 2, letters to Orwell I.

4. After Orwell's review of *Tropic of Cancer* in November 1935, Miller wrote to him sometime in the summer of 1936 to tell him about his next book, *Black Spring*. Miller had received a copy of *Down and Out*, and (from Orwell's reply) was clearly enquiring about his other works just at the point Orwell was writing *The Road to Wigan Pier*: letter, Orwell to Miller, from The Stores, Wallington, 26–7 Aug. 1936, *CW* x. 496.

5. Orwell, *Down and Out*, 17.
6. As Orwell put it, 'dealing with facts well known to everybody but never mentioned in print' '(e.g. when the chap is supposed to be making love to the woman but is dying for a piss all the while)': Orwell to Miller, 26–7 Aug. 1936, p. 495.
7. e.g. On the swindle of 'Progress': G. K. Chesterton, *Illustrated London News*, 19 April 1924. 'Inside the Whale', 111.
8. The period from the declaration of war in September 1939 to the German invasion of Norway in April 1940 is commonly called the 'Phoney War'. This was the period in which he wrote and brought together the collected volume *Inside the Whale and Other Essays*—comprising 'Inside the Whale' (also published in *New Directions in Prose and Poetry*, 1940), 'Boys' Weeklies' (also published in *Horizon*, March 1940), and 'Charles Dickens'—published by Gollancz on 11 March 1940.
9. Well into adolescence Orwell would make third-person commentary on his actions. He had been a lonely child, talking to himself about himself until at Eton he had entered more serious 'literary' activities: 'Why I Write', *Gangrel*, 4 (1946), *CW* xviii. 316–21.
10. J. M. Keynes, *The Economic Consequences of the Peace* (New York, 1920), ch. 4, 'Europe after the Treaty': 'This chapter must be one of pessimism.'
11. 'Inside the Whale', 107.
12. *Coming Up*, 76.
13. 'Inside the Whale', 111.
14. Nazi plebiscites were met with a League of Nations 'Peace Ballot' of overwhelming ambiguity. On 22 June 1937 the British were asked whether they were in favour of 'all round' arms reductions (they were), as well as military and non-military measures to repel invasions (they were): R. J. Q. Adams, *British Politics and Foreign Policy in an Age of Appeasement* (Basingstoke, 1993), 161.
15. Chamberlain's finest hour, according to G. A. H. Gordon, leaving the country primed for a long war by 1940 and outproducing and -resourcing Germany by 1941: *British Seapower and Procurement between the Wars* (Basingstoke, 1988), 289–90. Defence expenditure accounted for 48% of British government expenditure by 1939: R. P. Shay, *British Re-Armament in the Thirties* (Princeton, 1977), 297. Chamberlain was convinced before Munich that 'a visible force of overwhelming strength' 'is the only argument that Germany understands': letter to his sister, Hilda, 13 Mar. 1938, quoted in R. Self (ed.), *The Neville Chamberlain Diary Letters*, vol. 4, *1934–40* (Aldershot, 2005), 304. According to Morgan, Lloyd George managed to reach 'the rhetorical climax of inter-war appeasement' in a 1936 interview with the *Daily Express*: *Ages of Reform*, 89.
16. Chamberlain's political life had been devoted to social reform: Denis Smith, 'Englishness and the Liberal Inheritance after 1885', in Colls and Dodd, *Englishness*, 268–70, 273–4. After the Czech government's capitulation to the Munich agreement, Chamberlain and Hitler signed a separate treaty in the early hours of 30 September. 'Peace for our time', the British prime minister called it, to the great relief of almost everybody. At this point dissident Tories like Churchill, and the leadership of the Labour party, who opposed Munich, were in the minority. *Coming Up for Air*, then, was a Munich novel in the sense that it was written over the period of the possibility of peace or at any rate not war. Bowling's anti-war feelings represented the mass of British public opinion. But because it was written in Morocco, Orwell was out of touch with the swift changes in public opinion leading up to and following Hitler's taking of Prague in March 1939, so that when the novel was published in June it was already behind the curve. As for Chamberlain, no British politician of the twentieth century was more reviled for policy failure ('Appeasement')

than he, but his position in 1938–9 was more reasonable than Orwell's, and no more naive than 'Cato's', whose coarse, clichéd, but perfectly timed political tract *Guilty Men* (1940) blamed him and his fellow appeasers with all the authority of hindsight.

17. George Orwell, 'Why I Join the ILP', *New Leader*, 24 June 1938, *CW* xi. 168.

18. '...by the building of a new world order based on fellowship and justice': 'If War Comes We Shall Resist', *New Leader*, 30 Sept. 1938, *CW* xi. 213. Signatories included Vera Brittain, Havelock Ellis, C. E. M. Joad, J. S. Rowntree, Fenner Brockway, and James Maxton, MP. Orwell, letter to Jack Common, from rue Edmond Doutte, Marrakech, 29 Sept. 1938, *CW* xi. 211.

19. In his 'Notes on the Way' (*Time and Tide*, 10 Mar. and 6 Apr. 1940) Orwell was still describing Hitler as 'the extenuation and perpetuation of our own methods' (*CW* xii. 123), and the leader of the ILP was still balancing moral equivalences in 1947, this time with the Soviets, not the Nazis: Fenner Brockway, *Inside the Left: Thirty Years of Platform, Press, Prison, and Parliament* (London, 1947), preface.

20. Peace Pledge Union, Society of Friends, No More War Movement, ILP, International African Bureau, Labour Parliamentary Pacifist Group, 'Against War', *Manchester Guardian*, 28 Sept. 1938; letter, Orwell to John Sceats, from Gueliz, Marrakech, 26 Oct. 1938, *CW* xi. 227; letters to Herbert Read, from Gueliz, Marrakech, 4 Jan., 5 Mar. 1939, *CW* xi. 313, 340; on the governing class and the need for a mass party, 'Not Counting Niggers', *The Adelphi* (July 1939), *CW* xi. 359, 361; on treachery, *Wartime Diary*, 27 June 1940, *CW* xii. 198.

21. Eileen Blair to Geoffrey Gorer, from rue Edmond Doutte, Medina, Marrakech, 4 Oct. 1938: Orwell Archive, K27, and *CW* xi. 218.

22. The ILP specialized in 'moral outrage': Morgan, *Ages of Reform*, 162.

23. Eileen Blair to Marjorie Dakin, from rue Edmond Doutte, Medina, Marrakech, 27 Sept. 1938, *CW* xi. 207, 206.

24. Orwell's 'fascizing process' is somewhat present in both. 'The inhabitants of the post-war world knew with certainty that war would now rain down upon civilians; terror would come': Susan R. Grayzel, *At Home and Under Fire: Air Raids and Culture in Britain from the Great War to the Blitz* (New York, 2012), 119.

25. Eileen Blair to Marjorie Dakin, 27 Sept. 1938.

26. Orwell to Leonard Moore, from The Stores, Wallington, 25 Apr. 1939, *CW* xi. 352. Adrian Gregory reminds us that 'the vast majority of the men of military age in Britain during the First World War chose not to volunteer': *The Last Great War* (Cambridge, 2008), 89. Gregory reminds us too that the moral superiority of the Second World War made the First look futile. Orwell carried the First War round in his head right up to George Bowling.

27. Still against war in the month it breaks out, but we do not know the lead time between him writing the piece and seeing it published: 'Democracy in the British Army', *Left Forum* (Sept. 1939), *CW* xi. 406–7. By the time of his 'Don't Let Colonel Blimp Ruin the Home Guard' (*Evening Standard*, 8 Jan. 1941) his argument is that the Blimps are not treacherous, just stupid: *CW* xii. 363.

28. Orwell, 'Spilling the Spanish Beans' (1937), *CW* xi. 44.

29. Orwell, 'My Country Right or Left', *Folios of New Writing*, 2 (Autumn 1940), *CW* xii. 272.

30. Quoted in Richard Weight, 'State, Intelligentsia and the Promotion of National Culture in Britain 1939–45', *Historical Research*, 69 (1996), 89.

31. McKibbin, *Parties and People*, 122.

32. '[Churchill] responded... throughout the crisis by appealing to the Commons and to the nation at large. His appeal was through the emotions... [he] staked his own survival as Prime Minister upon a strategy of "no surrender". That was the badge

of his administration, that was his contact with the nation': John Charmley, *Churchill: The End of Glory* (London, 1995), 418–19.

33. Richard Weight, *Patriots: National Identity in Britain 1940–2000* (London, 2002), 24; Malcolm Smith, *Britain and 1940: History, Myth and Popular Memory* (London, 2000), 60–1.

34. Letter to Cicely Jennings, 20 Oct. 1940, in Mary-Lou Jennings (ed.), *Humphrey Jennings: Film-maker, Painter, Poet* (London, 1982), 25. McKibbin, *Parties and People*, 118.

35. McKibbin, *Parties and People*, 123, 117, 120, 136. Orwell's Spanish strategy was misconceived even in Spain, but Labour's key role in Churchill's government, 1940–5, and then in government on its own account, 1945–51, went some way to making the point that total wars and (peaceful) revolutions are not mutually exclusive. It is certainly the case that the British people experienced something of a glorious revolution starting May 1940, and they would not have done it without the threat of defeat and occupation. Richard Weight and Abigail Beach call it 'citizenship': *The Right to Belong: Citizenship and National Identity in Britain 1930–1960* (London, 1998), chs. 1–8.

36. 'My Country Right or Left', *CW* xii. 269–72.

37. His application to the Ministry of Labour and National Service does not survive but the reply does, made on 8 December 1939: Peter Davison (ed.), *Orwell and Politics* (London, 2001), 83. He was turned down twice more—by Field Security Recruiting, 25 May 1940, and by the Air Ministry, 3 April 1941, which advised him to reapply, this time to the Administrative and Special Duties branch: letters, Orwell Archive, Appendix 2, Letters to Orwell.

38. Orwell, 'Not Counting Niggers', review of *Union Now*, by Clarence K. Streit, *The Adelphi* (July 1939), *CW* xi. 360.

39. Orwell, 'Notes on the Way', *Time and Tide*, 10 Mar., 6 Apr. 1940, and review of *Mein Kampf*, *New English Weekly*, 21 Mar. 1940: *CW* xii. 123, 117.

40. *Wartime Dairy*, 27 June 1940, *CW* xii. 199.

41. Orwell, review of Alex Comfort, *The Adelphi* (Oct. 1941), *CW* xiii. 42.

42. 'Pacifism and the War: A Controversy', 12 July 1942, published *Partisan Review*, Sept.–Oct. 1942, *CW* xiii. 396–8. In response to Alex Comfort's charge that he was 'intellectual-hunting again', Orwell made the astonishing claim that he had never been anti-intellectual, and had 'never attacked "the intellectuals" or "the intelligentsia" *en bloc*' (p. 399). *En bloc* is an interesting phrase. His point about British pacifism being a branch of liberalism allowed to grow strong in a country comprehensively defended by its navy is richly endorsed by Bernard Semmel, *Liberalism and Naval Strategy* (Winchester, Mass., 1986).

43. In 'Looking back on the Spanish Civil War' (1942) he came clean, admitting that the 'Trotskyist thesis that the war could have been won if the revolution had not been sabotaged' was 'probably false' (p. 241).

44. 'This is not only dishonest; it also carries a severe penalty... If you disregard people's motives, it becomes much harder to foresee their actions': Orwell, in *Tribune*, 8 Dec. 1944, *CW* xvi. 495. Ethel Mannin wrote to him twice in 1939, once to praise *Coming Up for Air* as an anti-war novel, and again to express her puzzlement ('bitched buggered and bewildered', as she put it) at his reply, where he appears to have said he was keen to get into the army: 'I thought you thought it all crazy, this smashing of Nazi faces. For the love of Mike write a few lines to lighten our darkness': letter to Orwell, probably 30 Oct. 1939, *CW* xi. 413. Mannin was a Quaker, who had married Orwell's friend Reg Reynolds.

45. Salman Rushdie did not approve of whale talk, and forty years too late he took it upon himself to rescue us from it: S. Rushdie, 'Outside the Whale' (1984), in *Imaginary Homelands: Essays and Criticism 1981–91* (London, 1991), 97–9.

46. *Wartime Diary*, 28 May 1940, *CW* xii. 168.
47. Ibid. 31 May, 25 May, 2 June 1940. Orwell worked as a theatre critic for *Time and Tide*, 18 May 1940–9 August 1941.
48. Review of Wyndham Lewis, 'The Mysterious Mr Bull', *New English Weekly*, 8 June 1939, *CW* xii. 354.
49. Orwell, 'My Country Right or Left' (1940), *CW* xii. 271.
50. Waterloo and Victoria stations: *Wartime Diary*, Saturday, 1 June 1940, *CW* xii. 175; Orwell accounts for his dream in 'My Country Right or Left'.
51. Song first referenced as sung by an unturbulent people in *Wigan Pier Diary*, 19 Feb. 1936, *CW* x. 431; and referenced again as sung by a turbulent people in his *The English People* (London, 1947), 20. In their response to the crisis it would seem that Orwell's saloon-bar drinkers did not differ much from the Woodrow Wilson Professor of International Politics. From the professor's diary, 7 March 1936: 'Germans enter Rhineland. Home to lunch': Jonathan Hasland, *The Vices of Integrity: E. H. Carr 1892–1982* (London, 2000), 60.
52. *Wartime Diary*, Saturday 1 June 1940, *CW* xii. 272.
53. His contemporary, the Oxford philosopher Isaiah Berlin (1909–97), could have advised on giving up the liberty of outside the whale for the liberty inside it: *Four Essays on Liberty* (Oxford, 1982), 170.
54. Unlike the most famous socialist propagandist of his youth, Robert Blatchford (1851–1943), who instructed that under socialism 'costume should be simple, healthy, convenient and beautiful': *Merrie England* (London, 1908), 43.
55. *Wartime Diary*, 3 May 1941, *CW* xii. 490. He would change his mind on Tube station children: 'London Letter', *Partisan Review* (Fall 1944), *CW* xvi. 303. On known and knowable political communities, it is worth remembering that Orwell was a classicist. When he thought of democracy one thinks of him thinking of ancient Athens, and when he thought of war, Sparta: Eugenio F. Biagini (ed.), *Citizenship and Community: Liberals, Radicals and Collective Identities in the British Isles 1865–1931* (Cambridge, 1996), 50.
56. 'Colonel Blimp' (combination of 'blink' and 'limp'?): pompous and reactionary cartoon figure by David Low in the London *Evening Standard*, and subject of a popular Powell and Pressburger film, *The Life and Death of Colonel Blimp* (1943).
57. Orwell, letter to Geoffrey Gorer from The Stores, Wallington, 10 Jan. 1940, *CW* xii. 6.
58. 'Inside the Whale', *CW* xii. 107.
59. Orwell, 'My Country Right or Left', *CW* xii. 590.
60. '...the most powerful of the great powers', completely outgunning the German battle-fleet in 1939 and out-producing the Luftwaffe by 50 per cent by 1940: David Edgerton, *Warfare State: Britain 1920–70*, 58; *England and the Aeroplane*, 71.
61. '...the great mass of the English people were unmoved, or unmoved directly, by the culture of the country's intellectual elites': McKibbin, *Classes and Cultures*, preface.
62. Britain's scientific and engineering superiority was proved at 'Station X', or Bletchley Park, where German codes were broken and the first electronic computer was built, by Tommy Flowers and his colleagues from the GPO research establishment at Dollis Hill, London. At Bletchley, scholarship boys like Flowers (son of a bricklayer) and Bill Tutte (son of a gardener) mixed with a wide array of elite mathematical talent to make it an extreme version of Orwell's argument about the innovating propensities of the 'new' middle class. See Jack Copeland *et al.*, *Colossus: The Secrets of Bletchley Park's Code-Breaking Computers* (Oxford, 2006).

63. Mark Rawlinson, *British Writing of the Second World War* (Oxford, 2000), 142. Street myths testifying to local courage and resource circulated before the MoI had time to vet or invent them: Tom Harrison, *Living Through the Blitz* (London, 1976), 83–6.

64. 'The People'—'a moral, a physical, a political, a national regenerator', 'the homely, the personal, the concrete': Joyce, *Visions of the People*, 39, 318. See Angus Calder, *The People's War* (London, 1971), 188–306.

65. From 1940 to 1945 they lived at Dorset Chambers, Chagford Street, NW1; Langford Court, Abbey Road, NW8; Mortimer Crescent, NW6; and Canonbury Square, Islington, N1. Orwell's disregard for elite culture in favour of the people is unusual and brings him closer to an English nationalist tradition than the older way of writing about English national identity through the country's leading institutions. At the same time, he never quite threw off the old (left and right) idea that the people needed leading: 'the emphasis was not on the character of the people but rather on the ability of institutions to lead and hold them': Disraeli, in Mandler, *English National Character*, 123. On the dominant academic mode of writing about politics (totally ignored by Orwell), see Patrick Dunleavy, 'The Westminster Model', in Dunleavy et al., *Developments in British Politics* (Basingstoke, 2006).

66. In 1943 Orwell's salary was raised from £680 to £740 p.a. The BBC Empire Service made its first broadcast on 19 December 1932. India was one of five zones. It broadcast in English and Hindustani. Its remit was the same as the Home Service, though with a greater sense of countering anti-British propaganda. It never really knew who was listening and was the subject of long and bitter arguments over content and direction: Asa Briggs, *The Golden Age of Wireless* (London, 1965), 408–10; id., *The War of Words* (London, 1970), 505–18.

67. R. A. Randall, Assistant Controller Overseas, reported on Orwell's interview to the Director-General as 'distinguished... impressive... frank and honest... attractive... no misgivings... very suitable': Internal Memorandum, 25 June 1941, BBC Archive. He was appointed in preference to Edward Thompson, another old India hand and left-winger, though far, far better connected than Orwell (and the father of E. P. Thompson). See also D. Pearson Smith's report on Orwell: BBC Annual Report, E. A. Blair, Grade B 1 Talks Producer, 10 Aug. 1943, www.bbc.co.uk/archive, accessed 22 Jan. 2013. The only criticism seems to have come from J. B. Clark, Controller of Overseas Services, concerning the quality of Orwell's voice, which he thought 'might repel' (memo, 19 Jan. 1943).

68. 'I am tendering my resignation because for some time past I have been conscious that I was wasting my own time and public money on doing work that produces no result... I feel that by going back to my normal work of writing and journalism I could be more useful': internal memo, Orwell to Mr Rushbrooke-Williams, 24 Sept. 1943; 'He leaves at his own request to the regret of the whole Department', Leaving Note, Rushbrooke-Williams, 20 Nov. 1943, BBC Archive.

69. Taylor, *Orwell*, 311.

70. Letter to Alex Comfort, from 10a Mortimer Crescent, London NW6, 11 July 1943, *CW* xv. 165.

71. Forgiven perhaps since his edited volume *The Betrayal of the Left* (London 1941)—including an essay by Orwell. For Orwell's *Tribune* journalism, Richard Keeble, in Keeble and Wheeler (eds.), *Journalistic Imagination* (Abingdon, 2013) ch. 7.

72. Andrew Motion, *Philip Larkin: A Writer's Life* (London, 1994), 45. *The Times* ranked Orwell second to Larkin in a list of 'The 50 Greatest British Writers since 1945' (5 Jan. 2008).

73. Orwell wrote a highly appreciative profile of Bevan for the *Observer*, 14 Oct. 1945, where he showed how much he had learned since his Wigan days. He understood

now how it was possible for working-class men like Bevan to become intellectuals, thrust as they were into a politics more serious and more intense than anything parliament could offer.

74. Hilary Spurling, *The Girl from the Fiction Department: A Portrait of Sonia Orwell* (London, 2002), 67. It was not just the buildings that were shaken up by bombs: see Lara Feigel, *The Love Charm of Bombs: Restless Lives in the Second World War* (London, 2013).

75. See Crick, 'Broadcasting Days', *Orwell*, ch. 13; Taylor, *Orwell*, part 4; Bowker, *Orwell*, chs. 13, 14, 15.

76. Orwell, letter to Jack Common, from New Hostel, Preston Hall, Aylesford, Kent, 5 July 1938, *CW* xi. 171.

77. A 'family saga sort of thing', but 'I feel I have written myself out': Orwell to Geoffrey Gorer, from The Stores, Wallington, 10 Jan. 1940, *CW* xii. 7.

78. 'I have been ILL. Ever so ill. Bedridden for four weeks & still weak': Eileen Blair to Norah Myles, 5 Dec. 1940, from Greenwich, in Davison, *Lost Orwell*, 79.

79. Taylor, *Orwell*, 273; Bowker, *Orwell*, 265, 290.

80. Not counting abroad or his forays into the north of England, by the time Orwell moved into the Wallington cottage in 1936 one can count at least twenty addresses. Stansky and Abrahams' *Unknown Orwell* and *Orwell: The Transformation* are both particularly good on the types of locations, and Davison's magnificent *Complete Works* gets just about all of them.

81. Bernard Crick, lecture on Orwell at University of Leicester, 12 Feb. 2004; Allan Pond identified 'unabashed Englishness' as a classic trait of the English Radical tradition: 'Beyond Memory's Reach: The Particularities of English Radicalism', *Quarterly Review* (Winter 2008), 27.

82. Letter to the Editor, *Time and Tide*, 22 June 1940, and 'Colonel Blimp', *Evening Standard*, 8 Jan. 1941, *CW* xii. 192, 365. William Cobbett saw no reason why those who defended their country in time of war should be denied the right to bear arms in time of peace: 'the peasants of this country are brave, their forefathers were so, and notwithstanding the incessant efforts of cant and effeminacy to eradicate every manly sentiment from their minds, the sons also are brave': *Political Register*, 23 June 1804, in Ian Dyck, *William Cobbett and Rural Popular Culture* (Cambridge, 1992), 31.

83. The Local Defence Volunteers changed its name to the Home Guard in July 1940 on Churchill's instructions. Orwell was encouraged by these little platoons: *Wartime Diaries*, 1 June, 21 June; they are inspected by 'the usual senile imbecile' of a general along with the London battalions in Regents Park at the end of the month (*Wartime Diaries*, 30 June); and then again on 23 August: 'wretched old blimps…degenerate in everything but physical courage': *CW* xii. 202, 241.

84. *Lion and the Unicorn* (1941), *CW* xii. 405.

85. Harris, *Romantic Moderns*, 10, 11.

86. It was the first publication by Searchlight Books, planned in the summer of 1940 by Orwell, Oscar Fyvel, and Frederic Warburg. Eight more books followed in 1941, and two more in 1942.

87. 'Fascism and Democracy', *CW* xii. 377.

88. Orwell, letter to Gollancz, 8 Jan. 1940, from The Stores, Wallington, Nr. Baldock, *CW* xii. 5: 'the intellectuals who are at present pointing out that democracy and fascism are the same thing etc depress me horribly. However perhaps when the pinch comes the common people will turn out to be more intelligent than the clever ones.' Although it wasn't long since this line on democracy and fascism had been his own position, Orwell was rubbing Gollancz's nose in the Hitler–Stalin

pact. As he told Gorer two days later: Gollancz is 'furious with his Communist late friends, owing to their lies etc...perhaps the Left Book Club may become quite a power for good again': letter, 10 Jan. 1940 from The Stores, Wallington, *CW* xii. 7.

89. Orwell, letter to Geoffrey Gorer, ibid. The two titles he had in mind for this novel were 'The Quick and the Dead' or 'The Lion and the Unicorn'.

90. He had changed his mind on the royal badge. In *The Road to Wigan Pier* he had seen a 'slimy Anglicized form' of British Fascism emerging with 'the lion and the unicorn instead of the swastika' (p. 203).

91. See pp. 107, 148, 195.

92. *Lion and the Unicorn*, *CW* xii. 415. Even when talking about regionalism, or transnational phenomena such as industrialization, as he does briefly in *Wigan Pier*, and in spite of the fact that Eileen's father and brother were Irish, he rarely tarries over Scotland and Wales, still less the Irish in their own right. In a rare moment he addresses the 'so-called races of Britain' question, and concludes that although they feel very different, 'looked at from the outside...the differences sometimes fade away': *CW* xii. 398. Which was convenient.

93. 'his will is not his own': Vernon Bogdanor, *The Monarchy and the Constitution* (Oxford, 1997), 140.

94. Review for the *Listener*, 2 Dec. 1936, *CW* x. 525–6.

95. By 1914 the British state had secured a steep fall in violent crime since 1850, even though the population had doubled and the efficiency of the criminal-justice system had increased: V. A. C. Gattrell, 'Decline of Theft and Violence in Victorian and Edwardian England', in V. A. C. Gattrell, B. Lenman, and G. Parker (eds.), *Crime and the Law* (London, 1980), 239–41.

96. *Lion and the Unicorn*, *CW* xii. 432.

97. F. R. Leavis and Dennys Thompson, *Culture and Environment: The Training of Cultural Awareness* (London, 1933), 1–5; F. R. Leavis, *Education and the University* (1943; Cambridge, 1979), 146.

98. Colls, 'After Bagehot', *Political Quarterly* (2007).

99. Strathearn Gordon described the constitution in 1952 as connecting 'outward sameness' with 'hidden inner change': *Our Parliament*, Hansard Society (London, 1952), 32.

100. Ernest Renan referred to the importance of getting the national history 'wrong' while holding 'a daily plebiscite' of public opinion in order to confirm that it was right: 'What Is a Nation?' (1882), in H. K. Bhabha (ed.), *Nation and Narration* (London, 1990), 19.

101. 'Orwell's greatest single attempt to define the values of democratic socialism', 'by far his most important, positive political statement': Gregory Claeys, 'The Lion and the Unicorn: Patriotism and Orwell's Politics', *Review of Politics*, 47: 2 (1985), 186, 187.

102. *Lion and the Unicorn*, *CW* xii. 408–9, 393.

103. Ibid. 418. *Picture Post* front cover for 21 August 1940 showed an unusually well-armed soldier with the strap-line, 'The Home Guard Can Fight'.

104. *CW* xii. 422. Beveridge apart, Morgan assesses the degree to which the making of that welfare state was connected to wartime measures: K. O. Morgan, *Labour in Power 1945–51* (Oxford, 1984), 21–44.

105. Compare Humphrey Jennings's *Fires Were Started* (Crown Film Unit, 1942) with the Ministry of Information's *Front Line 1940–41: The Official Story of the Civil Defence of Britain* (HMSO, 1942).

106. *Lion and the Unicorn*, *CW* xii. 432.

107. Priestley had made a similar call in the *News Chronicle* two years before. In his core arguments—we have to dump the old leaders, embrace democracy, value the new middle class, and so on—we can see his similarities to Orwell and Orwell's similarities to him: 'Britain Wake Up' (10 Jan. 1939), 'Where is Our Democracy?' (11th), 'The Big Sham' (12th), 'Two Kinds of Unemployed' (13th), 'Thunder on the Left' (14th), 'Conclusion' (17th): Baxendale, *Priestley*, 69–70. In certain other respects—English non-intellectuality, instinct, civility, and so on—Priestley's 1939 novel *Let the People Sing* bears some resemblance to Orwell's *Coming Up for Air*.

108. Priestley was ahead of Orwell on the war but behind him in the theatre, apparently. Orwell reviewed his *Cornelius*, playing at the Westminster Theatre, as a 'period piece': *Time and Tide*, 7 Sept. 1940, *CW* xii. 251.

109. Priestley's radio *Postscript* of 5 June 1940 offered a thousand words on the seaside pleasure-steamers and amateur sailors who helped rescue the British and French armies off Dunkirk beach; he ended by saying that, 'before it is anything else', this country was their country: Baxendale, *Priestley*, 47–9.

110. In a review of Charlie Chaplin's film *The Great Dictator*, Orwell wishes McGill on Hitler. He thought it was Hitler's bad luck in looking so like Chaplin: 'a Jewish foundling with a tendency to fall into pails of whitewash': *Time and Tide*, 21 Dec. 1940, *CW* xii. 375.

111. Michael Lynch, *Hitler* (Abingdon, 2013), 12.

112. 'John Bull Peppering Bonaparte in the front and rear' (McCleary, Dublin 1801–2), John Johnson Collection, Bodleian Library, 6/6. Gillray's 'Little Boney' appears to have made his bow in 1803.

113. George Orwell, 'The Art of Donald McGill', *Horizon* (Sept. 1941), *CW* xiii. 29, 30. For his parallel musings on popular culture, see his review of Jack Hilton's *English Ways*, *The Adelphi* (July 1940), *CW* xii. 202–4.

114. George Orwell, 'Politics and the English Language', *Horizon* (Apr. 1946), *CW* xvii. 427. Poetry, for all these frightfully democratic reasons, he saw as the most abstract, 'the most discredited', and 'the most intellectually pretentious' of the arts: 'Poetry and the Microphone', *New Saxon Pamphlets*, 3 (March 1945), *CW* xvii. 79.

115. Orwell, *Wigan Pier*, 179. Dai Smith's biography of Raymond Williams shows how he spent his life trying to connect the high abstraction and difficulty of his left-intellectualizing to an obsessive reworking of his ordinary life in numerous biographical fictions: *A Warrior's Tale* (Cardigan, 2008).

116. Meyers, *Orwell*, 99.

117. Orwell, 'Why I Write' (1946), *CW* xviii. 320.

118. J. M. Keynes, 'Thomas Robert Malthus', *Essays in Biography* (1933); ed. Donald Winch (London, 2010), 86. Members of Keynes's High English Intelligentsia, which appeared to include 'Scotch and English thought', included Locke and Hume, Smith, Malthus, Darwin, and Mill.

119. Edward Gibbon, on Blackstone's *Commentaries on the Laws of England* (1765–9), quoted in Wilfred Prest, *William Blackstone: Law and Letters in the Eighteenth Century* (Oxford, 2008), 2.

120. Georgina Boyes, *The Imagined Village: Culture, Ideology and the English Folk Revival* (Manchester, 1993).

121. The thesis was called 'survivals in culture': E. B. Tylor, *Primitive Culture* (1871; London 1903), i. 21.

122. J. G. A. Pocock, *The Ancient Constitution and the Feudal Law* (1957; Cambridge, 1987), 34.

123. '...Englishness became an obsession for British Communists after the 7th Congress of the Comintern in 1935': Bounds, *Orwell and Marxism*, 41. Orwell was

familiar with Popular Front journals, especially *Left Review*, *Our Time*, and the book page of the *Daily Worker*.

124. On common law and common culture: Colls, *Identity of England*, 23–30.
125. Not all jurists agreed. Jeremy Bentham built his philosophy repudiating Whig and Tory common-law claims. Like the constitution itself, he saw it as open to manipulation by lawyers and landowners against the interests of the people: G. J. Postema, *Bentham and the Common Law Tradition* (Oxford, 1986), ch. 8.
126. David Lemmings, *Professors of the Law: Barristers and English Legal Culture in the Eighteenth Century* (Oxford, 2000), 309, 316.
127. Sir Matthew Hale, *History of the Common Law of England* (1739; Chicago, 1971), 30; Lord Mansfield quoted in Tom Bingham, *The Rule of Law* (London, 2010), 38.
128. Orwell, 'Boys' Weeklies', *Inside the Whale* (1940), and abridged version in *Horizon* (Mar. 1940), *CW* xii. 60.
129. Claudia Nelson, 'Ideals of Manliness and Sexuality in Victorian Literature for Boys', *Victorian Studies*, 32: 4 (1989). Orwell argued that the stories had not changed since his boyhood.
130. 'Boys' Weeklies', *CW* xii. 67; Orwell to Malcolm Muggeridge, from Barnhill, Isle of Jura, 4 Dec. 1948, in Davison, *Lost Orwell*, 117. His second wife, Sonia, said of his friends that they were all schoolboys, 'adolescent-hero-worshippers': Gordon Bowker, 'Orwell and the Biographers', in Rodden, *Companion to Orwell*, 18. In a later encounter with Sonia at least one of them did nothing to dispel her view: Kingsley Amis, *Memoirs* (London, 1991), 232.
131. 'At first glance such an idea merely makes one slightly sick. It is so horribly easy to imagine what a left-wing boys' paper would be like, if it existed': *CW* xii. 75.
132. The toasts were to the King, the College, and Those Who Have Gone Before: Eton Collegers' Dinner Menu, Thursday, 7 July 1938: Orwell Archive, J/11.
133. The essay drew a sparkling reply from one of the authors of stories for boys, Mr 'Frank Richards' (Charles Hamilton, 1876–1961). Richards, who wrote for the *Magnet*, took Orwell to task on a number of points, but his defence was well received, and enjoyed, by his tormentor. Richards writes in the same vein, with a countervailing intelligence: 'Anyone who disagrees with Mr Orwell is necessarily either an antiquated ass or an exploiter on the make!' 'To conclude, Mr Orwell hopes that a boys' paper with a left-wing bias may not be impossible. I hope that it is' ('Frank Richards Replies to George Orwell', *Horizon* (May 1940), *CW* xii. 79, 85). Richards also says something on national identity that may have caught Orwell's eye: 'Progress, I believe, goes on: but it moves to slow time. No real change is perceptible in the course of a single lifetime. But even if changes succeed one another with kaleidoscopic rapidity, the writer for young people should still endeavour to give his young readers a sense of stability and solid security, because it is good for them, and makes for happiness and peace of mind' (p. 84).
134. Domestic service was far and away the leading employer of occupied females and a significant employer of occupied males all through the nineteenth century, taken jointly, comprising more workers than mining and quarrying, or metals: Mitchell and Deane, *Historical Statistics*, Labour Force 1841–1921, p. 60; Raphael Samuel, 'Workshop of the World: Steam Power and Hand Technology in mid-Victorian Britain', *History Workshop Journal*, 3 (1977), 17.
135. Orwell, 'Charles Dickens', *Inside the Whale* (London, 1940), *CW* xii. 27.
136. Ibid. 33.
137. Ibid. 21.
138. 'There is a scarcely mistakable class-reaction when David Copperfield discovers that Uriah Heep is plotting to marry Agnes Wickfield': ibid. 39.

139. Ibid. 30, 22, 24, 23, 31.

140. Ibid. 35, 56.

141. He had written an appreciation of Kipling on the occasion of his death in 1936: 'now that he is dead, I for one cannot help wishing that I could offer some kind of tribute', *New English Weekly*, 23 Jan. 1936, *CW* x. 410.

142. Orwell concentrates on Kipling's poetry and misses, for instance, his novel *Kim*, which crosses the ethnic divide in search of a new trans-racial imperial state with Anglo-India at its centre: Rudyard Kipling, *Kim* (1901; Harmondsworth, 1994), 159. Kipling, however, could be inconsistent on this, and others have drawn attention to his racial hierarchies, as in *The Jungle Book* (1894) and 'Beyond the Pale', in *Plain Tales from the Hills* (1888): Jonah Raskin, *The Mythology of Imperialism* (New York, 1971), 40; Parry, *Delusions and Discoveries*, 29.

143. Orwell, *Burmese Days*, 70.

144. Richard Jefferies, *Hodge and his Masters* (1880; London, 1949), 303.

145. Orwell, 'Rudyard Kipling', *Horizon* (Feb. 1942), *CW* xiii. 156. Leonard Woolf went to Sri Lanka in 1904, and remembered thinking how much the real colonial world resembled Kipling's: *Growing: An Autobiography of the Years 1904–11* (London, 1961), 46.

146. Orwell, 'In Defence of P. G. Wodehouse', *The Windmill*, 2 (July 1945), *CW* xvii. 52.

147. Orwell, 'Charles Dickens', *CW* xii. 35.

148. 'I agree with every word of it': P. G. Wodehouse to Orwell, from 78 ave. Paul Doumer, Paris, 25 July 1945, Orwell Archive, Appendix 2, letters to Orwell I.

149. *The English People* was commissioned by Collins in 1943 and written by Orwell sometime in May 1944, but not published till August 1947.

150. Orwell, 'Charles Reade', *New Statesman and Nation*, 17 Aug. 1940, *CW* xii. 232–4.

151. He argued in the same piece that English writers before 1914 had also turned in on their own world: 'Literature Between the Wars', BBC Eastern Service, 10 Mar. 1942, *CW* xiii. 211–15.

152. 'First of all the physical memories, the sounds, the smells and the surfaces of things': Orwell, *Homage to Catalonia*, 31, and 'Looking Back on the Spanish War', 225.

153. Letter to Tosco Fyvel, from Ward 3, Hairmyres Hospital, East Kilbride, 31 Dec. 1947, *CW* xix. 241.

154. 'Eighteenth-century Englishmen identified their national culinary traditions not just as one set of tastes and techniques among others, but as the encapsulation of home and hearth': Ben Rogers, *Beef and Liberty: Roast Beef, John Bull and the English Nation* (London, 2004), 55.

155. Although he still received a fee big enough to feed a working-class family for a few months: letter from the British Council, 3 May 1946, Orwell Archive, A/4 e).

156. 'Decline of the English Murder', *Tribune*, 15 Feb.1946, *CW* xviii. 109. He is talking mainly of literature, but by this time he is a master-builder of small worlds connecting literature with politics and both with what he occasionally called 'culture'. George Orwell, 'The Case for the Open Fire', *Evening Standard*, 8 Dec. 1945, 'In Defence of English Cooking', *Evening Standard*, 15 Dec. 1945 (CW xvi); review of *Cricket Country* by Edmund Blunden, *Manchester Evening News*, 20 Apr. 1944 (*CW* xvi); 'Just Junk', *Evening Standard*, 5 Jan. 1946 (*CW* xviii); common conventions, 'Raffles and Miss Blandish', *Horizon* (Aug. 1944) (*CW* xvi); 'Some Thoughts on the Common Toad', *Tribune*, 12 Apr. 1946; 'Moon Under Water', *Evening Standard*, 9 Feb. 1946 (*CW* xviii), and review of *The Pub and the People*, Mass Observation, *Listener*, 21 Jan. 1943 (*CW* xiv); 'A Nice Cup of Tea', *Evening Standard*, 12 Jan. 1946

(*CW* xviii); 'British Cookery', unpublished MS, Mar. 1946, Orwell Archive A/4e); 'Bad Climates Are Best', *Evening Standard*, 2 Feb. 1946, and 'Songs We Used to Sing', *Evening Standard*, 19 Jan. 1946 (*CW* xviii). He was ahead of the field in his idea of the perfect pub. See Basil Oliver, *The Renaissance of the English Public House* (London, 1947).

157. A restraint cruelly broken by Ian Fleming's James Bond in *Casino Royale* in 1953 and restored again with John Le Carre's George Smiley, starting with *Call for the Dead* in 1961.

158. He asked that this 'little propaganda book' along with *A Clergyman's Daughter* and *Keep the Aspidistra Flying* not be reprinted in the event of his death. As if to remind us all that he did not always recognize his own best work, he included *The Lion and the Unicorn*: Notes for My Literary Executor, 31 Mar. 1945, Orwell Archive, J/28.

159. Orwell's *English People* appeared in Collins' celebrated 'Britain in Pictures' series. Its author had other things on his mind, however, referring to 'that silly little English people book', Orwell to Julian Symons, from Barnhill, Isle of Jura, 9 Oct. 1947, and 'I haven't the faintest interest in the book', Orwell to Leonard Moore, 17 July 1947: *CW* xix. 212, 172.

160. *English People*, 10, 21.

161. Ibid. 8–11. For the stability and order of post-war England, with class as 'the first and most vital of the Englishman's social charts', see Monica Redlich, *The Pattern of England* (Copenhagen, 1945), 107. In his influential book, Harold Perkin would also come to depict English stability as that of a 'mature' class society which, in the battle of ideas, had mostly come to agree. Orwell would have agreed with Perkin (or was it the other way?) that 'the class which was most successful in this educational and moral struggle, in uniting its own members and imposing its ideal upon others, would win the day and have most influence in determining the actual society in which all had to live...': *The Origins of Modern English Society 1780–1880* (London, 1978), 220. The battle of ideas allowed room for people like Orwell to leave their own class for another. The extent to which they could do this, of course, is one of Orwell's key arguments with the left.

162. Archbishop Temple complained about dishonesty, promiscuity, and the dissolution of moral codes threatening the war effort: *The Times*, 12 July 1943. Orwell said roughly the opposite. Lord David Cecil tried to prevent its publication. He told the publishers that it was a 'factious & inaccurate pamphlet [that] only blackens England's reputation': letter to W. J. Turner, from New College, Oxford, 1944?, Davison, *Lost Orwell*, 103.

163. Orwell, *English People*, 40.

164. Ibid. 41.

165. He is particularly prescient on regionalism here and in *The Road to Wigan Pier*, but does not follow it up. For others in broadcasting and the arts who were alive to regionalism before and after the war, see Natasha Vall, *Cultural Region: North East England 1945–2000* (Manchester, 2011), chs. 2–5.

166. He praised Stalin for 'a magnificent fighting speech' after the German invasion, but noted too its 'complete contradiction' of Soviet policy over the past two years: 'we are now more or less pro-Stalin. This disgusting murderer is temporarily on our side and so the purges etc are suddenly forgotten': *Wartime Diary*, 3 July 1941, *CW* xii. 522. In his preface to the Ukrainian edition of *Animal Farm* Orwell referred to the British people's innocence in these matters: Mar. 1947, *CW* xix. 88.

167. 'I did mean it to have a wider application... that that kind of revolution (violent conspiratorial...led by unconsciously power-hungry people) can only lead to a

change of masters': Orwell, letter to Dwight Macdonald, from 27B Canonbury Square, Islington, London, 5 Dec. 1946, *CW* xviii. 506.

168. Handled well by Crick, *Orwell*, 450–62.
169. The official was Peter Smollett, a Soviet agent: Taylor, *Orwell*, 337.
170. Crick, *Orwell*, 457.
171. Orwell, *English People*, 20.
172. George Orwell, 'Politics vs. Literature. An Examination of Gulliver's Travels', *Polemic*, 5 (Sept.–Oct. 1946), *CW* xviii. 426. Orwell shows he is alert to breakdowns in Swift's metaphors.
173. Walter Laqueur, *Europe in our Time: A History 1945–92* (New York, 1993), 37. Orwell was one of the very few journalists who drew attention to the British part in the forced repatriation and mistreatment of some 70,000 Cossacks and 2 million other Russians under the Yalta agreement: 'The Prevention of Literature', *Polemic*, 2 (Jan. 1946), *Atlantic Monthly* (Mar. 1947), *CW* xvii. 373; Orwell to Koestler, from Barnhill, Isle of Jura, 20 Sept. 1947, *CW* xix. 207. See Nikolai Tolstoy, *The Minister and the Massacres* (London, 1986), 257.

Chapter 6

1. Though he found the French view premature: 'The French Believe We Have Had a Revolution', *Manchester Evening News*, 20 Mar. 1945, *CW* xvii. 94.
2. Labour was elected in 1945 with a landslide 11,995,152 votes and 393 seats against the Conservatives' 9,988,306 and 213. Labour went out in 1951 with 13,948,883 votes and 295 seats against the Conservatives' 12,659,712 and 321.
3. Celia Kirwan, report to Information Research Department, 30 Mar. 1949 and Orwell, letter to Celia Kirwan, from Cranham, 6 Apr. 1949, *CW* xx. 318–22; and Peter Davison, 'Orwell's List of Unreliables', lecture at De Montfort University, Leicester, 10 Mar. 1999. In January 1948 Bevin decided to respond to Soviet anti-British propaganda and the IRD was set up to place articles with British agencies around the world and in the world's press. Kirwan worked for the IRD and had met Orwell through her brother-in-law Arthur Koestler in December 1945. Orwell did not write but he did provide a list of names of those whom he thought should not be asked because they were either Communists or dupes. He was smack on target with some (including Peter Smollett of the Russian desk of British Information Services), but slightly wide of the mark with others, though among those others J. B. Priestley is an instructive case. Orwell himself had been watched by British security service MI6 from 1928 to 1942. For more names see Davison, *Lost Orwell*, 209.
4. Moves supported by Bevan and Laski: Morgan, *Labour in Power*, 69–73. Morgan reports that unity was the 'dominant mood' (p. 45)
5. Report of R. A. Rendall, 25 June 1941, BBC Archive. Orwell did not expect to be asked to tell untruths (memo, Orwell to A. L. C. Bullock, European Section BBC, 25 Jan. 1943) and was judged 'a poor judge of political expediency' (D. Pearson Smith, BBC Annual Report, 10 Aug. 1943). And yet he accepted the need for propaganda and discipline—presumably only if it was his own.
6. J. B. Priestley, *Russian Journey* (London, 1946), 40. 'The Magic Tablecloth' is a Russian fairy-tale. Potemkin villages were façades. 'During the famines…the press depicted collective farms as happy and prosperous, with merry peasants gathering around laden tables in the evening to dance and sing to the accordion': Fitzpatrick, *Everyday Stalinism*, 9. Priestley made his support for the USSR personal and

emotional. But even calculating liberal rationalists like Sir William Beveridge could speak in 1945 of their trust and hope in the Soviet system: *The Price of Peace* (London, 1945), 85.

7. John Steinbeck, *A Russian Journal* (London, 1949), 76.
8. See Michael David-Fox, *Showcasing the Great Experiment: Cultural Diplomacy and Western Visitors to the Soviet Union 1921–41* (Oxford, 2012), and Katerina Clark, *Moscow, the Fourth Rome: Stalinism, Cosmopolitanism and the Evolution of Soviet Culture 1931–41* (Cambridge, Mass., 2011).
9. S. G. Wheatcroft, 'Anthropometric Data and Indicators of Crises and Secular Change in Soviet Welfare Levels 1880–1960', *Slavic Review*, 58: 1 (1999), 35–6. There had been famines in Russia before the Soviets of course, but not as a direct result of public policy: John Komlos, 'On the Biological Standard of Living in Russia and the Soviet Union', *Slavic Review*, 58: 1 (1999), 75.
10. Fact 1: *100 Facts on the Labour Party*, Smatterbooks 25 (London, 1950); and Fact 4: 'as British as roast beef and Yorkshire pudding'.
11. From the Cabinet's point of view at any rate: Peter Hennessey, *Never Again: Britain 1945–51* (London, 1992).
12. Stefan Collini sees his anti-intellectualism as evidence of bad faith. I see it as a recognition that in politics rational solutions are as rare as rational problems: Collini, *Absent Minds*, 353.
13. It is on these grounds that Orwell's two burliest minders insist on his socialism: John Newsinger, *Orwell's Politics* (Basingstoke, 1999), and Hitchens, *Orwell's Victory*.
14. Irving Howe, *Nineteen Eighty-Four Revisited* (New York, 1985), 188.
15. For the tradition of English non-statist socialism and the degree to which it did and did not accord with working-class associational life, see Stephen Yeo, 'Some Oppositional Englishness', in Colls and Dodd, *Englishness*.
16. Review essay of Arthur Koestler, typescript, 1944, Orwell Archive, A/3 e).
17. *New Leader*, 24 June 1938, *CW* xi. 168.
18. Point 2 of his six-point programme suggests the 'limitation of incomes on such a scale that the highest tax-free income in Britain does not exceed the lowest by more than ten to one': *Lion and the Unicorn*, *CW* xii. 422.
19. Will Lawther, 'Foreword' to Margot Heinemann, *Britain's Coal: A Study of the Mining Crisis* (London, 1944), 5–7. He was president of the Miners' Federation of Great Britain.
20. The occupations with the densest union memberships—in coal, cotton, textiles, rail, at around 84 per cent—were Labour's staunchest supporters: Chris Wrigley, *British Trade Unions Since 1933* (Cambridge, 2002), 21.
21. E. R. Manley, *Meet the Miner: The Yorkshire Miner at Work, at Home, and in Public Life* (Lofthouse, 1947), 87. McKibbin thinks the unions had not been historically assertive enough, but accepts the ties of informal connection: *Parties and People*, 74–7.
22. David Kynaston, *Austerity Britain 1945–51* (London, 2007), 267.
23. Apart from them, 'every significant member of Attlee's government was of middle or upper middle-lass origin': McKibbin, *Parties and People*, 141. There were more former public-school candidates for Labour in 1950, just as there were for the Conservatives.
24. Stephen Spender, *Citizens at War—and After* (London, 1945), 31, 98, Foreword by Herbert Morrison.
25. The minister responsible was jeered defending the New Towns bill at Stevenage in 1946 to cries of 'dictator!' and 'Gestapo!': Harrison, *Seeking a Role*, 63.

26. Clarke, *Hope and Glory*, 224. 'Planning' was the subject of great post-war debate. 'It all depends whether we can find ways of transferring democratic, parliamentary control to a planned society': Karl Mannheim, *Man and Society: In an Age of Reconstruction* (1944; London, 1955), 380.

27. Paul Addison thinks it did win votes: *The Road to 1945* (London, 1994), but H. L. Smith (ed.), *Britain in the Second World War* (Manchester, 1986) and G. H. Gallup (ed.), *The Gallup International Public Opinion Polls* (New York, 1976) do not.

28. Even so, nationalization did not redistribute wealth; coal and rail were about to lose their markets to oil; the unions were not interested in worker participation; planning was impossible; the government lacked ideas, the trade unions did not give them any, and Attlee was timid when it came to the bastions of middle- and upper-class privilege—McKibbin marshals his criticisms across a wide front: *Parties and People*, 149–63.

29. 'anything strongly defended ideologically, whether it be public schools or the sugar industry, was left alone by the Attlee government' (ibid. 162). Tosco Fyvel says Orwell told him in 1948 that he thought Bevan had got bogged down in 'all this administration about housing and hospitals', and that he was planning to attack the government in *Tribune* for not taking on the public schools, the House of Lords, and the aristocracy: Crick, *Orwell*, 519.

30. Harrison, *Seeking a Role*, p. xvi.

31. 'Bevan told difficult truths and never made a populist speech in his life': Mark Hayhurst, 'Duty Bound', *Guardian*, 28 May 2005. Orwell made the same point in 'Writers and Leviathan': 'the greatest difficulty of all [is that] the left is now in power and is obliged to take responsibility and make genuine decisions': *Politics and Letters* (Summer 1948), *CW* xix. 290.

32. After 1924 'Labour worked hard to allay middle-class suspicions... The idea that Labour had an official doctrine which it did not mean, and a real sense of responsibility which could be trusted, appealed to middle-class susceptibilities': Roy Lewis and Angus Maude, *The English Middle Classes* (1949; London, 1953), 53.

33. Orwell anonymously in the *Observer*, 14 Oct. 1948, *CW* xvii. 311–12.

34. In his *Orwell and the Left* (New Haven, 1974) Alex Zwerdling compares Sidney and Beatrice Webb's ideal type socialist administrator (*A Constitution for the Socialist Commonwealth*, 1920)—'disinterested professional expert who invents, discovers, inspects, audits, costs, tests or measures'—with Orwell's Totalitarian 'Ingsoc' party members 'brought together by the barren world of monopoly industry and centralized government', 'made up for the most part of bureaucrats, scientists, technicians', and others *including* academics and trade-union organizers (pp. 198, 210–11).

35. 'Culture and Democracy', lecture given Saturday, 22 Nov. 1941 to the Fabian Society: *CW* xiii. 71–2. The Fabian Society had started out utopian (the 'Fellowship of the New Life') before being led by the Webbs towards state rationalism: Peter Beilharz, *Labour's Utopias: Bolshevism, Fabianism, Social Democracy* (London, 1992), 56.

36. Review of H. G. Wells, *Observer*, 21 May 1944, *CW* xvi. 198. See also his 'Wells, Hitler and the World State', *CW* xii: 'If one had to choose among Wells' own contemporaries a writer who could stand towards him as a corrective, one might choose Kipling' (p. 540).

37. 'Writers and Leviathan', *CW* xix.

38. In 1941 he had invoked the political experience of East European intellectuals (Trotsky, Rauschning, Rosenberg, Silone, Borkenau, and Koestler) as superior: 'Wells, Hitler and the World State', *Horizon* (Aug. 1941), *CW* xii. 538.

39. Review of F. A. Hayek, *The Road to Serfdom, Observer*, 9 Apr. 1944 (*CW* xvi. 149–50); review of four works by Joseph Conrad, *Observer*, 24 June 1945 (*CW* xvii. 190–1); review of John Plamenatz's *What Is Communism?, Observer*, 15 Feb. 1948 (*CW* xix. 269); 'Arthur Koestler', 11 Sept. 1944, typescript (*CW* xvi. 393), and review of Arthur Koestler, *The Yogi and the Commissar, Common Wealth Review* Nov. 1945 (*CW* xvii. 344); foretaste of *Nineteen Eighty-Four* in reference to James Burnham, 'As I Please', *Tribune*, 2 Feb. 1945 (*CW* xvii. 39); 'Second Thoughts on James Burnham', *Polemic*, 3 (May 1946), and 'Burnham's View of Contemporary World Struggle', *New Leader* (New York), 29 Mar. 1947 (*CW* xviii. 268–84 and *CW* xix. 96–115); 'Freedom and Happiness', feature on E. I. Zamyatin's *We*, in *Tribune*, 4 Jan. 1946 (*CW* xviii. 13–16). Orwell was keen to help Victor Serge (1890–1947) publish his *Memoirs of a Revolutionary* in English through his own publisher Fred Warburg: letter, Orwell to Warburg, from 27B Canonbury Square, Islington, London, 11 Mar. 1946 (*CW* xviii. 148), but it was published first in Paris in 1951, where his *The Case of Comrade Tulayev*, the greatest of all the anti-Stalinist fictions, had been published in 1949. On the Austrian school of liberal conservativism, see Tony Judt, *Ill Fares the Land* (London, 2011), 95–6. On Jack London, see Orwell's 'Introduction' to his *Love of Life and Other Stories*, Oct. or Nov. 1945 (*CW* xvii. 352–7).

40. J. D. Bernal, unsigned editorial, in *Polemic*, 3 (May 1946) (*CW* xviii. 263–8); J.-P. Sartre, review of *Portrait of the Anti-Semite, Observer*, 7 Nov. 1948 (*CW* xix. 464–5); Oscar Wilde, *Observer*, 9 May 1948, whose *Soul of Man under Socialism* was judged dated, ridiculous, and if not 'altogether wrong', 'wrong' (*CW* xix. 334); T. S. Eliot, review of *Notes Towards the Definition of Culture, Observer*, 28 Nov. 1948—'he might be right but at some point his pessimism seems to be exaggerated' (*CW* xix. 475); Churchill, review of *Their Finest Hour, New Leader* (New York), 14 May 1949 (*CW* xx. 110–13); 'George Gissing', written May–June 1948? (*CW* xix. 347–52); Evelyn Waugh, written Apr. 1949 (*CW* xx. 76), and literary notebook, 1949, Orwell Archive, UCL B/3.

41. 'Evelyn Waugh' (1949), typescript, Orwell Archive, A/8 d), and ibid.

42. Tressell, in *Manchester Evening News*, 25 Apr. 1946, *CW* xviii. 256; Pound, in *Partisan Review* (May 1949), *CW* xx. 102.

43. 'Notes on Nationalism', *Polemic* 1 (Oct. 1945), *CW* xvii. 154.

44. St Cyprian's: 'for years I loathed its very name so deeply that I could not view it with enough detachment to see the significance of the things that happened to me there': Orwell, 'Such, Such Were the Joys', *Partisan Review* (Oct. 1952), *CW* xix. 385. He took his title from a line in William Blake's 'The Echoing Green', in his *Songs of Innocence* (1789).

45. 'The Labour Government after Three Years', *Commentary* (Oct. 1948), *CW* xix. 441.

46. 'Britain's Left-Wing Press', *Progressive* (Madison, Wisc.) (June 1948), *CW* xix. 297.

47. Attlee's government started falling apart once it had committed itself to a £4.7b rearmament programme it could not afford imposed by the Americans. Bevan resigned over the welfare cuts that followed, and the 'Bevanites' were born: Morgan, *Ages of Reform*, ch. 12, 'Labour and the Special Relationship', and ch. 14, 'Nye Bevan: Pragmatist and Prophet'.

48. 'Once the communal sector, in which the state controls all the means, exceeds a certain proportion of the whole, the effects of its actions dominate the whole system': F. A. Hayek, *The Road to Serfdom* (1944; London, 1986), 45.

49. Stephen Yeo, 'Three Socialisms', in W. Outhwaite and M. Mulkay (eds.), *Social Theory and Social Criticism* (Oxford, 1987), 103.

50. Woodcock, *Crystal Spirit*, 198.

51. Michael Walzer makes the people as they are the benchmark of Orwell's politics: 'George Orwell's England', in Graham Holderness *et al.* (eds.), *George Orwell* (Basingstoke, 1998). David Kubal makes it democracy: *Outside the Whale: George Orwell's Art and Politics* (London, 1972), 111. Orwell managed to raise two cheers for 'bourgeois' democracy while waiting for what England had never had—'a socialist party which meant business': 'Fascism and Democracy', *Left News* (Feb. 1941), *CW* xii. 380. He wrote to Gollancz on 8 January 1940 saying he was depressed by left intellectuals (who were saying exactly what he had been saying only months earlier): 'the intellectuals...are at present pointing out that democracy and fascism are the same thing ': ibid. 5.

52. Names of British directors and, crew for crew, among their films, *Target for Tonight* (1941), *In Which We Serve* (1943), *London Can Take It* (1941), *Fires Were Started* (1943), *Millions Like Us* (1943), *The Way Ahead* (1945), and *Went the Day Well?* (1942). These films showed a 'full-blooded love' for an England: James Chapman, *The British at War: Cinema, State and Propaganda 1939–45* (London, 2000), 165.

53. On the educational costs of removing the people from history: Gavin Kitching, *The Trouble with Theory: The Educational Costs of Postmodernism* (London, 2008).

54. *Lion and the Unicorn*, *CW* xii. 426–7.

55. Orwell, 'Politics vs. Literature', *CW* xviii. 425.

56. Colls, *Identity of England*, chs. 1 and 2.

57. Mill asked his readers to watch out for the 'beak and claws' of the central state: J. S. Mill, *On Liberty* (1859); ed. John Gray and G. W. Smith (London, 1991), 23.

58. Colls, *Identity of England*, 207–11, 71–4.

59. L. T. Hobhouse, *Liberalism* (1911; Oxford, 1979), 16, 48.

60. 'at bottom...free thought': John Skorupski, *Why Read Mill Today?* (Basingstoke, 2006), 5–6; 'Inside the Whale', 111.

61. Quoted in Donald Winch, 'Arnold Toynbee's Industrial Revolution', in J. Betts and D. C. S. Wilson (eds.), 'Before and After Arnold Toynbee', *History and Memory* (forthcoming, Sept. 2013).

62. Michael Bentley, *Modernizing England's Past: English Historiography in the Age of Modernism 1870–1970* (Cambridge, 2005), 24; Arthur Aughey, *The Politics of Englishness* (Manchester, 2007), 78.

63. Ernest Barker (ed.), *The Character of England* (Oxford, 1947), 562. For the foundational text on the crowd as gullible, intolerant, and 'everywhere distinguished by feminine characteristics': Gustave Le Bon, *The Crowd: A Study of the Popular Mind* (London, 1896), 21. The key feature of the 'Crowd' was that it was seen to denote the end of liberal civilization (pp. 2–11).

64. Herbert Butterfield, *The Englishman and his History* (1944; Cambridge, 1945), p. v.

65. Ibid. 82.

66. Anthony Brundage, *The People's Historian: John Richard Green and the Writing of History in Victorian England* (Westport, Conn., 1994), 90–102.

67. Toynbee, *Industrial Revolution*, 64; Beatrice Webb remembered the sin, citing Toynbee as her example: *My Apprenticeship* (Harmondsworth, 1938), i. 208.

68. In 1949 he told Reg Reynolds that he had been reading the Hammonds' 'The English Labourer' to advantage—believing, for example, that the game laws were 'a Norman survival' until he read them. He suggests to Reynolds that they find some pamphlet literature to match for volume 2 of their jointly edited *British Pamphleteers*, which never appeared: letter, 17 Jan. 1949, from Cotswold Sanatorium, Cranham, Gloucestershire, *CW* xx. 20. The book in question is J. L. and Barbara Hammond's *The Village Labourer* (1911), which was followed by *The Town Labourer* in 1917 and *The Skilled Labourer* in 1919.

69. '...liberty without equality is a name of noble sound and squalid result': Hobhouse, *Liberalism*, 48. Hobhouse addressed his book to younger up-and-coming Liberals. He restates the case for a liberal living tradition, and expands it: 'Thus individualism, when it grapples with the facts, is driven no small distance along Socialist lines' (p. 54). It is worth noting just for the liberal record that Orwell preferred Hayek's 'eloquent defence' of capitalism ('great deal of truth') over Zilliacus's 'vehement denunciations' of it: *Observer*, 9 Apr. 1944, *CW* xvi. 149–50.

70. In Paris in 1928 Lucien Febvre and Marc Bloch founded the *Annales* school of history committed to the study of deep collective experience: Peter Burke, *The French Historical Revolution: The Annales School 1929–1989* (Cambridge, 1990), 13–15.

71. There is plenty room for manoeuvre, it has to be said: 'liberal principles enjoin the limitation of government by stringent rules... [but] the liberal state need not... be a minimum state... [and] the minimum state could be a socialist state': John Gray, *Liberalism* (Milton Keynes, 1986), 73. Looking the other way, Ferdinand Mount claimed Orwell for the lesser state and even the Liberal Democrat half of the 2010 Cameron–Clegg coalition government: 'Orwell and the Oligarchs', George Orwell Memorial Lecture, 26 Nov. 2010, published in *Political Quarterly*, 82: 2 (2011), 154–5.

72. Yet D. J. Taylor marks it as Orwell's pre-eminent concern: *Orwell*, 2. Alan Sandison makes a strong case for Orwell as a Protestant writer in *The Last Man in Europe: An Essay on George Orwell* (London, 1975), p. 5 and chs. 5–7. Christopher Small makes a case for 'the fundamentally religious aspect of his writing' in *The Road to Miniluv: George Orwell, the State, and God*, 20. Mr Small quotes Blake on the frontispiece in a way Orwell would have approved: 'Man must and will have some religion. If he has not the religion of Jesus, he will have the religion of Satan...'

73. Jane to Rochester in Charlotte Brontë, *Jane Eyre* (1847; Harmondsworth, 2002), 282.

74. Orwell, *Inside the Whale, CW* xii. 105. Hitchens reverses this by seeing Ingsoc in *Nineteen Eighty-Four* as analogous to the sixteenth-century Reformation party: Christopher Hitchens, 'Hilary Mantel's Wolf Hall', *Atlantic* (Mar. 2010), repr. in *Arguably* (London, 2011), 149.

75. George Orwell and Reginald Reynolds (eds.), *British Pamphleteers*, vol. 1, *From the 16th century to the French Revolution* (London, 1948), 15; Michael Carter, *George Orwell and the Problem of Authentic Existence*, 52–3.

76. Katie Heathman, 'The English Hymnal of 1906', University of Leicester MA dissertation (2012), 1. On Catholic intellectuals: e.g. *Tribune*, 23 June 1944, CW xvi. 261–5.

77. Waugh identified the church with the theology, while Orwell identified the church with the tradition. Nevertheless, Waugh lays it out straight: 'what makes your vision [in *Nineteen Eighty-Four*] spurious to me is the disappearance of the Church... The Brotherhood which can confound the Party is one of love—not adultery in Berkshire... And men who love a crucified Lord will never think of torture as all-powerful': Waugh to Orwell, 17 July 1949, from Stinchcombe, Gloucestershire, Orwell Archive, Appendix 2.

78. Orwell, *Clergyman's Daughter*, 260–1.

79. Parson Thwackum: 'when I mention Religion', he said he meant only the Protestant Christian religion, 'and not only the Protestant religion, but the Church of England': Henry Fielding, *History of Tom Jones. A Foundling* (1749).

80. Orwell makes all these points in reviews of Malcolm Muggeridge's *The Thirties*, *New English Weekly*, 25 Apr. 1940, *CW* xii. 150, and F. J. Sheed's *Communism and Man*, *Peace News*, 27 Jan. 1939, *CW* xi. 323. Burnham alerted him to the religious propensities

of Communist party membership: 'Burnham's View', *CW* xix. 97. On Protestant writers, see Orwell's collection of *British Pamphleteers*, Introduction; and on at least one Puritan's reasons for writing such powerful prose: N. H. Keeble, *Richard Baxter: Puritan Man of Letters* (Oxford, 1982)—'I obey my conscience…I durst not stand by in silence to see all this, no more than to see men drowning, or the City on Fire, without endeavouring to save' (p. 6). In Orwell's own day, with the population going up, all Anglican and Nonconformist numbers were stagnating or going down: in beneficed clergy and ministers; in Anglican communicants (2.2 million); in Nonconformist members, including Methodists (from 750,000 in 1937 to 622,916 in 1960), Baptists (from 254,908 in 1920 to 198,577 in 1960), and Congregationalists (from 288,784 in 1920 to 193,341 in 1960). Church congregations were generally bigger than their memberships, but still the downward trend was clear: S. J. D. Green, *The Passing of Protestant England: Secularism and Social Change 1920–1960* (Cambridge, 2011), 60–76. In *The English People* Orwell remarked that Puritanism had all but gone, except for the 'small traders and manufacturers' type. Green rejoins: 'would that his mind's eye could have been turned towards Councillor Roberts' grocery in Grantham' (p. 140). A. J. P. Taylor dated the passing of Protestant England from the Prayer Book controversy of 1927: *English History*, 259.

81. William C. Lubenow, *Liberal Intellectuals and Public Culture in Modern Britain 1815–1914* (Woodbridge, 2010).

82. 'Arthur Koestler', 11 Sept. 1944, typescript, *CW* xvi. 399.

83. 'Notes on the Way', *CW* xii. 123–5.

84. He told *Adelphi* people in the 1930s that he was a 'Tory Anarchist', possibly to distance himself from John Middleton Murry, who founded the journal. He told Southwold people the same. Crick is right to take the term seriously: *Orwell*, 239, 254. Ian Williams, 'Orwell and the British Left', Rodden, *Cambridge Companion*, ch. 8.

85. Along with John Betjeman and Evelyn Waugh, in John Brannigan, *Orwell to the Present: Literature in England 1945–2000* (Basingstoke, 2003), 4–26; and Patrick Parrinder, *Nation and Novel* (Oxford, 2006), 316. Baines and Johnson complain about unwarranted post-war assumptions about a 'stable, resigned, and inward looking' working class: 'In Search of the Traditional Working Class', *Economic History Review*, 52: 4 (1999), 700.

86. Rodden, *Literary Reputation*, 186–202; Scott Lucas, 'Policing Dissent: "Orwell" and Cold War Culture 1945–2004', in D Field (ed.), *American Cold War Culture* (Edinburgh, 2005), 133.

87. Havel, Miłosz, Bahro, Haraszti, Kołakowski, Smecka, Michnik, and others—Hitchens considers the list of East European dissident intellectuals who made their tribute: *Orwell's Victory*, 41. Orwell was particularly popular in West and East Germany. Florian Henckel von Donnersmarck's film *The Lives of Others* (2006) is a powerful rendition of Orwellian themes.

88. Alison Light, *Forever England: Femininity, Literature and Conservatism between the Wars* (London, 1991), 8.

89. For Seeley, a test case for Tories over Liberals: J. R. Seeley, *The Expansion of England* (1883; London, 1897), 1–10.

90. Roger Fry, in Christopher Butler, *Modernism: A Very Short Introduction* (Oxford, 2010), 18.

91. The essay form also suited Orwell's taste for personal encounter: 'I myself am the subject of my book', said Montaigne: see Marks, *Orwell the Essayist*, 6–9, and Graham Good, *The Observing Self: Rediscovering the Essay* (London, 1988). Pearson

Smith's report on Orwell (staff member 9889) that he was capable of shocking the more 'Conservatively minded' listeners probably stemmed from his inability to address them in the usual way: BBC Annual Report, 10 Aug. 1943, BBC Archive.

92. Stuart Ball, *Portrait of a Party: The Conservative Party in Britain 1918–1945* (Oxford, 2013), ch. 1, 'Conservatism: Principles and Temperament'.

93. Arthur Bryant, *The Spirit of Conservatism* (London, 1929), 11; Dorothy Crisp (ed.), *The Rebirth of Conservatism* (London, 1931), 111, 251; H. M. Adam, *The Fallacies of Socialism* (London, 1926), 5; F. J. C. Hearnshaw, *Conservatism in England* (London, 1933), 13. Inter-war Conservatism was itself rethinking its philosophy and appeal, drawing heavily from Lord Hugh Cecil's modernizing text, *Conservatism* (London, 1913).

94. Oswald Mosley, *Fascism Explained: Read and Enrol* (n.p., n.d.), 'Point I', 'Patriotism and Revolution'. Both Liberal and Conservative philosophers had to accept the revolution of 1688–9 as a legitimate part of the national identity—the Conservatives reluctantly so.

95. Mrs Cecil Chesterton, *I Lived in a Slum* (London, 1936), 64. Gollancz was the publisher.

96. William Blackstone (1723–80), judge, jurist, and MP, author of *Commentaries on the Laws of England* (1766). Prest asserts Blackstone's 'Country'-party Tory cast of mind and its 'central emphasis on English liberties', but also invokes Harris's view of Blackstone's politics, where 'change [is] conceived as restoration', and restoration has a 'strong populist, even republican edge': R. Harris, *Politics and the Nation*, quoted in Prest, *Law and Letters*, 129. Prest also makes the case for the influence of Blackstone's *Commentaries*, 'not least among radicals, reformers, and non-lawyers' and, in the USA, among revolutionaries (pp. 9, 292).

97. Edmund Burke, 'Letter to a Member of the National Assembly' (1791), in R. Kirk (ed.), *The Portable Conservative Reader* (Harmondsworth, 1982), 48.

98. Richard Rees, *George Orwell: Fugitive from the Camp of Victory* (London, 1961), 48; id., 'George Orwell', in G. Panichas (ed.), *Politics and 20th Century Novelists* (New York, 1974), 86. On Burke's counter-revolutionary Englishness and pro-revolutionary Irishness: Conor Cruise O'Brien, 'Introduction', to Burke, *Reflections on the Revolution in France* (1790; Harmondsworth, 1978), 33–41. For Burke, like Blackstone, the expert in English common law, see Peter J. Stanlis, *Edmund Burke and the Natural Law* (Ann Arbor, Mich., 1965), 35–6. He said the law rendered man 'full of resources'.

99. Philip Harling, 'Re-thinking Old Corruption', *Past and Present* (May 1995).

100. Orwell, 'The Freedom of the Press', Introduction to 1945 edition of *Animal Farm*, *CW* xvii. 259: italics mine.

101. John Newsinger notes how Orwell missed the true significance of the Holocaust: 'Orwell, Anti-Semitism and the Holocaust', in Rodden, *Cambridge Companion*, 191.

102. ' "All tobacconists are Fascists!" as though this was something so obvious that no one could possibly question his statement. Momentarily one was swept along. Yes, there was something in it; those little men in their kiosks...then the sheer craziness of it took hold of one, and one began to laugh helplessly, until—such was his persuasiveness—one reflected inside one's laughter: after all, they are rather rum birds, those tobacconists' (Malcolm Muggeridge, 'A Knight of the Woeful Countenance', in Gross, *World of George Orwell*, 169). Woodcock's Anarchism no less than Orwell's socialism depended on small, knowable communities who could survey themselves without recourse to coercion, or legal rational force from the central state: George Woodcock, *Anarchism* (Harmondsworth, 1962), 78.

103. 'give me England every time': 'Spanish Prison', *Observer*, 24 Dec. 1944, *CW* xvi. 502.
104. Orwell, *Wigan Pier*, 129; *Homage*, 220; *Lion and the Unicorn*, *CW* xii. 392; 'London Letter', *Partisan Review* (Summer 1945), *CW* xvii. 164–5.
105. 'Patriotism has got nothing to do with Conservatism': *Lion and Unicorn*, *CW* xii. 428; Woodcock, *Crystal Spirit*, 196.
106. We find Orwell in what Collini calls 'John Bullish contrasts' with France, 'pitting stability and practical good sense against evolution and political over-excitability, pragmatic empiricism against abstract rationalism': Collini, *Absent Minds*, 69–73.
107. As explained by Joyce, *Rule of Freedom*, 3–4.
108. Ferdynand Zweig, *The British Worker* (Harmondsworth, 1952), 87. Zweig's 'worker' is male only, and he looks for typologies, but no more than any other sociological study of the period and with a lot more insight.
109. We can find traces of all the leading twentieth-century historians of England in Orwell—including Trevelyan, Halevy, Namier, and Tawney: Collini, *English Pasts*, chs. 1, 3, 9.
110. On how the foregrounds of J. M. W. Turner's *Picturesque Views in England and Wales* (1826–35) were 'unusually full of human activity', and how John Clare's poems were 'bred in a village full of strife and noise', and how William Cobbett liked to show that wasteland was not waste but had once been full of folk: Elizabeth Helsinger, 'Turner and the Representation of England', in W. J. T. Mitchell (ed), *Landscape and Power* (Chicago, 2002), 110; Jonathan Bate, *John Clare: A Biography* (London, 2003), 226; Cobbett writing about Horton Heath, Surrey, in the *Political Register* quoted in T. Williamson and L. Bellamy, *Property and Landscape* (London, 1987), 115.
111. 'Was he a socialist?' 'No' (Humphrey Dakin, his brother-in-law); 'I don't think he was ever a socialist' (Fred Warburg, his publisher); 'we discussed politics generally but none of us were very well versed' (Kate Ekevall, his friend); 'tended to be rather sketchy and naïve in lots of domestic political matters' (Richard Rees, his friend); 'he belongs to no group, he joins no side…entirely on his own' (V. S. Pritchett, in review);'lone wolf' (Denys King-Farlow, at Eton); 'He judged everything…by the standards of what it ought to be in terms of living' (Stephen Spender, his friend): all from Coppard and Crick, *Orwell Remembered*, 129, 194, 99, 124, 57, 263. 'Very much the Eton boy' (Mabel Friez, his friend); 'He struck me as a gentleman' (Carlton Melling, Wigan Public Library); 'Orwell you see always *reacted* to situations, to people, to individuals' (Jon Kimche, bookshop colleague); 'The main thing was he was awfully *personal*' (Henry Swanzy, BBC colleague): all from Wadhams, *Remembering Orwell*, 46, 63, 95, 124.
112. There was wealth on both sides—the Blairs in West Indian plantations and land, the Limouzins in Burmese timber and distilling—but none trickled down to Orwell.
113. Orwell, *Road to Wigan Pier*, 107, 133, 147, 203, 204.
114. George Santayana, *Soliloquies in English. And later soliloquies* (London, 1922), 31.
115. Orwell, *English People*, 12. For his allusion to physical types, see Thomas Rowlandson's *Portsmouth Point* (1811). On making poetry ordinary, see his 'Poetry and the Microphone', *New Saxon Pamphlets*, 3 (Mar. 1945), *CW* xvii. 75–80.
116. Stanlis, *Burke*, 39, 98; Sir Matthew Hale, *History of the Common Law in England* (1713; Chicago, 1971), p. xxxi.
117. 'On Being Conservative', in Michael Oakeshott, *Rationalism in Politics and Other Essays* (1962; Indianapolis, 1991), 408.
118. 'National characteristics are not easy to pin down, and when pinned down, they often turn out to be trivialities': *Lion and Unicorn*, *CW* xii. 393.

119. '... how many of the values by which our grandfathers lived could be taken seriously? Patriotism, religion, the Empire, the family, the sanctity of marriage, the Old School Tie, birth, breeding, honour discipline—anyone of ordinary education could turn the whole lot of them inside out in three minutes': 'Inside the Whale', *CW* xii. 102.

120. Literary Notebook, 1949, Orwell Archive, B/3. See also early drafts, *Burmese Days* (1928–33), 'Hop-Picking' (Oct. 1931), and 'Clink' (Aug. 1932): A/1 u), v), w).

121. He dined with Anthony Powell and Malcolm Muggeridge, and occasionally with their friends—not really his friends—Hughie Kingsmill and Hugh Trevor-Roper. Muggeridge described Orwell as having a 'conservative undertow in his leftist course': Gross, *World of George Orwell*, 172. In Labour Britain, he likened Eton College to Napoleon's baggage-wagons after the battle of Sedan, 'rather a nuisance ... full of chefs and hairdressers, blocking up the roads': 'For Ever Eton', *Observer*, 1 Aug. 1948, *CW* xix. 412. On the Conservative party, see his 'Labour Government after Three Years', *Commentary* (Oct. 1948), *CW* xix. 441; letter, Orwell to Duchess of Atholl, from 27B Canonbury Square, Islington, London, 15 Nov. 1945, *CW* xvii. 384–5.

122. After Spain, letter, Orwell to Spender, from Preston Hall, Aylesford, Kent, 2 Apr. 1938, *CW* xi. 130.

123. Michael Oakeshott, 'The Political Economy of Freedom' (1949), in *Rationalism*, 409, 406.

124. 'To assume that all values can be graded on one scale, so that it is a mere matter of inspection to determine the highest, seems to me to falsify our knowledge that men are free agents': Berlin, 'Two Concepts of Liberty', in *Four Essays*, 171–2.

125. Spotted by Margery Sabin in her chapter on Orwell's 1930s non-fiction in Rodden, *Cambridge Companion*—'partial truths in an open ended process' (p. 58). She recognizes that the artlessness is artful as well.

Chapter 7

1. Eileen Blair, letter to Denys King-Farlow, 22 June 1938, from The Stores, Wallington, *CW* xi. 165.

2. 'In London they said I couldn't have any kind of operation without a preparatory month of blood transfusions etc; here I'm going in next Wednesday to be done on Thursday.' 'They don't take as many precautionary measures as London doctors (who have a fear of patients dying on them) ...': Eileen Blair, letter to Lettice Cooper, from Greystone, Carlton, near Stockton on Tees, 23 Mar. 1945, *CW* xvii. 104–5. *Animal Farm* was published in August. Her husband was a famous writer at last.

3. Eileen O'Shaughnessy (1905–45) was born in South Shields, where her, father was Collector of Customs and Excise. She read English at St Hugh's College, Oxford, followed by various teaching and secretarial jobs. Her brother Laurence, also known as 'Eric', was a thoracic surgeon who treated Orwell's TB. Laurence was killed on active service with the British Expeditionary Force in France. See his obituaries in the *Irish Independent* and *Irish Times*, both 6 June 1940.

4. Orwell Archive, J/10; J/12 a) b).

5. 'Dearest, You really are a wonderful wife': Orwell to Eileen, from Hospital, Monflorite, 5? Apr. 1937, *CW* xi. 15.

6. Stansky and Abrahams note an improvement in his writing after meeting her, and a return to the early bitterness and rancour after losing her: *Orwell*, 147.

7. Writing under her pen-name, Elisaveta Fen, 'George Orwell's First Wife', *The Twentieth Century* (Aug. 1960), 168, 118. Fen once heard someone call Eileen 'a woman of the people'. 'No two words', she averred, 'could be less appropriate in describing Eileen O'Shaughnessy' (p. 115). About one of Orwell's typescripts, Eileen said she gave him it back 'covered with…emendations that he can't read': letter, Eileen Blair to Norah Myles, New Years Day 1938, from The Stores, Wallington, in Davison, *Lost Orwell*, 70–1.

8. Letter, Orwell to Stanley Kunitz and Howard Haycraft, from The Stores, Wallington, 17 Apr. 1940, *CW* xii. 148.

9. Telegram, Southwold, 4 May 1937: Orwell Archive, K20.

10. Letter, Eileen Blair to her Mother ('Mummy'), 22 Mar. 1937, from Seccion Inglesa, 10 Rambla de los Estudios, Barcelona, *CW* xi. 13.

11. Letter, Eileen Blair to Norah Myles (formerly of St Hugh's College, with Eileen), from 24 Croom's Hill, Greenwich, 16 Feb. 1937, in Davison, *Lost Orwell*, 68; Eileen Blair to Marjorie Dakin, Orwell's sister, 27 Sept. 1938, from rue Edmond Doutte, Marrakech, *CW* xi. 205.

12. Letter, Eileen Blair to Ida Mabel Blair, Orwell's mother, from Majestic Hotel, Marrakech, 15 Sept. 1938, *CW* xi. 198.

13. Letter, Eileen Blair to Geoffrey Gorer, from rue Edmond Doutte, Marrakech, 4 Oct. 1938, *CW* xi. 218, and letter to Marjorie Dakin, 27 Sept. 1938.

14. Letter, Eileen Blair to Norah Myles, from 24 Croom's Hill, Greenwich, 5 Dec. 1940, in Davison, *Lost Orwell*, 80; 'Eileen brought not just an intimate female presence into his life…but also an intellectual companionship that he rarely found with other women': Bowker, *Orwell*, 189.

15. 'the Spanish War…still dominates our lives in a most unreasonable manner': letter, Eileen Blair to Norah Myles, 1 Jan. 1938, from Wallington, ibid. 70.

16. As well as the prostitutes of Burma, Paris, London, and Marrakech there is a leading group of other contenders including Jacintha Buddicom, Brenda Salkeld, Eleanor Jacques, Mabel Friez, Rosalind Obermeyer, Kay Walton, Sally Jerome, Stevie Smith, Lydia Jackson, Inez Holden, Celia Paget, Ruth Graves, Anne Popham, Audrey Jones, Sally McEwan, and Orwell's second wife, Sonia Brownell. From what we know of these women, and their relationship with Orwell, if they were sexual partners we can be sure they were not only sexual partners. Orwell could be extraordinarily loyal. Salkeld held his love from teens to the end. So, it seems, did Buddicom. We find him writing to Brenda on his thirty-seventh birthday (he says Eileen allowed him a treat) inviting her to resume their sexual relationship: 25 June 1940, Davison, *Lost Orwell*, 96. Friez encouraged him in his writing from the start and found him a literary agent. Brownell was a forceful editor who shared his views.

17. For instance, she told Norah Myles that she bitterly regretted encouraging, or not discouraging, Georges Kopp, Orwell's commanding officer, on one occasion, in Barcelona: letter, 1 January 1938, from Wallington, Davison, *Lost Orwell*, 71. Kopp wrote from prison to Eileen through Laurence her brother. He ended a very serious and sober letter with, 'tell her I am intensely thinking of her and give her my love. Shake hands to Eric': 7 July 1937, Orwell Archive, K25c. Orwell got sight of this letter but, as Eileen told Norah, he has been 'extraordinarily magnanimous about the whole business'.

18. Eileen to Orwell, from Greystones, Carlton, Stockton on Tees, 25 Mar. 1945, *CW* xvii. 108.

19. Eileen to Orwell, 21 Mar. 1945, from Greystones, Carlton, Stockton on Tees, *CW* xvii. 98–9; Fen, 'Orwell's First Wife', 122–5. Greystones belonged to Eileen's sister

in law Gwen's family. Like her husband Laurence, Gwen was also a doctor. Eileen told Norah Myles she was depressed in March 1941—'Please write a letter': letter from 18 Dorset Chambers, Chagford Street, NW1, Davison, *Lost Orwell*, 82.

20. Eileen to Orwell, from Fernwood House, Clayton Road, Newcastle upon Tyne, 29 Mar. 1945, *CW* xvii. 112.

21. Letter, Orwell to Lydia Jackson, from Greystones, *CW* xvii. 118. 'He was a person who was always playing a role, but with great pathos and sincerity': Stephen Spender, in Wadhams, *Remembering Orwell*, 104. 'She effaced herself and, well, he was a sort of God about the place. It wasn't what I would call an ordinary husband and wife set up': Dennis Collings, in Coppard and Crick, *Orwell Remembered*, 81.

22. 'charming...nice...intelligent...independent...very pretty...totally worthy': Cyril Connolly, in 1970: Bowker, *Orwell*, 189, 254.

23. 'Men are too easily seen as having a natural and undifferentiated proclivity for domination, because their subjective experiences are left unexplored': John Tosh and Michael Roper (eds.), *Manful Assertions: Masculinities in Britain since 1800* (London, 1991), 9.

24. In eleven volumes of the *Complete Works*, and in the complementary volume, Peter Davison produces over 1,700 letters by George Orwell but only one is to Eileen— a very loving letter in fact, from the Monflorite field hospital in Spain where he was suffering from a poisoned hand: 5? April 1937, CW xi, 15–17. Davison discusses untraced letters in his General Introduction (*CW* x, p.xx), and in his (ed.) *Orwell: A Life in Letters* (London 2010), xii–xv, but offers no clue as to what happened to the letters to Eileen. In a peripatetic life, we know that they wrote many letters to each other, and that his letters to her were valued and eagerly awaited (Eileen to Orwell, 21, 25 March 1945, *CW* xvii, 98–9, 108), but we do not know what happened to them. It is true they were not in a position to know their future value, and it is true that Orwell 'tended to be business-like' in his correspondence (*Life in Letters*, xiv). It seems they did not keep personal letters.

25. Letter, Humphey Dakin to T. R. Fyvel, 1 June 1958, Orwell Archive, M/12.

26. As we have seen, Daphne Patai claimed misogyny and androcentrism. Stevie Smith included an unflattering portrait of Orwell in her novel *The Holiday* (1949), as did Inez Holden in a short story she wrote for radio: Bowker, *Orwell*, 284.

27. 'Inside the Whale', *CW* xii. 107.

28. 'Do not get into arguments about religion or politics': *Instructions for British Servicemen in France* (Foreign Office, London, 1944), 44.

29. 'Toward European Unity', *Partisan Review* (July–Aug.) 1947, *CW* xix. 165.

30. Ibid. 166.

31. From Gregor Dallas, *Poisoned Peace: 1945, the War that Never Ended* (London, 2005), 608–14.

32. Federal aims as stated in article 9 of the Treaty of the European Coal and Steel Community, 16 Apr. 1951: Richard Vaughan, *Post-War Integration in Europe* (London, 1976), 64.

33. He earned the princely sum of £967 before tax in 1945—hard luck for Eileen, who had spent her entire married life husbanding scarce resources: 'I guard my five English pounds, which I could exchange at a fairly decent rate, because I must have something to use when we—whoever "we" may be—cross the frontier again': letter to her Mother, from Barcelona, 22 Mar. 1937.

34. His Diary carefully plots his physical deterioration from first entering Hairmyres Hospital, East Kilbride, on 20 December 1947 up to 28 July 1948 when he returned to Barnhill. Treatment included paralysis of the diaphragm and filling the diseased lung with air, and injections of streptomycin, obtained by David

Astor from the USA, which Orwell reacted against with rashes, baldness, ulcers, and inflammations of the mouth. His doctor observed, 'most people would have been round the bend': *CW* xix. 309. The first draft of *Nineteen Eighty-Four* was completed on the Isle of Jura (7 Nov. 1947); the second draft was completed in Hairmyres Hospital (May 1948); the final typescript was finished back in Jura (4 Dec. 1948), followed by an immediate collapse in Orwell's condition. He left Jura never to return on 2 January 1949, and was admitted to the Cotswold Sanatorium, Cranham, in Gloucestershire, on 6 January.

35. Letter, Orwell to Anthony Powell, from Barnhill, Jura, 29 Nov. 1947. He tells Tosco Fyvel from Hairmyres Hospital on 31 December 1947 that he has been 'deadly sick' for the last three months. He tells David Astor on the same day that Richard is 'getting very big and rowdy...this is the first Christmas that he has more or less understood what it is all about, so I was glad to get away just beforehand and not be a skeleton at the Christmas dinner': letters, *CW* xix. 228, 238–40.

36. Spurling, *The Girl*, 46–9.

37. After describing the nightmare journey: letter, Orwell to Sonia Brownell, from Barnhill, Jura, 12 Apr. 1947, *CW* xix. 123; Heppenstall was warned there was no hot water, no transport, no facilities, and 'Bring any food'—plus towel: letter Orwell to Rayner Heppenstall, from Barnhill, Jura, 4 June, 16 June, 5 Sept. 1946, BBC Archive. Heppenstall asked if they had a French dictionary (letter, 18 June 1946).

38. Letter, Orwell to Sonia Brownell, from Cranham Lodge, Cranham, Gloucestershire, 24 May 1949, *CW* xx. 120.

39. Including oysters and Supreme de Volaille a la Ritz: 'Alfresco at Ritz', 13 Oct. 1949, Orwell Archive, J/36.

40. Spurling, *The Girl*, 77–80, 67–8, 95–6. In July 1946 she wrote a piece for *Horizon* on Roman Catholic boarding-schools which prefigures major themes in Orwell's 'Such, Such Were the Joys' (1939–47) and *Nineteen Eighty-Four* (p. 68). Merleau-Ponty was a professor of philosophy at the Sorbonne.

41. Letter, Andrew Morland, later to be Orwell's doctor, to Fred Warburg, Orwell's publisher, from University College Hospital, 25 May 1949, *CW* xx. 122.

42. Spurling defends her from all charges, particularly 'the myth of the cold and grasping Widow Orwell' (*The Girl*, p. xii). The case against Sonia begins, 'She turned to Orwell on the rebound': Jeffrey Meyers, *Orwell: Wintry Conscience of a Generation* (New York, 2001), 300; Shelden, *Orwell*, 485–8, and 'Was Mrs Orwell a Gold Gigger?', *Daily Telegraph*, 31 May 2002; and Bowker, who sees the publisher, the girlfriend, the lawyer, and the doctor in a conspiracy: *Orwell*, 411–12. Between 18 October 1949 and 19 January 1950 Orwell spent marginally more on his wife than he did on his hospital fees, and four times more than he spent on his son, or his hospital consultant: cheque-books, Barclays Bank, Highbury, Orwell Archive, J/37.

43. *Language, Truth and Logic*, by A. J. Ayer (1910–89), was published by Victor Gollancz in 1936, and again in 1945. It is likely Orwell knew the work. Some parts of *Nineteen Eighty-Four* appear to turn on its arguments. Ayer was an Old Etonian working for British Intelligence when Orwell first met him in Paris in 1945. After the war he held chairs of philosophy at UCL and at Oxford.

44. In 1948 *Picture Post* had run a feature on the English Fascist leader Sir Oswald Mosley, whose message it summarized in Freudian terms as 'the longing for an all powerful parent': *Picture Post*, 1 May 1948.

45. Typical debating point in a self-regarding student debating society: W. C. Lubenow, *The Cambridge Apostles 1820–1914* (Cambridge, 1998), 53.

46. George Orwell, *Nineteen Eighty-Four* (1949; Harmondsworth, 1973), 12.

47. Ibid. 11, 145.
48. Ibid. 49.
49. Ibid. 29, 27, 204.
50. Ibid. 37–8.
51. Edmund Burke, 'Appeal to the Old Whigs from the New' (1791), in *Works* (1826; Oxford, 1906–7), i. 96.
52. *Nineteen Eighty-Four*, 29. Orwell was sure there would be an atomic war in about five years: 'You and the Atom Bomb', *Tribune*, 19 Oct. 1945, *CW* xvii. 319. American policy committees saw the future rather differently: 'The atomic bomb altered the face of war and changed the course of history...We hold the power...To us has been granted greatness...Ours is the future': Hanson Baldwin, *The Price of Power* (New York, 1948), 321.
53. *Nineteen Eighty-Four*, 45–6.
54. Ibid. 213.
55. A. J. Ayer, *Language, Truth, and Logic* (1946; London, 1947), 131.
56. *Nineteen Eighty-Four*, 170–1.
57. Ibid. 41.
58. Ibid. 55.
59. Pubs were recommended sites for interviews with old men: C. S. Burne, *The Handbook of Folk-Lore* (London, Folk-Lore Society, 1913), 6–15.
60. 'Survivals in culture only survived by force of habit': E. B. Tylor, *Primitive Culture* (1871; London, 1903), i. 21; 'All that the peasantry practise, believe, and relate on the strength of immemorial custom' is 'sanctioned by unbroken succession from one generation to another'. But they do not understand what they do: G. L. Gomme, *Ethnology in Folklore* (London, 1892), 14.
61. *Nineteen Eighty-Four*, 78.
62. Ibid. 175.
63. Ibid. 218.
64. First published in 1947 as *Jeder stirbt fur sich allein* ('Everyone Dies For Himself Alone'). First published in English as 'Alone in Berlin': this translation Hans Fallada (Rudolf Ditzen), *Alone in Berlin* (London, 2009). Orwell's 'A Hanging' was published in *The Adelphi* (Aug. 1931).
65. Orwell reviewed James Burnham's *The Managerial Revolution* at length in 1945. First published in 1941 and subtitled 'What Is Happening In The World Now?', the book saw a failing capitalism and a techno-managerial new order replacing it in Germany, the USSR, the United States, and elsewhere. Burnham invoked Machiavelli's 'Letter to a Friend', possibly to Orwell's advantage in view of Orwell's future intentions in *Nineteen Eighty-Four*. 'If I have been a little too punctual in describing these monsters...I hope mankind will know them, the better to avoid them, my treatise being both a satire against them, and a true character of them...': *The Managerial Revolution* (Harmondsworth, 1945), 65–6. Orwell's review appeared in *Polemic*, 3 May 1946, and as a pamphlet: *CW* xviii. 268–84.
66. *Nineteen Eighty-Four*, 103.
67. Ibid. 111.

Chapter 8

1. He asked for no memorial service and no biography: Last Will and Testament, 18 Jan. 1950, *CW* xx. 237.
2. Literary Notebook, reading-list, Jan.–Dec. 1949, Orwell Archive, B/3.

3. On the tea: T. R. Fyvel, 'A Writer's Life', Mar. 1950, Orwell Archive, M/I.
4. Muggeridge, *Diaries*, 11 Nov. 1949 (p. 362), 20 Dec. 1949 (p. 366), 26 Jan. 1950 (p. 376).
5. 'New Labour's version of market liberalism has deprived manual work of dignity and social legitimacy': Avner Offer, 'British Manual Workers: From Producers to Consumers 1950–2000', *Contemporary British History*, 22: 4 (Dec. 2008), 561.
6. Declaration on the occasion of the fiftieth anniversary of the signature of the Treaties of Rome (German Presidency of the European Union 2007)—sixty abstract nouns in forty-five lines.

Life after Death

1. Tit for tat, Alexei Sayle's Communist trade-unionist parents were as much against Orwell as they were against Hitler, Churchill, and Mickey Mouse: *Stalin Ate My Homework* (London, 2010), 35.
2. A. L. Rowse, 'The Contradictions of George Orwell', *Contemporary Review* (Oct. 1982), 189, 191, 187.
3. Orwell, *Wigan Pier*, 128.
4. Orwell, *Down and Out*, 18. Politicians are said to have started minding their language following the siege of Latvian Anarchists in a house in Sidney Street, Stepney, in January 1911. 'Immigrant' or 'alien' was preferred to 'Jew'. In the early 1930s politicians were quick to distance themselves from the increasingly anti-Semitic speeches of Oswald Mosley's British Union of Fascists: L. Trubowitz, *Civil Anti-Semitism, Modernism, and British Culture 1902–39* (New York, 2012), 2, 6–9.
5. Orwell, *Burmese Days*, 38; Orwell, review of *Mein Kampf*, *New English Weekly*, 21 Mar. 1940—where he also said he would kill Hitler if he got the chance: *War Diary*, 25 Oct. 1940, *CW* xii. 278.
6. 'extraordinary Manichaean construction': Brian Cheyette, *Constructions of 'The Jew' in English Literature and Society* (Cambridge, 1993), 56.
7. Fyvel, *Personal Memoir*, 99.
8. 'He never got beyond regarding it as a particularly large-scale pogrom': Newsinger, 'Orwell, Anti-Semitism and the Holocaust', in Rodden, *Cambridge Companion*, 121; 'There are about 400,000 known Jews in Britain...': George Orwell, 'Antisemitism in Britain', *Contemporary Jewish Record*, Apr. 1945, *CW* xvii. 64–70.
9. Russell, 'George Orwell', *World Review*, 16 (1950), 6. Melvyn New, 'Orwell and Anti-Semitism', *Modern Fiction Studies*, 21: 1 (Spring 1975), 84. See also Hannah Arendt, *The Origins of Totalitarianism* (New York, 1951). Muggeridge noted the preponderance of Jews at his funeral service and wilfully remarked that he found it odd in view of the fact that Orwell 'was at heart strongly anti-Semitic': *Diaries*, 26 Jan. 1950 (p. 376). Fyvel's 1982 *Personal Memoir* defended him from the charge, and on Fyvel's own capacity to make judgement, see P. Worsthorne, in *Encounter* (Dec. 1985), 76.
10. Patai, *Orwell Mystique*, 234, and 'Gamesmanship and Andro-centrism in *Nineteen Eighty-Four*', in Harold Bloom (ed.), *George Orwell's 'Nineteen Eighty-Four'* (New Haven, 1987). Dana Nelson takes the mystique idea and reduces it to an all-American college frat: *National Manhood: Capitalist Citizenship and the Imagined Fraternity of White Men* (Durham, NC, 1998).
11. Beatrix Campbell, 'Orwell: Paterfamilias or Big Brother?', in Christopher Norris (ed.), *Inside the Myth: Orwell: Views from the Left*, 128–36.
12. Where the Jewish mother tries to protect her child from the bomb and sets in train Winston's memories of his own mother—a train of thought which eventually

restores his emotional health: Erika Gottlieb in Rodden, *Every Intellectual's Big Brother*, 152–3. Anne Mellor, 'Orwell's View of Women', in Peter Stansky (ed.), *On 'Nineteen Eighty-Four'* (New York, 1983); Urmila Seshagiri, 'Misogyny and Anti-Imperialism in *Burmese Days*', and Ana Moya, 'Discourses of Power in *Burmese Days*', in Alberto Lazaro (ed.), *The Road from George Orwell: His Achievement and Legacy* (Bern, 2001). Jenny Taylor sees Oceania as a depiction of 'the ultimate form of patriarchy', in Paul Chilton and Crispin Aubrey (eds.), *'Nineteen Eighty-Four': Autonomy, Control and Communication* (London, 1983), 29.

13. 'Certainly not a misogynist': Buddicom, *Eric and Us*, 182; 'gentle friend yet a man with a poor attitude to women': Bowker, *Orwell*, 427; Patai, *Orwell Mystique*, 19.

14. In six pages of poison, Heppenstall, who shared a flat with Orwell, accused him of being a racist, a snob, a bore, and, rather ungallantly one might think, having 'squinting' mistresses: 'Memoir of George Orwell: The Shooting Stick', *Twentieth Century* (Apr. 1955), 369–72.

15. Sonia Brownell, quoted in Gordon Bowker, 'Orwell and the Biographers', in Rodden, *Cambridge Companion*, 18.

16. Anthony Burgess, 'Ingsoc Considered', in Bloom, *Nineteen Eighty-Four*.

17. E. P. Thompson, 'Outside the Whale' (1960), and 'Open Letter to Leszek Kołakowski' (1973), in E. P. Thompson, *The Poverty of Theory and Other Essays* (London, 1978). Kołakowski was professor of the History of Philosophy at the University of Warsaw from 1959 to 1968, and thereafter at McGill, Berkeley, and Oxford, where he stayed. Like Thompson, he moved away from Communism after the Soviet Union's invasion of Hungary in 1956. Unlike Thompson, he did not stay loyal to what his interlocutor called the 'Marxist tradition' and broke with it definitively in his *Main Currents of Marxism* (Oxford, 1978). Kołakowski's altogether shorter reply to Thompson's letter appeared in the *Socialist Register* (1974) and is called 'My Correct Views On Everything'.

18. Latin preposition 'ob', and French noun 'rien', meaning 'out of' or 'from' 'nothing': Sue Lonoff, 'Art of Nightmare', in Rose, *Revised Orwell*, 32. His anti-intellectualism: 'How is it that he treats himself as exempt from these strictures?': Collini, *Absent Minds*, 355; John Rodden, 'On the Political Sociology of Intellectuals', in Holderness, *George Orwell*.

19. Bounds, *Orwell and Marxism*, 2 and *passim*.

20. 'Nothing is more artificial than plain speaking': Terry Eagleton, 'Reach Me Down Romantic', *London Review of Books*, 19 June 2003.

21. David Lodge, *The Modes of Modern Writing* (London, 1977), 46; essays by Margery Sabin, Michael Levenson, and William E. Cain, in Rodden, *Cambridge Companion*, chs. 4, 5, 6. Patrick Collinson refers to Puritan admiration for 'plain, honest, even artless' prose: *The Birthpangs of Protestant England* (Basingstoke, 1991), 97.

22. Simon Dentith, 'Orwell and Propaganda', in J. Pettifer (ed.), *Cockburn in Spain* (London, 1986); Richard Filloy, 'Orwell's Political Persuasion', in Holderness, *George Orwell*; Daniel Kies, 'Fourteen Types of Passivity', in Rose, *Revised Orwell*; Lynette Hunter, *George Orwell: The Search for a Voice* (Milton Keynes, 1984), 90–1.

23. Paul Roazen, 'Orwell, Freud and 1984', in Bloom, *Nineteen Eighty-Four*; Chilton and Aubrey, *Control and Communication*, 2; Paul Robinson, 'The Sexual Politics of *Nineteen Eighty-Four*', in Stansky, *On 'Nineteen Eighty-Four'*.

24. Laurence M. Porter, 'Psychomachia versus Socialism in 1984: A Psychoanalytical View', in Rose, *Revised Orwell*, 71; Richard I. Smyer, *Primal Dream and Primal Crime: Orwell's Development as a Psychological Novelist* (Columbia, Mo., 1979), chs. 6, 7.

25. Mason Harris, 'The Politics of Sado-Masochism in 1984', in Peter Buitenhuis and Ira B. Nadel (eds.), *George Orwell: A Reassessment* (Basingstoke, 1988); David Wykes,

A Preface to Orwell (London, 1987), 37–44; Patrick Wright, 'The Conscription of History', in Chilton and Aubrey, *Control and Communication*; *Manchester Guardian*, 16 Feb. 1950.

26. In Hendon the Conservatives had a constituency majority of 41,387 and there was to be no general election until 1945: letter, Mary Colebrook to Orwell, 5 Oct. 1941, Orwell Archive, Appendix 2, letters to Orwell 1928–37. His friend Kay Ekevall, his brother-in-law Humphrey Dakin, and his publisher Fred Warburg, quoted in Coppard and Crick, *Orwell Remembered*, 99, 129, 194.

27. Stephen Spender, 'Homage to Catalonia', *World Review*, 16 (1950). Peter Stansky agrees: 'truly a socialist', *On 'Nineteen Eighty-Four'*, 12; Tosco Fyvel, 'A Writer's Life', ibid.

28. David Smith and Michael Mosher, *Orwell for Beginners* (London, 1984), 6.

29. 'an ethical socialist'—Bernard Crick, 'Orwell and English Socialism', in Butenhuis and Nadel, *Reassessment*, 14.

30. Isaac Deutscher, '1984: The Mysticism of Cruelty', in *Russia in Transition and Other Essays* (New York, 1957); Tony Cliff, in David Widgery, *The Left in Britain 1958–68* (Harmondsworth, 1976), 17. On the claim that Orwell was a Trotskyite, or the literary equivalent of a Trotskyite, whatever that is, Newsinger, *Orwell's Politics*, 91, and Malcolm Pittock, 'George Orwell', *Cambridge Quarterly*, 39: 2 (2010).

31. 'gross...filthy...last word in counter revolutionary politics' (A. L. Morton), 'slobbering with poisonous spittle' (*Pravda*), in Chilton and Aubrey, *Control and Communication*, 11; serving 'every kind of reactionary populist creed', Norris, *Inside the Myth*, 8. Rather than make a proper case, Scott Lucas cuffs Orwell with ironic apostrophes: 'Policing Dissent', Field, *Cold War Culture*.

32. Woodcock, *Crystal Spirit*, 185.

33. Muggeridge observed that although he dressed 'in a sort of proletarian fancy dress', 'the truth is he was by temperament deeply conservative': 'Orwell', 10 Feb. 1971, in Orwell Archive M/18. Rees stressed the libertarian *and* traditional sides: Orwell Archive M/1, 1950, and *DNB* (1959). Testimonials of genuineness ('no sort of fake about him', Dakin, p. 136) from those who knew him personally include Astor, Common, Connolly Cottman, Dakin, Deiner, King-Farlow, Rees, Runciman, Spender, and Woodcock, in Coppard and Crick, *Orwell Remembered*; and for his gentlemanliness, Mabel Friez ('very much the Eton boy'), Common, Melling, Denny, Dunn, Braithwaite, Morgan, and Cooper, in Wadham, *Remembering Orwell*.

34. Zola's famous letter in defence of Dreyfus (*J'Accuse*, 1 Feb. 1898) attacked the French political, legal, military, and religious establishment and was followed on the next day by a manifesto of the left signed by 1,200 people grouped under their academic qualifications (*L'Aurore*, 2 Feb. 1898). Georges Clemenceau, the newspaper's editor, called it 'la protestation des Intellectuels'. Red rag to a bull, the judges, generals, and other patriots understood the nature of the challenge, and identified their own anti-intellectual position accordingly.

35. Two arguments in favour of Orwell's conservatism are Robert Nisbet's '*1984* and the Conservative Imagination', in Irving Howe (ed.), *'Nineteen Eighty-Four' Revisited: Totalitarianism in our Century* (New York, 1983) which starts: 'George Orwell was no conservative...' (p. 180); and William E Laskowski Jr.'s 'George Orwell and the Tory Radical Tradition', in Rose, *Revised Orwell*, which accurately points to literary likenesses in Swift, Cobbett, Hazlitt, Chesterton, and Belloc.

36. First quotation taken from O'Brien, second from Rousseau, and third from the Jacobin Committee of Public Safety: all in Nisbet, '*1984* and the Conservative Imagination', 193, who takes up Orwell's argument that totalitarianism was a

movement 'as rational and modern as any other large scale structure of the 20th Century' (p. 188). John Gray moves the same argument forward in his *Al Qaeda and What It Means to be Modern* (London, 2003).

37. Louis Menand, 'Honest, Decent, Wrong', *New Yorker*, 27 Jan. 2003.

38. Definitely a liberal—'He is, precisely, distinctively, a twentieth century liberal': Alok Rai, *Orwell and the Politics of Despair* (Cambridge, 1988), 1; and 'As a writer... [he] had to be a liberal': B. T. Oxley, *George Orwell* (London, 1967), 136. Definitely not a liberal—Patrick Reilly, *George Orwell: The Age's Adversary* (London, 1986), p. xi; mainly a liberal—George Woodcock, *The Writer and Politics* (London, 1948), 124.

39. Ian Watts, 'Winston Smith: The Last Humanist', and Robert Conquest, 'Totali-terror', in Stansky, *On 'Nineteen Eighty-Four'*.

40. Modernist in Kristin Bluemel, *George Orwell and the Radical Eccentrics: Intermodernism in Literary London* (New York, 2004), and Robert E. McGinn, 'Politics of Technol-ogy', in Stansky, *On 'Nineteen Eighty-Four'*; anti-modernist in John Mander, 'George Orwell's Politics', *Contemporary Review*, 197 (1960), and Peter Lowe, 'Englishness in a Time of Crisis, George Orwell, John Betjeman and the Second World War', *Cambridge Quarterly*, 38: 3 (2009).

41. 'too unphilosophical even to be properly anti-philosophical': Collini, *Absent Minds*, 369.

42. John Morris, typescript, Mar. 1950, Orwell Archive, M/I.

43. His alertness was noticed early: Ifor Evans, review of *Inside the Whale*, *Manchester Guardian*, 13 June 1939. Roy Harris thinks he was a poor linguistic philosopher ('The Misunderstanding of Newspeak', Bloom, *Nineteen Eighty-Four*) but Elizabeth Closs Transgott thinks he was a good one ('Newspeak: Could It Really Work?' in Stansky, *On 'Nineteen Eighty-Four'*). Samuel Macey considers Orwell's use of chron-ological time in 'The Future that Becomes the Past', in Buitenhuis and Nadel, *Reassessment*.

44. Where he 'offers no guarantee of impartiality, accuracy or special knowledge': Stephen Ingle, *The Social and Political Thought of George Orwell* (London, 2006), 24–5. 'Remark should be modified. I have no good evidence that prostitution decreased 75 per cent': 'Further notes for my literary executor', after June 1949, Orwell Archive, J/32.

45. Carter, *George Orwell and the Problem of Authentic Existence*, 53.

46. To be followed by second encounters with small communities of committed readers in small committed journals. Part of Orwell's strength as an essayist is his conversational tone.

47. Christopher Hollis, *A Study of George Orwell, the Man and his Works* (London, 1956), and Sandison, *Last Man in Europe*, 106.

48. Arthur Eckstein shows how the liberating words in *Nineteen Eighty-Four* have classi-cal roots while the dead words are all Anglo-Saxon—quite against the etymologi-cal practices recommended in Orwell's 'Politics and the English Language' (1946): 'The Classical Heritage of Airstrip One', in Rose, *Revised Orwell*.

49. Worldly—'free of pieties', 'posed no riddles, elaborated no myths': Richard Rovere, 'The Importance of George Orwell', in *The American Establishment* (New York, 1962), 169, 178; otherworldly—Rees, *Fugitive from the Camp of Victory*, 114.

50. Reilly, *Age's Adversary*, 11.

51. Tom Hopkinson, *George Orwell* (London, British Council and National Book League, 1953); John Atkins, *George Orwell: A Literary Study* (London, 1954).

52. Communists—Norris, *Inside the Myth*, 8; prep-school supporter—Robert Pearce, 'Truth and Falsehood, George Orwell's Prep School Woes', *Review of English*

Studies, 43: 197 (Aug. 1992), 386; his BBC boss reported that 'in early days [he] would have been either canonized—or burnt at the stake' (D. Pearson Smith, Annual Report, 10 Aug. 1943, BBC Archive); Alex Comfort came up with Church-ill, 'George Orwell and the Vision of Judgement', in Stansky, *On 'Nineteen Eighty-Four'*, 20. Anthony Stewart calls him 'elastic' and no wonder: 'George Orwell's Elastic Politics', *English Studies in Canada*, 28: 4 (Dec. 2002).

53. Ian Slater, *Orwell: The Road to Airstrip One* (New York, 1985), 241. Bertrand Russell thanked him for showing 'elderly radicals like Wells and myself' what centralized power could do, but seemed to forget that English radicalism, elderly or not, had always been focused on the abuse of central power above all else: Russell quoted in Meyers, *Orwell*, 241, 301; and K. O. Morgan, 'Le Pouvoir politique britannique et sa representation', *Revue Française de Civilisation Britannique*, 17: 1 (2012).

54. Meyers puts Wigan in the 'industrial Midlands': Jeffrey Meyers, *Orwell: Life and Art* (Urbana, Ill., 2010), 203–15, 194.

55. Orwell, review of 'The Mysterious Mr Bull', in *New English Weekly*, 8 June 1939, *CW* xi. 354.

56. Zwerdling's *Orwell and the Left* was a path-breaking study, but assumes there is a composite position to analyse—whether it be Orwell's hatred of hierarchies 'in any form' (though he lived them in all forms), or the 'strong Utopian element' in his work (though many would call him 'Dystopian'), or his dislike of 'bourgeois socialism' (though on other occasions he said it was the only sort), and so on.

57. Marks, *Orwell the Essayist*, 202; 'from first to last Orwell...was always writing the same novel': William Steinhoff, *The Road to 'Nineteen Eighty-Four'* (London, 1975), 123.

58. Mark Rawlinson, 'George Orwell and Spain', in A. Gomis and S. Onega (eds.), *George Orwell: A Centenary Celebration* (Heidelberg, 2005), 74.

59. 'When poverty is in question, the author of *Down and Out in Paris and London* knows all the answers': Harold Brighouse, *Manchester Guardian*, 21 Apr. 1936.

60. *Manchester Guardian*, 23 Jan. and 30 Dec. 1950. Orwell Archive, J/41, empty enve-lope, 10 Downing Street, addressed to Orwell at University College Hospital, p.m., 7 Jan. 1950; V. S. Pritchett, 'Living Writers', broadcast 11.30–11.50 p.m., BBC radio, Saturday, 23 Nov. 1946, and radio productions of *Animal Farm* in Janu-ary 1947 and September 1950, plus talk by T. R. Fyvel, in the 'Contemporary English Novel' series, 27 June 1950.

61. John Rodden has traced every phase in the *Politics of Literary Reputation* (1989), *Every Intellectual's Big Brother* (2006), *The Cambridge Companion to George Orwell* (2007), and *The Unexamined Orwell* (2011). Lionel Trilling famously referred to Orwell as a virtuous man.

62. V. S. Pritchett, *New Statesman and Nation*, 28 Jan. 1950.

63. Stephen Spender, 'Homage to Catalonia', *World Review*, 16 (June, 1950), 51. Orwell began his 'reflections on Gandhi' with the injunction that 'Saints should always be judged guilty until they are proven innocent': *Partisan Review* (Jan. 1949), *CW* xx. 5.

64. Anthony Hartley's description of the Movement's poetry in the *Spectator* for 27 August 1954 sounds like a description of Orwell's politics—'distrustful of too much fanaticism, austere and sceptical...egalitarian and anti-aristocratic...pro-foundly opposed to fashion in the metropolitan sense..."dissenting" and non-conformist'. On the Movement's major poet, see Stephen Regan, *Philip Larkin* (Basingstoke, 1992), ch. 1; on the Movement's language, see D. Cameron, 'The Virtues of Good Prose', in Z Leader (ed.), *The Movement Reconsidered* (Oxford, 2009); and on the Movement's direct reference to Orwell, see Rodden, *Orwell's Big Brother*, ch. 2.

65. Kingsley Amis sets the context: 'Speaking Up for Excellence', in Patrick Cormack (ed.), *Right Turn* (London, 1978); Kubal, *Art and Politics*, 51.
66. Rodden, *Unexamined Orwell*, 29.
67. Irving Howe, 'George Orwell', *Harper's Magazine* (Jan. 1969).
68. Rodden, *Every Intellectual's Big Brother*, 64, 68. Howe described the ideological turn thus: 'Within [Orwell's] generation of left-wing writers and intellectuals, some have turned to the right, some have tried to refine their socialist values towards a greater stress on democracy, and others have abandoned their interest in politics entirely': 'Enigmas of Power', in Irving Howe (ed.), *'Nineteen Eighty-Four' Revisited* (New York, 1983), 17.
69. American left-liberals included Lionel and Diana Trilling, Herbert Matthews, Mary McCarthy, Daniel Bell, Philip Rahv, and Arthur Schlesinger (Rodden, *Every Intellectual's Big Brother* , ch. 3, and Meyers, *Critical Heritage*, 143–9, 549, 117). European dissident liberals included Václav Havel, Czesław Miłosz, Rudolf Bahro, Miklós Haraszti, Leszek Kołakowski, Milan Simecka, and Adam Michnik (Hitchens, *Orwell's Victory*, 41). There are essays on Orwell by Kołakowski and Milovan Djilas in Howe, *'Nineteen Eighty-Four' Revisited*, chs. 8 and 12. On Orwell in Germany, Rodden, *Unexamined Orwell*, part 2. Soviet military parity and intransigence towards dissident movements edged East European and American (but not West European) liberals into more aggressive anti-Soviet foreign-policy positions.
70. Art Spiegelman, *Metamaus* (London, 2011), 130.
71. *The Uses of Literacy*, published in 1957. Hoggart duly acknowledged his debt to Orwell: Nicholas Wroe, 'The Uses of Decency', *Guardian*, 7 Feb. 2004. Orwell told Gorer that he found 'this kind of semi sociological literary criticism very interesting': letter from The Stores, Wallington, 3 Apr. 1940, *CW* xii. 137.
72. 'The ideal type traditional proletarian worker is rarely found...': Jim Cousins and Richard Brown, 'Shipbuilding Workers' Images of Society', in Martin Bulmer (ed.), *Working Class Images of Society* (London, 1975), 79.
73. See e.g. David Lockwood, 'Sources of Variation in Working-Class Images of Society', ibid.
74. Colls, 'When We Lived in Communities'.
75. 'So you have whole populations settling down, as it were, to a lifetime on the PAC [Public Assistance Committee]': Orwell, *Wigan Pier*, 78.
76. *Guardian*, 31 Oct. 2008. He would have had fun with 'chavs', whose caravan he spotted coming a long way off: 'Every middle-class person has a dormant class prejudice which needs only a small thing to arouse it... The notion that the working class have been absurdly pampered, hopelessly demoralized by doles, old age pensions, free education etc... is still widely held; it has merely been a little shaken perhaps, by the recent recognition that unemployment does exist': *The Road to Wigan Pier*, also quoted in Owen Jones, *Chavs: The Demonization of the Working Class* (London, 2012), 13.
77. David Marquand, 'The New Left at Oxford': 'What are they concerned with instead? The short, superficial answer is, culture': *Manchester Guardian*, 18 Aug. 1958. For the anti-theatrical ones see pieces by John Arden, Albert Finney, John Osborne, Alan Sillitoe, Harold Pinter, and Arnold Wesker in *Twentieth Century* (Feb. 1961), 191–4: 'I wish people didn't talk so much about The Theatre', 'The less I say the better I like it', 'art is beginning to have no meaning for me', and 'What one wants is bloody revolution' (Wesker). Becket's *Waiting for Godot* arrived in London in 1955, Brecht in 1956, John Osborne's *Look Back in Anger* at the Royal Court, 8 May 1956.

78. But Mary McCarthy (*Writing on the Wall*) and George Woodcock (*Crystal Spirit*) also acknowledged Orwell's contribution: John Coleman, 'The Critic of Popular Culture', in Gross, *World of George Orwell*. Ask not what Cultural Studies can do for Englishness, but see for an example Simon Gikandi, *Maps of Englishness: Writing Identity in the Culture of Colonialism* (New York, 1996).

79. Gyan Prakash, 'Subaltern Studies as Post-Colonial Criticism', *American Historical Review*, 95: 5 (Dec. 1994), 1488; Pratt, *Imperial Eyes*, 6–7.

80. Benedict Anderson, *Imagined Communities: Reflections on the Origin and Spread of Nationalism* (London, 1985).

81. 'What is felt and lived as a personal life but which is always inescapably a social life': Light, *Forever England*, 5.

82. E. P. Thompson, 'Outside the Whale' (1960), 32; Raymond Williams, 'George Orwell', in Bloom, *Nineteen Eighty-Four*, 10. For other coded indictments of Orwell see Williams's *Culture and Society*, 281, and *Orwell*, 63, 73, 79, 91.

83. 'disillusioned loathing represents a main line of continuity between the attitudes voiced towards Orwell by the Stalinists [and] Williams and the *New Left Review*, and the post-structuralist Left [and] post-New Left feminists of the 1980s': Rodden, *Politics of Literary Reputation*, 223.

84. 'Moral courage, creative reflection on one's environment, difficult choices in the shifting of one's allegiances': Bess might have been describing Orwell's trajectory when describing Thompson's: Michael D. Bess, 'E. P. Thompson: The Historian as Activist', *American Historical Review* (Feb. 1993), 22.

85. D. A. N. Jones for instance, who thought Orwell's criticisms of the USSR were 'beneath contempt': 'Arguments against Orwell', in Gross, *World of George Orwell*; see also David Pryce-Jones's 'Orwell's Reputation', in the same volume.

86. Hitchens turned Larkin's finely tuned phrase 'the less deceived' into the 'No Bullshit Brigade'—*Orwell's Victory*, 41. For a selection of less-deceived essays and journalism, see Martin Amis, *The Second Plane* (London, 2008) and Hitchens's *Arguably* (London, 2011).

87. Stefan Collini noted Orwell's place in Hitchens's pantheon, as well as their mutual hatred of cant—'especially pious cant, especially pious radical academic cant': *London Review of Books*, 23 Jan. 2003. Larkin published his second volume of poetry, *The Less Deceived*, in Hull in 1955. Martin Amis defended Larkin from what he saw as pious radical academic cant in his 'The Ending: Don Juan in Hull', published in *The War against Cliché* (London, 2001).

88. F. S. Saunders, *Who Paid the Piper? The CIA and the Cultural Cold War* (London, 1999), 290, and knowingly funding some of his key supporters (pp. 397–404). Soviet intelligence pushed the line that *Nineteen Eighty-Four* was a satire on the United States: D. Hencke and R. Evans, 'How Big Brothers Used Orwell to Fight Cold War', *Guardian*, 30 June 2000.

89. Mary McCarthy, *The Writing on the Wall* (New York, 1970), 168–9.

90. Norman Podhoretz, 'If Orwell Were Alive Today', *Harper's* (Jan. 1983). This piece should be yoked to Arthur M. Eckstein's recognition of Orwell's crucial 1941 conflation of economic liberty and personal liberty (Orwell, 'Will Freedom Die with Capitalism?', *Left News* (Apr. 1941), and 'Literature and Totalitarianism', BBC broadcast, 21 May 1941, *CW* xii. 458–64, 502–5): Eckstein, 'George Orwell's Second Thoughts on Capitalism', in Rose, *Revised Orwell*, 200.

91. 'What we always forget is that the overwhelming bulk of the British proletariat do not live in Britain': Orwell, review of *Union Now* by Clarence K. Streit, *The Adelphi* (July 1939), *CW* xi. 360.

92. For American cultural conservative admirers Russell Kirk and John Lukacs: Rodden, *Every Intellectual's Big Brother*, 81, and *Unexamined Orwell*, 111.

93. On at least one occasion, literally so. Clifford Collins wrote to Sonia in 1959 saying he had found the Gissing essay Orwell had submitted to him and Raymond Williams as editors of the journal *Politics and Letters* back in 1947. He had found it in an old packing-case—and it seemed to him 'a characteristic and interesting piece'. Raymond Williams meanwhile had written strongly on Gissing in his *Culture and Society*, published in 1958. Collins had the nerve to suggest that Sonia now send the essay to *Universities and Left Review*, which had 'rather similar aims and readership to *Politics and Letters*': letters, Collins to Sonia Pitt Rivers, 1 Aug., 6 Sept. 1959, in Orwell Archive, A/8 b).

94. Thompson, 'Open Letter to Leszek Kołakowski' (1973), 95–8.

95. *Journal of the History Group of the Communist Party*, 11 Jan. 1987, p. 3. For a view of life inside the Communist Party of Great Britain in the 1950s, 'absurd', 'poisonous', 'grim', 'depressing': Doris Lessing, *Walking in the Shade*, vol. ii, *1949–62* (London, 1997), 22, 106.

96. McKibbin, *Classes and Cultures*, 528–36; Harrison, *Seeking a Role*, Introduction, ch. 1.

97. Richard Sennett, *The Corrosion of Character: The Personal Consequences of Work in the New Capitalism* (New York, 1998), 16–24.

98. On the erosion of 'manifest doctrines' of Britishness: K. O. Morgan, 'The British National Identity 1851–2008', *British Scholar*, 1 (2008), 6.

99. Mandler, *English National Character*, 193.

100. Julia Stapleton, *Political Intellectuals and Public Identities in Britain since 1850* (Manchester, 2001), 168; Mandler provides the immediate context in chapters 5 and 6, 'Little England' and 'England after Character' (ibid.). Other works on the return of Englishness include Robert Colls and Philip Dodd (eds.), *Englishness: Politics and Letters 1880–1920* (London, 1986); Linda Colley, *Britons* (London, 1992); Stefan Collini, *English Pasts* (Oxford, 1999); Robert Colls, *Identity of England* (Oxford, 2002); Krishan Kumar, *The Making of English National Identity* (Cambridge, 2003); and Simon Featherstone *Englishness* (Edinburg 2009). For a review: Peter Mandler, 'What Is "National Identity"? Definitions and Applications in Modern British Historiography', *Modern Intellectual History*, 3: 2 (2006). Roger Scruton calls the new Englishness 'The Forbidding of England', but there are recent signs that the forbidding has reached its limit: *England: An Elegy* (London, 2001), 248–9. Peter Hitchens wrote in a similar vein with his *The Abolition of Britain* (London, 1999).

101. On the political consequences of the weakening of national identity in the face of transnational forces and ideologies: Robert Colls, 'The Lion and the Eunuch: National Identity and the British Genius', *Political Quarterly*, 82: 4 (2011). A recent commentator has said that the contemporary relevance of Orwell's work is in danger of being lost in 'an ocean of posthumous revision': C. J. Fusco, *Our Orwell Right or Left* (Newcastle upon Tyne, 2008), 100.

102. Katharine Cockin, 'Locating the Literary North', in Cockin (ed.), *The Literary North* (Basingstoke, 2012), 241; Geoffrey Moorhouse, *Britain in the Sixties: The Other England* (Harmondsworth, 1964).

103. Taylor, *Orwell*, 4.

104. Simon Heffer, 'The Undiluted Joys of a Literary Genius', *Daily Telegraph*, 8 May 2010; Julian Barnes, *New York Review of Books*, 12 Mar. 2009.

105. A statue intended for London and sponsored by the Orwell Memorial Trust and the BBC: 'I wish Orwell was here with us now to hear his views on the mess that we are in. We need heroes like Orwell but there aren't any with his vision of the

world today' (Ben Whitaker, chair, Orwell Memorial Trust, *Islington Tribune*, 30 Aug. 2012).

106. Rodden sees John Wain, a member of the 'Movement', as the first 'second' Orwell (*Every Intellectual's Big Brother*, 34). Hitchens made no bones about it: 'The Importance of Being Orwell', *Vanity Fair* (Aug. 2012), and had his supporters (Francis Saunders, *Guardian*, 17 Dec. 2011, and Ron Rosenbaum, *Every Intellectual's Big Brother*, 94), as did Judt (front cover of the *New Left Review*, Sept.–Oct. 2011),'The New Orwell', and front cover of his *Ill Fares the Land* (London, 2010), the 'latter-day Orwell'. Both men, Hitchens (1949–2011) and Judt (1948–2010), had more in common than being Orwell, but neither was like him really. For the American contenders: Rodden, *Every Intellectual's Big Brother*, 70, and *Unexamined Orwell*, 29. Feminist critics of Orwell might find Alice Holt's identification of strong similarities between him and Simone Weil interesting: 'Une rencontre manquée? La pensée politique de George Orwell et Simone Weil', *Esprit* (Aug. 2012).

107. For the posh end of the cliché: Sean O'Hagen, 2009 George Orwell Memorial Lecture, republished in the *Guardian*, 9 Jan. 2009. For the down-and-out end, with bad journalism and poor scholarship: Stephen Armstrong and Danny Dorling, 'What Would Orwell Say?', *Big Issue*, 26 Mar.–1 Apr. 2012.

108. Terry Eagleton, 'Reach Me Down Romantic', *London Review of Books*, 19 June 2003.

109. Robert Colls, 'Ethics Man: John Gray's New Moral World', *Political Quarterly*, 69:1 (1998), 59–71.

Text Acknowledgements

Picture Acknowledgements

Plates 10, **11**, **13**: Getty Images; **Plates 16**, **17**: Estate of Mary Kent Harrison, Courtesy of Stephen Harrison; **Plate 5**: Photo: © Rheinisches Bildarchiv Köln, rba_d029031; **Plates 1**, **2**, **3**, **4**, **6**, **7**, **12**, **14**, **15**, **18**: UCL Special Collections; **Plates 8**, **9**: Woodhorn Museum and Northumberland Archives

Index

Abercrombie, Sir Patrick 118
Abingdon 123
Adam Bede, fictional character in George
    Eliot's *Adam Bede* 186
Adam, Eugene 91, 210
Adelphi, [*The*] 33, 35, 36, 42, 47, 48, 65, 68,
    99, 124, 189
Adenauer, Konrad 202
Affairs of the Heart 217
Afghan War 21
Africanistas 89
Afrikaaners 25
Agnes Terrace, Barnsley 70–1, 218
Airstrip One, fictional country in *Nineteen
    Eighty-Four* 224
Albacete 94
Alfred the Great 122
Alington, Revd Dr C. A, headmaster Eton
    College 13
Alone in Berlin 215
Amalgamated Society of Woodworkers 52
ambulance stations 182
Amis, Kingsley 228
Amis, Martin 231
Amritsar massacre 27
An Inspector Calls 173
Anarchists 180, 182
Anarchist–Communist struggles, in
    Spain 76, 85, 88–9, 93
Anarquistas 88
Anderson, Benedict 230
Angell, Norman 82
Anglican Communion 187
Angus, Ian 205
'Anschluss' 134
'Anti-Fascism' 76
'anti-intellectualism', right against
    left 224
'Apostles', Cambridge 206
Appeasement 134–6; defeated 139
Aragon 8, 73, 83, 99; Battle of 88
Aristotle 222
Army Bureau of Current Affairs 145

Arnedo 88
Arnold, Matthew 66
Ashanti 25
aspidistra 37
Astor, David 146, 147, 217, 224
Asturias 88
Atkins, John 4, 5, 226
atheists 180
atomic bomb 167, 203
Attlee, Clement 19–20, 105, 138, 154, 172,
    174, 177, 223, 227
Auden, W. H. 98–102, 130, 148
Auschwitz 220
Austria 135
Austrian school, liberal
    conservatives 179
Autobiography of a Super Tramp, The 32
Avenue Clichy 83
Ayer, A. J. 211

babus 20, 24
back to backs, houses 53
Bagehot, Walter 42, 151
Baldwin, Stanley 103, 233
Bank of England 48
Barcelona 72, 74, 76, 77, 78, 81, 88, 108,
    141, 165, 218
Barker, Ernest 184
Barlow Commission 119
Barnes, Julian 5, 235
Barnsley 56, 58, 64, 70, 71, 150, 218
Battersea Park 219
Beaton, Cecil 148
Beavan, John 55, 147
beer (and skittles) 176
Bell, Vanessa 148
Belsen 49
benchmarks, of British-ness 233
Benda, Julien 84, 106
Bergonzi, Bernard 5
Berlin 166, 201, 202
Bethnal Green 229
Betjeman, John 218

Bevan, Aneurin 146, 174, 175, 176, 177
   admired by Orwell 178–9; as Prime
   Minister 235
Beveridge, William 154, 283 n. 6
Bevin, Ernest 145, 172, 176, 177, 207
Bihar province, India 21, 204
Birmingham 48, 49
Bitter Cry of Outcast London, [The] 32
Blackpool 56
Blackstone, Sir William 158, 189
Blair family, 1, 11, 12, 16, 17, 29, 31,
   202–3, 204, 253 n. 88
Blair, Avril, Orwell's younger sister 203, 204
Blair, Ida, Orwell's mother 11, 12, 202,
   203, 249 n. 13
Blair, Marjorie, Orwell's older sister 11,
   199, 203
Blair, Richard, Orwell's father 11, 15, 202
Blair, Richard Horatio, Orwell's son 147,
   160, 167, 182, 197, 199, 203, 204, 205
Bletchley Park 274 n. 62
Bloomsbury 115, 227
Bolsheviks 162
Bolton 57
bombers (always get through) 138–9
Bonaparte, Napoleon, 'The Corsican
   Fairy' 156
Booth, Charles 30, 112
Booth, William 32
Borkenau, Franz 91
Bosanquet, Bernard 185
Boston Evening Transcript 36
bourgeois morality 65–6;
   and bourgeois self-destruction 68–9
Bowker, Gordon 5, 205, 221
Boyle, Danny 234–5
boys, fictional characters, Bunter, Cherry,
   Merry etc 160–1, 170
'Bozo', fictional character in *Down and Out in
   Paris and London* 222
Bradbury, Malcolm 5
Braine, John 229
Brandt, Bill 148
brainworkers 182
Brannigan, John 5
Breton, André 68
Bristol 49
British Army 165, 172
British battalion, XV International Brigade 88
British Broadcasting Corporation (BBC) 48,
   145, 173; creative people 138, 146

British cookery 167
British Council 167
British economy 25–6
British Empire: for and against 24–7;
   Empire Day 28; and Kipling 165;
   as agent of liberty 185, and
   genocide 243 n. 71;
   disappearance 233
British Expeditionary Force 141, 145
British Institute of Public Opinion 126
British military capability 144–5
British/English national identity 129,
   141, 148, 150, 182, 233; and
   India 240 n. 36, 241 nn. 45, 47
British Pathe News 41
British people, left politicization
   ('People's War') 139, 145,
   152–3, 178
British security services 107, 172–3
British Worker [The] 192
Britten, Benjamin 182
Broadcasting House (BBC) 145
Brockway, Fenner 137
Bronte, Charlotte 190
Brooke, Rupert 120, 130
Brooker family, Wigan, *The Road to Wigan
   Pier* 60, 63
Brown, Ivor 146
Brown, James 69
Brownell, Sonia (Sonia Orwell) 147, 204–5,
   217, 218, 219, 221
Brunette, Battle of 88
Bryant, Arthur 123
Buchenwald 221
Buckingham Palace 48
Buddhism 18, 19, 23, 235
Bukharin, Nikolai 93
Burckhardt, Jacob 224
Burgess, Anthony 222
Burillo, Ricardo 91
Burke, Edmund, and national cultures
   189–90, 209, 224
Burma, 18–22, 27, 218
Burnham, James 179, 215, 295 n. 65
Burslem 51
Butlin's, Filey 175
Butterfield, Herbert 184–5

Caballero, Francisco Largo 76
Cabinet Reconstruction Committee 177
Calcutta 22

Calder, Jenni 4, 81
Calder-Marshall, Arthur 98
Cambridge University 15, 227
'camp', English 228
Campaign for Nuclear Disarmament 219
Campbell, Beatrix 221
Camus, Albert 201
Canonbury Square, Essex Road, Islington 147
Cape, Jonathan 169
Cape Town 219
Capitalism 2
car workers 219, 228, 230
Carlyle, Thomas 50
Carr, E. H. 217
Casas Viejas 88
Castiblanco 88
Cavalcade 153
cavalry horses 73–4
Central Intelligence Agency (CIA) 232
Chamberlain, Neville 134, 135
Chaplin, Charlie 32
'character' 233
Chauri Chaura 28
Cheam, Sir Joseph, fictional character in *Coming Up for Air* 114, 117
Cheap Bread 183
checkweighman 54
Chesterfield, Lord 42
Chichele Professor of Economic History, Oxford 218, 296 n. 5
China War 21
Church of England 145
Churchill, Winston 82, 122, 139, 145, 202, 233
cinema 182, 230
City and Guilds, technical qualifications 117
City of London 37, 48, 116–17, 128, 155
Civil War, English 183
Civil War in Spain 98
'Civilians', top rung of the Indian Civil Service 20–1, 26
Clare, John 192
Clarke, Ben 5
class relations, in Britain 30, 31, 35, 60, 62–3, 112–13, 230; connotations 115–17
Cliff, Tony 223
clubs, expatriate 23–4

Clutton-Brock, Arthur 13
coal industry 46–7, 181; and royal commissions (Sankey and Samuel) 224
Cobbett, William 81, 130, 148, 190, 192, 276 n. 82
Cold War 219
Cole, Margaret 176
Collini, Stefan 9, 222
Collins, publishers 168, 169
Cologne 201
Commentary 232
Commission for Racial Equality 230
Common, Jack 47, 65–6, 69, 224
Communist International 87, 91, 94
Communist Party of Great Britain 8, 48, 62, 226; dress sense 64; General Secretary 98; Gollancz, Laski, and Strachey 104; Historians' Group 233; and Labour party 173, 223; New Left 231; and W. H. Auden 99
Communist Fifth Regiment, Spain 88
'community centres', fictional institutes in *Nineteen Eighty-Four* 208
commuters 116
'Comstockery' 40, 45, 73, 247 n. 119
Confederacion Nacional del Trabajo (CNT) 76, 85
Congo 219
Connolly, Cyril 36, 52, 147, 204
Conquest, Robert 228
Conrad, Joseph 179, 217
conscription 139, 172
Conservative party 103, 188–9, 233
conservatism, anti-philosophical 194
Constitutional History 184
Controversy 84, 85
Cooperative movement 176
Cortada, Roldan 76
Coser, Lewis 229
Cottman, Stafford 79
Coventry 48, 51
Coward, Noel 153, 182
Cranham, Gloucestershire 182
Crankshaw, Edward 91
Crick, Bernard 5, 148, 205
Crimea 201
Cripps, Stafford 90
Crossland, Margaret 146

Crossman, Richard 146
Crown Derby 170
Crown Film Unit 145, 154
Crystal Spirit [The] 190
Cuba 228, 232
Cultural Studies 230
Curzon, Lord 20
Czechoslovakia 134, 135, 138, 139, 232

Dagenham 110, 228
Daily Chronicle 82
Daily Herald 181
Daily Mail 82
Daily Mirror 154, 170
Daily Telegraph 226
Daily Worker 62, 64, 84, 98, 181
Dakin, Humphrey 55, 223
Dakin, Marjorie (née Blair) 11, 55, 69, 112,
    119, 136, 199, 203
Daladier, Edouard 134
Dalton, Hugh 177
Darlington Street, Wigan 48
Davie, Donald 228
Davies, Sir John 159
Davies, W. H. 32
Davison, Peter 6
Darkest England and the Way Out 32
de-industrialization 191, 234
de Montfort, Simon 183
'deep' England 122–3
democracy 234
Dennis, Norman 229
Dentith, Simon 222
destroyer crews 182
Deutscher, Isaac 223
devaluation 181
Dewey, Clive 23
Dialectical Materialism 96, 212
Dialectics of Nature 96
Dickens, Charles 162–4, 170, 186
District Officer's court 17
documentarists 81, 188
dole 54
dominions, British Empire 20
Dorothy Hare, fictional character in
    A Clergyman's Daughter 36, 38–9, 44,
    128, 186–7, 201
Dr Veraswami, fictional character in *Burmese
    Days* 24
Dreyfus Affair 253 n. 82, 298 n. 34
Durbin, Evan 61

Durham coalfield 49
Durham Miners' Gala 178
Dundee 160
Dunkirk 145
Dunn, Bill, husband of Avril Blair 203

Eagleton, Terry 235
Ealing 115
East Germany 202
East India Company 19
East Kent Regional Plan (1925) 119
Eastbourne Workhouse 12
Eastern Europe 229
Ebro, Battle of 88, 90
Eden Commission 19
Edgerton, David 117, 144
Edward VIII 150
Edward Watkin, fictional (and
    non-fictional) character in *Coming Up
    for Air* 124
Egypt 21
Ekevall, Kay 223
Elgar, Edward 123
Eliot, T. S. 130, 146, 169, 170
Elizabeth Lackersteen, fictional character in
    Burmese Days 23, 201
Ellesmere Road, fictional (and non-fictional)
    road in *Coming Up for Air* 109, 119,
    267 n. 43
embourgeoisified 176
Emergency Powers (Defence) Act
    (1939) 138
Empson, William 146
Engels, Friedrich 96, 97
England, north and south 48–9, 121–5, 234;
    starvation in the south 124
English Constitution [The] 151
English history, liberal view 183
English nation 3–4, 128–9
English Social History 129
Englishman and his History [The] 185
Englishness, guardians 6; riddle 9;
    of the left 145, 150–2, 153, 156,
    158–9, 163–4, 229–30, 278 n. 123;
    of the right 102–3, 160–1, 165;
    southern iconic 122–3; modern
    renaissance 148; conservation and
    development 124; liberal 182–5;
    cultural 230; new academic
    interest 234
Enright, D. J. 228

Epsom Derby 41
Esperantism 91, 210
Estcourt Avenue, Headingley, Leeds 69
Essex Road, Islington 147
Eton Boating Song 13
Eton College 13–15
European Coal and Steel Community 202
European Commission 219
European futures, in 1945 202
European Union 234
Evening Standard [*The*] 114, 147, 148, 153

Faber, publishers 169
Fabian Society 146, 182
fags 13
Falklands War 234
Fallada, Hans 215
Falmer, University of Sussex 218
Farson, Daniel 218
Faulkner, William 83
Featherstone 229
Federal Bureau of Investigation (FBI) 232
feminism 221
Festival of Britain 178, 219, 233
Fierz, Mabel 245 n. 107
Fields, Gracie 56
fifth columnists 173
Filloy, Richard 222
Finest Hour 180
fish 229
flaneurs 113–14
Fleet Street 48
'Flip', fictional character in 'Such, Such
    were the Joys' 200
Fontana Modern Masters 5
Foot, Michael 147
football 176
Foreign Office 173, 201
foreign policy 181
Formby, George 56
Forster E. M. 15, 146
Fortnightly 98
Foucault, Michel 192
France 202
Franco, General Francisco 85, 87, 89, 145
Frankford F. A. 84
Frankfurter Zeitung 221
Free Trade 183
Freedom Defence Committee 182
French left 91
French Morocco 28, 126

French positivism 66
French Revolution 209
friendly societies 56
Fry, Roger 148
Fyvel, Tosco 146, 221, 223

Gaitskell, Hugh 61
Gandhi, M. K. 16, 20, 22, 26–7, 28
garden cities 123
Gasset, José Ortega y 126
Gaulle, Charles de 202
Geddes, Sir Patrick 118
Gellhorn, Martha 83
general elections 103, 140, 177
General Strike 30, 46, 103
genocide 25–6, 243 n. 71
gentlemanliness 42–3, 113–17, 120–1, 132
George, Henry 184
George Orwell Productions 205, 218
Germany 201, 202
Gervais, David 5
Gilliat, Sidney 182
Gillray, John 156
Glasgow 204
globalization 234
Glorious Revolution 183
Gloucestershire 204
Goldring, Douglas 98
Goldthorpe, J. H. 230
Gollancz, Victor 48, 58, 98, 104, 137, 146,
    149, 169
Gorer, Geoffey 57, 127, 135, 149, 199
Gordon Comstock, fictional character in
    Keep the Aspidistra Flying 37–40, 44,
    247 n. 119
Gottlieb, Erika 221
Government of India Act 22
Graham, Helen 90
grammar schools 117
Gramsci, Antonio 11
Grant, Duncan 148
Grapes of Wrath [*The*] 83
Gray, John 235
Great Reform Act 183
Greece 172
Green, J. R. 185
Green, Martin 5
Green, T. H. 185
Green Belt (London and Home Counties)
    Act (1938) 119
Greene, Grahame 28, 40, 146

Greenwood, Walter 98
Gresford, colliery disaster 47
Grey family, Barnsley, *The Road to Wigan Pier* 70–1
Grimethorpe 58, 70
Guadalajara, Battle of 90
Guillotine 162
gulag 92, 171
Gulliver's Travels 169
Gurkhas 21

Hacha, Emil 135
Hale, Sir Matthew 159
Hamlet 150
Hammond, J. L. and B. 185
Hammond, J. R. 5
Hampstead 197
Hampstead Garden Suburb 223
Hanley 48
Harcourt and Brace, publishers 169
Hard Times 162
Harris, Alexandra 3
Harrison, Brian 233
Harrisson, Tom 57
Hayek, Friedrich von 179, 186
Hayes 34, 35, 152
Hazlitt, William 81
Headingley, Leeds 69
Hearst, William Randolph 82
Heffer, Simon 235
Hegel's dialectic 96–7
Hemingway, Ernest 82–3, 101, 201
Hendon Labour party 223
Henley on Thames 11, 12, 108, 121
Henriques, Fernando 229
Heppenstall, Rayner 146, 204, 221
Hertfordshire 72, 107, 113
Hertfordshire Appeal for Co Durham 56
highbrows 115
Hilda Bowling, fictional character in *Coming Up for Air* 110, 111, 115–16, 118, 119, 120, 201
Hindswaraj 16
Historical Materialism 95
History of Mr Polly [*The*] 114
Hitchens, Christopher 5, 231, 235
Hitler, Adolf 202, 233
Hobhouse, L. T. 183, 185
Hobson, J. A. 26, 82, 123
Hoggart, Richard 229

Holborn Empire 155
Hollis, Christopher 225
Hollywood 207–8
Holocaust 229
Home Counties 48, 122
Home Guard 148
Home Office 145
Home Rule 103
homosexuals 180, 251 n. 54
Homo Sovieticus 96
Hopkinson, Tom 4, 153, 226
Horizon 147, 204
Hotel Florida, Madrid 83
Hotel Scribe, Paris 83
housing boom 119
Housman, A. E. 130
Houyhnhnms 169, 170
Howe, Irving 229
Hsaya San rebellion, Burma 23
Huddersfield 229
Huesca 98
Hughes, Thomas 159
Hull 229
human nature 12, 95–6, 144, 156, 180, 224
humanities, knowledge 6
Hungary 219, 232
Hunslet 229
Hunter, Lynette 222
Hurricane, fighter aircraft 139
Huxley, Aldous 217
Hymns Ancient and Modern 186

I Lived in a Slum 189
identity 6–7
Imagined Communities 230
Imperialism 123
Independent Labour Party 8, 47, 64, 72; Glasgow POUM Defence Committee 80; manifesto against war 134–5
India, rupee against the pound 11; *Raj*, size, governance, and jurisdiction 16–21, 25–6; warrants of precedence 17, 21; class structure 17; 'Mutiny' 19, 25; civil service 19–20, 23; dominion status 20; army, 21; white women 23; census 1881 25; independence 28, 153, 233; British national identity 240 n. 35, 241 nn. 45, 47

Indian National Congress 17, 20, 26
Industrial Revolution 46, 47, 50, 233
industrial working class 175–6
INGSOC, fictional English Socialism
    party in *Nineteen Eighty-Four* 181–2,
    210, 212–13, 215, 216
intellectuals, technical and scientific 145
inter-war building boom 119
International Brigades 77, 87, 90;
    British battalion 88, and
    executions 94
Irrawaddy, River 18, 24
Isherwood, Christopher 102
Isoniazid 218

Jackson, Brian 229
Jackson, Lydia 146, 198, 200
Jacobins, in Charles Dickens' *A Tale of Two
    Cities* 162
Jarama, Battle of 88, 90
Jarrow Marchers 71
Jay, Douglas 61
Jellinek, Frank 98, 102
Jennings, Humphrey 57, 139, 182
Jefferies, Richard 165
Jews 133
John Flory, fictional character in *Burmese
    Days* 4, 23, 24, 26, 27, 37, 38, 40,
    44, 128
Johnson, Dr 189
Joppen's map, of Burma 18
journalism, American and British
    81–3, 231
Joyce, James 36, 158, 167
Joyce, Patrick 15
Julia, fictional character in *Nineteen
    Eighty-Four* 208, 209, 214–16
Jura, Hebrides 167, 203, 218

Kamenev, Lev 93
Karl Marx Allee, East Berlin 202
Keane, Nigel 228
Keeble, Richard 80
Kensal Rise 41
Kenya 25
Kerr, Madeline 229
Keynes, J. M. 15, 104–5, 158, 185
Kies, Daniel 222
King's College, Cambridge 15
Kipling, Rudyard 27, 82, 159

Ko S'la, fictional character in *Burmese
    Days* 27
Koestler, Arthur 146, 174, 179, 221, 224
Kolakowski, Leszek 220, 233, 297 n. 17
Kopp, Georges 78, 79, 80, 94
Korean War 172, 232
Krushchev, N. 219
Kyauktada, fictional town in *Burmese
    Days* 23

L'Ami du Peuple 33
La Batalla 78
Labour governments 46, 103, 172–82;
    support within and without party 173,
    176, 181;
    swing against 177
labour movement 175–6
Labour party 56, 61, 66, 230;
    standing for the nation 139–40, 175–6
Labour party conference, at
    Scarborough 175
labour value 60;
    and surplus 96
Laidler, Graham 126
Lake District 49
Lambeth Palace 48
Lancashire 49, 55, 86
Lancashire Steel Corporation 50
Langham, Essex 64, 124
Language, Truth and Logic 211
Lansbury, George 105
lardy cake 125
Larkin, Philip 146, 228, 300 n. 64
Laski, Harold 104, 157
Lasswell, Harold 82
Launder, Frank 182
Lawrence, D. H. 114, 124, 130
Lawrence, T. E. 28
Laws of Motion 96
Lawther, Will 175
Le Trahison des clercs 106
League of Youth 55
Lean, David 182
Left Book Club 48, 56, 83, 98, 104, 105–6,
    157, 227
Left News 149
left patriotism 233, 234–5
Lenin Barracks 72, 73
Lenin Division 73, 78
Leninism 55, 77, 91, 182

Lerida 77
Letchworth, Herts 64, 124, 152
Lévi-Strauss, Claude 22
Lewis, Wyndham 226
liberalism, sceptical of state 183–5
Liberal party 103
Light, Alison 188
Limouzin, Nellie 91
Linlithgow, Lord 19–20
Lippman, Walter 82
Little Dorritt 162
Liverpool 59
living tradition 129, 184–5, 223
Llobregat 88
Lloyd George, David 134
Lockwood, David 230
Look Back in Anger 230
London commuters 116
London crowd 184
London fire crews 154, 182
London, Jack 32, 179
London Midland Scottish Railway 50
London, north 40, 145
London 2012 Olympiad 234
London Passenger Transport Authority 61
London, regional dominance 48, 122
London suburbs, Wembley, Harrow, Ruislip,
    Northwood, Uxbridge 109; and
    building legislation 119
London, west 109
Lothar, Hans 221
Lower Binfield, fictional town
    (Henley-on-Thames) in *Coming Up for
    Air* 110–11, 121, 123, 124, 125, 128
Luton, 230
Lyons, Eugene 91
Lyttelton, Revd E., headmaster Eton
    College 13

Ma Hla May, fictional character in *Burmese
    Days* 27
Macaulay, T. B. 19
Macdonald, Dwight 229
Macdonald, Ramsay 61, 103
machines 66
Madge, Charles 57
Madrid 76, 77, 88, 99
magic tablecloths 173
Magna Carta 183
Mais, S. P. B. 49
malnutrition 52
Malraux, André 201

Malthus, T. R. 215
Manchester 48, 51, 62
Manchester Chamber of Commerce 18
Manchester Evening News 147
Manchester Guardian 82, 98, 127,
    223, 227
Mandalay 18, 19
Mannoni, Octave 27
Mansfield, Lord 159
Maori 25
Marcuse, Herbert 232
Margate 110
markets 176
Marrakech, French Morocco 109,
    135, 191
Marsden, Dennis 229
Marshall Aid 172, 181, 201–2
Martin, Kingsley 84, 147
Marx, Karl 215; as a dog 97;
    as a pig 170
Marxism 65, 94–9
Marxist historians 97
Marylebone Cricket Club 48
Mass Observation 56, 57
masses, the 82, 83, 111–12
Masterman C. F. G. 126
Maus 229
Mauser rifle 76
Mayhew, Henry 32
McCarthy, Joseph 219
McCarthy, Mary 232
McEwan, Ian 231
McKibbin, Ross 139
McNair, John 79
Meade, Frank 51–2, 62
Mearns, Andrew 32
Mellor, Ann 221
Melville, Herman 144
Memphis, TN 219
Menand, Louis 225
Merleau-Ponty, Maurice 204
mess 49–50
Methodist men's meeting (The
    Brotherhood) 55
'Metroland' 109
Meyers, Jeffrey 205, 226
middle class 71, 218; and types of middle
    class-ness 112–13; salaries and
    qualifications of new middle class 117;
    social and geographic mobility 118;
    geographic concentration 122;
    technical and scientific 145

Middlesbrough 48
Miles, Hamish 98
Millenium Dome 233
Miller, Henry 4, 45, 50, 52, 54, 69, 72, 83,
    131–2, 133, 143–4, 155, 158
Miller, Max 155
Miners' Federation of Great Britain 56
miners' unions 46–7, 219
Ministry of Food 146
Ministry of Information 138, 145,
    154, 169
Modern Literary Association 2
Modernism 148, 178
Mogey, John 229
Monde 32
Morning Post 82
Mortimer Crescent, Kilburn 146
Morton, H. V. 49, 51
Morris, William 66, 123
Morrison, Herbert 172, 176, 177, 178
Moscovitas 88
Moscow premier 173
Moscow show trials 93, 105
Mosley, Oswald 64, 70, 120, 189
'Mother of Parliaments' 183
Moulmein 21
'Movement', The, 228, 231
Moya, Ana 221
Mr MacGregor, fictional character in
    Burmese Days 27
Mr Warburton, fictional character in
    A Clergyman's Daughter 27
Mrs Creevey, fictional character in
    A Clergyman's Daughter 36, 200
Mrs Pither, fictional character in *A Clergyman's
    Daughter* 36
Muggeridge, Malcolm 127, 146, 217, 218,
    224, 226
multiculturalism 234
Munich agreement (1938) 134, 199,
    271 n. 16
Mussolini, Benito 134
Mutually Assured Destruction, nuclear
    doctrine 219
Mysterious Mr Bull [*The*] 226

Nash, John 148
National Geographic Magazine 49
National government 1931
National Health Service 218
National Unemployed Workers' Movement
    (NUWM) 52, 54–5, 105, 161

National Union of Mineworkers 175
nationalization 61
Nazi plebiscites 133–4
Negrin, Juan 76, 78, 86, 88, 90, 94
Nevinson, Henry 82
New College Oxford 104
New English Weekly 85
New Labour 219
New Leader 8, 75, 134
New Liberalism 183, 185
New Republic 98
New Statesman and Nation 33, 36, 84, 98, 121,
    147, 181
New York Times 36
New Yorker 4
Newcastle upon Tyne 65, 197
Newman, John Henry 66
News From Nowhere 123
Newsom, John 56
Nin, Andres 78, 90–1
'9/11' 231
'No Bullshit Brigade' 231
Non-Aggression Pact, Germany and USSR
    (1939) 138
Nonconformist Conscience 183
North American Newspaper Alliance 83
North Atlantic Treaty Organization
    (NATO) 172, 231
Northcliffe, Alfred, Lord 82
Notes Towards the Definition of Culture 180
Nuremburg 201

O'Brien, fictional character in *Nineteen
    Eighty-Four* 207
O'Shaughnessy, Eileen (Eileen Blair) 47,
    76, 78–9, 97, 113, 136, 145, 146, 147,
    186, 197–201; and his writing 197–9;
    with Richard 199; and London
    life 200; death 198, 200; 291–3 nn. 3,
    7, 17, 24, 33
O'Shaughnessy, Gwen, at Greenwich 146;
    family property at Greystones,
    N. Yorks 199
O'Shaughnessy, Laurence, brother-in-law
    141, 142, 200, 202
Oakeshott, Michael 194, 195, 235
Oastler, Richard 190
Observer [*The*] 146, 147, 167, 190
'Old Corruption' 190
Old 'Daddy' 43
Old Porteous, fictional character in *Coming
    Up for Air* 120–1, 124

Orwell Archive 205
Orwell for Beginners 223
Orwell Fund 235
Orwell, George *and*:
Abdication, Edward VIII 150
abstraction 11, 96, 106–7
addresses 275 n. 65, 276 n. 80
aesthetics 3
aggression 226
air raid shelter 198
allegory 171
American book sales 169
American contemporaries 82–4
American left intellectuals 228–9
American politicians 181, 219
American right 231, 232
American violence 167
andro-centrism 221
Animal Farm, English and not English 170
anti-Auden 99–102
anti-British Empire 220
anti-Communist 10, 84–91, 100–1, 172,
    188, 226, 232
anti-Englishness 207–10
anti-Fascist 72–9
anti-Freudian 222
anti-intellectuals 222, 223;
    and denial 273 n. 42
anti-imperialist proto-feminist 221
anti-imperialist misogynist 221
anti-Marxist 94–9
anti-politics 230
anti-Semitic 118, 214, 220–1, 227;
    pro-Jewish 221; 296 nn. 4, 8, 9
anti-Soviet 91–4, 169–70, 232
anti-prep school 226
anti-women 200–1, 221–2
anti-Zionist 221
antithetical 10, 39, 45, 219, 220–1, 230
appeaser 132;
    anti-appeaser 229
apple dumplings 166
Aragon Front 76
army intelligence 201
aspidistras 37
assassination 167
atheism 187–8, 225–6
atomic war 203, 209, 218
Auden, W. H. 99–102, 106
August bathing 167
bad taste 155

Barcelona 201, 223
barmaids 141, 166
Barnet 152
Barnhill, Jura 203, 204
Barnsley 201
BBC 106, 144, 194, 227, 228; in and
    out 145–6; pay 147; not
    censorious 173; hagiographical
    226–7; and becoming a national
    figure 228, 264 n. 145, 275 nn. 66–8,
    282 n. 5
beasts of England, fictional proletariat in
    Animal Farm 170
bed-ridden and sanatoria 11, 138, 167,
    180, 203, 217, 246 n. 108, 265 n. 1
beetles 39, 51, 60, 214
beliefs 2–3, 86–7, 125, 128, 144, 145,
    172–5, 180, 187, 195, 225–6
'belly-to-earth' attitudes 45, 125, 144, 191,
    216, 218
Benda, Julien 106
Bennett, Arnold 115
Bernal, J. D. 180
Bevan, Aneurin 146, 174, 175, 176, 177;
    admired by Orwell 178–9
Bevan wing of the Labour party 228
Big Brother, fictional fictional character in
    Nineteen Eighty-Four 213, 216
'big-dipper' singing 37
Billy Bunter and his pals 160, 161, 170
'Bill Sikes', fictional character in Charles
    Dickens'*Oliver Twist* 162
biographers 226
Black Spring 45
'Blimps' 144, 148, 194
bodies, and facial marks 201
bombed-out 146
Book Lover's Corner 35
book reviewing 80, 84, 98; theatre
    reviewing 141
bourgeois, anti-bourgeois 69, 112
'Boxer', fictional horse in *Animal Farm* 170
boys' comics, *Gem, Magnet, Triumph,
    Champion, Rover, Skipper* 159;
    Beano 160, 165; mental world 160–1,
    167, 194
'Bozo', fictional character in *Down and Out in
    Paris and London* 222
British, and English people 107, 108, 129,
    141, 148, 150, 182, 192, 229, 233
British cookery 167

British Empire 15–28, 173, 220, 232
British nation-state 149–50, 172–3, 182–3, 187, 193–4, 195
Brooker family, Wigan, *The Road to Wigan Pier* 60, 63
Brotherhood, fictional organization in *Nineteen Eighty-Four* 215
Brownell, Sonia 204–5
burial 217
Burma 16, 21–8, 106, 191
capitalism 10, 37, 153, 180, 186, 190, 193, 201, 232
cartoons 155
Catalans 74, 86
character 233
'Chavs' 301 n. 76
Chesterton, G. K. 71, 82, 101, 143, 185
childhood 12, 103
Christianity 225–6
Church of England 5–6, 144, 186–8, 201
Churchill, W. S. 180, 226
cigarettes, 36, 147, 203; roll ups 190
civil society 174, 208–9, 211
classes 63, 112–21, 152, 168
class sex theme 163–4
classics 13, 121, 226
climate 167
'Clover', fictional horse in *Nineteen Eighty-Four* 170
clutter 166
coal-face 57–61
Cobbett, W. 143
Colchester 209
Cold War 188
Collected Essays, Letters, and Journalism, ed. Angus and Orwell 205, 231
Common, Jack 65–6, 134
common culture 66, 155, 208–9
common folk 159
common law 158–9, 183, 208–9
common language 158, 208–9
common sense 159, 211
common sense histories 211
common toads 166
Communism, as 'Animalism' 169
Communist front organizations 105, 173
Conrad, Joseph 115
conscientious objection 132
conservative modernity 188, 231
Conservative party 188–9, 195

conservatism 144, 171, 179, 180, 188–96, 209, 223; American and East European neo-conservatism and liberalism 225, 229, 232
constitutionalism 151, 183, 188, 209
contrarian 1–3, 9; as a 'scrub' 8–15, 140, 142–3, 179–80, 187–8, 189, 220, 222, 226, 227
conventions 224
corporal 76
'country party' 190
Cox's orange pippins 167
cranks 63–4, 67, 182
cricket 166, 194
Critical Essays 229
critical moments 29, 72, 99–100, 132, 141–2, 144, 147, 171, 195, 203
Crucifixion 14
cup of tea 166, 192, 217
Dagenham 110, 152
death 203–5, and burial 217
'death stoppage' 185
decadence 51
deceived and deceiving, non-deceived and non-deceiving: Gordon Comstock deceived 44; role of intellectuals 84, 108, 212, 215, 219, 231; and the press 83, 87; Orwell *not* deceived—by the USSR 91, 93, or by Marxism 95–7, but Orwell deceived (in part) by his country 29, in Spain 79–80, 85–6, over Czechoslovakia 134–5, by approaching war 136–7, 140–1, and by POUM revolutionary strategy 85–6, 138; W. H. Auden not deceived 100–2; the left deceived 105–6; Old Porteous deceived 121; George Bowling not deceived 125–6, 129; the masses not deceived 127–9, 154; Ernest Bevin not deceived 177; INGSOC deceiving itself 211–13; Orwell's reputation in these matters, 222, 228, 231; Priestley and Steinbeck deceived 173–4; Webbs deceived 260 n. 91; Shaw deceived 95, 259 n. 90; Larkin one of the less deceived 228, 302 n. 87; Hitchens and others too 231, 302 n. 86
democratic socialism 10, 182, 233

deracination and displacement 44, 64, 103, 147, 148, 159, 207–9
Dickens, Charles 162–4, 194; free spirit 170; freethinking 185
diet 54, 167, 182
Dissent 186
Dorothy Hare, fictional character in *A Clergyman's Daughter* 186–7, 201
doublethink 136, 195, 212
dreams 141–2;
    sleepwalking 223
economics 185, 186
Edward Watkin, fictional (and non-fictional) character in *Coming Up for Air* 124
Eliot, T. S. 180
Elizabeth Lackersteen, fictional character in *Burmese Days* 201
Emmanuel Goldstein, fictional fictional character in *Nineteen Eighty-Four* 215
empirical verification 208–9, 211–12, 213
England 121–5; feelings for 141–7; feelings without 205–8; war and post-war 206–7
England, looked at from abroad 127, 190–1, 206
English accents 168
English folk 124, 158, 170, 213, 214
English history 182–8, 208–9
English people 148, 182–3, 189, 195; and British 107, 150; change and stay the same 151, 152–3, 194; a family 153, 194; vulgar 155; immovable 155–6, 194; gentle 168, 226; freeborn 170; and getting freer 183; socialistic 190; conservative 191; commitment 196, abandonment 207; noticed and not noticed 226
English Toryism 97, 103, 188–96, 224
Englishness 1–2, 3–7, 9, 16–17, 39, 44, 59–60, 103, 107, 112, 121–5, 127, 128–9, 143–4, 148, 162–8, 194, 196; powerfully re-interpreted by him 148–71, 188, 191, 229, 234; but untypical 206; organic 158, 209; in Dickens, Kipling, and Wodehouse 162–6; in shorter pieces 166–7; in *The English People* 168; as socialist, liberal, and Tory hybrid 191; Orwell reconciled 206; personally meaningful 234

ephemera 190
epiphanies, at the coal face 58, and elsewhere 141–2, 143
Eric Blair 41–5, 98, 111, 118
Eton College 13–15, 102, 106, 144, 148, 195;
Eton Collegers Dinner 161
Evelyn's School 34–5
everyday life 11, 12, 15, 103, 133, 146
existential questions 41, 126, 128, 130–2, 143–4, 160, 193–4, 216, 225
family saga, unwritten 149
famine 199
Fascism 10, 89–91; anti-Fascism 120; in Britain 135, 140
Feuerbachian 226
fillers 58
finance capitalism 218
financial security 202
firesides 167
first-person, writing 194
fishing 133, 203
Flip, fictional character in 'Such, Such were the Joys' 200
football 55, 102
Fray's School 34–5
freethinking 185, 187;
    free speech 194
French publications and translator 42
Freudian, with maternal, Oedipal, sadomasochistic, 'Trotskyesque', Marxian, Adlerian, psycho-historical, and Aspergerian themes 222–3
friends, comrades, acquaintances 29, 35, 36, 47, 52, 53, 59, 77, 79, 81, 85, 86, 93–4, 127, 189, 190, 200, 203, 204; in London, including Old Etonians, Adelphians, and Southwoldians 146–7, 195; Jewish 221;
    female 221; intellectual 222; distinguished 227; faithful 228
Galsworthy, John 115
George Bowling, character in *Coming Up for Air* 111–12; class-less 113; class as a performance 113–14; implausible 118; and England's future 121, 125, 129; northern and southern qualities 126, not deceived 125–9; not easily

'placed' 126, 128; like Orwell 126, 128; like 'you', like 'us' 127; of his time 128; quietist 133; autobiographical 136; wants it both ways 137
general elections 103, 140, 177
generalizations, rash 225
gentlemanliness 43, 115
gloomy 41
Glyn, Elinor 115
goodness and virtue 228
'governmentality' 191
'Greyfriars', fictional public school 161
grocer 72, 73
Hammersmith 168
Hayek, Friedrich von 186
Hayes 152
health and treatment 147, 154, 172, 197, 203, 293–4 n. 34; sanatoria 126, 167, 180, 182, 203, 204; a 'good chronic' 205, 217
Henley-on-Thames 121
high-brows 148
Hilda Bowling, fictional character in *Coming Up for Air* 201
Hitler, Adolf 101, 133–5, 140, 220; Cpl Schicklgruber 156
Hocking, Silas 115
Holocaust 221
home, returning to it 121, 126, 127
home cooking 52, 166, 167, 194
Home Guard (Local Defence Volunteers) 140, 141, 145
homosexuality 102
hop-picking 37
Hope, Anthony 115
Hospital Cochin 33–4
hotel dishwashing 60
humanism, anti-humanism 225
'iconic' 226
idealism 211
identities 41–5, 127–9; transmuted 145; transformed 152–3
ideology 10–11; end of 138; Carlist, Jesuist, Falangiste, Nazi, Communist ideologies 157; free from 178, 189, 195, 206
Imperial Police 15, 17–18, 21–3, 106
imperialism, anti-imperialism 10, 25–8, 37, 132, 140, 144, 185, 188, 220

income tax 153
Independent Labour Party (ILP) 89–90; manifesto against war 134; moral equivalence with Germany 134–5; Orwell's departure 138; reverses his opinion 140–1, 175
Indian independence 153
individualism and collectivism 186–7
infidelity 199, 204–5
INGSOC, English Socialist Party 206, 208, 210–11, 213, 214, 216
inheritors, those who felt closest 228–33
insurance, white collar occupation 112
intellectuals 9, 11, 40, 41–2, 44, 55, 59, 63–4, 67, 71, 83, 84, 97, 100, 104–6, 132, 172–3, 211, 212; anti-intellectualism 106, 111–12, 114–15, 141, 145, 166, 170, 178, 179–80, 182, 194, 196, 211; and denial of it 273 n. 42
Israel 221
Jane Eyre, fictional character in Charlotte Bronte's *Jane Eyre* 186
Jews 214, 220–1
John Flory, Dorothy Hare, Gordon Comstock, early fictional characters 36–40, 44, 128, 155, 186–7
journalism 79–84, 97, 98–9, 100, 197
Joyce, James 158
Julia, fictional character in *Nineteen Eighty-Four* 215–16, 221
junk 166
Jura, Hebridean island 203–4
Kensington 168
Keynesian 132
Kipling, Rudyard 115, 194; like Orwell 164–5
kippers 166
'kips' 34, including 'the rope' 185
labour movement 56, 102, 174
Labour party 61, 89, 102–3, 135–6, 190; Labour supporter and critic 172–82, 219, 223; and 'third way' 181
labour value 60
ladies' social 54, 141, 142–3
Lancashire and Yorkshire 74, 86
language 157, 168, 194, 207–10
'Last Man in Europe' [The] 203
Lee & Perrin's sauce 198

[the] left 68, 89, 90, 101, 103–4, 132, 137, 172, 179
left and national culture 229, 233
left and left in Spanish politics 88
left and right, and left to right, in politics 9, 86, 87, 104, 174, 179–80, 191, 228, 229
Letchworth, Herts 152
letters to Eileen 200, 293 n. 24
liberal 174, 183–4; not a liberal, or a Liberal, or a New Liberal 185, and neo-conservativism 225, 229
life, a failure 130–1; rising expectations 146, 172
literary realism 161
living tradition 129, 151–3, 183–5, 187, 190–1, 209–11, 223–4
local cultures ('little platoons') 90, 96, 140, 143, 144, 177, 182–3, 188, 190–1, 194, 209
lodgings 48, 60
London County Council 34
London, policies and financial markets 116–17
London gossip 227
London left 102, 104,120, 182, 223, 228
London, peaceful 116, 121–2, linked to Henley on Thames 121; ordinary 124–5; Soho and Fitzrovia 147, 182; pleasures 200
Lord Mauleverer, fictional character in 'Billy Bunter' 161
Lower Binfield, fictional town (Henley-on-Thames) in *Coming Up for Air* 110
loyalties 74, 86, 94, 172
Mackenzie, Compton 115
March winds 167
Margate 110
Marrakech, French Morocco 191, 197, 199
marriage 71, 197
'Marx', their dog 97
Marxism 10, 91, 97, 211, 232
masculinity 120–1, 200, 201
masses 39, 50–1, 109–12, 115
'material culture' 191
mathematical axioms 212–13
Maugham, Somerset 241 n. 108
Meade family, Manchester, *The Road to Wigan Pier* 51–2

'Merrie England' 124
metaphors 170
'middlebrow' literature 115
middle class 68; income 192–3; new middle class 107, 'techno-class' 195, 215–16; old and new middle class 112–13, at war 145, 152; as pigs 170; old middle class 192–3
Midsummer Eve 170
military virtues 140–1, 170
mill girls 46
Miller, Henry 45, 52, 131–2, 133, 138, 143, 159
Miller, Max 155
Milton, John 190
miners 50, 53, 57–60, 74, 103
Minister of Culture 235
Ministry of Truth, fictional government agency in *Nineteen Eighty-Four* 208
misanthropic 36, 38–40
misogyny 221, 227
modernism, 3, 33, 34, 116; and anti-modernism 225
moral rectitude 226
mouldy potatoes 199
Mrs Creevy, fictional character in *A Clergyman's Daughter* 201
Mrs Gamp, fictional character in Charles Dickens' *Martin Chuzzlewit* 162
muffins 166
murder, English style 167, 194
myth-making 188
name change, Blair's 41
'Napoleon', fictional pig in *Animal Farm* 170
narodnik tendencies 70
National Coal Board 175
National Health Service 175
national importance 227, 228
national types 4, 108
nationalism 9, 10, 144
nationalization 153
natural self 216
Navy League 161
Nazis 213
New Left 231; not so 'New' 233
News of the World 167
Newspeak 210–11
'1910' illusions 161
noms des plumes 41

northern England 56, 60, 71, 122
Observer [*The*] 190
Old 'Daddy' 43
Old Left 231
Old Porteous, fictional character in *Coming Up for Air* 121, 124
Old Major, fictional pig in *Animal Farm* 170
open fires 166, 167
ordinariness 158, 168, 182–3, 188, 190–1, 194
'Orwell' as an identity 41–2, 68; essential and complete 226, 228
pacifism 106, 120, 132, 136–7; critique 140, 232
pamphleteers 186
parliament 144
pastries 167
penny knowledge 166
personal restraint 167, 200
Peters brothers 81
philosophy, and anti-philosophy 194, 196, 225
photograph 197
pigs 169, 170, 232
plain speaking, and not plain speaking 222
playing, with Richard 203
pneumonia 33, 35
poetry 98–9, 101, 102, 130, 194
policy 175
politics and anti-politics 136, 143–4, 182–8, 190, 192–3
political parties 103, 172, 183
Popular Front 86, 105, 120, 159
Porter, Gene Stratton 115
postcards 154–6, 170, 194
post modernism 3
POUM line 84–91, in Britain 135–8; anti-POUM line in Britain 140
Pound, Ezra 180
PPE (Philosophy, Politics, Economics), Oxford University course 185
preparatory schools 12, 34, 35, 181
prejudices 192–3, 204
Priestley, J. B. 82, 101, 173
privacy 6, 70, 200, 208
progress 132, 183
proles 213–14, 216
propagandists 172–3
Protestants 186–8, 195, 225
prudishness 200
public ownership 181–2
public school mores, in comics 160

pubs 166, 194; 'Moon Under Water' 167
queer theory 231
quietism 131–2
Ragged Trousered Philanthropist [*The*] 180
rats 52, 223
Ravelston, fictional character in *Keep the Aspidistra Flying* 189
Reade, Charles 166
rebel 14, 15–16, 81, 97, 126, 140, 180, 187–9, 216, 222, 225–6, 228
Rees, Richard 189
regions 168
Report of the Burma Police Enquiry 224
repressive tolerance, theory 232
reputation 2, 14–15, 146–7, 169–70, 199, 203; wide range of opinions 226–7; in a different age 227, 228–35; as one of the Less Deceived, a Crystal Spirit, Fugitive from Camp of Victory, Age's Adversary, Wintry Conscience, saint, knight, champion, hero, victor, mystic, true patriot, plain speaker, great writer, moral force, good man, straight as an arrow, and National Treasure 235
revolution 74–7, 79, 81, 86, 87, 91, 121; 'Red Militias' 137–8; part of national character 151, 152–3, 183, 189; inevitable failure 169–70, 175; Labour's success 172; and counter-revolutionary radicals 190 riding a bicycle 65
Roman Catholic intellectuals 186
Roman Catholicism 10
Room 101, fictional room in *Nineteen Eighty-Four* 216
Royal Marines 142
rue du Coq d'Or 33
rue de la Montagne St-Geneviève 220
ruling class, potentially Fascist 135
Russian Revolution 169
sadism, sado-masochism 200, 221, 222
sailors 194
sainthood 226, 228
salvation 186, 225
Salvation Army 34
Sam Weller, fictional character in Charles Dickens' *The Pickwick Papers* 162
Sartre, J. P. 106, 180, 225
Schadenfreude 201
scholarships 12, 13, 15

scientific laws 211–12
Scots 5
Searchlight Books 221
Searle family, Sheffield, *The Road to Wigan Pier* 69
secularization 218–19
security services 107, 172–3, 264 n. 151, 282 n. 3
self-understanding 6, 125–9, 144; self-destruction 68–9; self-destruction and deception 212
semi-detached houses 109, 119
'semi-sociological' studies 229
sex 27, 33, 38, 147, 163–4, 199, 200, 204, 213, 216, 221, 222, 230, 292 n. 16
Sheffield 52, 69
shooting, an elephant 21–2, 77–8
shooting, rabbits 203
shot, in the throat 77–8, 198
silly song 142–3
Slough 152
slums 63–4, 214
smells and dirt 51, 62–3, 67, 69, 73, 75, 101, 110, 165, 192, 207, 223, 251 n. 60
snobbery 14, 15, 31, 35, 37, 62, 63, 74, 81
socialism 61–4, 66–9, 132, 153–4, 172, 182, 223–4; anti-socialism 179–80, 192; equality 174, 182, 185; statist and non-statist 174–5; and the life of the people 190, 195; as charity 193
sociological studies, in work and community 229–30
soldiering in Spain 8, 74–6, 167, 198
solipsism 211
southern England 121–5
Southwold 116
Soviet Union 169, 201
Spanish Civil War, 72–9; encounters 80–1; unrealistic assessment 89–90, 94; instructive 100–1, 106–7, 126, 169, 191, 223
Spender, Stephen 100, 106, 130
sport 13
spying and treachery 78–9, 85, 94
St Cyprian's 181
St Jim's, fictional public school 161
St Pancras railway station 214
Stalin, Joseph, as 'Big Brother' 213

starvation 33, 131–2
state intervention, for and against 174, 183–4, 208–10, 223
Stilton cheese 167
street communities, of women 56
structuralism 192
suburbs 34, 103, 109; conurbations 110; prejudice against 118; positive aspects 119; without tradition 123; with tradition 152; and women 201
Sunday roast 167
Swift, Jonathan 183, 189, 194
synecdoche 190
[as a] teacher 81
television adaptation of *Nineteen Eighty-Four* (1954) 228
temperament 189–90, 194
Tennyson, Alfred Lord 186
theology 186, 187
Theory and Practice of Oligarchical Collectivism, fictional fictional book in *Nineteen Eighty-Four* 215
'thought crime' 209–10, 211
tobacconists 219, 289 n. 102
totalitarianism 9, 83, 179, 228, 232
tramping 31, 33, 106
treacle tart 166
Tressell, Robert 180
Tribune 147, 174, 181
Tropic of Cancer 45, 131
trust in each other 129, 172–3, 212
truth (and hope) 215–16
tuberculosis (TB) 130, 132, 186, 203
turbulence, lack of 141; no shortage 142
unemployed 48, 52
United States of Europe 202
universalism 95, 191
university 15
upper class 150
Vatican 84
Vietnam War 229
'Voice of the People' 136, 141
volunteers for forces 140
war 116, 120, 129; anti-war 132–8; pro-war 138–41; war diaries 132, 141; personal toll 202–3
war correspondent (*The Observer*) 201
wedding, to Eileen 197; to Sonia 204
welfare dependency 230
Welfare State 154

Wells H. G. 106, 115, 179
Westminster politics 233
Whiteways Anarchist Commune 182
Wigan 46–69, and its pier 47; housing and
women's lives 51–3, 62; lessons 79,
108, 126, 141, 201
Wigan girl, with stick 51–2, 270 n. 83
Wilde, Oscar 115, 180
will and testament 204
Winston Smith, fictional character in
Nineteen Eighty-Four 207, 214
Winter 167
Wodehouse, P. G. 165–6
women 9, 29–30, 54, 70, 119–20, 141,
199, 200–1, 214, 215–16, 221–2,
231, 248 n. 8
Woolworth's roses 182
working-class people 12, 47, 50–1, 53,
54–5, 56, 59–60, 61, 62–3, 67,
69–71, 74, 79, 131, 152, 170; and
patriotism 138, 141–2; regenerative
qualities 168, 213–14; dreary 170,
213; mindless 214; traditional 192;
'white' 230
working-class family life 70–1
worldly, other worldly 226
writer 29–40
writing 2, 11, 30–4, 37, 39, 42, 43–4, 45,
68, 79, 80–1, 86–7, 126, 128, 131–3,
150, 156–8, 180, 189; essayist 44;
national 128; metaphorical 170;
informal 194; artless 196, 222;
committed 197–8; rhetorical 222;
rash 225; and other writers 1–2, 83,
222, 228; truthful 256 n. 32; not a
novelist 270 n. 86
Yorkshire and Lancashire 74, 86

Orwell's works consulted:
A Clergyman's Daughter 35, 36–7, 187, 197
'A Day in the Life of a Tramp' 42
'A Farthing Newspaper' 32–3, 82
'A Hanging' 33, 42–4, 80, 215
'A Nice Cup of Tea' 280 n. 156
'A Peep into the Future' 14, 214
'Aneurin Bevan' 275 n. 73
Animal Farm 10, 149, 168–71,
181, 202, 203, 229; Russian
translation 173
'Antisemitism in Britain', 296 n. 8
'Arthur Koestler' 285 n. 39
'Bad Climates Are Best' 167

'Beggars in London' 42
'Bookshop Memories' 245 n. 108
'Boys' Weeklies' 149, 159–61, 165
'Britain's Left-Wing Press' 285 n. 46
'British Cookery' 167
Burmese Days 23–4, 26–7, 28, 36, 42, 44, 80,
127, 165
'Burnham's View of Contemporary World
Struggle' 285 n. 39
'Charles Dickens' 149, 162–4
'Charles Reade' 280 n. 150
'Clink' 33
'Colonel Blimp' 276 n. 82
Coming Up for Air 4, 5, 109–29, 136; behind
public opinion 137, 151
'Common Lodging Houses' 33
'Culture and Democracy' 284 n. 35
'Decline of the English Murder' 167
'Democracy in the British Army'
272 n. 27
'Don't Let Colonel Blimp Ruin the Home
Guard' 272 n. 27
Down and Out in Paris and London 4, 31, 33,
35, 36, 42, 80, 106, 131–2, 145, 169,
220–1, 222, 227
'Evelyn Waugh' 180
'Eye Witness in Barcelona' 84, 85
'Fascism and Democracy' 149
'For Ever Eton' 240 n. 24
'Freedom and Happiness' 285 n. 39
'George Gissing' 180
Homage to Catalonia 75, 79, 80, 81, 84–5,
91, 127, 197
'Hop Picking' 33
'How the Poor Die' 244 n. 90
'In Defence of English Cooking'
280 n. 156
'In Defence of P. G. Wodehouse' 166
'India Next' 256 n. 30
'Inside the Whale' 99, 130–1
'Introduction', to *British Pamphleteers*
288 n. 80
'Introduction' to *Jack London's Love of Life and
Other Stories* 285 n. 39
'Just Junk' 280 n. 156
Keep the Aspidistra Flying 37, 45, 52, 84,
189, 197
'La Censure en Angleterre' 32–3, 82
'Literature and Totalitarianism'
302 n. 90
'Literature Between the Wars' 280 n. 151

'Looking Back on the Spanish Civil War' 56
'Marrakech' 244 n. 83
'Mood of Moment' 256 n. 30
'Moon Under Water' 167
'My Country Right or Left' 137, 149
Nineteen Eighty Four 10, 43, 83, 84, 92, 96, 179, 181–2, 200, 203, 205–16, 221, 222, 231, 232; and its references to other works 207
'Not Counting Niggers' 272 n. 20
'Notes on Nationalism' 180
'Notes on the Way' 270 n. 82
'On a Ruined Farm Near His Master's Voice Gramophone Factory (somewhere near the A40)' 40
'Oscar Wilde' 285 n. 40
'Our Opportunity' 149
'Pacifism and the War. A Controversy' 273 n. 42
'Poetry and the Microphone' 278 n. 114
'Political Reflections on the Crisis' 262 n. 115
'Politics and the English Language' 149, 156–9, 210, 222
'Politics v Literature. An Examination of Gulliver's Travels' 282 n. 172
'Raffles and Miss Blandish' 280 n. 156
'Reflections on Gandhi' 240 n. 33
'Revolt in Urban Desert' 256 n. 30
'Rudyard Kipling' 164–5, and obituary 280 n. 141
'Second Thoughts on James Burnham' 285 n. 39
'Some Thoughts on the Common Toad' 280 n. 156
'Songs We Used To Sing' 281 n. 156
'Spanish Prison' 290 n. 103
'Spilling the Spanish Beans' 85
'Such, Such Were the Joys' 181
'The Adventure of the Lost Meat Card' 14
'The Art of Donald McGill' 149, 154–6
'The British Empire in Burma' 42
'The Case for the Open Fire' 167
The English People 5, 56, 149, 166, 168, 170
'The French Believe We Have Had A Revolution' 282 n. 1

'The Italian Soldier Shook My Hand' 73, 106–7, 205
'The Labour Government After Three Years' 181
The Lion and the Unicorn 5, 149–54, 170, 175, 189, 193, 199, 205–6, 221, 223, 226
'The Man and the Maid' 14
'The Prevention of Literature' 282 n. 173
The Road to Wigan Pier 45, 50, 51–71, 72, 74, 79, 80, 84, 89, 91, 93, 98, 104, 105, 124, 127, 132, 155, 157, 170, 175, 192–3, 197, 212, 227
'The Slack-bob' 14
'The Spike' 33, 42–4, 80
'The Sporting Spirit' 239 n. 18
'The Tale of John Flory' 4
'The Quick and the Dead' 4
'Towards European Unity' 238 n. 4
'Unemployment' 42
'Wells, Hitler and the World State' 179
'Why I Join the ILP' 258 n. 68
'Why I Write' 238 n. 4
'Will Freedom Die with Capitalism?' 302 n. 90
'Writers and Leviathan' 179
'You and the Atom Bomb' 295 n. 52
Orwell Memorial Prize 235
Orwell Mystique [*The*] 221
Orwell Society 235
Orwell Trust 235
'Orwellian' 9, 196, 226–7, 228–9
Orwell's Victory 231
Osborne, John 40
Owen, Frank 153
owner occupation 119
Oxfam 161
Oxford 123
Oxford University 113
Oxford University Democratic Social Club 146
Oxford University English Club 146

pacifists 180
'Packingtown' 83
Paine, Thomas 82
Paris 31, 32, 33, 82, 91, 106, 132, 167, 197, 201, 210
parish councils 182

Park Lane Hotel, London 161
Parson Thwackum, fictional character in
    Henry Fielding's *Tom Jones* 187
Parsons, fictional character in *Nineteen
    Eighty-Four* 208
Partido Obrero de Unificacion Marxista
    (POUM) 72, 78, 85–8; trial 90; leader
    assassinated 90–1
Partisan Review 147, 229
Passage to India [A] 36
Patai, Daphne 119–20, 221
Pathan 21
Pearson and Knowles Coal & Iron Co 50
People of the Abyss, [The] 32
People's War 145, 154
Penguin Books 145, 205
pension, Richard Blair's 11
Perak War 21
Perkin, Harold 121
Picture Post 153, 154
pigs, fictional animals (or humans) in *Animal
    Farm* 170
Piper, John 148
Plamenatz, John 179
planning and collectivism 177
Player's tobacco 219
Podhoretz, Norman 232
Poland 138, 201
Political and Planning Group 145
politics 127–8
Pollitt, Harry 62, 98, 137
popular culture 230, 234
Popular Front 48, 85, 87
Portobello Road, Notting Hill 31
Post-Christian society 218–19
Post-Impressionism 188
Potemkin villages 173
Potts, Paul 146
POUM militia 76; strategy 149, 258 n. 65
Pound, Ezra 130
poverty, investigations 30, 32, 47, 81, 112
Powell, Anthony 146
Pravda 93
Priestley, J. B. 49, 51, 101, 114–15, 153,
    173; three Englands 118, 125
Prince of Wales 19
Pritchett, V. S. 228
Proletkult 95–6
propaganda 84
*Prospero and Caliban. The Psychology of
    Colonization* 27

Public Assistance Committee 54,
    301 n. 75
public moralists 9, 66
Puigcerda 76
Pulitzer Prize 229
Punjabi 21
Putin, Vladimir 232

Queen St, Southwold 31
Queen Victoria 28

radar 139
Rahv, Philip 147
Ramblas, Barcelona 76
Randolph Hotel, Oxford 146
Rangoon 18, 21, 22; University 24
rape 201
Rawlinson, Mark 227
Red Army 201
Rees, Richard 5, 36, 59, 60, 65, 195, 224
Reform Acts 151
Regent's Park, London 148
Reilly, Patrick 226
Reith, Sir John 138
Renier, G. J. 126
reserve, middle-class 6
Restriction of Ribbon Development Act
    (1935) 119
Revd Charles Hare, fictional character in
    A Clergyman's Daughter 36
Revolution Betrayed [The] 169
Reynold's News 181
Rhineland 133, 135
Richards, Frank (Mr Charles Hamilton)
    279 n. 133
Right Book Club 49, 123
Ritz Hotel, London 137, 138, 185, 204, 218
Ritz Super, Wigan 56
River Thames 122, 123, 124
Road to Morocco [The] 199
Road to Serfdom [The] 186
Rodden, John 2, 5
Rojo, Vicente 90
Roman Catholics 180
Rolling Stones [The] 218
Romantic Exiles [The] 217
Room at the Top 229
Rose's Lime Juice 4
Rotary Club 145
Rowntree, Seebohm 112
Rowse, A. L. 220

Royal Academy of Dramatic Art
(RADA) 230
Royal Air Force (RAF) 110, 135, 139
Royal Army Medical Corps
(RAMC) 142
Royal Marines 142
Royal Navy 21, 30, 134
Rudge Bicycles 4
Rule Britannia 183
Runnymede 123
Ruskin, John 17, 66, 190
Russell, Bertrand 182, 221
Russia Today 174
Russian Journal, incurious 174
Russian Journey, incurious 173
Russian people 169

Saarland 133, 135
Sackville-West, Vita 148
Salinas Valley 83
Salisbury, Lord 19, 20
Salkeld, Brenda 41
Sam Weller, fictional character in Charles
Dickens' *The Pickwick Papers* 162
Sandison, Alan 225
Santayana, George 193
Saturday Night and Sunday Morning 229
Satyagraha 20
Sayers, Michael 195
schoolchildren 229
Searle family, Sheffield, in *The Road to Wigan
Pier* 69
Secker & Warburg, publishers 149, 169
semi-detached houses 118–19
Serge, Victor 179
Servicio Investigacion Militar 94
Seshagiri, Urmila 221
Shape of Things to Come [The] 136
Sharp, Thomas 49
Shaw, George Bernard 95, 146
Sheffield 71
Shelden, Michael 205
Ship Street, Liverpool 229
Shiplake, Oxon 123
shop floor 182
Short History of the English People 185
Shute, Nevil 136
Sikhs 7, 21
Sillitoe, Alan 229
Simon Commission 28

Sinclair, Upton 83
Singapore 28
skilled and unskilled workers 113
Skylon 219
Slaughter, Clifford 229
slums 63
Smillie, Bob 78, 79
Smith, Adam 214
Smith, Stevie 146
Socialist Realism 95–6
Socialist Sunday Schools 55
Society for Cultural Relations with the
USSR 173
Society for Cultural Ties Abroad
(VOKS) 174
sociological investigations 229–30
Sons and Lovers 114
South African War 21, 28, 82
South Downs Preservation Bill
(1934) 119
South Shields 47
Southey, Robert 190
Southwold 11, 29, 31, 35, 116
Soviet Genetics 217
Soviet News 174
Soviet Union, invasion 10, 168;
progressivism 66, 94–5; influence in
Spain 85, 94; collectivization,
industrialization, abolition of classes,
politics, terror quotas 92–3;
executions 94; famine 95, 127, and
scarcity 96; building a new
humanity 96; sympathizers, in
Britain and US 172–4;
atrocities 201
Soviet secret police (NKVD) and Spanish
terror 90, 93, 169
Spain, 'Black' and 'Red' 74
'Spain', poem by W. H. Auden 99–101
Spanish Civil War 72–102; internecine
struggles 76–8, 88; strategy and
tactics 77, 89, 101; equipment 77;
torture and execution 78–9;
Orwell's reflections 84–91, 101,
191, 224; acronyms and sides 85;
Spanish Communists (PCE) 87–8,
89, 90, 140; Second Republican
disasters and reforms 88–90
Spectator (The) 104
Spencer, Stanley 148

Spender, Stephen 57, 100, 177, 195, 223, 228
Spengler, Oswald 116, 215
Spiegelman, Art 229
St Cyprian's preparatory school, Eastbourne 12–13
St Ebbes, Oxford 229
St John's Wood, London 145
Stafford 48, 51
Stalinism 91, 93, 94, 168, 170, 182; and umanity 95; and murder 101; non-aggression pact 137; Great Patriotic War 169, and after 202
Stalky & Co 159
standard of living 25, 112
state intervention 177, 234
statesmen 3–4
Steinbeck, John 83, 174
sterling crisis 181
Stern, James 98
Stevens, G. W. 17
Strachey, John 90, 104
Strauss, George 147
Strube, Sidney 126
Stubbs, William 184
Student Christian Movement 218
students, 1960s 219
Stunde null 202
Stuttgart 201
Subaltern Studies 230
suburbs, and connotations 109–11, 118–20, 121
Sudan Wars 21
Sudetenland 134, 135
Suez 219
Surrey Appeal for Jarrow 56
Sutton Courtenay, Berks 217
swaraj (*Hindswaraj*) 16
Swift, Jonathan 189
Sylvester, David 146
Syme, fictional character in *Nineteen Eighty-Four* 208
Symons, Julian 146

Tale of Two Cities [*A*] 162
Taine, Hippolyte 224
Tawney, R. H. 61
Taylor, D. J. 5, 234
Taylor, Jenny 221
teenagers 234

Tehran 201
television 218
Temple, Dr William, archbishop of Canterbury 168
Thalmann, Ernst 54
Thames Valley 124–5
Thatcher, Margaret 219
The Times 36, 227
The Times Literary Supplement 36
The Tramp 32
theatrical, anti-theatrical 230
Thomas, Dylan 146
Thomas, Hugh 90
Thompson, E. P. 212, 222, 231, 233
Time & Tide 98, 148
Tit Bits 170
Tocqueville, Alexis de 224
Tom Brown's Schooldays 15
Tory history 185
town planning 119
Toynbee, Arnold 50, 184, 185
trade unions 102, 176, 177
trans-cultural 230
transitions, capitalism to socialism 67–8, 143–4, 145
trans-national 234
Trevelyan, George Macaulay 129
Trevelyan, Julian 56, 57
Tribune 98, 146, 157, 223
Trilling, Lionel 4, 5
Trotsky, Leon 169
Trotskyists 89, 90
Truman, Harry 202
Tudor Reformation 183
Tunstall, Jeremy 229
Turner, J. M. W. 192
Twentieth Party Congress 219

U Ottama, Burmese nationalist 23
Ukraine 127
Ulysses 36, 167
unemployed 46–7, 55, 112, 228
Union Flag 234
United States 89, 102, 201, 229, 231
University College, London 197
University College Hospital, London 203, 204
Upper Binfield, fictional place in *Coming Up for Air* 124
Uses of Literacy [*The*] 229

Utopian socialism 66
Uxbridge 34, 35

Valencia 76, 88, 99
vernacular architecture 124
Verrall, fictional character in *Burmese Days* 23
Versailles Treaty 133–5
Victoria railway station, London 142
Vietnam War 219, 228, 232

wages and oncosts 53–4
Wain, John 228
Wallace, Edgar 82
Wallingford 123
Wallington, Herts 107, 124, 136, 141,
    147, 197
Walzer, Michael 5
war reporting 81
Warburg, Fred 146, 181, 221, 223
Wardour Street 48
Wargrave, Berks 123
Warre, Dr Edmund, headmaster Eton
    College 13
Warrington 49
Warrington Lane, Wigan 48
Warsaw Pact 231
Washington DC 181, 219
Watford 123
Watkin, Sir Edward 268 n. 59
Watson, Susan 203
Watt, Harry 182
Waugh, Evelyn 146, 148, 180
We 179
'weak ties syndrome' 233
Webb, Sidney and Beatrice 61, 182
Wells, H. G. 114, 136, 146
Wessex 122
West Bletchley, fictional town ('Metroland')
    in *Coming Up for Air* 109, 110, 111, 116,
    118, 121, 123, 124, 125, 128
West Germany 202
West Hampstead 35

Westropes, Hampstead 245 n. 108
Westminster School 15
What Happened to the Corbetts? 136
Whig Liberty 183
Whig Interpretation of History [*The*] 184
Whitechapel 185
Wigan 150, 218, 228
Wigan Coal Corporation 50
Wigan Coal and Iron Company 50
Wikipedia 223
William Brown, fictional character 95,
    260 nn. 93, 94
Williams, Raymond 4, 5, 231
Williams, Vaughan 124, 148
Willmott, Peter 229
Windsor 123
Winston Smith, fictional character in
    Nineteen Eighty-Four 205–8, 213–15
Women's Institute 145
women's streets 176
Women's Suffrage 183
Woodcock, George 4, 190–1, 195,
    223, 224
Woolf, Virginia 114–15
workhouse 32, 33, 34, 165
working class, death of a culture 218
Workingmen's Club and Institute
    Union 55–6, 70
World in Action, television programme 218
World Review 4
Wordsworth, William 190

Yahoos 169, 170
Yalta 201
Yeltsin, Boris 232
Yoknapatawpha County 83
Young, Michael 229

Zamyatin, E. I. 179
Zinoviev, Grigory 93
Zulu 25
Zweig, Ferdynand 192